2002

MASS COMMUNICATION LAW AND ETHICS

A CASEBOOK

MASS COMMUNICATION LAW AND ETHICS
A CASEBOOK

Roy L. Moore
University of Kentucky

LAWRENCE ERLBAUM ASSOCIATES, PUBLISHERS
1999   Mahwah, New Jersey   London

Lawrence Erlbaum Associates, Inc., Publishers
10 Industrial Avenue
Mahwah, NJ 07430

Cover design by Kathryn Houghtaling Lacey

Library of Congress Cataloging-in-Publication Data

Moore, Roy L.
    Mass communication law and ethics: a casebook / Roy L. Moore.
      p.   cm.
    ISBN 0-8058-3278-5
    1. Mass media—Law and legislation—United States—Cases.   2. Mass
media—Moral and ethical aspects—Case studies.   I. Title.
KF2750.A7M66   1999
343.7309'9—dc21   99-17431
                                                               CIP

Books published by Lawrence Erlbaum Associates are printed on acid-free
paper, and their bindings are chosen for strength and durability.

Printed in the United States of America
10 9 8 7 6 5 4 3 2 1

Contents

Page

SOURCES AND TYPES OF U.S. LAW

Introduction vii

1. *Clinton v. City of New York* (1998) [separation of powers] 1

2. *Marbury v. Madison* (1803) [authority of federal judiciary] 8

THE U.S. LEGAL SYSTEM

3. *Arizonans for Official English v. Arizona* (1997) [mootness] 21

THE JUDICIAL PROCESS

4. *J.E.B. v. Alabama ex rel. T.B.* (1994) [jury selection -- gender] 31

5. *Victor v. Nebraska* and *Sandoval v. California* (1994)
    [jury instructions -- beyond a reasonable doubt] 47

PRIOR RESTRAINT

6. *Near v. Minnesota* (1931) [constitutionality of state statute
    imposing prior restraint on publications] 58

7. *United States v. Eichman* and *United States v. Haggerty* (1990)
    [First Amendment protection for flag burning] 71

8. *City of Ladue v. Gilleo* (1994) [prior restraint on residential
    sign] 80

9. *National Endowment for the Arts v. Finley* (1998) [prior restraint
    on artistic expression] 89

CORPORATE AND COMMERCIAL SPEECH

10. *Central Hudson Gas & Electric Corp. v. Public Service
    Commission of New York* (1980) [First Amendment protection
    for commercial speech] 101

11. *Florida Bar v. Went For It, Inc.* (1995) [regulation of mail
    solicitations by attorneys] 109

12. *44 Liquormart, Inc. v. Rhode Island* (1996) [regulation of
    advertising for alcoholic beverages] 126

ELECTRONIC MASS MEDIA AND TELECOMMUNICATIONS

13. *Red Lion Broadcasting v. Federal Communications Commission*
     (1969) [regulation of broadcasting -- Fairness Doctrine] 143

14. *Turner Broadcasting System v. Federal Communications*
     Commission (Turner Broadcasting II) (1997) [regulation of cable
     television -- "must carry provisions"] 158

LIBEL

15. *New York Times v. Sullivan* (1964) [actual malice rule --
     Public officials] 182

16. *Gertz v. Robert Welch* (1974) [state standards -- private
     Individuals] 202

17. *Hustler v. Falwell* (1988) [intentional infliction of emotional
     Distress] 218

RIGHT OF PRIVACY

18. *Zacchini v. Scripps Howard Broadcasting* (1977)
     [appropriation right of publicity] 226

19. *Florida Star v. B. J. F.* (1989) [public records -- publication
     of rape victim's name] 236

ACCESS

20. *Richmond Newspapers v. Virginia* (1980) [First Amendment
     right of access to criminal trials] 246

21. *Chandler v. Florida* (1981) [free press v. fair trial -- cameras
     in the courtroom] 261

22. *Sheppard v. Maxwell* (1966) [free press v. fair trial --
     prejudicial publicity] 275

INTELLECTUAL PROPERTY

23. *Campbell v. Acuff-Rose Music* (1994) [copyright -- parody] ... 293

OBSCENITY AND INDECENCY

24. *Miller v. California* (1973) [test for obscenity]..................... 308

25. *Reno v. American Civil Liberties Union* (1997) [Internet
     indecency] 317

Introduction

This casebook includes extensive excerpts from 25 major mass communication decisions by the Supreme Court of the United States. The cases are presented in the order in which they are discussed in the second edition of *Mass Communication Law and Ethics,* but the casebook is designed to be used as a supplemental text in any media law course. I have included a brief overview with each case, and they have all has been edited, particularly to delete detailed citations and highly technical material. Every effort has been made, however, to preserve the Court's original language, including its recitation of the *facts,* its *reasoning* and the *holding* in the case. Most of the cases also include excerpts from the Court's *syllabus,* a summary prepared by the Court's Reporter of Decisions. A few of the cases include excerpts from concurring and/or dissenting opinions, where those opinions illustrate the complexity of the case or were influential in later decisions.

Brackets [ ] indicate that one or more citations have been omitted from the official decision and **ellipses** ... indicate that one or more paragraphs have been omitted. **Text within brackets** [text] indicate information has been added for clarity.

The cases cover a wide range of areas of mass communication law, including the judicial process; prior restraint; commercial speech; electronic media and telecommunications; libel; privacy; media access; intellectual property; and indecency and obscenity. The page numbers in the in the overviews refer to the first page on which the case is discussed in *Mass Communication Law and Ethics* (second edition) (MCLE).

You are encouraged to read other cases as well, including decisions by other courts. There are several comprehensive sources for complete texts of court decisions, especially those of the United States Supreme Court, on the Internet. You will find them listed at my course web site:

http://www.uky.edu/~moore/JAT531

My special thanks to Clayton R. Smalley, President and Executive Editor of InfoSynthesis, Inc. (195 East Fifth Street, Suite 807, St. Paul, MN 55101-1984 or 800-784-7036) for granting me permission to copy the cases directly from USSC+, a CD-ROM database of full-text decisions of the United States Supreme Court. I also wish to thank LEA editor, Linda Bathgate, for her encouragement and assistance.

This casebook is dedicated with love to my wife, Pamela, and my son, Derek.

In *Clinton v. City of New York* (MCLE, page 4), the justices held 6–3 that the Line Item Veto Act of 1996 violated the Presentment Clause of the U.S. Constitution, which the Court said requires the veto of an entire bill, not individual spending items. According to the Court, line item veto authority could be granted to the president only through a constitutional amendment. The case illustrates how the U.S. Constitution both limits and defines the powers of the federal government and the role the Supreme Court plays in interpreting the Constitution.

Clinton v. City of New York

Argued April 27, 1998
Decided June 25, 1998

114 S.Ct. 2091, 141 L.Ed.2d 393

APPEAL FROM THE UNITED STATES DISTRICT COURT
FOR THE DISTRICT OF COLUMBIA

Syllabus

Last Term, this Court determined on expedited review that Members of Congress did not have standing to maintain a constitutional challenge to the Line Item Veto Act ... because they had not alleged a sufficiently concrete injury. [   ] Within two months, the President exercised his authority under the Act by cancelling § 4722(c) of the Balanced Budget Act of 1997, which waived the Federal Government's statutory right to recoupment of as much as $2.6 billion in taxes that the State of New York had levied against Medicaid providers, and § 968 of the Taxpayer Relief Act of 1997, which permitted the owners of certain food refiners and processors to defer recognition of capital gains if they sold their stock to eligible farmers' cooperatives. Appellees, claiming they had been injured, filed separate actions against the President and other officials challenging the cancellations. The plaintiffs in the first case are the City of New York, two hospital associations, one hospital, and two unions representing health care employees. The plaintiffs in the second are the Snake River farmers' cooperative and one of its individual members. The District Court consolidated the cases, determined that at least one of the plaintiffs in each had standing under Article III, and ruled, *inter alia,* that the Act's cancellation procedures violate the Presentment Clause, Art. I, § 7, cl. 2. This Court again expedited its review.

Held:

1. The appellees have standing to challenge the Act's constitutionality.

1

They invoked the District Court's jurisdiction under a section entitled "Expedited Review," which, among other things, expressly authorizes "any individual adversely affected" to bring a constitutional challenge ...

2. The Act's cancellation procedures violate the Presentment Clause.

STEVENS, J., delivered the opinion of the Court, in which REHNQUIST, C. J., and KENNEDY, SOUTER, THOMAS, and GINSBURG, JJ., joined. KENNEDY, J., filed a concurring opinion. SCALIA, J., filed an opinion concurring in part and dissenting in part, in which O'CONNOR, J., joined, and in which BREYER, J., joined as to Part III. BREYER, J., filed a dissenting opinion, in which O'CONNOR and SCALIA, JJ., joined as to Part III.

STEVENS, J., lead opinion

[Justice Stevens begins his analysis by summarizing the budget items cancelled by President Clinton and then describes the plaintiffs in the case.]

III

As in the prior challenge to the Line Item Veto Act, we initially confront jurisdictional questions. The appellees invoked the jurisdiction of the District Court under the section of the Act entitled "Expedited Review." That section, 2 U.S.C. § 692(a)(1), expressly authorizes "[a]ny Member of Congress or any individual adversely affected" by the Act to bring an action for declaratory judgment or injunctive relief on the ground that any provision of the Act is unconstitutional. Although the Government did not question the applicability of that section in the District Court, it now argues that, with the exception of Mike Cranney, the appellees are not "individuals" within the meaning of § 692(a)(1). Because the argument poses a jurisdictional question (although not one of constitutional magnitude), it is not waived by the failure to raise it in the District Court. The fact that the argument did not previously occur to the able lawyers for the Government does, however, confirm our view that, in the context of the entire section, Congress undoubtedly intended the word "individual" to be construed as synonymous with the word "person."

The special section authorizing expedited review evidences an unmistakable congressional interest in a prompt and authoritative judicial determination of the constitutionality of the Act. Subsection (a)(2) requires that copies of any complaint filed under subsection (a)(1) "shall be promptly delivered" to both Houses of Congress, and that each House shall have a right to intervene. Subsection (b) authorizes a direct appeal to this Court from any order of the District Court, and requires that the appeal be filed within 10 days. Subsection (c) imposes a duty on both the District Court and this Court "to advance on the docket and to expedite to the greatest possible extent the disposition of any matter brought under subsection (a)." There is no plausible reason why

Congress would have intended to provide for such special treatment of actions filed by natural persons, and to have precluded entirely jurisdiction over comparable cases brought by corporate persons. Acceptance of the Government's new-found reading of § 692 "would produce an absurd and unjust result which Congress could not have intended." [ ]

We are also unpersuaded by the Government's argument that appellees' challenge to the constitutionality of the Act is nonjusticiable. We agree, of course, that Article III of the Constitution confines the jurisdiction of the federal courts to actual "Cases" and "Controversies," and that "the doctrine of standing serves to identify those disputes which are appropriately resolved through the judicial process." [ ] Our disposition of the first challenge to the constitutionality of this Act demonstrates our recognition of the importance of respecting the constitutional limits on our jurisdiction, even when Congress has manifested an interest in obtaining our views as promptly as possible. But these cases differ from *Raines* [*v. Byrd* (1997)] not only because the President's exercise of his cancellation authority has removed any concern about the ripeness of the dispute, but, more importantly, because the parties have alleged a "personal stake" in having an actual injury redressed, rather than an "institutional injury" that is "abstract and widely dispersed." [ ]

In both the New York and the Snake River cases, the Government argues that the appellees are not actually injured, because the claims are too speculative and, in any event, the claims are advanced by the wrong parties. We find no merit in the suggestion that New York's injury is merely speculative because HHS has not yet acted on the State's waiver requests. The State now has a multi-billion dollar contingent liability that had been eliminated by § 4722(c) of the Balanced Budget Act of 1997 ...

The self-evident significance of the contingent liability is confirmed by the fact that New York lobbied Congress for this relief, that Congress decided that it warranted statutory attention, and that the President selected for cancellation only this one provision in an act that occupies 536 pages of the Statutes at Large. His action was comparable to the judgment of an appellate court setting aside a verdict for the defendant and remanding for a new trial of a multi-billion dollar damages claim. Even if the outcome of the second trial is speculative, the reversal, like the President's cancellation, causes a significant immediate injury by depriving the defendant of the benefit of a favorable final judgment. The revival of a substantial contingent liability immediately and directly affects the borrowing power, financial strength, and fiscal planning of the potential obligor.

We also reject the Government's argument that New York's claim is advanced by the wrong parties, because the claim belongs to the State of New York, and not appellees. Under New York statutes that are already in place, it is clear that both the City of New York and the

3

appellee health care providers will be assessed by the State for substantial portions of any recoupment payments that the State may have to make to the Federal Government. To the extent of such assessments, they have the same potential liability as the State does.

The Snake River farmers' cooperative also suffered an immediate injury when the President cancelled the limited tax benefit that Congress had enacted to facilitate the acquisition of processing plants. Three critical facts identify the specificity and the importance of that injury. First, Congress enacted § 968 for the specific purpose of providing a benefit to a defined category of potential purchasers of a defined category of assets. The members of that statutorily defined class received the equivalent of a statutory "bargaining chip" to use in carrying out the congressional plan to facilitate their purchase of such assets. Second, the President selected § 968 as one of only two tax benefits in the Taxpayer Relief Act of 1997 that should be cancelled. The cancellation rested on his determination that the use of those bargaining chips would have a significant impact on the Federal budget deficit. Third, the Snake River cooperative was organized for the very purpose of acquiring processing facilities, it had concrete plans to utilize the benefits of § 968, and it was engaged in ongoing negotiations with the owner of a processing plant who had expressed an interest in structuring a tax-deferred sale when the President cancelled § 968. Moreover, it is actively searching for other processing facilities for possible future purchase if the President's cancellation is reversed, and there are ample processing facilities in the State that Snake River may be able to purchase. By depriving them of their statutory bargaining chip, the cancellation inflicted a sufficient likelihood of economic injury to establish standing under our precedents. [ ] ...

As with the New York case, the Government argues that the wrong parties are before the Court -- that, because the sellers of the processing facilities would have received the tax benefits, only they have standing to challenge the cancellation of § 968. This argument not only ignores the fact that the cooperatives were the intended beneficiaries of § 968, but also overlooks the self-evident proposition that more than one party may have standing to challenge a particular action or inaction.{GO>23} Once it is determined that a particular plaintiff is harmed by the defendant, and that the harm will likely be redressed by a favorable decision, that plaintiff has standing -- regardless of whether there are others who would also have standing to sue. Thus, we are satisfied that both of these actions are Article III "Cases" that we have a duty to decide.

IV

The Line Item Veto Act gives the President the power to "cancel in whole" three types of provisions that have been signed into law: "(1) any dollar amount of discretionary budget authority; (2) any item of new direct spending; or (3) any limited tax benefit." [ ] It is undisputed that the New York case involves an "item of new direct spending," and that the Snake River case involves a "limited tax benefit" as those terms are defined in the Act. It is also undisputed that each of those provisions had been signed into law pursuant to Article I, § 7, of the Constitution before it was cancelled.

In both legal and practical effect, the President has amended two Acts of Congress by repealing a portion of each ... [ ] There is no provision in the Constitution that authorizes the President to enact, to amend, or to repeal statutes. Both Article I and Article II assign responsibilities to the President that directly relate to the lawmaking process, but neither addresses the issue presented by these cases ...

There are important differences between the President's "return" of a bill pursuant to Article I, § 7, and the exercise of the President's cancellation authority pursuant to the Line Item Veto Act. The constitutional return takes place *before* the bill becomes law; the statutory cancellation occurs *after* the bill becomes law. The constitutional return is of the entire bill; the statutory cancellation is of only a part. Although the Constitution expressly authorizes the President to play a role in the process of enacting statutes, it is silent on the subject of unilateral Presidential action that either repeals or amends parts of duly enacted statutes.

There are powerful reasons for construing constitutional silence on this profoundly important issue as equivalent to an express prohibition. The procedures governing the enactment of statutes set forth in the text of Article I were the product of the great debates and compromises that produced the Constitution itself. Familiar historical materials provide abundant support for the conclusion that the power to enact statutes may only "be exercised in accord with a single, finely wrought and exhaustively considered, procedure." [ ] Our first President understood the text of the Presentment Clause as requiring that he either "approve all the parts of a Bill, or reject it *in toto*." What has emerged in these cases from the President's exercise of his statutory cancellation powers, however, are truncated versions of two bills that passed both Houses of Congress. They are not the product of the "finely wrought" procedure that the Framers designed ...

V

The Government advances two related arguments to support its position that, despite the unambiguous provisions of the Act, cancellations do not amend or repeal properly enacted statutes in violation of the Presentment Clause. First, relying primarily on *Field v. Clark*, 143 U.S. 649 (1892), the Government contends that the cancellations were merely exercises of discretionary authority granted to the President by the Balanced Budget Act and the Taxpayer Relief Act read in light of the previously enacted Line Item Veto Act. Second, the Government submits that the substance of the authority to cancel tax and spending items

is, in practical effect, no more and no less than the power to "decline to

5

spend" specified sums of money, or to "decline to implement" specified tax measures.

Brief for Appellants 40. Neither argument is persuasive ...

Neither are we persuaded by the Government's contention that the President's authority to cancel new direct spending and tax benefit items is no greater than his traditional authority to decline to spend appropriated funds. The Government has reviewed in some detail the series of statutes in which Congress has given the Executive broad discretion over the expenditure of appropriated funds. For example, the First Congress appropriated "sum[s] not exceeding" specified amounts to be spent on various Government operations. [ ] In those statutes, as in later years, the President was given wide discretion with respect to both the amounts to be spent and how the money would be allocated among different functions. It is argued that the Line Item Veto Act merely confers comparable discretionary authority over the expenditure of appropriated funds. The critical difference between this statute and all of its predecessors, however, is that, unlike any of them, this Act gives the President the unilateral power to change the text of duly enacted statutes. None of the Act's predecessors could even arguably have been construed to authorize such a change.

VI

Although they are implicit in what we have already written, the profound importance of these cases makes it appropriate to emphasize three points.

First, we express no opinion about the wisdom of the procedures authorized by the Line Item Veto Act. Many members of both major political parties who have served in the Legislative and the Executive Branches have long advocated the enactment of such procedures for the purpose of "ensur[ing] greater fiscal accountability in Washington." [ ] The text of the Act was itself the product of much debate and deliberation in both Houses of Congress, and that precise text was signed into law by the President. We do not lightly conclude that their action was unauthorized by the Constitution. We have, however, twice had full argument and briefing on the question, and have concluded that our duty is clear.

Second, although appellees challenge the validity of the Act on alternative grounds, the only issue we address concerns the "finely wrought" procedure commanded by the Constitution. [ ] We have been favored with extensive debate about the scope of Congress' power to delegate lawmaking authority, or its functional equivalent, to the President. The excellent briefs filed by the parties and their *amici curiae* have provided us with valuable historical information that illuminates the delegation issue, but does not really bear on the narrow issue that is dispositive of these cases. Thus, because we conclude that the Act's cancellation provisions violate Article I, § 7, of the Constitution, we find it unnecessary to consider the District Court's alternative holding that the

Act "impermissibly disrupts the balance of powers among the three branches of government." [ ]

Third, our decision rests on the narrow ground that the procedures authorized by the Line Item Veto Act are not authorized by the Constitution. The Balanced Budget Act of 1997 is a 500-page document that became "Public Law 105-33" after three procedural steps were taken: (1) a bill containing its exact text was approved by a majority of the Members of the House of Representatives; (2) the Senate approved precisely the same text; and (3) that text was signed into law by the President. The Constitution explicitly requires that each of those three steps be taken before a bill may "become a law." Art. I, § 7. If one paragraph of that text had been omitted at any one of those three stages, Public Law 105-33 would not have been validly enacted. If the Line Item Veto Act were valid, it would authorize the President to create a different law -- one whose text was not voted on by either House of Congress or presented to the President for signature. Something that might be known as "Public Law 105-33 as modified by the President" may or may not be desirable, but it is surely not a document that may "become a law" pursuant to the procedures designed by the Framers of Article I, § 7, of the Constitution.

If there is to be a new procedure in which the President will play a different role in determining the final text of what may "become a law," such change must come not by legislation, but through the amendment procedures set forth in Article V of the Constitution. [ ]

The judgment of the District Court is affirmed.

It is so ordered

In *Marbury v. Madison* (MCLE, page 6), the Supreme Court for the first time established the authority of the judicial branch to determine whether specific acts of Congress were constitutional. Today, legal scholars still differ on the breadth of the judicial power delineated in the case -- i.e., whether the courts play a broad, special role or a more restrictive role shared with the other two branches of government in interpreting the Constitution. The Court itself appears to have taken the former approach, often serving as the final arbiter of the meaning of the U.S. Constitution.

Marbury v. Madison

Decided 1803

5 U.S. 137, 2 L.Ed. 60, 1 Cranch 137

Syllabus

The clerks of the Department of State of the United States may be called upon to give evidence of transactions in the Department which are not of a confidential character.

The Secretary of State cannot be called upon as a witness to state transactions of a confidential nature which may have occurred in his Department. But he may be called upon to give testimony of circumstances which were not of that character.

Clerks in the Department of State were directed to be sworn, subject to objections to questions upon confidential matters.

Some point of time must be taken when the power of the Executive over an officer, not removable at his will, must cease. That point of time must be when the constitutional power of appointment has been exercised. And the power has been exercised when the last act required from the person possessing the power has been performed. This last act is the signature of the commission.

If the act of livery be necessary to give validity to the commission of an officer, it has been delivered when executed, and given to the Secretary of State for the purpose of being sealed, recorded, and transmitted to the party.

In cases of commissions to public officers, the law orders the Secretary of State to record them. When, therefore, they are signed and sealed, the order for their being recorded is given, and, whether inserted inserted into the book or not, they are recorded.

When the heads of the departments of the Government are the political or confidential officers of the Executive, merely to execute the will of the President, or rather to act in cases in which the Executive possesses a constitutional or legal discretion, nothing can be more perfectly clear than that their acts are only politically examinable. But where a specific duty is assigned by law, and individual rights depend upon the performance of that duty, it seems equally clear that the individual who considers himself injured has a right to resort to the laws of his country for a remedy ...

The authority given to the Supreme Court by the act establishing the judicial system of the United States to issue writs of mandamus to public officers appears not to be warranted by the Constitution.

It is emphatically the duty of the Judicial Department to say what the law is. Those who apply the rule to particular cases must, of necessity, expound and interpret the rule. If two laws conflict with each other, the Court must decide on the operation of each.

If courts are to regard the Constitution, and the Constitution is superior to any ordinary act of the legislature, the Constitution, and not such ordinary act, must govern the case to which they both apply.

MARSHALL, J., lead opinion

Mr. Chief Justice MARSHALL delivered the opinion of the Court.

At the last term, on the affidavits then read and filed with the clerk, a rule was granted in this case requiring the Secretary of State to show cause why a mandamus should not issue directing him to deliver to William Marbury his commission as a justice of the peace for the county of Washington, in the District of Columbia.

No cause has been shown, and the present motion is for a mandamus. The peculiar delicacy of this case, the novelty of some of its circumstances, and the real difficulty attending the points which occur in it require a complete exposition of the principles on which the opinion to be given by the Court is founded.

These principles have been, on the side of the applicant, very ably argued at the bar. In rendering the opinion of the Court, there will be some departure in form, though not in substance, from the points stated in that argument.

In the order in which the Court has viewed this subject, the following questions have been considered and decided.

1. Has the applicant a right to the commission he demands?

2. If he has a right, and that right has been violated, do the laws

of his country afford him a remedy?

3. If they do afford him a remedy, is it a mandamus issuing from this court?

The first object of inquiry is:

1. Has the applicant a right to the commission he demands?

His right originates in an act of Congress passed in February, 1801, concerning the District of Columbia.

After dividing the district into two counties, the eleventh section of this law enacts,

that there shall be appointed in and for each of the said counties such number of discreet persons to be justices of the peace as the President of the United States shall, from time to time, think expedient, to continue in office for five years.

It appears from the affidavits that, in compliance with this law, a commission for William Marbury as a justice of peace for the County of Washington was signed by John Adams, then President of the United States, after which the seal of the United States was affixed to it, but the commission has never reached the person for whom it was made out.

In order to determine whether he is entitled to this commission, it becomes necessary to inquire whether he has been appointed to the office. For if he has been appointed, the law continues him in office for five years, and he is entitled to the possession of those evidences of office, which, being completed, became his property.

The second section of the second article of the Constitution declares,

The President shall nominate, and, by and with the advice and consent of the Senate, shall appoint ambassadors, other public ministers and consuls, and all other officers of the United States, whose appointments are not otherwise provided for.

The third section declares, that "He shall commission all the officers of the United States."

An act of Congress directs the Secretary of State to keep the seal of the United States,

to make out and record, and affix the said seal to all civil commissions to officers of the United States to be appointed by the President, by and with the consent of the Senate, or by the President alone; provided that the said seal shall not be affixed to any commission before the same shall have been signed by the President of the United States.

These are the clauses of the Constitution and laws of the United States which affect this part of the case. They seem to contemplate three distinct operations:

    1. The nomination. This is the sole act of the President, and is completely voluntary.

    2. The appointment. This is also the act of the President, and is also a voluntary act, though it can only be performed by and with the advice and consent of the Senate.

    3. The commission. To grant a commission to a person appointed might perhaps be deemed a duty enjoined by the Constitution. "He shall," says that instrument, "commission all the officers of the United States."

    The acts of appointing to office and commissioning the person appointed can scarcely be considered as one and the same, since the power to perform them is given in two separate and distinct sections of the Constitution. The distinction between the appointment and the commission will be rendered more apparent by adverting to that provision in the second section of the second article of the Constitution which authorises Congress

to vest by law the appointment of such inferior officers as they think proper in the President alone, in the Courts of law, or in the heads of departments;

thus contemplating cases where the law may direct the President to commission an officer appointed by the Courts or by the heads of departments. In such a case, to issue a commission would be apparently a duty distinct from the appointment, the performance of which perhaps could not legally be refused.

    Although that clause of the Constitution which requires the President to commission all the officers of the United States may never have been applied to officers appointed otherwise than by himself, yet it would be difficult to deny the legislative power to apply it to such cases. Of consequence, the constitutional distinction between the appointment to an office and the commission of an officer who has been appointed remains the same as if in practice the President had commissioned officers appointed by an authority other than his own ...

    This is an appointment made by the President, by and with the advice and consent of the Senate, and is evidenced by no act but the commission itself. In such a case, therefore, the commission and the appointment seem inseparable, it being almost impossible to show an appointment otherwise than by proving the existence of a commission; still, the commission is not necessarily the appointment; though conclusive evidence of it.

But at what stage does it amount to this conclusive evidence?

    The answer to this question seems an obvious one. The appointment, being the sole act of the President, must be completely evidenced when it is shown that he has done everything to be performed by him.

Should the commission, instead of being evidence of an appointment, even be considered as constituting the appointment itself, still it would be made when the last act to be done by the President was performed, or, at furthest, when the commission was complete.

The signature is a warrant for affixing the great seal to the commission, and the great seal is only to be affixed to an instrument which is complete. It attests, by an act supposed to be of public notoriety, the verity of the Presidential signature.

It is never to be affixed till the commission is signed, because the signature, which gives force and effect to the commission, is conclusive evidence that the appointment is made.

The commission being signed, the subsequent duty of the Secretary of State is prescribed by law, and not to be guided by the will of the President. He is to affix the seal of the United States to the commission, and is to record it.

This is not a proceeding which may be varied if the judgment of the Executive shall suggest one more eligible, but is a precise course accurately marked out by law, and is to be strictly pursued. It is the duty of the Secretary of State to conform to the law, and in this he is an officer of the United States, bound to obey the laws. He acts, in this respect, as has been very properly stated at the bar, under the authority of law, and not by the instructions of the President. It is a ministerial act which the law enjoins on a particular officer for a particular purpose ...

The appointment being, under the Constitution, to be made by the President personally, the delivery of the deed of appointment, if necessary to its completion, must be made by the President also. It is not necessary that the livery should be made personally to the grantee of the office; it never is so made. The law would seem to contemplate that it should be made to the Secretary of State, since it directs the secretary to affix the seal to the commission after it shall have been signed by the President. If then the act of livery be necessary to give validity to the commission, it has been delivered when executed and given to the Secretary for the purpose of being sealed, recorded, and transmitted to the party ...

The transmission of the commission is a practice directed by convenience, but not by law. It cannot therefore be necessary to constitute the appointment, which must precede it and which is the mere act of the President. If the Executive required that every person appointed to an office should himself take means to procure his commission, the appointment would not be the less valid on that account. The appointment is the sole act of the President; the transmission of the commission is the sole act of the officer to whom that duty is assigned, and may be accelerated or retarded by circumstances which can have no influence on the appointment. A commission is transmitted to a person already appointed, not to a person to be appointed or not, as the letter enclosing the commission should happen to get into the post office and reach him in safety, or to miscarry ...

A commission bears date, and the salary of the officer commences from his appointment, not from the transmission or acceptance of his commission. When a person appointed to any office refuses to accept that office, the successor is nominated in the place of the person who has declined to accept, and not in the place of the person who had been previously in office and had created the original vacancy.

It is therefore decidedly the opinion of the Court that, when a commission has been signed by the President, the appointment is made, and that the commission is complete when the seal of the United States has been affixed to it by the Secretary of State.

Where an officer is removable at the will of the Executive, the circumstance which completes his appointment is of no concern, because the act is at any time revocable, and the commission may be arrested if still in the office. But when the officer is not removable at the will of the Executive, the appointment is not revocable, and cannot be annulled. It has conferred legal rights which cannot be resumed.

The discretion of the Executive is to be exercised until the appointment has been made. But having once made the appointment, his power over the office is terminated in all cases, where by law the officer is not removable by him. The right to the office is then in the person appointed, and he has the absolute, unconditional power of accepting or rejecting it.

Mr. Marbury, then, since his commission was signed by the President and sealed by the Secretary of State, was appointed, and as the law creating the office gave the officer a right to hold for five years independent of the Executive, the appointment was not revocable, but vested in the officer legal rights which are protected by the laws of his country.

To withhold the commission, therefore, is an act deemed by the Court not warranted by law, but violative of a vested legal right.

This brings us to the second inquiry, which is:

2. If he has a right, and that right has been violated, do the laws of his country afford him a remedy?

The very essence of civil liberty certainly consists in the right of every individual to claim the protection of the laws whenever he receives an injury. One of the first duties of government is to afford that protection. In Great Britain, the King himself is sued in the respectful form of a petition, and he never fails to comply with the judgment of his court ...

The Government of the United States has been emphatically termed a government of laws, and not of men. It will certainly cease to deserve this high appellation if the laws furnish no remedy for the violation of a vested legal right.

If this obloquy is to be cast on the jurisprudence of our country, it must arise from the peculiar character of the case.

It behooves us, then, to inquire whether there be in its composition any ingredient which shall exempt from legal investigation or exclude the injured party from legal redress. In pursuing this inquiry, the first question which presents itself is whether this can be arranged with that class of cases which come under the description of *damnum absque injuria* -- a loss without an injury.

This description of cases never has been considered, and, it is believed, never can be considered, as comprehending offices of trust, of honour or of profit ...

Is it in the nature of the transaction? Is the act of delivering or withholding a commission to be considered as a mere political act belonging to the Executive department alone, for the performance of which entire confidence is placed by our Constitution in the Supreme Executive, and for any misconduct respecting which the injured individual has no remedy?

That there may be such cases is not to be questioned. but that every act of duty to be performed in any of the great departments of government constitutes such a case is not to be admitted ...

Whatever the practice on particular occasions may be, the theory of this principle will certainly never be maintained. No act of the Legislature confers so extraordinary a privilege, nor can it derive countenance from the doctrines of the common law ...

It follows, then, that the question whether the legality of an act of the head of a department be examinable in a court of justice or not must always depend on the nature of that act.

If some acts be examinable and others not, there must be some rule of law to guide the Court in the exercise of its jurisdiction.

In some instances, there may be difficulty in applying the rule to particular cases; but there cannot, it is believed, be much difficulty in laying down the rule.

By the Constitution of the United States, the President is invested with certain important political powers, in the exercise of which he is to use his own discretion, and is accountable only to his country in his political character and to his own conscience. To aid him in the performance of these duties, he is authorized to appoint certain officers, who act by his authority and in conformity with his orders.

In such cases, their acts are his acts; and whatever opinion may be entertained of the manner in which executive discretion may be used, still there exists, and can exist, no power to control that discretion. The subjects are political. They respect the nation, not individual rights, and, being entrusted to the Executive, the decision of the Executive is conclusive. The application of this remark will be perceived by adverting to the act of Congress for establishing the Department of Foreign Affairs. This officer, as his duties were prescribed by that act, is to conform precisely to the will of the President. He is the mere organ by whom that will is communicated. The acts of such an officer, as an officer, can never be examinable by the Courts.

But when the Legislature proceeds to impose on that officer other duties; when he is directed peremptorily to perform certain acts; when the rights of individuals are dependent on the performance of those acts; he is so far the officer of the law, is amenable to the laws for his conduct, and cannot at his discretion, sport away the vested rights of others.

The conclusion from this reasoning is that, where the heads of departments are the political or confidential agents of the Executive, merely to execute the will of the President, or rather to act in cases in which the Executive possesses a constitutional or legal discretion, nothing can be more perfectly clear than that their acts are only politically examinable. But where a specific duty is assigned by law, and individual rights depend upon the performance of that duty, it seems equally clear that the individual who considers himself injured has a right to resort to the laws of his country for a remedy ...

The question whether a right has vested or not is, in its nature, judicial, and must be tried by the judicial authority ...

It is then the opinion of the Court:

1. That, by signing the commission of Mr. Marbury, the President of the United States appointed him a justice of peace for the County of Washington in the District of Columbia, and that the seal of the United States, affixed thereto by the Secretary of State, is conclusive testimony of the verity of the signature, and of the completion of the appointment, and that the appointment conferred on him a legal right to the office for the space of five years.

2. That, having this legal title to the office, he has a consequent right to the commission, a refusal to deliver which is a plain violation of that right, for which the laws of his country afford him a remedy.

It remains to be inquired whether,

3. He is entitled to the remedy for which he applies. This depends on: ...

1. The nature of the writ.

1. With respect to the officer to whom it would be directed. The intimate political relation, subsisting between the President of the United States and the heads of departments, necessarily renders any legal investigation of the acts of one of those high officers peculiarly irksome, as well as delicate, and excites some hesitation with respect to the propriety of entering into such investigation. Impressions are often received without much reflection or examination, and it is not wonderful that, in such a case as this, the assertion by an individual of his legal claims in a court of justice, to which claims it is the duty of that court to attend, should, at first view, be considered by some as an attempt to intrude into the cabinet and to intermeddle with the prerogatives of the Executive.

If one of the heads of departments commits any illegal act under colour of his office by which an individual sustains an injury, it cannot be pretended that his office alone exempts him from being sued in the ordinary mode of proceeding, and being compelled to obey the judgment of the law. How then can his office exempt him from this particular mode of deciding on the legality of his conduct if the case be such a case as would, were any other individual the party complained of, authorize the process? ...

It is true that the mandamus now moved for is not for the performance of an act expressly enjoined by statute ...

This, then, is a plain case of a mandamus, either to deliver the commission or a copy of it from the record, and it only remains to be inquired:

Whether it can issue from this Court.

The act to establish the judicial courts of the United States authorizes the Supreme Court

to issue writs of mandamus, in cases warranted by the principles and usages of law, to any courts appointed, or persons holding office, under the authority of the United States.

The Secretary of State, being a person, holding an office under the authority of the United States, is precisely within the letter of the description, and if this Court is not authorized to issue a writ of mandamus to such an officer, it must be because the law is unconstitutional, and therefore absolutely incapable of conferring the authority and assigning the duties which its words purport to confer and assign.

The Constitution vests the whole judicial power of the United States in one Supreme Court, and such inferior courts as Congress shall, from time to time, ordain and establish. This power is expressly extended to all cases arising under the laws of the United States; and consequently, in some form, may be exercised over the present case, because the right claimed is given by a law of the United States.

16

In the distribution of this power. it is declared that

The Supreme Court shall have original jurisdiction in all cases affecting ambassadors, other public ministers and consuls, and those in which a state shall be a party. In all other cases, the Supreme Court shall have appellate jurisdiction.

It has been insisted at the bar, that, as the original grant of jurisdiction to the Supreme and inferior courts is general, and the clause assigning original jurisdiction to the Supreme Court contains no negative or restrictive words, the power remains to the Legislature to assign original jurisdiction to that Court in other cases than those specified in the article which has been recited, provided those cases belong to the judicial power of the United States.

If it had been intended to leave it in the discretion of the Legislature to apportion the judicial power between the Supreme and inferior courts according to the will of that body, it would certainly have been useless to have proceeded further than to have defined the judicial power and the tribunals in which it should be vested. The subsequent part of the section is mere surplusage -- is entirely without meaning -- if such is to be the construction. If Congress remains at liberty to give this court appellate jurisdiction where the Constitution has declared their jurisdiction shall be original, and original jurisdiction where the Constitution has declared it shall be appellate, the distribution of jurisdiction made in the Constitution, is form without substance.

Affirmative words are often, in their operation, negative of other objects than those affirmed, and, in this case, a negative or exclusive sense must be given to them or they have no operation at all.

It cannot be presumed that any clause in the Constitution is intended to be without effect, and therefore such construction is inadmissible unless the words require it ...

When an instrument organizing fundamentally a judicial system divides it into one Supreme and so many inferior courts as the Legislature may ordain and establish, then enumerates its powers, and proceeds so far to distribute them as to define the jurisdiction of the Supreme Court by declaring the cases in which it shall take original jurisdiction, and that in others it shall take appellate jurisdiction, the plain import of the words seems to be that, in one class of cases, its jurisdiction is original, and not appellate; in the other, it is appellate, and not original. ,If any other construction would render the clause inoperative, that is an additional reason for rejecting such other construction, and for adhering to the obvious meaning.

To enable this court then to issue a mandamus, it must be shown to be an exercise of appellate jurisdiction, or to be necessary to enable them to exercise appellate jurisdiction ...

It is the essential criterion of appellate jurisdiction that it revises and corrects the proceedings in a cause already instituted, and does not create that case. Although, therefore, a mandamus may be directed to courts, yet to issue such a writ to an officer for the delivery of a paper is, in effect, the same as to sustain an original action for that paper, and therefore seems not to belong to appellate, but to original jurisdiction. Neither is it necessary in such a case as this to enable the Court to exercise its appellate jurisdiction.

The authority, therefore, given to the Supreme Court by the act establishing the judicial courts of the United States to issue writs of mandamus to public officers appears not to be warranted by the Constitution, and it becomes necessary to inquire whether a jurisdiction so conferred can be exercised ...

This original and supreme will organizes the government and assigns to different departments their respective powers. It may either stop here or establish certain limits not to be transcended by those departments ...

Between these alternatives there is no middle ground. The Constitution is either a superior, paramount law, unchangeable by ordinary means, or it is on a level with ordinary legislative acts, and, like other acts, is alterable when the legislature shall please to alter it.

If the former part of the alternative be true, then a legislative act contrary to the Constitution is not law; if the latter part be true, then written Constitutions are absurd attempts on the part of the people to limit a power in its own nature illimitable.

Certainly all those who have framed written Constitutions contemplate them as forming the fundamental and paramount law of the nation, and consequently the theory of every such government must be that an act of the Legislature repugnant to the Constitution is void.

It is emphatically the province and duty of the Judicial Department to say what the law is. Those who apply the rule to particular cases must, of necessity, expound and interpret that rule. If two laws conflict with each other, the Courts must decide on the operation of each.

So, if a law be in opposition to the Constitution, if both the law and the Constitution apply to a particular case, so that the Court must either decide that case conformably to the law, disregarding the Constitution, or conformably to the Constitution, disregarding the law, the Court must determine which of these conflicting rules governs the case. This is of the very essence of judicial duty.

If, then, the Courts are to regard the Constitution, and the Constitution is superior to any ordinary act of the Legislature, the Constitution, and not such ordinary act, must govern the case to which they both apply.

Those, then, who controvert the principle that the Constitution is to be considered in court as a paramount law are reduced to the necessity of maintaining that courts must close their eyes on the Constitution, and see only the law.

This doctrine would subvert the very foundation of all written Constitutions. It would declare that an act which, according to the principles and theory of our government, is entirely void, is yet, in practice, completely obligatory. It would declare that, if the Legislature shall do what is expressly forbidden, such act, notwithstanding the express prohibition, is in reality effectual. It would be giving to the Legislature a practical and real omnipotence with the same breath which professes to restrict their powers within narrow limits. It is prescribing limits, and declaring that those limits may be passed at pleasure.

That it thus reduces to nothing what we have deemed the greatest improvement on political institutions -- a written Constitution, would of itself be sufficient, in America where written Constitutions have been viewed with so much reverence, for rejecting the construction. But the peculiar expressions of the Constitution of the United States furnish additional arguments in favour of its rejection.

The judicial power of the United States is extended to all cases arising under the Constitution ...

In some cases then, the Constitution must be looked into by the judges. And if they can open it at all, what part of it are they forbidden to read or to obey?

There are many other parts of the Constitution which serve to illustrate this subject.

It is declared that "no tax or duty shall be laid on articles exported from any State." Suppose a duty on the export of cotton, of tobacco, or of flour, and a suit instituted to recover it. Ought judgment to be rendered in such a case? ought the judges to close their eyes on the Constitution, and only see the law?

The Constitution declares that "no bill of attainder or *ex post facto* law shall be passed."

If, however, such a bill should be passed and a person should be prosecuted under it, must the Court condemn to death those victims whom the Constitution endeavours to preserve?

"No person," says the Constitution, "shall be convicted of treason unless on the testimony of two witnesses to the same overt act, or on confession in open court."

Here. the language of the Constitution is addressed especially to the Courts. It prescribes, directly for them, a rule of evidence not to be departed from. If the Legislature should change that rule, and declare one witness, or a confession out of court, sufficient for conviction, must the constitutional principle yield to the legislative act?

19

From these and many other selections which might be made, it is apparent that the framers of the Constitution contemplated that instrument as a rule for the government of courts, as well as of the Legislature.

Why otherwise does it direct the judges to take an oath to support it? This oath certainly applies in an especial manner to their conduct in their official character. How immoral to impose it on them if they were to be used as the instruments, and the knowing instruments, for violating what they swear to support! ...

Why does a judge swear to discharge his duties agreeably to the Constitution of the United States if that Constitution forms no rule for his government? if it is closed upon him and cannot be inspected by him?

If such be the real state of things, this is worse than solemn mockery. To prescribe or to take this oath becomes equally a crime.

It is also not entirely unworthy of observation that, in declaring what shall be the supreme law of the land, the Constitution itself is first mentioned, and not the laws of the United States generally, but those only which shall be made in pursuance of the Constitution, have that rank.

Thus, the particular phraseology of the Constitution of the United States confirms and strengthens the principle, supposed to be essential to all written Constitutions, that a law repugnant to the Constitution is void, and that courts, as well as other departments, are bound by that instrument.

The rule must be discharged.

Arizonans for Official English v. Arizona (MCLE, page 39) illustrates the concept of *mootness* -- the refusal of the Court to hear a case when the outcome has already been determined. The unanimous decision also provides insight into the complexity of the judicial process, especially appeals. Note how the opinion emphasizes that the "actual controversy" requirement of the U.S. Constitution must be satisfied at all stages of a case. The Court was highly critical of the Ninth Circuit U.S. Court of Appeals' failure to either reverse the or vacate the lower court decision, noting that the appellate court should have given stronger deference to the state attorney general's request that the case be certified to the Arizona Supreme Court to determine the effect and constitutionality of the amendment in question.

Arizonans for Official English v. Arizona

Argued December 4, 1996
Decided March 3, 1997

520 U.S. 43, 117 S.Ct. 1055, 137 L.Ed.2d 170

CERTIORARI TO THE UNITED STATES COURT OF APPEALS

FOR THE NINTH CIRCUIT

Syllabus

Maria-Kelly F. Yniguez, an Arizona state employee at the time, sued the State and its Governor, Attorney General, and Director of the Department of Administration under 42 U.S.C. § 1983, alleging that State Constitution Article XXVIII -- key provisions of which declare English "the official language of the State," require the State to "act in English and in no other language," and authorize state residents and businesses "to bring [state court] suit[s] to enforce th[e] Article" -- violated, *inter alia*, the Free Speech Clause of the First Amendment. Yniguez used both English and Spanish in her work, and feared that Article XXVIII, if read broadly, would require her to face discharge or other discipline if she did not refrain from speaking Spanish while serving the State. She requested injunctive and declaratory relief, counsel fees, and "all other relief that the Court deems just and proper." During the early phases of the suit, the State Attorney General released an Opinion expressing his view that Article XXVIII is constitutional in that, although it requires the expression of "official acts" in English, it allows government employees to use other languages to facilitate the delivery of governmental services. The Federal District Court heard testimony, and, among its rulings, determined that only the Governor, in her official capacity, was a proper defendant. The court at the same time, dismissed the State because of its Eleventh Amendment immunity, the State Attorney General because he had no authority to enforce Article XXVIII against state employees, and the Director because there was no showing that she had undertaken or threatened any action adverse to Yniguez; rejected the Attorney General's interpretation of the Article on the ground that it conflicted with the measure's plain language; declared the Article fatally overbroad after reading it to impose a sweeping ban on the use of any language other than English by all of Arizona officialdom; and declined to allow the Arizona courts the initial opportunity to determine the scope of Article XXVIII. Following the Governor's announcement that she would not appeal, the District Court denied the State Attorney General's request to certify the pivotal state law question -- the Article's correct construction -- to the Arizona Supreme Court. The District Court also denied the State Attorney General's motion to intervene on behalf of the State, under 28 U.S.C. § 2403(b), to contest on appeal the court's holding that the Article is unconstitutional. In addition, the court denied the motion of newcomers Arizonans for Official English Committee (AOE) and its Chairman Park, sponsors of the ballot initiative that became Article XXVIII, to intervene to support the Article's constitutionality. The day after AOE, Park, and the State Attorney General filed their notices of appeal, Yniguez resigned from state employment to accept a job in the private sector. The Ninth Circuit then concluded that AOE and Park met standing requirements under Article III of the Federal Constitution, and could proceed as party appellants, and that the Attorney General, having successfully obtained dismissal below, could not reenter as a party, but could present an argument, pursuant to § 2403(b), regarding the constitutionality of Article XXVIII. Thereafter, the State Attorney General informed the Ninth Circuit of Yniguez'ss resignation and suggested that, for lack of a viable plaintiff, the case was moot. The court disagreed, holding that a plea for nominal damages could be read into the complaint's "all other relief' clause to save the case. The en banc Ninth Circuit ultimately affirmed the District Court's ruling that Article XXVIII was unconstitutional, and announced that Yniguez was entitled to nominal damages from the State. Finding the Article's "plain language" dispositive, and noting that the State Attorney General had never conceded that the Article would be unconstitutional if construed as Yniguez asserted it should be, the Court of Appeals also rejected the Attorney General's limiting construction of the Article and declined to certify the matter to the State Supreme Court. Finally, the Ninth Circuit acknowledged a state court challenge to Article XXVIII's constitutionality, *Ruiz v. State,* but found that litigation no cause to stay the federal proceedings.

Held: Because the case was moot, and should not have been retained for adjudication on the merits, the Court vacates the Ninth Circuit's judgment and remands the case with directions that the action be dismissed by the District Court. This Court expresses no view on the correct interpretation of Article XXVIII or on the measure's constitutionality.

69 F.3d 920, vacated and remanded.

GINSBURG, J., delivered the opinion for a unanimous Court.

GINSBURG, J., lead opinion

Federal courts lack competence to rule definitively on the meaning of state legislation [ ], nor may they adjudicate challenges to state measures absent a showing of actual impact on the challenger [ ]. The Ninth Circuit, in the case at hand, lost sight of these limitations. The initiating plaintiff, Maria-Kelly F. Yniguez, sought federal court resolution of a novel question: the compatibility with the Federal Constitution of a 1988 amendment to Arizona's Constitution declaring English "the official language of the State of Arizona" -- "the language of . . . all government functions and actions." Ariz.Const., Art. XXVIII, §§ 1(1), 1(2). Participants in the federal litigation, proceeding without benefit of the views of the Arizona Supreme Court, expressed diverse opinions on the meaning of the amendment.

Yniguez commenced and maintained her suit as an individual, not as a class representative. A state employee at the time she filed her complaint, Yniguez voluntarily left the State's employ in 1990 and did not allege she would seek to return to a public post. Her departure for a position in the private sector made her claim for prospective relief moot. Nevertheless, the Ninth Circuit held that a plea for nominal damages could be read into Yniguez'ss complaint to save the case, and therefore pressed on to an ultimate decision. A three-judge panel of the Court of Appeals declared Article XXVIII unconstitutional in 1994, and a divided en banc court, in 1995, adhered to the panel's position.

The Ninth Circuit had no warrant to proceed as it did. The case had lost the essential elements of a justiciable controversy, and should not have been retained for adjudication on the merits by the Court of Appeals. We therefore vacate the Ninth Circuit's judgment, and remand the case to that court with directions that the action be dismissed by the District Court. We express no view on the correct interpretation of Article XXVIII or on the measure's constitutionality.

I

...

Prior to the Ninth Circuit's July 1991 opinion, indeed, the very day after AOE, Park ,and the Arizona Attorney General filed their notices of appeal, a development of prime importance occurred. On April 10, 1990, Yniguez resigned from state employment in order to accept another job. Her resignation apparently became effective on April 25, 1990. Arizona's Attorney General so informed the Ninth Circuit in September 1991, "suggest[ing] that this case may lack a viable plaintiff and, hence, may be moot." [ ]

One year later, on September 16, 1992, the Ninth Circuit rejected the mootness suggestion. *Yniguez v. Arizona,* 975 F.2d 646. The court's ruling adopted in large part Yniguez's argument opposing a mootness disposition. [ ] "[T]he plaintiff may no longer be affected by the English only provision," the Court of Appeals acknowledged. [ ] Nevertheless, the court continued, "[her] constitutional claims may entitle her to an award of nominal damages." [ ] Her complaint did "not expressly request nominal damages," the Ninth Circuit noted, but "it did request `all other relief that the Court deems just and proper under the circumstances.'" [ ] Thus, the Court of Appeals reasoned, one could regard the District Court's judgment as including an "implicit denial" of nominal damages. [ ]

[In the next several paragraphs, J. Ginsburg describes the various proceedings involved prior to the case ultimately reaching the Supreme Court.] ...

After construing Article XXVIII as sweeping in scope, the en banc Court of Appeals condemned the provision as manifestly overbroad, trenching untenably on speech rights of Arizona officials and public employees. [ ] For prevailing in the § 1983 action, the court ultimately announced, Yniguez was "entitled to nominal damages." [ ] On remand, the District Court followed the en banc Court of Appeals' order and, on November 3, 1995, awarded Yniguez $1.00 in damages. [ ]

AOE and Park petitioned this Court for a writ of certiorari to the Ninth Circuit. They raised two questions: (1) Does Article XXVIII violate the Free Speech Clause of the First Amendment by "declaring English the official language of the State and requiring English to be used to perform official acts"?; (2) Do public employees have "a Free Speech right to disregard the [State's] official language" and perform official actions in a language other than English? This Court granted the petition and requested the parties to brief as threshold matters (1) the standing of AOE and Park to proceed in this action as defending parties, and (2) Yniguez's continuing satisfaction of the case or controversy requirement. [ ]

III

Article III, § 2, of the Constitution confines federal courts to the decision of "Cases" or "Controversies." Standing to sue or defend is an aspect of the case or controversy requirement. [ ] To qualify as a party with standing to litigate, a person must show, first and foremost, "an invasion of a legally protected interest" that is "concrete and particularized" and "`actual or imminent.'" [ ] An interest shared generally with the public at large in the proper application of the Constitution and laws will not do. [ ] Standing to defend on appeal in the place of an original defendant, no less than standing to sue, demands that the litigant possess "a direct stake in the outcome." [ ]

The standing Article III requires must be met by persons seeking appellate review, just as it must be met by persons appearing in courts of first instance. [ ] The decision to seek review "is not to be placed in the

24

hands of `concerned bystanders,'" persons who would seize it "as a `vehicle for the vindication of value interests.'" [ ] An intervenor cannot step into the shoes of the original party unless the intervenor independently "fulfills the requirements of Article III." [ ]

In granting the petition for a writ of certiorari in this case, we called for briefing on the question whether AOE and Park have standing, consonant with Article III of the Federal Constitution, to defend in federal court the constitutionality of Arizona Constitution Article XXVIII. Petitioners argue primarily that, as initiative proponents, they have a *quasi*-legislative interest in defending the constitutionality of the measure they successfully sponsored. AOE and Park stress the funds and effort they expended to achieve adoption of Article XXVIII. We have recognized that state legislators have standing to contest a decision holding a state statute unconstitutional if state law authorizes legislators to represent the State's interests. [ ] AOE and its members, however, are not elected representatives, and we are aware of no Arizona law appointing initiative sponsors as agents of the people of Arizona to defend, in lieu of public officials, the constitutionality of initiatives made law of the State. Nor has this Court ever identified initiative proponents as Article III-qualified defenders of the measures they advocated. [ ]

AOE also asserts representational or associational standing. An association has standing to sue or defend in such capacity, however, only if its members would have standing in their own right. [ ] The requisite concrete injury to AOE members is not apparent. As nonparties in the District Court, AOE's members were not bound by the judgment for Yniguez. That judgment had slim precedential effect [ ] and it left AOE entirely free to invoke Article XXVIII, § 4, the citizen suit provision, in state court, where AOE could pursue whatever relief state law authorized. Nor do we discern anything flowing from Article XXVIII's citizen suit provision -- which authorizes suits to enforce Article XXVIII in state court -- that could support standing for Arizona residents in general, or AOE in particular, to defend the Article's constitutionality in federal court.

We thus have grave doubts whether AOE and Park have standing under Article III to pursue appellate review. Nevertheless, we need not definitively resolve the issue. Rather, we will follow a path we have taken before, and inquire, as a primary matter, whether originating plaintiff Yniguez still has a case to pursue. [ ] For purposes of that inquiry, we will assume, *arguendo,* that AOE and Park had standing to place this case before an appellate tribunal. [ ] We may resolve the question whether there remains a live case or controversy with respect to Yniguez's claim without first determining whether AOE or Park has standing to appeal because the former question, like the latter, goes to the Article III jurisdiction of this Court and the courts below, not to the merits of the case. [ ]

IV

To qualify as a case fit for federal court adjudication, "an actual controversy must be extant at all stages of review, not merely at the time the complaint is filed." [ ] As a state employee subject to Article XXVIII, Yniguez had a viable claim at the outset of the litigation in late 1988. We need not consider whether her case lost vitality in January, 1989,

25

when the Attorney General released Opinion No. I89-009. That opinion construed Article XXVIII to require the expression of "official acts" in English, but to leave government employees free to use other languages "if reasonably necessary to the fair and effective delivery of services" to the public. [ ] ... Yniguez left her state job in April, 1990, to take up employment in the private sector, where her speech was not governed by Article XXVIII. At that point, it became plain that she lacked a still vital claim for prospective relief. [ ]

The Attorney General suggested mootness, but Yniguez resisted, and the Ninth Circuit adopted her proposed method of saving the case. [ ] It was not dispositive, the court said, that Yniguez "may no longer be affected by the English only provision," [ ] for Yniguez had raised in response to the mootness suggestion "[t]he possibility that [she] may seek nominal damages," [ ]. At that stage of the litigation, however, Yniguez's plea for nominal damages was not the possibility the Ninth Circuit imagined.

Yniguez's complaint rested on 42 U.S.C. § 1983. [ ] Although Governor Mofford, in her official capacity, was the sole defendant against whom the District Court's February 1990 declaratory judgment ran [ ], the Ninth Circuit held the State answerable for the nominal damages Yniguez requested on appeal. [ ] .... We have held, however, that § 1983 actions do not lie against a State. [ ] Thus, the claim for relief the Ninth Circuit found sufficient to overcome mootness was nonexistent. The barrier was not, as the Ninth Circuit supposed, Eleventh Amendment immunity, which the State could waive. The stopper was that § 1983 creates no remedy against a State.

Furthermore, under the Ninth Circuit's ruling on intervention, the State of Arizona was permitted to participate in the appeal, but not as a party. [ ] The Court of Appeals never revised that ruling. To recapitulate, in July, 1991, two months prior to the Attorney General's suggestion of mootness, the Court of Appeals rejected the Attorney General's plea for party status, as representative of the State. [ ] The Ninth Circuit accorded the Attorney General the "right [under 28 U.S.C. § 2403(b)] to argue the constitutionality of Article XXVIII . . . contingent upon AOE and Park's bringing the appeal." [ ] ... AOE and Park, however, were the sole participants recognized by the Ninth Circuit as defendants-appellants. The Attorney General "ha[d] asked the district court to dismiss him as a party," the Court of Appeals noted, hence he "cannot now become one again." [ ]. While we do not rule on the propriety of the Ninth Circuit's exclusion of the State as a party, we note this lapse in that court's accounting for its decision: The Ninth Circuit did not explain how it arrived at the conclusion that an intervenor the court had designated a nonparty could be subject, nevertheless, to an obligation to pay damages.

True, Yniguez and the Attorney General took the steps the Ninth Circuit prescribed: Yniguez filed a cross-appeal notice, [ ]; the Attorney General waived the State's right to assert the Eleventh Amendment as a defense to an award of nominal damages [ ]. But the earlier, emphatic Court of Appeals ruling remained in place: the State's intervention, although proper under § 2403(b), the Ninth Circuit maintained, gave Arizona no status as a party in the lawsuit. [ ]

In advancing cooperation between Yniguez and the Attorney General regarding the request for and agreement to pay nominal damages, the Ninth Circuit did not home in on the federal courts' lack of authority to act in friendly or feigned proceedings. [ ] ... It should have been clear to the Court of Appeals that a claim for nominal damages, extracted late in the day from Yniguez's general prayer for relief and asserted solely to avoid otherwise certain mootness, bore close inspection. [ ] ... On such inspection, the Ninth Circuit might have perceived that Yniguez's plea for nominal damages could not genuinely revive the case.

When a civil case becomes moot pending appellate adjudication, [t]he established practice . . . in the federal system . . . is to reverse or vacate the judgment below and remand with a direction to dismiss.

[ ] Vacatur "clears the path for future relitigation" by eliminating a judgment the loser was stopped from opposing on direct review. [ ] Vacatur is in order when mootness occurs through happenstance -- circumstances not attributable to the parties -- or, relevant here, the "unilateral action of the party who prevailed in the lower court." [ ] ...

As just explained, Yniguez's changed circumstances -- her resignation from public sector employment to pursue work in the private sector -- mooted the case stated in her complaint. We turn next to the effect of that development on the judgments below. Yniguez urges that vacatur ought not occur here. She maintains that the State acquiesced in the Ninth Circuit's judgment, and that, in any event, the District Court judgment should not be upset, because it was entered before the mooting event occurred, and was not properly appealed. [ ]

Concerning the Ninth Circuit's judgment, Yniguez argues that the State's Attorney General effectively acquiesced in that court's dispositions when he did not petition for this Court's review. [ ] We do not agree that this Court is disarmed in the manner suggested.

We have taken up the case for consideration on the petition for certiorari filed by AOE and Park. Even if we were to rule definitively that AOE and Park lack standing, we would have an obligation essentially to search the pleadings on core matters of federal court adjudicatory authority -- to inquire not only into this Court's authority to decide the questions petitioners present, but to consider also the authority of the lower courts to proceed ... [ ] ...

Because the Ninth Circuit refused to stop the adjudication when Yniguez's departure from public employment came to its attention, we set aside the unwarranted en banc Court of Appeals judgment.

As to the District Court's judgment, Yniguez stresses that the date of the mooting event -- her resignation from state employment effective April 25, 1990 -- was some 2 months after the February 6, 1990, decision she seeks to preserve. Governor Mofford was the sole defendant bound by the District Court judgment, and Mofford declined to appeal. Therefore, Yniguez contends, the District Court's judgment should remain untouched.

But AOE and Park had an arguable basis for seeking appellate review, and the Attorney General promptly made known his independent interest in defending Article XXVIII against the total demolition declared by the District Court. First, the Attorney General repeated his plea for certification of Article XXVIII to the Arizona Supreme Court. [ ] And if that plea failed, he asked, in his motion to intervene, "to be joined as a defendant so that he may participate in all post-judgment proceedings." [ ] Although denied party status, the Attorney General had at a minimum, a right secured by Congress, a right to present argument on appeal "on the question of constitutionality." [ ] He was in the process of pursuing that right when the mooting event occurred.

We have already recounted the course of proceedings thereafter. First, Yniguez did not tell the Court of Appeals that she had left the State's employ. [ ] When that fact was disclosed to the court by the Attorney General, a dismissal for mootness was suggested, and rejected. A mootness disposition at that point was in order, we have just explained. Such a dismissal would have stopped in midstream the Attorney General's endeavor, premised on § 2403(b), to defend the State's law against a declaration of unconstitutionality, and so would have warranted a path-clearing vacatur decree.

The State urges that its current plea for vacatur is compelling in view of the extraordinary course of this litigation. [ ] ... The "exceptional circumstances" that abound in this case, [ ] and the federalism concern we next consider, lead us to conclude that vacatur down the line is the equitable solution.

V

In litigation generally, and in constitutional litigation most prominently, courts in the United States characteristically pause to ask: is this conflict really necessary? When anticipatory relief is sought in federal court against a state statute, respect for the place of the States in our federal system calls for close consideration of that core question. [ ]

Arizona's Attorney General, in addition to releasing his own opinion on the meaning of Article XXVIII [ ], asked both the District Court and the Court of Appeals to pause before proceeding to judgment; specifically, he asked both federal courts to seek, through the State's certification process, an authoritative construction of the new measure from the Arizona Supreme Court. [ ]

Certification today covers territory once dominated by a deferral device called "*Pullman* abstention," after the generative case, *Railroad Comm'n of Tex. v. Pullman Co.*, 312 U.S. 496 (1941). Designed to avoid federal court error in deciding state law questions antecedent to federal constitutional issues, the *Pullman* mechanism remitted parties to the state courts for adjudication of the unsettled state law issues. If settlement of the state law question did not prove dispositive of the case, the parties could return to the federal court for decision of the federal issues. Attractive in theory because it placed state law questions in courts equipped to rule authoritatively on them, *Pullman* abstention proved protracted and expensive in practice, for it entailed a full round of litigation in the state court system before any resumption of proceedings in federal court. [ ]

Certification procedure, in contrast, allows a federal court faced with a novel state law question to put the question directly to the State's highest court, reducing the delay, cutting the cost, and increasing the assurance of gaining an authoritative response. [ ] Most States have adopted certification procedures. [ ]. Arizona's statute [ ] permits the State's highest court to consider questions certified to it by federal district courts, as well as courts of appeals and this Court.

Both lower federal courts in this case refused to invite the aid of the Arizona Supreme Court because they found the language of Article XXVIII "plain," and the Attorney General's limiting construction unpersuasive. [ ] Furthermore, the Ninth Circuit suggested as a proper price for certification a concession by the Attorney General that Article XXVIII "would be unconstitutional if construed as [plaintiff Yniguez] contended it should be." [ ]. Finally, the Ninth Circuit acknowledged the pendency of a case similar to Yniguez's in the Arizona court system, but found that litigation no cause for a stay of the federal court proceedings. [ ]

A more cautious approach was in order. Through certification of novel or unsettled questions of state law for authoritative answers by a State's highest court, a federal court may save "time, energy, and resources and hel[p] build a cooperative judicial federalism." [ ] ... It is true, as the Ninth Circuit observed [   ], in our decision certifying questions in *American Booksellers Assn., Inc.,* 484 U.S. 383 (1988), we noted the State's concession that the statute there challenged would be unconstitutional if construed as plaintiffs contended it should be [ ]. But neither in that case nor in any other did we declare such a concession a condition precedent to certification.

The District Court and the Court of Appeals ruled out certification primarily because they believed Article XXVIII was not fairly subject to a limiting construction. [ ] The assurance with which the lower courts reached that judgment is all the more puzzling in view of the position the initiative sponsors advanced before this Court on the meaning of Article XXVIII.

At oral argument on December 4, 1996, counsel for petitioners AOE and Park informed the Court that, in petitioners' view, the Attorney General's reading of the Article was "the correct interpretation." [ ] ... The Ninth Circuit found AOE's "explanations as to the initiative's scope . . . confused and self-contradictory" [ ], and we agree that AOE wavered in its statements of position [ ]. Nevertheless, the Court of Appeals understood that the ballot initiative proponents themselves at least "partially endorsed the Attorney General's reading." [ ] Given the novelty of the question and its potential importance to the conduct of Arizona's business, plus the views of the Attorney General and those of Article XXVIII's sponsors, the certification requests merited more respectful consideration than they received in the proceedings below.

Federal courts, when confronting a challenge to the constitutionality of a federal statute, follow a "cardinal principle": they "will first ascertain whether a construction . . . is fairly possible" that will

29

contain the statute within constitutional bounds. [ ] State courts, when interpreting state statutes, are similarly equipped to apply that cardinal principle. [ ]

Warnings against premature adjudication of constitutional questions bear heightened attention when a federal court is asked to invalidate a State's law, for the federal tribunal risks friction-generating error when it endeavors to construe a novel state Act not yet reviewed by the State's highest court. [ ] ...

Blending abstention with certification, the Ninth Circuit found "no unique circumstances in this case militating in favor of certification." [ ] Novel, unsettled questions of state law, however, not "unique circumstances," are necessary before federal courts may avail themselves of state certification procedures. Those procedures do not entail the delays, expense, and procedural complexity that generally attend abstention decisions. [ ] Taking advantage of certification made available by a State may "greatly simplif[y]" an ultimate adjudication in federal court. [ ]

The course of Yniguez's case was complex. The complexity might have been avoided had the District Court, more than eight years ago, accepted the certification suggestion made by Arizona's Attorney General. The Arizona Supreme Court was not asked by the District Court or the Court of Appeals to say what Article XXVIII means. But the State's highest court has that very question before it in *Ruiz v. Symington* [ ], the case the Ninth Circuit considered no cause for federal court hesitation. In *Ruiz,* which has been stayed pending our decision in this case [ ], the Arizona Supreme Court may now rule definitively on the proper construction of Article XXVIII. Once that court has spoken, adjudication of any remaining federal constitutional question may indeed become greatly simplified.

*   *   *   *

For the reasons stated, the judgment of the Court of Appeals is vacated, and the case is remanded to that court with directions that the action be dismissed by the District Court.

It is so ordered.

In *J.E.B. v. Alabama ex rel. T.B.* (MCLE, page 640), the Supreme Court held 6-3 that litigants may not strike potential jurors based solely upon gender. In *Batson v. Kentucky* eight years earlier the Court had ruled that the equal protection clause of the 14th Amendment to the U.S. Constitution barred a prosecutor from exercising peremptory challenges in the trial of a criminal defendant to eliminate potential jurors solely because of race or because the prosecutor believed that members of a particular racial group would not render a fair and impartial verdict. The concurring and dissenting opinions are included to illustrate the struggle the Court had with this decision. *J.E.B. v. Alabama ex rel. T.B.*, unlike *Batson*, was a civil trial involving paternity and child support. (The Court had already extended *Batson* to civil trial in earlier decisions.) Note that J. O'Connor, in her concurring opinion, expresses her belief that the holding should be limited to the *government*'s use of gender-based peremptory strikes. In their dissenting opinions, C.J. Rehnquist and J. Scalia articulate their concern that this extension of *Batson* will undermine the jury selection process.

J.E.B. v. Alabama ex rel. T.B.

Argued November 2, 1993
Decided April 19, 1994

511 U.S. 127, 114 S.Ct. 1419, 128 L.Ed.2d 89

CERTIORARI TO THE COURT OF CIVIL APPEALS OF ALABAMA

Syllabus

At petitioner's paternity and child support trial, respondent State used 9 of its 10 peremptory challenges to remove male jurors. The court empaneled an all-female jury after rejecting petitioner's claim that the logic and reasoning of *Batson v. Kentucky,* 476 U.S. 79 -- in which this Court held that the Equal Protection Clause of the Fourteenth Amendment prohibits peremptory strikes based solely on race -- extend to forbid gender-based peremptory challenges. The jury found petitioner to be the father of the child in question and the trial court ordered him to pay child support. The Alabama Court of Civil Appeals affirmed.

Held: The Equal Protection Clause prohibits discrimination in jury selection on the basis of gender, or on the assumption that an individual will be biased in a particular case solely because that person happens to be a woman or a man. Respondent's gender-based peremptory challenges cannot survive the heightened equal protection scrutiny that this Court affords distinctions based on gender. Respondent's rationale -- that its decision to strike virtually all males in this case may reasonably have been based on the perception, supported by history, that men

31

otherwise totally qualified to serve as jurors might be more sympathetic and receptive to the arguments of a man charged in a paternity action, while women equally qualified might be more sympathetic and receptive to the arguments of the child's mother -- is virtually unsupported and is based on the very stereotypes the law condemns. The conclusion that litigants may not strike potential jurors solely on the basis of gender does not imply the elimination of all peremptory challenges. So long as gender does not serve as a proxy for bias, unacceptable jurors may still be removed, including those who are members of a group or class that is normally subject to "rational basis" review and those who exhibit characteristics that are disproportionately associated with one gender. [ ]

606 So.2d 156, reversed and remanded.

BLACKMUN, J., delivered the opinion of the Court, in which Stevens, O'CONNOR, SOUTER, and GINSBURG, JJ., joined. O'CONNOR, J., filed a concurring opinion. KENNEDY, J., filed an opinion concurring in the judgment, *post*. REHNQUIST, C.J., filed a dissenting opinion. SCALIA, J., filed a dissenting opinion, in which REHNQUIST, C.J., and THOMAS, J., joined.

BLACKMUN, J., lead opinion

In *Batson v. Kentucky*, 476 U.S. 79 (1986), this Court held that the Equal Protection Clause of the Fourteenth Amendment governs the exercise of peremptory challenges by a prosecutor in a criminal trial. The Court explained that, although a defendant has "no right to a `petit jury composed in whole or in part of persons of his own race,'" [ ] ... Since *Batson*, we have reaffirmed repeatedly our commitment to jury selection procedures that are fair and nondiscriminatory. We have recognized that, whether the trial is criminal or civil, potential jurors, as well as litigants, have an equal protection right to jury selection procedures that are free from state-sponsored group stereotypes rooted in, and reflective of, historical prejudice. [ ]

Although premised on equal protection principles that apply equally to gender discrimination, all our recent cases defining the scope of *Batson* involved alleged racial discrimination in the exercise of peremptory challenges. Today we are faced with the question whether the Equal Protection Clause forbids intentional discrimination on the basis of gender, just as it prohibits discrimination on the basis of race. We hold that gender, like race, is an unconstitutional proxy for juror competence and impartiality.

I

On behalf of relator T.B., the mother of a minor child, respondent State of Alabama filed a complaint for paternity and child support against petitioner J.E.B. in the District Court of Jackson County, Alabama. On October 21, 1991, the matter was called for trial and jury selection began. The trial court assembled a panel of 36 potential jurors,

12 males and 24 females. After the court excused three jurors for cause, only 10 of the remaining 33 jurors were male. The State then used 9 of its 10 peremptory strikes to remove male jurors; petitioner used all but one of his strikes to remove female jurors. As a result, all the selected jurors were female.

Before the jury was empaneled, petitioner objected to the State's peremptory challenges on the ground that they were exercised against male jurors solely on the basis of gender, in violation of the Equal Protection Clause of the Fourteenth Amendment. [ ] Petitioner argued that the logic and reasoning of *Batson v. Kentucky,* which prohibits peremptory strikes solely on the basis of race, similarly forbids intentional discrimination on the basis of gender. The court rejected petitioner's claim and empaneled the all-female jury. [ ] The jury found petitioner to be the father of the child and the court entered an order directing him to pay child support. On post-judgment motion, the court reaffirmed its ruling that *Batson* does not extend to gender-based peremptory challenges. App. 33. The Alabama Court of Civil Appeals affirmed [ ], relying on Alabama precedent [ ]. The Supreme Court of Alabama denied certiorari.

We granted certiorari [ ] to resolve a question that has created a conflict of authority -- whether the Equal Protection Clause forbids peremptory challenges on the basis of gender as well as on the basis of race. Today we reaffirm what, by now, should be axiomatic: intentional discrimination on the basis of gender by state actors violates the Equal Protection Clause, particularly where, as here, the discrimination serves to ratify and perpetuate invidious, archaic, and overbroad stereotypes about the relative abilities of men and women.

II

Discrimination on the basis of gender in the exercise of peremptory challenges is a relatively recent phenomenon. Gender-based peremptory strikes were hardly practicable for most of our country's existence, since, until the 19th century, women were completely excluded from jury service. So well-entrenched was this exclusion of women that, in 1880, this Court, while finding that the exclusion of African-American men from juries violated the Fourteenth Amendment, expressed no doubt that a State "may confine the selection [of jurors] to males." [ ].

Many States continued to exclude women from jury service well into the present century, despite the fact that women attained suffrage upon ratification of the Nineteenth Amendment in 1920. States that did permit women to serve on juries often erected other barriers, such as registration requirements and automatic exemptions, designed to deter women from exercising their right to jury service. [ ] ...

The prohibition of women on juries was derived from the English common law which, according to Blackstone, rightfully excluded women from juries under "the doctrine of *propter defectum sexus,* literally, the

33

`defect of sex.'" [ ] In this country, supporters of the exclusion of women from juries tended to couch their objections in terms of the ostensible need to protect women from the ugliness and depravity of trials. Women were thought to be too fragile and virginal to withstand the polluted courtroom atmosphere. [ ] ...

This Court in *Ballard v. United States,* 329 U.S. 187 (1946), first questioned the fundamental fairness of denying women the right to serve on juries. Relying on its supervisory powers over the federal courts, it held that women may not be excluded from the venire in federal trials in States where women were eligible for jury service under local law ... [ ]

Fifteen years later, however, the Court still was unwilling to translate its appreciation for the value of women's contribution to civic life into an enforceable right to equal treatment under state laws governing jury service. In *Hoyt v. Florida,* 368 U.S. at 61, the Court found it reasonable, "despite the enlightened emancipation of women," to exempt women from mandatory jury service by statute, allowing women to serve on juries only if they volunteered to serve. The Court justified the differential exemption policy on the ground that women, unlike men, occupied a unique position "as the center of home and family life." [ ]

In 1975, the Court finally repudiated the reasoning of *Hoyt* and struck down, under the Sixth Amendment, an affirmative registration statute nearly identical to the one at issue in *Hoyt.* [ ] We explained:

Restricting jury service to only special groups or excluding identifiable segments playing major roles in the community cannot be squared with the constitutional concept of jury trial.

[ ] The diverse and representative character of the jury must be maintained

"partly as assurance of a diffused impartiality and partly because sharing in the administration of justice is a phase of civic responsibility."

[ ]

III

Taylor relied on Sixth Amendment principles, but the opinion's approach is consistent with the heightened equal protection scrutiny afforded gender-based classifications. Since *Reed v. Reed,* 404 U.S. 71 (1971), this Court consistently has subjected gender-based classifications to heightened scrutiny in recognition of the real danger that government policies that professedly are based on reasonable considerations in fact may be reflective of "archaic and overbroad" generalizations about gender [ ], or based on "outdated misconceptions concerning the role of females in the home rather than in the `marketplace and world of ideas.'" [ ] ...

Despite the heightened scrutiny afforded distinctions based on gender, respondent argues that gender discrimination in the selection of

34

the petit jury should be permitted, though discrimination on the basis of race is not. Respondent suggests that "gender discrimination in this country . . . has never reached the level of discrimination" against African-Americans, and therefore gender discrimination, unlike racial discrimination, is tolerable in the courtroom. [ ]

While the prejudicial attitudes toward women in this country have not been identical to those held toward racial minorities, the similarities between the experiences of racial minorities and women, in some contexts, "overpower those differences." [ ] ...

Certainly, with respect to jury service, African-Americans and women share a history of total exclusion, a history which came to an end for women many years after the embarrassing chapter in our history came to an end for African-Americans.

We need not determine, however, whether women or racial minorities have suffered more at the hands of discriminatory state actors during the decades of our Nation's history. It is necessary only to acknowledge that "our Nation has had a long and unfortunate history of sex discrimination," [ ] a history which warrants the heightened scrutiny we afford all gender-based classifications today. Under our equal protection jurisprudence, gender-based classifications require "an exceedingly persuasive justification" in order to survive constitutional scrutiny. [ ] Thus, the only question is whether discrimination on the basis of gender in jury selection substantially furthers the State's legitimate interest in achieving a fair and impartial trial. In making this assessment, we do not weigh the value of peremptory challenges as an institution against our asserted commitment to eradicate invidious discrimination from the courtroom. Instead, we consider whether peremptory challenges based on gender stereotypes provide substantial aid to a litigant's effort to secure a fair and impartial jury.

Far from proffering an exceptionally persuasive justification for its gender-based peremptory challenges, respondent maintains that its decision to strike virtually all the males from the jury in this case

may reasonably have been based upon the perception, supported by history, that men otherwise totally qualified to serve upon a jury in any case might be more sympathetic and receptive to the arguments of a man alleged in a paternity action to be the father of an out-of-wedlock child, while women equally qualified to serve upon a jury might be more sympathetic and receptive to the arguments of the complaining witness who bore the child.

[ ]

We shall not accept as a defense to gender-based peremptory challenges "the very stereotype the law condemns." [ ] Respondent's rationale, not unlike those regularly expressed for gender-based strikes, is reminiscent of the arguments advanced to justify the total exclusion of women from juries. Respondent offers virtually no support for the

35

conclusion that gender alone is an accurate predictor of juror's attitudes; yet it urges this Court to condone the same stereotypes that justified the wholesale exclusion of women from juries and the ballot box. Respondent seems to assume that gross generalizations that would be deemed impermissible if made on the basis of race are somehow permissible when made on the basis of gender.

Discrimination in jury selection, whether based on race or on gender, causes harm to the litigants, the community, and the individual jurors who are wrongfully excluded from participation in the judicial process. The litigants are harmed by the risk that the prejudice which motivated the discriminatory selection of the jury will infect the entire proceedings. [ ] The community is harmed by the State's participation in the perpetuation of invidious group stereotypes and the inevitable loss of confidence in our judicial system that state-sanctioned discrimination in the courtroom engenders.

When state actors exercise peremptory challenges in reliance on gender stereotypes, they ratify and reinforce prejudicial views of the relative abilities of men and women. Because these stereotypes have wreaked injustice in so many other spheres of our country's public life, active discrimination by litigants on the basis of gender during jury selection "invites cynicism respecting the jury's neutrality and its obligation to adhere to the law." [   ] The potential for cynicism is particularly acute in cases where gender-related issues are prominent, such as cases involving rape, sexual harassment, or paternity. Discriminatory use of peremptory challenges may create the impression that the judicial system has acquiesced in suppressing full participation by one gender or that the "deck has been stacked" in favor of one side. [ ] ....

In recent cases, we have emphasized that individual jurors themselves have a right to nondiscriminatory jury selection procedures. [ ] Contrary to respondent's suggestion, this right extends to both men and women. [ ] ... All persons, when granted the opportunity to serve on a jury, have the right not to be excluded summarily because of discriminatory and stereotypical presumptions that reflect and reinforce patterns of historical discrimination. Striking individual jurors on the assumption that they hold particular views simply because of their gender is "practically a brand upon them, affixed by law, an assertion of their inferiority." [ ] It denigrates the dignity of the excluded juror, and, for a woman, reinvokes a history of exclusion from political participation. The message it sends to all those in the courtroom, and all those who may later learn of the discriminatory act, is that certain individuals, for no reason other than gender, are presumed unqualified by state actors to decide important questions upon which reasonable persons could disagree.

IV

Our conclusion that litigants may not strike potential jurors

36

solely on the basis of gender does not imply the elimination of all peremptory challenges. Neither does it conflict with a State's legitimate interest in using such challenges in its effort to secure a fair and impartial jury. Parties still may remove jurors whom they feel might be less acceptable than others on the panel; gender simply may not serve as a proxy for bias. Parties may also exercise their peremptory challenges to remove from the venire any group or class of individuals normally subject to "rational basis" review. [ ] Even strikes based on characteristics that are disproportionately associated with one gender could be appropriate, absent a showing of pretext. [ ]

If conducted properly, *voir dire* can inform litigants about potential jurors, making reliance upon stereotypical and pejorative notions about a particular gender or race both unnecessary and unwise. *Voir dire* provides a means of discovering actual or implied bias and a firmer basis upon which the parties may exercise their peremptory challenges intelligently. [ ] ...   The   experience   in   the   many jurisdictions that have barred gender-based challenges belies the claim that litigants and trial courts are incapable of complying with a rule barring strikes based on gender. [ ] ... As with race-based *Batson* claims, a party alleging gender discrimination must make a prima facie showing of intentional discrimination before the party exercising the challenge is required to explain the basis for the strike. [ ] When an explanation is required, it need not rise to the level of a "for cause" challenge; rather, it merely must be based on a juror characteristic other than gender, and the proffered explanation may not be pretextual. [ ]

Failing to provide jurors the same protection against gender discrimination as race discrimination could frustrate the purpose of *Batson* itself. Because gender and race are overlapping categories, gender can be used as a pretext for racial discrimination. Allowing parties to remove racial minorities from the jury not because of their race, but because of their gender, contravenes well-established equal protection principles and could insulate effectively racial discrimination from judicial scrutiny.

V

Equal opportunity to participate in the fair administration of justice is fundamental to our democratic system. It not only furthers the goals of the jury system. It reaffirms the promise of equality under the law -- that all citizens, regardless of race, ethnicity, or gender, have the chance to take part directly in our democracy. [ ] ... When persons are excluded from participation in our democratic processes solely because of race or gender, this promise of equality dims, and the integrity of our judicial system is jeopardized.

In view of these concerns, the Equal Protection Clause prohibits discrimination in jury selection on the basis of gender, or on the assumption that an individual will be biased in a particular case for no reason other than the fact that the person happens to be a woman or

37

happens to be a man. As with race, the

core guarantee of equal protection, ensuring citizens that their State will not discriminate . . . , would be meaningless were we to approve the exclusion of jurors on the basis of such assumptions, which arise solely from the jurors' [gender].

Batson, 476 U.S. at 97-98.

The judgment of the Court of Civil Appeals of Alabama is reversed and the case is remanded to that court for further proceedings not inconsistent with this opinion.

It is so ordered.

O'CONNOR, J., concurring

JUSTICE O'CONNOR, concurring.

I agree with the Court that the Equal Protection Clause prohibits the government from excluding a person from jury service on account of that person's gender. [ ] The State's proffered justifications for its gender-based peremptory challenges are far from the "exceedingly persuasive" showing required to sustain a gender-based classification. [ ] I therefore join the Court's opinion in this case. But today's important blow against gender discrimination is not costless. I write separately to discuss some of these costs, and to express my belief that today's holding should be limited to the *government's* use of gender-based peremptory strikes.

Batson v. Kentucky, 476 U.S. 79 (1986), itself was a significant intrusion into the jury selection process. *Batson* mini-hearings are now routine in state and federal trial courts, and *Batson* appeals have proliferated as well. Demographics indicate that today's holding may have an even greater impact than did *Batson* itself. In further constitutionalizing jury selection procedures, the Court increases the number of cases in which jury selection -- once a sideshow -- will become part of the main event.

For this same reason, today's decision further erodes the role of the peremptory challenge ... The peremptory challenge is "a practice of ancient origin" and is "part of our common law heritage." [ ] ...

The peremptory's importance is confirmed by its persistence: it was well established at the time of Blackstone, and continues to endure in all the States. [ ] ...

Indeed, often a reason for it cannot be stated, for a trial lawyer's judgments about a juror's sympathies are sometimes based on experienced hunches and educated guesses, derived from a juror's responses at voir dire or a juror's "bare looks and gestures." [ ] That a trial lawyer's instinctive assessment of a juror's predisposition cannot meet the high standards of a challenge for cause does not mean that the lawyer's instinct is erroneous. [ ] ... Our belief that experienced lawyers will often correctly intuit which jurors are likely to be the least sympathetic, and our understanding that the lawyer will often be unable to explain the intuition, are the very reason we cherish the peremptory challenge. But, as we add, layer by layer, additional constitutional restraints on the use of the peremptory, we force lawyers to articulate what we know is often inarticulable.

In so doing, we make the peremptory challenge less discretionary and more like a challenge for cause. We also increase the possibility that biased jurors will be allowed onto the jury, because sometimes a lawyer will be unable to provide an acceptable gender-neutral explanation even though the lawyer is in fact correct that the juror is unsympathetic. Similarly, in jurisdictions where lawyers exercise their strikes in open court, lawyers may be deterred from using their peremptories, out of the fear that if they are unable to justify the strike the court will seat a juror who knows that the striking party thought him unfit. Because I believe the peremptory remains an important litigator's tool and a fundamental part of the process of selecting impartial juries, our increasing limitation of it gives me pause.

Nor is the value of the peremptory challenge to the litigant diminished when the peremptory is exercised in a gender-based manner. We know that, like race, gender matters. A plethora of studies make clear that in rape cases, for example, female jurors are somewhat more likely to vote to convict than male jurors. [ ] ... Moreover, though there have been no similarly definitive studies regarding, for example, sexual harassment, child custody, or spousal or child abuse, one need not be a sexist to share the intuition that, in certain cases, a person's gender and resulting life experience will be relevant to his or her view of the case. "'Jurors are not expected to come into the jury box and leave behind all that their human experience has taught them.'" [ ] Individuals are not expected to ignore as jurors what they know as men -- or women.

Today's decision severely limits a litigant's ability to act on this intuition, for the import of our holding is that any correlation between a juror's gender and attitudes is irrelevant as a matter of constitutional law. But to say that gender makes no difference as a matter of law is not to say that gender makes no difference as a matter of fact ... [ ] Today's decision is a statement that, in an effort to eliminate the potential discriminatory use of the peremptory [ ], gender is now governed by the special rule of relevance formerly reserved for race. Though we gain much from this statement, we cannot ignore what we lose. In extending *Batson* to gender, we have added an additional burden to the state and federal trial process, taken a step closer to eliminating the peremptory challenge, and diminished the ability of litigants to act on sometimes accurate gender-based assumptions about juror attitudes.

These concerns reinforce my conviction that today's decision should be limited to a prohibition on the government's use of gender-based peremptory challenges. The Equal Protection Clause prohibits only discrimination by state actors ... Clearly, criminal defendants are not state actors ...

Accordingly, I adhere to my position that the Equal Protection Clause does not limit the exercise of peremptory challenges by private civil litigants and criminal defendants. This case itself presents no state action dilemma, for here the State of Alabama itself filed the paternity suit on behalf of petitioner. But what of the next case? Will we, in the name of fighting gender discrimination, hold that the battered wife -- on trial for wounding her abusive husband -- is a state actor? Will we preclude her from using her peremptory challenges to ensure that the jury of her peers contains as many women members as possible? I assume we will, but I hope we will not.

KENNEDY, J., concurring

JUSTICE KENNEDY, concurring in the judgment.

I am in full agreement with the Court that the Equal Protection Clause prohibits gender discrimination in the exercise of peremptory challenges. I write to explain my understanding of why our precedents lead to that conclusion.

Though, in some initial drafts, the Fourteenth Amendment was written to prohibit discrimination against "persons because of race, color or previous condition of servitude," the Amendment submitted for consideration and later ratified contained more comprehensive terms: "No State shall . . . deny to any person within its jurisdiction the equal protection of the laws." [ ] In recognition of the evident historical fact that the Equal Protection Clause was adopted to prohibit government discrimination on the basis of race, the Court most often interpreted it in the decades that followed in accord with that purpose. In *Strauder v. West Virginia*, 100 U.S. 303 (1880), for example, the Court invalidated a West Virginia law prohibiting blacks from serving on juries. In so doing, the decision said of the Equal Protection Clause: "What is this but declaring that the law in the States shall be the same for the black as for the white." [ ] And while the Court held that the State could not confine jury service to whites, it further noted that the State could confine jury service "to males, to freeholders, to citizens, to persons within certain ages, or to persons having educational qualifications." [ ]

As illustrated by the necessity for the Nineteenth Amendment in 1920, much time passed before the Equal Protection Clause was thought to reach beyond the purpose of prohibiting racial discrimination and to apply as well to discrimination based on sex. In over 20 cases beginning in 1971, however, we have subjected government classifications based on sex to heightened scrutiny. Neither the State nor any Member of the Court questions that principle here. And though the intermediate scrutiny test we have applied may not provide a very clear standard in all instances [ ], our case law does reveal a strong presumption that gender classifications are invalid. [ ]

40

There is no doubt under our precedents, therefore, that the Equal Protection Clause prohibits sex discrimination in the selection of jurors. [ ] The only question is whether the Clause also prohibits peremptory challenges based on sex. The Court is correct to hold that it does. The Equal Protection Clause and our constitutional tradition are based on the theory that an individual possesses rights that are protected against lawless action by the government. The neutral phrasing of the Equal Protection Clause, extending its guarantee to "any person," reveals its concern with rights of individuals, not groups (though group disabilities are sometimes the mechanism by which the State violates the individual right in question) ... [ ]

For purposes of the Equal Protection Clause, an individual denied jury service because of a peremptory challenge exercised against her on account of her sex is no less injured than the individual denied jury service because of a law banning members of her sex from serving as jurors. [ ] The injury is to personal dignity and to the individual's right to participate in the political process. [ ] The neutrality of the Fourteenth Amendment's guarantee is confirmed by the fact that the Court has no difficulty in finding a constitutional wrong in this case, which involves males excluded from jury service because of their gender.

The importance of individual rights to our analysis prompts a further observation concerning what I conceive to be the intended effect of today's decision. We do not prohibit racial and gender bias in jury selection only to encourage it in jury deliberations. Once seated, a juror should not give free rein to some racial or gender bias of his or her own. The jury system is a kind of compact by which power is transferred from the judge to jury, the jury in turn deciding the case in accord with the instructions defining the relevant issues for consideration. The wise limitations on the authority of courts to inquire into the reasons underlying a jury's verdict does not mean that a jury ought to disregard the court's instructions. A juror who allows racial or gender bias to influence assessment of the case breaches the compact and renounces his or her oath.

In this regard, it is important to recognize that a juror sits not as a representative of a racial or sexual group, but as an individual citizen. Nothing would be more pernicious to the jury system than for society to presume that persons of different backgrounds go to the jury room to voice prejudice. [ ] The jury pool must be representative of the community, but that is a structural mechanism for preventing bias, not enfranchising it. [ ] "Jury competence is an individual rather than a group or class matter. That fact lies at the very heart of the jury system." [ ] Thus, the Constitution guarantees a right only to an impartial jury, not to a jury composed of members of a particular race or gender. [ ]

*   *   *   *

For these reasons, I concur in the judgment of the Court holding that peremptory strikes based on gender violate the Equal Protection

41

Clause.

REHNQUIST, J., dissenting

CHIEF JUSTICE REHNQUIST, dissenting.

I agree with the dissent of JUSTICE SCALIA, which I have joined. I add these words in support of its conclusion. Accepting *Batson v. Kentucky*, 476 U.S. 79 (1986), as correctly decided, there are sufficient differences between race and gender discrimination such that the principle of *Batson* should not be extended to peremptory challenges to potential jurors based on sex.

That race and sex discrimination are different is acknowledged by our equal protection jurisprudence, which accords different levels of protection to the two groups. Classifications based on race are inherently suspect, triggering "strict scrutiny," while gender-based classifications are judged under a heightened, but less searching standard of review. [ ] Racial groups comprise numerical minorities in our society, warranting, in some situations, a greater need for protection, whereas the population is divided almost equally between men and women. Furthermore, while substantial discrimination against both groups still lingers in our society, racial equality has proved a more challenging goal to achieve on many fronts than gender equality. [ ]

Batson, which involved a black defendant challenging the removal of black jurors, announced a sea-change in the jury selection process. In balancing the dictates of equal protection and the historical practice of peremptory challenges, long recognized as securing fairness in trials, the Court concluded that the command of the Equal Protection Clause was superior. But the Court was careful that its rule not "undermine the contribution the challenge generally makes to the administration of justice." [ ] *Batson* is best understood as a recognition that race lies at the core of the commands of the Fourteenth Amendment. Not surprisingly, all of our post-*Batson* cases have dealt with the use of peremptory strikes to remove black or racially identified venirepersons, and all have described *Batson* as fashioning a rule aimed at preventing purposeful discrimination against a cognizable racial group ... [ ]

Under the Equal Protection Clause, these differences mean that the balance should tilt in favor of peremptory challenges when sex, not race, is the issue. Unlike the Court, I think the State has shown that jury strikes on the basis of gender "substantially further" the State's legitimate interest in achieving a fair and impartial trial through the venerable practice of peremptory challenges. [ ] ... The two sexes differ, both biologically and, to a diminishing extent, in experience. It is not merely "stereotyping" to say that these differences may produce a difference in outlook which is brought to the jury room. Accordingly, use of peremptory challenges on the basis of sex is generally not the sort of derogatory and invidious act which peremptory challenges directed at black jurors may be.

42

JUSTICE O'CONNOR's concurrence recognizes several of the costs associated with extending *Batson* to gender-based peremptory challenges -- lengthier trials, an increase in the number and complexity of appeals addressing jury selection, and a "diminished . . . ability of litigants to act on sometimes accurate gender-based assumptions about juror attitudes." [ ] These costs are, in my view, needlessly imposed by the Court's opinion, because the Constitution simply does not require the result which it reaches.

SCALIA, J., dissenting

JUSTICE SCALIA, with whom THE CHIEF JUSTICE and JUSTICE THOMAS join, dissenting.

Today's opinion is an inspiring demonstration of how thoroughly up-to-date and right-thinking we Justices are in matters pertaining to the sexes (or as the Court would have it, the genders), and how sternly we disapprove the male chauvinist attitudes of our predecessors. The price to be paid for this display -- a modest price, surely -- is that most of the opinion is quite irrelevant to the case at hand. The hasty reader will be surprised to learn, for example, that this lawsuit involves a complaint about the use of peremptory challenges to exclude *men* from a petit jury. To be sure, petitioner, a man, used all but one of *his* peremptory strikes to remove *women* from the jury (he used his last challenge to strike the sole remaining male from the pool), but the validity of *his* strikes is not before us. Nonetheless, the Court treats itself to an extended discussion of the historic exclusion of women not only from jury service, but also from service at the bar (which is rather like jury service, in that it involves going to the courthouse a lot). [ ] All this, as I say, is irrelevant, since the case involves state action that allegedly discriminates against men. The parties do not contest that discrimination on the basis of sex is subject to what our cases call "heightened scrutiny," and the citation of one of those cases ... [ ] is all that was needed.

The Court also spends time establishing that the use of sex as a proxy for particular views or sympathies is unwise, and perhaps irrational. The opinion stresses the lack of statistical evidence to support the widely held belief that at least in certain types of cases, a juror's sex has some statistically significant predictive value as to how the juror will behave. [ ] This assertion seems to place the Court in opposition to its earlier Sixth Amendment "fair cross-section" cases. [ ] ... But times and trends do change, and unisex is unquestionably in fashion. Personally, I am less inclined to demand statistics, and more inclined to credit the perceptions of experienced litigators who have had money on the line. But it does not matter. The Court's fervent defense of the proposition *il n'y a pas de différence entre les hommes et les femmes* (it stereotypes the opposite view as hateful "stereotyping") turns out to be, like its recounting of the history of sex discrimination against women, utterly irrelevant. Even if sex was a remarkably good predictor in certain cases, the Court would find its use in peremptories unconstitutional. [ ]

Of course, the relationship of sex to partiality *would have been* relevant if the Court had demanded in this case what it ordinarily demands: that the complaining party have suffered some injury. Leaving aside for the moment the reality that the defendant himself had the opportunity to strike women from the jury, the defendant would have some cause to complain about the prosecutor's striking male jurors if male jurors tend to be more favorable towards defendants in paternity suits. But if men and women jurors are (as the Court thinks) fungible, then the only arguable injury from the prosecutor's "impermissible" use of male sex as the basis for his peremptories is injury to the stricken juror, not to the defendant. Indeed, far from having suffered harm, petitioner, a state actor under our precedents [ ], has himself actually *inflicted* harm on female jurors. The Court today presumably supplies petitioner with a cause of action by applying the uniquely expansive third-party standing analysis of [ ], according petitioner a remedy because of the wrong done to male jurors. This case illustrates why making restitution to Paul when it is Peter who has been robbed is such a bad idea. Not only has petitioner, by implication of the Court's own reasoning, suffered no harm, but the scientific evidence presented at trial established petitioner's paternity with 99.92% accuracy. Insofar as petitioner is concerned, this is a case of harmless error if there ever was one; a retrial will do nothing but divert the State's judicial and prosecutorial resources, allowing either petitioner or some other malefactor to go free.

The core of the Court's reasoning is that peremptory challenges on the basis of any group characteristic subject to heightened scrutiny are inconsistent with the guarantee of the Equal Protection Clause. That conclusion can be reached only by focusing unrealistically upon individual exercises of the peremptory challenge, and ignoring the totality of the practice. Since all groups are subject to the peremptory challenge (and will be made the object of it, depending upon the nature of the particular case) it is hard to see how any group is denied equal protection. [ ] That explains why peremptory challenges coexisted with the Equal Protection Clause for 120 years. This case is a perfect example of how the system as a whole is even-handed. While the only claim before the Court is petitioner's complaint that the prosecutor struck male jurors, for every man struck by the government, petitioner's own lawyer struck a woman. To say that men were singled out for discriminatory treatment in this process is preposterous. The situation would be different if both sides systematically struck individuals of one group, so that the strikes evinced group-based animus and served as a proxy for segregated venire lists. [ ] The pattern here, however, displays not a systemic sex-based animus, but each side's desire to get a jury favorably disposed to its case. That is why the Court's characterization of respondent's argument as "reminiscent of the arguments advanced to justify the total exclusion of women from juries," [ ] is patently false. Women were categorically excluded from juries because of doubt that they were competent; women are stricken from juries by peremptory challenge because of doubt that they are well disposed to the striking party's case. [ ] There is discrimination and dishonor in the former, and not in the latter -- which explains the 106-year interlude between our holding that exclusion from juries on the basis of race was unconstitutional [ ], and our holding that peremptory challenges on the basis of race were unconstitutional [ ].

Although the Court's legal reasoning in this case is largely obscured by anti-male-chauvinist oratory, to the extent such reasoning is discernible, it invalidates much more than sex-based strikes. After identifying unequal treatment (by separating individual exercises of peremptory challenge from the process as a whole), the Court applies the "heightened scrutiny" mode of equal protection analysis used for sex-based discrimination, and concludes that the strikes fail heightened scrutiny because they do not substantially further an important government interest. The Court says that the only important government interest that could be served by peremptory strikes is "securing a fair and impartial jury" [ ]. It refuses to accept respondent's argument that these strikes further that interest by eliminating a group (men) which may be partial to male defendants, because it will not accept any argument based on "`the very stereotype the law condemns.'" [ ] This analysis, entirely eliminating the only allowable argument, implies that sex-based strikes do not even rationally further a legitimate government interest, let alone pass heightened scrutiny. That places *all* peremptory strikes based on *any* group characteristic at risk, since they can all be denominated "stereotypes." Perhaps, however (though I do not see why it should be so), only the stereotyping of groups entitled to heightened or strict scrutiny constitutes "the very stereotype the law condemns" -- so that other stereotyping (*e.g.,* wide-eyed blondes and football players are dumb) remains OK. Or perhaps when the Court refers to "impermissible stereotypes" [ ], it means the adjective to be limiting, rather than descriptive -- so that we can expect to learn from the Court's peremptory stereotyping jurisprudence in the future which stereotypes the Constitution frowns upon and which it does not.

Even if the line of our later cases guaranteed by today's decision limits the theoretically boundless *Batson* principle to race, sex, and perhaps other classifications subject to heightened scrutiny (which presumably would include religious belief [ ], much damage has been done. It has been done, first and foremost, to the peremptory challenge system, which loses its whole character when (in order to defend against "impermissible stereotyping" claims) "reasons" for strikes must be given. The right of peremptory challenge "`is, as Blackstone says, an arbitrary and capricious right; and it must be exercised with full freedom, or it fails of its full purpose.'" [ ] The loss of the real peremptory will be felt most keenly by the criminal defendant [ ], whom we have until recently thought "should not be held to accept a juror, apparently indifferent, whom he distrusted for any reason or for no reason." [ ] And make no mistake about it: there really is no substitute for the peremptory. *Voir dire* (though it can be expected to expand as a consequence of today's decision) cannot fill the gap. The biases that go along with group characteristics tend to be biases that the juror himself does not perceive, so that it is no use asking about them. It is fruitless to inquire of a male juror whether he harbors any subliminal prejudice in favor of unwed fathers.

And damage has been done, secondarily, to the entire justice system, which will bear the burden of the expanded quest for "reasoned peremptories" that the Court demands. The extension of *Batson* to sex, and almost certainly beyond [ ], will provide the basis for extensive collateral litigation, which especially the criminal defendant (who litigates full-time and cost-free) can be expected to pursue. While demographic reality places some limit on the number of cases in which race-based challenges will be an issue, every case contains a potential sex-based claim. Another consequence, as I have mentioned, is a lengthening of the *voir dire* process that already burdens trial courts.

The irrationality of today's strike-by-strike approach to equal protection is evident from the consequences of extending it to its logical conclusion. If a fair and impartial trial is a prosecutor's only legitimate goal; if adversarial trial stratagems must be tested against that goal in abstraction from their role within the system as a whole; and if, so tested, sex-based stratagems do not survive heightened scrutiny -- then the prosecutor presumably violates the Constitution when he selects a male or female police officer to testify because he believes one or the other sex might be more convincing in the context of the particular case, or because he believes one or the other might be more appealing to a predominantly male or female jury. A decision to stress one line of argument or present certain witnesses before a mostly female jury -- for example, to stress that the defendant victimized women -- becomes, under the Court's reasoning, intentional discrimination by a state actor on the basis of gender.

*   *   *   *

In order, it seems to me, not to eliminate any real denial of equal protection, but simply to pay conspicuous obeisance to the equality of the sexes, the Court imperils a practice that has been considered an essential part of fair jury trial since the dawn of the common law. The Constitution of the United States neither requires nor permits this vandalizing of our people's traditions.

For these reasons, I dissent.

46

In Victor v. Nebraska and *Sandoval v. California* (MCLE, page 68), the Supreme Court upheld jury instructions defining "reasonable doubt" in two criminal cases even though the instructions included archaic language with which the justices were clearly uncomfortable. The Court found that, taken as a whole, the instructions met constitutional muster. The consolidated decisions illustrate the flexibility the Court is willing to grant trial courts in instructing juries on the meaning of "beyond a reasonable doubt."

Victor v. Nebraska and *Sandoval v. California*

Argued January 18, 1994
Decided March 22, 1994

511 U.S. 1, 114 S.Ct. 1239, 127 L.Ed.2d 583

CERTIORARI TO THE SUPREME COURT OF NEBRASKA

Syllabus

The government must prove beyond a reasonable doubt every element of a charged offense. *In re Winship,* 397 U.S. 358. In upholding the first degree murder convictions and death sentences of petitioners Sandoval and Victor, the Supreme Courts of California and Nebraska, respectively, rejected contentions that due process was violated by the pattern jury instructions defining "reasonable doubt" that were given in both cases.

Held: Taken as a whole, the instructions in question correctly conveyed the concept of reasonable doubt, and there is no reasonable likelihood that the jurors understood the instructions to allow convictions based on proof insufficient to meet the *Winship* standard. [ ]

(a) The Constitution does not dictate that any particular form of words be used in advising the jury of the government's burden of proof, so long as, "taken as a whole, the instructions correctly conve[y] the concept of reasonable doubt" ...

(b) The instructions given in Sandoval's case defined reasonable doubt as, among other things, "not a mere possible doubt," but one "depending on moral evidence," such that the jurors could not say they felt an abiding conviction, "to a moral certainty," of the truth of the charge. [ ] ...

(c) Sandoval's objection to the charge's use of the 19th century phrases "moral evidence" and "moral certainty" is rejected. Although the former phrase is not a mainstay of the modern lexicon, its meaning today is consistent with its original meaning: evidence based on the general observation of people, rather than on what is demonstrable. Its use here is unproblematic, because the instructions given correctly pointed the jurors' attention to the facts of the case before them, not (as Sandoval contends) the ethics or morality of his criminal acts. Similarly, whereas "moral certainty," standing alone, might not be recognized by modern jurors as a synonym for "proof beyond a reasonable doubt," its use in conjunction with the abiding conviction language must be viewed as having impressed upon the jury the need to reach the subjective state of near certitude of guilt [ ], and thus as not having invited conviction on less than the constitutionally required proof ...

(d) Sandoval's objection to the portion of the charge declaring that a reasonable doubt is "not a mere possible doubt" is also rejected. That the instruction properly uses "possible" in the sense of fanciful is made [ ] clear by the fact that it also notes that everything "is open to some possible or imaginary doubt." [ ]

(e) The instructions given in Victor's case defined reasonable doubt as, among other things, a doubt that will not permit an abiding conviction,"to a moral certainty," of the accused's guilt, and an "actual and substantial doubt" that is not excluded by the "strong probabilities of the case." [ ]

(f) Victor's primary argument -- that equating a reasonable doubt with a "substantial doubt" overstated the degree of doubt necessary for acquittal -- is rejected ...

(g) The inclusion of the "moral certainty" phrase in the Victor charge did not render the instruction unconstitutional.

(h) The reference to "strong probabilities" in the Victor charge does not unconstitutionally understate the government's burden, since the charge also informs the jury that the probabilities must be strong enough to prove guilt beyond a reasonable doubt [ ]

No. 92-8894, 242 Neb. 306, 494 N.W.2d 565, and No. 92-9049, 4 Cal.4th 155, modified, 4 Cal.4th 928a, 841 P.2d 862, affirmed.

O'CONNOR, J., delivered the opinion for a unanimous Court with respect to Part II, and the opinion of the Court with respect to Parts I, III, and IV, in which REHNQUIST, C.J., and STEVENS, SCALIA, KENNEDY, and THOMAS, JJ., joined, and in Parts III-B and IV of which GINSBURG, J., joined. KENNEDY, J., filed a concurring opinion [ ]. GINSBURG, J., filed an opinion concurring in part and concurring in the judgment [ ]. BLACKMUN, J., filed an opinion concurring in part and dissenting in part, in all but Part II of which SOUTER, J., joined [ ] .

O'CONNOR, J., lead opinion

The government must prove beyond a reasonable doubt every element of a charged offense. *In re Winship,* 397 U.S. 358 (1970). Although this standard is an ancient and honored aspect of our criminal justice system, it defies easy explication. In these cases, we consider the constitutionality of two attempts to define "reasonable doubt."

I

The "beyond a reasonable doubt" standard is a requirement of due process, but the Constitution neither prohibits trial courts from defining reasonable doubt nor requires them to do so as a matter of course. [ ] Indeed, so long as the court instructs the jury on the necessity that the defendant's guilt be proven beyond a reasonable doubt [ ], the Constitution does not require that any particular form of words be used in advising the jury of the government's burden of proof. [ ] Rather, "taken as a whole, the instructions [must] correctly conve[y] the concept of reasonable doubt to the jury." [ ]

In only one case have we held that a definition of reasonable doubt violated the Due Process Clause. *Cage v. Louisiana*, 498 U.S. 39 (1990) (per curiam). There, the jurors were told:

> "[A reasonable doubt] is one that is founded upon a real tangible substantial basis, and not upon mere caprice and conjecture. *It must be such doubt as would give rise to a grave uncertainty,* raised in your mind by reasons of the unsatisfactory character of the evidence or lack thereof. A reasonable doubt is not a mere possible doubt. *It is an actual substantial doubt.* It is a doubt that a reasonable man can seriously entertain. What is required is not an absolute or mathematical certainty, but a *moral certainty.*"

Id. at 40 (emphasis added by this Court in *Cage*). We held that the highlighted portions of the instruction rendered it unconstitutional ...

In a subsequent case, we made clear that the proper inquiry is not whether the instruction "could have" been applied in unconstitutional manner, but whether there is a reasonable likelihood that the jury *did* so apply it. [ ] The constitutional question in the present cases, therefore, is whether there is a reasonable likelihood that the jury understood the instructions to allow conviction based on proof insufficient to meet the *Winship* standard. Although other courts have held that instructions similar to those given at petitioners' trials violate the Due Process Clause [ ], both the Nebraska and the California Supreme Courts held that the instructions were constitutional. We granted certiorari, 509 U.S. 954 (1993), and now affirm both judgments.

II

On October 14, 1984, petitioner Sandoval shot three men, two of them fatally, in a gang-related incident in Los Angeles. About two weeks later, he entered the home of a man who had given information to the police about the murders and shot him dead; Sandoval then killed the man's wife because she had seen him murder her husband. Sandoval was convicted on four counts of first degree murder. The jury found that

Sandoval personally used a firearm in the commission of each offense, and found the special circumstance of multiple murder. [   ] He was sentenced to death for murdering the woman and to life in prison without possibility of parole for the other three murders. The California Supreme Court affirmed the convictions and sentences. [   ]

The jury in Sandoval's case was given the following instruction on the government's burden of proof:

> A defendant in a criminal action is presumed to be innocent until the contrary is proved, and, in case of a reasonable doubt whether his guilt is satisfactorily shown, he is entitled to a verdict of not guilty. This presumption places upon the State the burden of proving him guilty beyond a reasonable doubt.
>
> Reasonable doubt is defined as follows: it is *not a mere possible doubt;* because everything relating to human affairs, and *depending on moral evidence,* is open to some possible or imaginary doubt. It is that state of the case which, after the entire comparison and consideration of all the evidence, leaves the minds of the jurors in that condition that they cannot say they feel an abiding conviction, *to a moral certainty,* of the truth of the charge.

[   ] The California Supreme Court rejected Sandoval's claim that the instruction, particularly the highlighted passages, violated the Due Process Clause. [   ]

The instruction given in Sandoval's case has its genesis in a charge given by Chief Justice Shaw of the Massachusetts Supreme Judicial Court more than a century ago:

> [W]hat is reasonable doubt?   It is a term often used, probably pretty well understood, but not easily defined. It is not mere possible doubt; because every thing relating to human affairs, and depending on moral evidence, is open to some possible or imaginary doubt. It is that state of the case, which, after the entire comparison and consideration of all the evidence, leaves the minds of jurors in that condition that they cannot say they feel an abiding conviction, to a moral certainty, of the truth of the charge. The burden of proof is upon the prosecutor.   All the presumptions of law independent of evidence are in favor of innocence; and every person is presumed to be innocent until he is proved guilty. If upon such proof there is reasonable doubt remaining, the accused is entitled to the benefit of it by an acquittal. For it is not sufficient to establish a probability, though a strong on, arising from the doctrine of chances, that the fact charged is more likely to be true than the contrary; but the evidence must establish the truth of the fact to a reasonable and moral certainty; a certainty that convinces and directs

the understanding, and satisfies the reason and judgment, of those who are bound to act conscientiously upon it. This we take to be proof beyond reasonable doubt.

Commonwealth v. Webster, 59 Mass. 295, 320 (1850).

The *Webster* charge is representative of the time when "American courts began applying [the "beyond a reasonable doubt" standard] in its modern form in criminal cases." [ ] ...

A

Sandoval's primary objection is to the use of the phrases "moral evidence" and "moral certainty" in the instruction. As noted, this part of the charge was lifted verbatim from Chief Justice Shaw's *Webster* decision; some understanding of the historical context in which that instruction was written is accordingly helpful in evaluating its continuing validity.

By the beginning of the Republic, lawyers had borrowed the concept of "moral evidence" from the philosophers and historians of the 17th and 18th centuries. [ ] ...

Thus, when Chief Justice Shaw penned the *Webster* instruction in 1850, moral certainty meant a state of subjective certitude about some event or occurrence ... [ ]

Indeed, we have said that "[p]roof to a `moral certainty' is an equivalent phrase with `beyond a reasonable doubt.'" [ ] ...

We recognize that the phrase "moral evidence" is not a mainstay of the modern lexicon, though we do not think it means anything different today than it did in the 19th century. The few contemporary dictionaries that define moral evidence do so consistently with its original meaning. [ ] ...

Moreover, the instruction itself gives a definition of the phrase. The jury was told that "everything relating to human affairs, and depending on moral evidence, is open to some possible or imaginary doubt" -- in other words, that absolute certainty is unattainable in matters relating to human affairs. Moral evidence, in this sentence, can only mean empirical evidence offered to prove such matters -- the proof introduced at trial.

This conclusion is reinforced by other instructions given in Sandoval's case. The judge informed the jurors that their duty was "to determine the facts of the case from the evidence received in the trial and not from any other source." [ ] The judge continued:

> Evidence consists of testimony of witnesses, writings, material objects, or anything presented to the senses and offered to prove the existence or nonexistence of a fact.

[ ] The judge also told the jurors that "you must not be influenced by pity for a defendant or by prejudice against him," and that "[y]ou must not be swayed by mere sentiment, conjecture, sympathy, passion, prejudice, public opinion or public feeling." [ ] These instructions correctly pointed the jurors' attention to the facts of the case before them, not (as Sandoval contends) the ethics or morality of Sandoval's criminal acts. Accordingly, we find the reference to moral evidence unproblematic.

We are somewhat more concerned with Sandoval's argument that the phrase "moral certainty" has lost its historical meaning, and that a modern jury would understand it to allow conviction on proof that does not meet the beyond a reasonable doubt standard. Words and phrases can change meaning over time: a passage generally understood in 1850 may be incomprehensible or confusing to a modern juror. And although some contemporary dictionaries contain definitions of moral certainty similar to the 19th century understanding of the phrase, see Webster's Third New International Dictionary 1468 (unabridged 1981) ("virtual, rather than actual, immediate, or completely demonstrable"); 9 Oxford English Dictionary, *supra,* at 1070 ("a degree of probability so great as to admit of no reasonable doubt"), we are willing to accept Sandoval's premise that "moral certainty," standing alone, might not be recognized by modern jurors as a synonym for "proof beyond a reasonable doubt." But it does not necessarily follow that the California instruction is unconstitutional.

Sandoval first argues that moral certainty would be understood by modern jurors to mean a standard of proof lower than beyond a reasonable doubt. In support of this proposition, Sandoval points to contemporary dictionaries that define moral certainty in terms of probability. *E.g.,* Webster's New Twentieth Century Dictionary, *supra,* at 1168 ("based on strong probability"); Random House Dictionary of the English Language 1249 (2d ed. 1983) ("resting upon convincing grounds of probability"). But the beyond a reasonable doubt standard is, itself, probabilistic.

Although, in this respect, moral certainty is ambiguous in the abstract, the rest of the instruction given in Sandoval's case lends content to the phrase. The jurors were told that they must have "an abiding conviction, to a moral certainty, of the truth of the charge." [ ] An instruction cast in terms of an abiding conviction as to guilt, without reference to moral certainty, correctly states the government's burden of proof. [ ] ... And the judge had already informed the jury that matters relating to human affairs are proven by moral evidence [ ]; giving the same meaning to the word moral in this part of the instruction, moral certainty can only mean certainty with respect to human affairs. As used in this instruction, therefore, we are satisfied that the reference to moral certainty, in conjunction with the abiding conviction language, "impress[ed] upon the factfinder the need to reach a subjective state of near certitude of the guilt of the accused." [ ] Accordingly, we reject Sandoval's contention that the moral certainty element of the California

52

instruction invited the jury to convict him on proof below that required by the Due Process Clause.

Sandoval's second argument is a variant of the first. Accepting that the instruction requires a high level of confidence in the defendant's guilt, Sandoval argues that a juror might be convinced to a moral certainty that the defendant is guilty even though the government has failed to *prove* his guilt beyond a reasonable doubt. A definition of moral certainty in a widely used modern dictionary lends support to this argument, *see* The American Heritage Dictionary of the English Language 1173 (3d ed. 1992) ("Based on strong likelihood or firm conviction, rather than on the actual evidence"), and we do not gainsay its force. As we have noted,

> [t]he constitutional standard recognized in the *Winship* case was expressly phrased as one that protects an accused against a conviction except on *"proof* beyond a reasonable doubt."

[ ]. Indeed, in *Cage,* we contrasted "moral certainty" with "evidentiary certainty." [ ]

But the moral certainty language cannot be sequestered from its surroundings. In the *Cage* instruction, the jurors were simply told that they had to be morally certain of the defendant's guilt; there was nothing else in the instruction to lend meaning to the phrase. Not so here. The jury in Sandoval's case was told that a reasonable doubt is

> that state of the case which, *after the entire comparison and consideration of all the evidence,* leaves the minds of the jurors in that condition that they cannot say they feel an abiding conviction, to a moral certainty, of the truth of the charge.

[ ] (emphasis added). The instruction thus explicitly told the jurors that their conclusion had to be based on the evidence in the case. Other instructions reinforced this message. The jury was told "to determine the facts of the case from the evidence received in the trial and not from any other source." [ ] The judge continued that "you must not be influenced by pity for a defendant or by prejudice against him. . . . You must not be swayed by mere sentiment, conjecture, sympathy, passion, prejudice, public opinion or public feeling." [ ] Accordingly, there is no reasonable likelihood that the jury would have understood moral certainty to be disassociated from the evidence in the case.

We do not think it reasonably likely that the jury understood the words moral certainty either as suggesting a standard of proof lower than due process requires or as allowing conviction on factors other than the government's proof. At the same time, however, we do not condone the use of the phrase. As modern dictionary definitions of moral certainty attest, the common meaning of the phrase has changed since it was used in the *Webster* instruction, and it may continue to do so to the point that

53

it conflicts with the *Winship* standard. Indeed, the definitions of reasonable doubt most widely used in the federal courts do not contain any reference to moral certainty. [ ] But we have no supervisory power over the state courts, and, in the context of the instructions as a whole, we cannot say that the use of the phrase rendered the instruction given in Sandoval's case unconstitutional.

B

Finally, Sandoval objects to the portion of the charge in which the judge instructed the jury that a reasonable doubt is "not a mere possible doubt." The *Cage* instruction included an almost identical reference to "not a mere possible doubt," but we did not intimate that there was anything wrong with that part of the charge. [ ] That is because "[a] 'reasonable doubt,' at a minimum, is one based upon 'reason.'" [ ] A fanciful doubt is not a reasonable doubt. As Sandoval's defense attorney told the jury: "[A]nything can be possible. . . . [A] planet could be made out of blue cheese. But that's really not in the realm of what we're talking about." [ ] That this is the sense in which the instruction uses "possible" is made clear from the final phrase of the sentence, which notes that everything "is open to some possible or imaginary doubt." We therefore reject Sandoval's challenge to this portion of the instruction as well.

III

On December 26, 1987, petitioner Victor went to the Omaha home of an 82 year-old woman for whom he occasionally did gardening work. Once inside, he beat her with a pipe and cut her throat with a knife, killing her. Victor was convicted of first degree murder. A three-judge panel found the statutory aggravating circumstances that Victor had previously been convicted of murder [ ], and that the murder in this case was especially heinous, atrocious, and cruel [ ]. Finding none of the statutory mitigating circumstances, the panel sentenced Victor to death. The Nebraska Supreme Court affirmed the conviction and sentence. [ ]

At Victor's trial, the judge instructed the jury that

> [t]he burden is always on the State to prove beyond a reasonable doubt all of the material elements of the crime charged, and this burden never shifts.

[ ] The charge continued:

> "Reasonable doubt" is such a doubt as would cause a reasonable and prudent person, in one of the graver and more important transactions of life, to pause and hesitate before taking the represented facts as true and relying and acting thereon. It is such a doubt as will not permit you, after full, fair, and impartial consideration of all the evidence,

to have an abiding conviction, *to a moral certainty,* of the guilt of the accused. At the same time, absolute or mathematical certainty is not required. You may be convinced of the truth of a fact beyond a reasonable doubt and yet be fully aware that possibly you may be mistaken. You may find an accused guilty upon the *strong probabilities of the case,* provided such probabilities are strong enough to exclude any doubt of his guilt that is reasonable. A reasonable doubt is an *actual and substantial doubt* arising from the evidence, from the facts or circumstances shown by the evidence, or from the lack of evidence on the part of the state, as distinguished from a doubt arising from mere possibility, from bare imagination, or from fanciful conjecture.

[ ] (emphasis added). On state postconviction review, the Nebraska Supreme Court rejected Victor's contention that the instruction, particularly the emphasized phrases, violated the Due Process Clause. [ ] Because the last state court in which review could be had considered Victor's constitutional claim on the merits, it is properly presented for our review despite Victor's failure to object to the instruction at trial or raise the issue on direct appeal. [ ]

The instruction given in Victor's case can be traced to two separate lines of cases. Much of the charge is taken from Chief Justice Shaw's *Webster* instruction. [ ] ... The rest derives from a series of decisions approving instructions cast in terms of an "actual doubt" that would cause a reasonable person to hesitate to act. [ ] In 1968, a committee appointed by the Nebraska Supreme Court developed model jury instructions; a court rule in effect at the time Victor was tried directed that those instructions were to be used where applicable. [ ] The model instruction on reasonable doubt [ ], is the one given at Victor's trial. (Since Victor was tried, a revised reasonable-doubt instruction [ ], has been adopted, although the prior version may still be used.)

A

Victor's primary argument is that equating a reasonable doubt with a "substantial doubt" overstated the degree of doubt necessary for acquittal. We agree that this construction is somewhat problematic. On the one hand, "substantial" means "not seeming or imaginary"; on the other, it means "that specified to a large degree." Webster's Third New International Dictionary, *supra,* at 2280. The former is unexceptionable, as it informs the jury only that a reasonable doubt is something more than a speculative one; but the latter could imply a doubt greater than required for acquittal under *Winship.* Any ambiguity, however, is removed by reading the phrase in the context of the sentence in which it appears:

A reasonable doubt is an actual and substantial doubt . . . *as distinguished from* a doubt arising from mere possibility, from

55

bare imagination, or from fanciful conjecture.

[ ]

This explicit distinction between a substantial doubt and a fanciful conjecture was not present in the *Cage* instruction. We did say in that case that

> the words "substantial" and "grave," as they are commonly understood, suggest a higher degree of doubt than is required for acquittal under the reasonable doubt standard.

[ ] But we did not hold that the reference to substantial doubt alone was sufficient to render the instruction unconstitutional. [ ] ... Rather, we were concerned that the jury would interpret the term "substantial doubt" in parallel with the preceding reference to "grave uncertainty," leading to an overstatement of the doubt necessary to acquit. In the instruction given in Victor's case, the context makes clear that "substantial" is used in the sense of existence rather than magnitude of the doubt, so the same concern is not present.

In any event, the instruction provided an alternative definition of reasonable doubt: a doubt that would cause a reasonable person to hesitate to act. This is a formulation we have repeatedly approved [ ], and to the extent the word substantial denotes the quantum of doubt necessary for acquittal, the hesitate to act standard gives a common-sense benchmark for just how substantial such a doubt must be. We therefore do not think it reasonably likely that the jury would have interpreted this instruction to indicate that the doubt must be anything other than a reasonable one.

B

Victor also challenges the "moral certainty" portion of the instruction ...

The moral certainty to which the *Cage* instruction referred was clearly related to the defendant's guilt; the problem in *Cage* was that that the rest of the instruction provided insufficient context to lend meaning to the phrase. But the Nebraska instruction is not similarly deficient.

Instructing the jurors that they must have an abiding conviction of the defendant's guilt does much to alleviate any concerns that the phrase moral certainty might be misunderstood in the abstract [ ]. The instruction also equated a doubt sufficient to preclude moral certainty with a doubt that would cause a reasonable person to hesitate to act. In other words, a juror morally certain of a fact would not hesitate to rely on it; and such a fact can fairly be said to have been proven beyond a reasonable doubt. [ ] The jurors were told that they must be convinced of Victor's guilt "after full, fair, and impartial consideration of all the evidence." [ ] The judge also told them:

> In determining any issues of fact presented in this case, you should be governed solely by the evidence introduced before

56

you. You should not indulge in speculation, conjectures, or inferences not supported by the evidence.

[ ] There is accordingly no reasonable likelihood that the jurors understood the reference to moral certainty to allow conviction on a standard insufficient to satisfy *Winship,* or to allow conviction on factors other than the government's proof. Though we reiterate that we do not countenance its use, the inclusion of the moral certainty phrase did not render the instruction given in Victor's case unconstitutional.

C

Finally, Victor argues that the reference to "strong probabilities" in the instruction unconstitutionally understated the government's burden. But in the same sentence, the instruction informs the jury that the probabilities must be strong enough to prove the defendant's guilt beyond a reasonable doubt. We upheld a nearly identical instruction in *Dunbar v. United States* [ ] ...

That conclusion has lost no force in the course of a century, and we therefore consider *Dunbar* controlling on this point.

IV

The Due Process Clause requires the government to prove a criminal defendant's guilt beyond a reasonable doubt, and trial courts must avoid defining reasonable doubt so as to lead the jury to convict on a lesser showing than due process requires. In these cases, however, we conclude that, "taken as a whole, the instructions correctly conveyed the concept of reasonable doubt to the jury." [ ] There is no reasonable likelihood that the jurors who determined petitioners' guilt applied the instructions in a way that violated the Constitution. The judgments in both cases are accordingly

Affirmed.

Near v. Minnesota (MCLE, page 112) is generally considered the most significant prior restraint decision handed down by the Supreme Court. Today, when the Court deals with prior restraint cases, as it occasionally does, it consistently cites the holding in *Near* as controlling even though the case was decided by the narrowest of margins (5-4). The Court struck down as unconstitutional a state statute that allowed authorities to halt publication of "obscene, lewd and lascivious" or "malicious, scandalous and defamatory" publications as a public nuisance. The Court made it clear that prior restraint can be imposed in "exceptional cases," but the opinion also noted that the chief purpose of the First Amendment was to prevent the evil of governmental prior restraint.

Near v. Minnesota

Argued January 30, 1931
Decided June 1, 1931

283 U.S. 697, 51 S.Ct. 625, 75 L.Ed. 1357, 1 Med.L.Rptr. 1001

APPEAL FROM THE SUPREME COURT OF MINNESOTA

Syllabus

1. A Minnesota statute declares that one who engages "in the business of regularly and customarily producing, publishing," etc., "a malicious, scandalous and defamatory newspaper, magazine or other periodical," is guilty of a nuisance, and authorizes suits, in the name of the State, in which such periodicals may be abated and their publishers enjoined from future violations. In such a suit, malice may be inferred from the fact of publication. The defendant is permitted to prove, as a defense, that his publications were true and published "with good motives and for justifiable ends." Disobedience of an injunction is punishable as a contempt. *Held* unconstitutional, as applied to publications charging neglect of duty and corruption upon the part of law-enforcing officers of the State. [ ]

2. Liberty of the press is within the liberty safeguarded by the due process clause of the Fourteenth Amendment from invasion by state action. [ ]

3. Liberty of the press is not an absolute right, and the State may punish its abuse. [ ]

4. In passing upon the constitutionality of the statute, the court has regard for substance, and not for form; the statute must be tested by its operation and effect. [ ]

5. Cutting through mere details of procedure, the operation and

effect of the statute is that public authorities may bring a publisher before a judge upon a charge of conducting a business of publishing scandalous and defamatory matter -- in particular, that the matter consists of charges against public officials of official dereliction -- and, unless the publisher is able and disposed to satisfy the judge that the charges are true and are published with good motives and for justifiable ends, his newspaper or periodical is suppressed and further publication is made punishable as a contempt. This is the essence of censorship. P. GO>713.

6. A statute authorizing such proceedings in restraint of publication is inconsistent with the conception of the liberty of the press as historically conceived and guaranteed. [ ]

7. The chief purpose of the guaranty is to prevent previous restraints upon publication. The libeler, however, remains criminally and civilly responsible for his libels. [ ]

8. There are undoubtedly limitations upon the immunity from previous restraint of the press, but they are not applicable in this case. [ ]

9. The liberty of the press has been especially cherished in this country as respects publications censuring public officials and charging official misconduct. [ ]

10. Public officers find their remedies for false accusations in actions for redress and punishment under the libel laws, and not in proceedings to restrain the publication of newspapers and periodicals. [ ]

11. The fact that the liberty of the press may be abused by miscreant purveyors of scandal does not make any the less necessary the immunity from previous restraint in dealing with official misconduct. [ ]

12. Characterizing the publication of charges of official misconduct as a "business," and the business as a nuisance, does not avoid the constitutional guaranty; nor does it matter that the periodical is largely or chiefly devoted to such charges. [ ]

13. The guaranty against previous restraint extends to publications charging official derelictions that amount to crimes. [ ]

14. Permitting the publisher to show in defense that the matter published is true and is published with good motives and for justifiable ends does not justify the statute. [ ]

15. Nor can it be sustained as a measure for preserving the public peace and preventing assaults and crime. [ ]

179 Minn. 40; 228 N.W. 326, reversed.

APPEAL from a decree which sustained an injunction abating the publication of a periodical as malicious, scandalous and defamatory, and restraining future publication. The suit was based on a Minnesota statute. [ ]

HUGHES, J., lead opinion

MR. CHIEF JUSTICE HUGHES delivered the opinion of the Court.

Chapter 285 of the Session Laws of Minnesota for the year 1925 provides for the abatement, as a public nuisance, of a "malicious, scandalous and defamatory newspaper, magazine or other periodical." Section one of the Act is as follows:

> Section 1. Any person who, as an individual, or as a member or employee of a firm, or association or organization, or as an officer, director, member or employee of a corporation, shall be engaged in the business of regularly or customarily producing, publishing or circulating, having in possession, selling or giving away

> (a) an obscene, lewd and lascivious newspaper, magazine, or other periodical, or

> (b) a malicious, scandalous and defamatory newspaper, magazine or other periodical,

is guilty of a nuisance, and all persons guilty of such nuisance may be enjoined, as hereinafter provided.

> Participation in such business shall constitute a commission of such nuisance and render the participant liable and subject to the proceedings, orders and judgments provided for in this Act. Ownership, in whole or in part, directly or indirectly, of any such periodical, or of any stock or interest in any corporation or organization which owns the same in whole or in part, or which publishes the same, shall constitute such participation.

> In actions brought under (b) above, there shall be available the defense that the truth was published with good motives and for justifiable ends and in such actions the plaintiff shall not have the right to report (*sic*) to issues or editions of periodicals taking place more than three months before the commencement of the action.

Section two provides that, whenever any such nuisance is committed or exists, the County Attorney of any county where any such periodical is published or circulated, or, in case of his failure or refusal to proceed upon written request in good faith of a reputable citizen, the Attorney General, or, upon like failure or refusal of the latter, any citizen of the county may maintain an action in the district court of the county in the name of the State to enjoin perpetually the persons committing or maintaining any such nuisance from further committing or maintaining it. Upon such evidence as the court shall deem sufficient, a temporary injunction may be granted. The defendants have the right to plead by demurrer or answer, and the plaintiff may demur or reply as in other cases.

The action, by section three, is to be " governed by the practice and procedure applicable to civil actions for injunctions," and, after trial, the court may enter judgment permanently enjoining the defendants found guilty of violating the Act from continuing the violation, and, "in and by such judgment, such nuisance may be wholly abated." The court is empowered, as in other cases of contempt, to punish disobedience to a temporary or permanent injunction by fine of not more than $1,000 or by imprisonment in the county jail for not more than twelve months.

Under this statute, clause (b), the County Attorney of Hennepin County brought this action to enjoin the publication of what was described as a " malicious, scandalous and defamatory newspaper, magazine and periodical" known as " The Saturday Press," published by the defendants in the city of Minneapolis. The complaint alleged that the defendants, on September 24, 1927, and on eight subsequent dates in October and November, 1927, published and circulated editions of that periodical which were "largely devoted to malicious, scandalous and defamatory articles" concerning Charles G. Davis, Frank W. Brunskill, the Minneapolis Tribune, the Minneapolis Journal, Melvin C. Passolt, George E. Leach, the Jewish Race, the members of the Grand Jury of Hennepin County impaneled in November, 1927, and then holding office, and other persons, as more fully appeared in exhibits annexed to the complaint, consisting of copies of the articles described and constituting 327 pages of the record. While the complaint did not so allege, it appears from the briefs of both parties that Charles G. Davis was a special law enforcement officer employed by a civic organization, that George E. Leach was Mayor of Minneapolis, that Frank W. Brunskill was its Chief of Police, and that Floyd B. Olson (the relator in this action) was County Attorney.

Without attempting to summarize the contents of the voluminous exhibits attached to the complaint, we deem it sufficient to say that the articles charged in substance that a Jewish gangster was in control of gambling, bootlegging and racketeering in Minneapolis, and that law enforcing officers and agencies were not energetically performing their duties. Most of the charges were directed against the Chief of Police; he was charged with gross neglect of duty, illicit relations with gangsters, and with participation in graft. The County Attorney was charged with knowing the existing conditions and with failure to take adequate measures to remedy them. The Mayor was accused of inefficiency and dereliction. One member of the grand jury was stated to be in sympathy with the gangsters. A special grand jury and a special prosecutor were demanded to deal with the situation in general, and, in particular, to investigate an attempt to assassinate one Guilford, one of the original defendants, who, it appears from the articles, was shot by gangsters after the first issue of the periodical had been published. There is no question but that the articles made serious accusations against the public officers named and others in connection with the prevalence of crimes and the failure to expose and punish them.

At the beginning of the action, on November 22, 1927, and upon the

61

verified complaint, an order was made directing the defendants to show cause why a temporary injunction should not issue and meanwhile forbidding the defendants to publish, circulate or have in their possession any editions of the periodical from September 24, 1927, to November 19, 1927, inclusive, and from publishing, circulating, or having in their possession, "any future editions of said The Saturday Press" and

> any publication, known by any other name whatsoever containing malicious, scandalous and defamatory matter of the kind alleged in plaintiff's complaint herein or otherwise.

The defendants demurred to the complaint upon the ground that it did not state facts sufficient to constitute a cause of action, and on this demurrer challenged the constitutionality of the statute. The District Court overruled the demurrer and certified the question of constitutionality to the Supreme Court of the State. The Supreme Court sustained the statute [ ], and it is conceded by the appellee that the Act was thus held to be valid over the objection that it violated not only the state constitution, but also the Fourteenth Amendment of the Constitution of the United States.

Thereupon, the defendant Near, the present appellant, answered the complaint. He averred that he was the sole owner and proprietor of the publication in question. He admitted the publication of the articles in the issues described in the complaint, but denied that they were malicious, scandalous or defamatory as alleged. He expressly invoked the protection of the due process clause of the Fourteenth Amendment. The case then came on for trial. The plaintiff offered in evidence the verified complaint, together with the issues of the publication in question, which were attached to the complaint as exhibits. The defendant objected to the introduction of the evidence, invoking the constitutional provisions to which his answer referred. The objection was overruled, no further evidence was presented, and the plaintiff rested. The defendant then rested without offering evidence. The plaintiff moved that the court direct the issue of a permanent injunction, and this was done.

The District Court made findings of fact which followed the allegations of the complaint and found in general terms that the editions in question were "chiefly devoted to malicious, scandalous and defamatory articles" concerning the individuals named. The court further found that the defendants, through these publications,

> did engage in the business of regularly and customarily producing, publishing and circulating a malicious, scandalous and defamatory newspaper,

and that "the said publication" "under said name of The Saturday Press, or any other name, constitutes a public nuisance under the laws of the State." Judgment was thereupon entered adjudging that "the newspaper, magazine and periodical known as The Saturday Press," as a public nuisance, "be and is hereby abated." The Judgment perpetually enjoined the defendants

> from producing, editing, publishing, circulating, having in their possession,
> selling or giving away any publication whatsoever which is a malicious,
> scandalous or defamatory newspaper, as defined by law,

and also "from further conducting said nuisance under the name and title of said The Saturday Press or any other name or title."

The defendant Near appealed from this judgment to the Supreme Court of the State, again asserting his right under the Federal Constitution, and the judgment was affirmed upon the authority of the former decision. [ ] With respect to the contention that the judgment went too far, and prevented the defendants from publishing any kind of a newspaper, the court observed that the assignments of error did not go to the form of the judgment, and that the lower court had not been asked to modify it. The court added that it saw no reason

> for defendants to construe the judgment as restraining them from operating
> a newspaper in harmony with the public welfare, to which all must yield,

that the allegations of the complaint had been found to be true, and, though this was an equitable action, defendants had not indicated a desire "to conduct their business in the usual and legitimate manner."

From the judgment as thus affirmed, the defendant Near appeals to this Court.

This statute, for the suppression as a public nuisance of a newspaper or periodical, is unusual, if not unique, and raises questions of grave importance transcending the local interests involved in the particular action. It is no longer open to doubt that the liberty of the press, and of speech, is within the liberty safeguarded by the due process clause of the Fourteenth Amendment from invasion by state action. It was found impossible to conclude that this essential personal liberty of the citizen was left unprotected by the general guaranty of fundamental rights of person and property. [ ] In maintaining this guaranty, the authority of the State to enact laws to promote the health, safety, morals and general welfare of its people is necessarily admitted. The limits of this sovereign power must always be determined with appropriate regard to the particular subject of its exercise. Thus, while recognizing the broad discretion of the legislature in fixing rates to be charged by those undertaking a public service, this Court has decided that the owner cannot constitutionally be deprived of his right to a fair return, because that is deemed to be of the essence of ownership. [ ] So while liberty of contract is not an absolute right, and the wide field of activity in the making of contracts is subject to legislative supervision [ ], this Court has held that the power of the State stops short of interference with what are deemed to be certain indispensable requirements of the liberty assured, notably with respect to the fixing of prices and wages. [ ] Liberty of speech, and of the press, is also not an absolute right, and the

State may punish its abuse. [ ] Liberty, in each of its phases, has its history and connotation, and, in the present instance, the inquiry is as to the historic conception of the liberty of the press and whether the statute under review violates the essential attributes of that liberty.

The appellee insists that the questions of the application of the statute to appellant's periodical, and of the construction of the judgment of the trial court, are not presented for review; that appellant's sole attack was upon the constitutionality of the statute, however it might be applied. The appellee contends that no question either of motive in the publication, or whether the decree goes beyond the direction of the statute, is before us. The appellant replies that, in his view, the plain terms of the statute were not departed from in this case, and that, even if they were, the statute is nevertheless unconstitutional under any reasonable construction of its terms. The appellant states that he has not argued that the temporary and permanent injunctions were broader than were warranted by the statute; he insists that what was done was properly done if the statute is valid, and that the action taken under the statute is a fair indication of its scope.

With respect to these contentions, it is enough to say that, in passing upon constitutional questions, the court has regard to substance, and not to mere matters of form, and that, in accordance with familiar principles, the statute must be tested by its operation and effect. [ ] That operation and effect we think is clearly shown by the record in this case. We are not concerned with mere errors of the trial court, if there be such, in going beyond the direction of the statute as construed by the Supreme Court of the State. It is thus important to note precisely the purpose and effect of the statute as the state court has construed it.

First. The statute is not aimed at the redress of individual or private wrongs. Remedies for libel remain available and unaffected. The statute, said the state court, "is not directed at threatened libel, but at an existing business which, generally speaking, involves more than libel." It is aimed at the distribution of scandalous matter as "detrimental to public morals and to the general welfare," tending "to disturb the peace of the community" and "to provoke assaults and the commission of crime." In order to obtain an injunction to suppress the future publication of the newspaper or periodical, it is not necessary to prove the falsity of the charges that have been made in the publication condemned. In the present action, there was no allegation that the matter published was not true. It is alleged, and the statute requires the allegation, that the publication was "malicious." But, as in prosecutions for libel, there is no requirement of proof by the State of malice in fact, as distinguished from malice inferred from the mere publication of the defamatory matter. The judgment in this case proceeded upon the mere proof of publication. The statute permits the defense not of the truth alone, but only that the truth was published with good motives and for justifiable ends. It is apparent that, under the statute, the publication is to be regarded as defamatory if it injures reputation, and that it is scandalous if it circulates charges of reprehensible conduct, whether criminal or otherwise, and the publication is thus deemed to invite public reprobation and to constitute a public scandal ...

Second. The statute is directed not simply at the circulation of scandalous and defamatory statements with regard to private citizens, but at the continued publication by newspapers and periodicals of charges against public officers of corruption, malfeasance in office, or serious neglect of duty. Such charges, by their very nature, create a public scandal. They are scandalous and defamatory within the meaning of the statute, which has its normal operation in relation to publications dealing prominently and chiefly with the alleged derelictions of public officers.

Third. The object of the statute is not punishment, in the ordinary sense, but suppression of the offending newspaper or periodical. The reason for the enactment, as the state court has said, is that prosecutions to enforce penal statutes for libel do not result in "efficient repression or suppression of the evils of scandal." Describing the business of publication as a public nuisance does not obscure the substance of the proceeding which the statute authorizes. It is the continued publication of scandalous and defamatory matter that constitutes the business and the declared nuisance. In the case of public officers, it is the reiteration of charges of official misconduct, and the fact that the newspaper or periodical is principally devoted to that purpose, that exposes it to suppression. In the present instance, the proof was that nine editions of the newspaper or periodical in question were published on successive dates, and that they were chiefly devoted to charges against public officers and in relation to the prevalence and protection of crime. In such a case, these officers are not left to their ordinary remedy in a suit for libel, or the authorities to a prosecution for criminal libel. Under this statute, a publisher of a newspaper or periodical, undertaking to conduct a campaign to expose and to censure official derelictions, and devoting his publication principally to that purpose, must face not simply the possibility of a verdict against him in a suit or prosecution for libel, but a determination that his newspaper or periodical is a public nuisance to be abated, and that this abatement and suppression will follow unless he is prepared with legal evidence to prove the truth of the charges and also to satisfy the court that, in addition to being true, the matter was published with good motives and for justifiable ends.

This suppression is accomplished by enjoining publication, and that restraint is the object and effect of the statute.

Fourth. The statute not only operates to suppress the offending newspaper or periodical, but to put the publisher under an effective censorship. When a newspaper or periodical is found to be "malicious, scandalous, and defamatory," and is suppressed as such, resumption of publication is punishable as a contempt of court by fine or imprisonment. Thus, where a newspaper or periodical has been suppressed because of the circulation of charges against public officers of official misconduct, it would seem to be clear that the renewal of the publication of such charges would constitute a contempt, and that the judgment would lay a permanent restraint upon the publisher, to escape which he must satisfy the court as to the character of a new publication. Whether he would be permitted again to publish matter deemed to be derogatory to the same or other public officers would depend upon the court's ruling. In the present instance, the judgment restrained the defendants from

> publishing, circulating, having in their possession, selling or giving away any publication whatsoever which is a malicious, scandalous or defamatory newspaper, as defined by law.

The law gives no definition except that covered by the words "scandalous and defamatory," and publications charging official misconduct are of that class. While the court, answering the objection that the judgment was too broad, saw no reason for construing it as restraining the defendants "from operating a newspaper in harmony with the public welfare to which all must yield," and said that the defendants had not indicated "any desire to conduct their business in the usual and legitimate manner," the manifest inference is that, at least with respect to a new publication directed against official misconduct, the defendant would be held, under penalty of punishment for contempt as provided in the statute, to a manner of publication which the court considered to be "usual and legitimate" and consistent with the public welfare.

If we cut through mere details of procedure, the operation and effect of the statute, in substance, is that public authorities may bring the owner or publisher of a newspaper or periodical before a judge upon a charge of conducting a business of publishing scandalous and defamatory matter -- in particular, that the matter consists of charges against public officers of official dereliction -- and, unless the owner or publisher is able and disposed to bring competent evidence to satisfy the judge that the charges are true and are published with good motives and for justifiable ends, his newspaper or periodical is suppressed and further publication is made punishable as a contempt. This is of the essence of censorship.

The question is whether a statute authorizing such proceedings in restraint of publication is consistent with the conception of the liberty of the press as historically conceived and guaranteed. In determining the extent of the constitutional protection, it has been generally, if not universally, considered that it is the chief purpose of the guaranty to prevent previous restraints upon publication. The struggle in England, directed against the legislative power of the licenser, resulted in renunciation of the censorship of the press. The liberty deemed to be established was thus described by Blackstone:

> The liberty of the press is indeed essential to the nature of a free state; but this consists in laying no *previous* restraints upon publications, and not in freedom from censure for criminal matter when published. Every freeman has an undoubted right to lay what sentiments he pleases before the public;

to forbid this is to destroy the freedom of the press; but if he publishes what is improper, mischievous or illegal, he must take the consequence of his own temerity.

[ ] The distinction was early pointed out between the extent of the freedom with respect to censorship under our constitutional system and that enjoyed in England ... [} ...

The criticism upon Blackstone's statement has not been because immunity from previous restraint upon publication has not been regarded as deserving of special emphasis, but chiefly because that immunity cannot be deemed to exhaust the conception of the liberty guaranteed by state and federal constitutions. The point of criticism has been "that the mere exemption from previous restraints cannot be all that is secured by the constitutional provisions", and that

> the liberty of the press might be rendered a mockery and a delusion, and the phrase itself a byword, if, while every man was at liberty to publish what he pleased, the public authorities might nevertheless punish him for harmless publications.

[ ] But it is recognized that punishment for the abuse of the liberty accorded to the press is essential to the protection of the public, and that the common law rules that subject the libeler to responsibility for the public offense, as well as for the private injury, are not abolished by the protection extended in our constitutions. [ ] The law of criminal libel rests upon that secure foundation. There is also the conceded authority of courts to punish for contempt when publications directly tend to prevent the proper discharge of judicial functions. [ ] In the present case, we have no occasion to inquire as to the permissible scope of subsequent punishment. For whatever wrong the appellant has committed or may commit by his publications the State appropriately affords both public and private redress by its libel laws. As has been noted, the statute in question does not deal with punishments; it provides for no punishment, except in case of contempt for violation of the court's order, but for suppression and injunction, that is, for restraint upon publication.

The objection has also been made that the principle as to immunity from previous restraint is stated too broadly, if every such restraint is deemed to be prohibited. That is undoubtedly true; the protection even as to previous restraint is not absolutely unlimited. But the limitation has been recognized only in exceptional cases:

> When a nation is at war, many things that might be said in time of peace are such a hindrance to its effort that their utterance will not be endured so long as men fight, and that no Court could regard them as protected by any constitutional right.

Schenck v. United States, 249 U.S. 47. No one would question but that a government might prevent actual obstruction to its recruiting service or the publication of the sailing dates of transports or the number and location of troops. On similar grounds, the primary requirements of decency may be enforced against obscene publications. The security of the community life may be protected against incitements to acts of violence and the overthrow by force of orderly government. The constitutional guaranty of free speech does not

> protect a man from an injunction against uttering words that may have all the effect of force. *Gompers v. Buck Stove & Range Co.,* 221 U.S. 418, 439.

Schenck v. United States, supra. These limitations are not applicable here. Nor are we now concerned with questions as to the extent of authority to prevent publications in order to protect private rights according to the principles governing the exercise of the jurisdiction of courts of equity.

The exceptional nature of its limitations places in a strong light the general conception that liberty of the press, historically considered and taken up by the Federal Constitution, has meant, principally, although not exclusively, immunity from previous restraints or censorship. The conception of the liberty of the press in this country had broadened with the exigencies of the colonial period and with the efforts to secure freedom from oppressive administration. That liberty was especially cherished for the immunity it afforded from previous restraint of the publication of censure of public officers and charges of official misconduct ...

The fact that, for approximately one hundred and fifty years, there has been almost an entire absence of attempts to impose previous restraints upon publications relating to the malfeasance of public officers is significant of the deep-seated conviction that such restraints would violate constitutional right. Public officers, whose character and conduct remain open to debate and free discussion in the press, find their remedies for false accusations in actions under libel laws providing for redress and punishment, and not in proceedings to restrain the publication of newspapers and periodicals. The general principle that the constitutional guaranty of the liberty of the press gives immunity from previous restraints has been approved in many decisions under the provisions of state constitutions.

The importance of this immunity has not lessened. While reckless assaults upon public men, and efforts to bring obloquy upon those who are endeavoring faithfully to discharge official duties, exert a baleful influence and deserve the severest condemnation in public opinion, it cannot be said that this abuse is greater, and it is believed to be less, than that which characterized the period in which our institutions took shape. Meanwhile, the administration of government has become more complex, the opportunities for malfeasance and corruption have multiplied, crime has grown to most serious proportions, and the danger of its protection by unfaithful officials and of the impairment of the fundamental security of life and property by criminal alliances and official neglect, emphasizes the primary need of a vigilant and courageous press, especially in great cities. The fact that the liberty of the press may be abused by miscreant purveyors of scandal does not make any the less necessary the immunity of the press from previous restraint in dealing with official misconduct. Subsequent punishment for such abuses as may exist is the appropriate remedy consistent with constitutional privilege.

In attempted justification of the statute, it is said that it deals not with publication *per se,* but with the "business" of publishing defamation. If, however, the publisher has a constitutional right to publish, without previous restraint, an edition of his newspaper charging official derelictions, it cannot be denied that he may publish subsequent editions for the same purpose. He does not lose his right by exercising it. If his right exists, it may be exercised in publishing nine editions, as in this case, as well as in one edition. If previous restraint is permissible, it may be imposed at once; indeed, the wrong may be as serious in one publication as in several. Characterizing the publication as a business, and the business as a nuisance, does not permit an invasion of the constitutional immunity against restraint. Similarly, it does not matter that the newspaper or periodical is found to be "largely" or "chiefly" devoted to the publication of such derelictions. If the publisher has a right, without previous restraint, to publish them, his right cannot be deemed to be dependent upon his publishing something else, more or less, with the matter to which objection is made.

Nor can it be said that the constitutional freedom from previous restraint is lost because charges are made of derelictions which constitute crimes. With the multiplying provisions of penal codes, and of municipal charters and ordinances carrying penal sanctions, the conduct of public officers is very largely within the purview of criminal statutes. The freedom of the press from previous restraint has never been regarded as limited to such animadversions as lay outside the range of penal enactments. Historically, there is no such limitation; it is inconsistent with the reason which underlies the privilege, as the privilege so limited would be of slight value for the purposes for which it came to be established.

The statute in question cannot be justified by reason of the fact that the publisher is permitted to show, before injunction issues, that the matter published is true and is published with good motives and for justifiable ends. If such a statute, authorizing suppression and injunction on such a basis, is constitutionally valid, it would be equally permissible for the legislature to provide that at any time the publisher of any newspaper could be brought before a court, or even an administrative officer (as the constitutional protection may not be regarded as resting on mere procedural details) and required to produce proof of the truth of his publication, or of what he intended to publish, and of his motives, or stand enjoined. If this can be done, the legislature may provide machinery for determining in the complete exercise of its discretion what are justifiable ends, and restrain publication accordingly. And it would be but a step to a complete system of censorship. The

69

recognition of authority to impose previous restraint upon publication in order to protect the community against the circulation of charges of misconduct, and especially of official misconduct, necessarily would carry with it the admission of the authority of the censor against which the constitutional barrier was erected. The preliminary freedom, by virtue of the very reason for its existence, does not depend, as this Court has said, on proof of truth. [ ]

Equally unavailing is the insistence that the statute is designed to prevent the circulation of scandal which tends to disturb the public peace and to provoke assaults and the commission of crime. Charges of reprehensible conduct, and in particular of official malfeasance, unquestionably create a public scandal, but the theory of the constitutional guaranty is that even a more serious public evil would be caused by authority to prevent publication ....

There is nothing new in the fact that charges of reprehensible conduct may create resentment and the disposition to resort to violent means of redress, but this well understood tendency did not alter the determination to protect the press against censorship and restraint upon publication. [ ] ...

The danger of violent reactions becomes greater with effective organization of defiant groups resenting exposure, and if this consideration warranted legislative interference with the initial freedom of publication, the constitutional protection would be reduced to a mere form of words.

For these reasons we hold the statute, so far as it authorized the proceedings in this action under clause (b) of section one, to be an infringement of the liberty of the press guaranteed by the Fourteenth Amendment. We should add that this decision rests upon the operation and effect of the statute, without regard to the question of the truth of the charges contained in the particular periodical. The fact that the public officers named in this case, and those associated with the charges of official dereliction, may be deemed to be impeccable cannot affect the conclusion that the statute imposes an unconstitutional restraint upon publication.

Judgment reversed.

United States v. Eichman (consolidated with *United States v. Haggerty*) (MCLE, page 150) is the second of two cases in which the Supreme Court considered whether flag desecration enjoyed First Amendment protection. The first case, *Texas v. Johnson*, involved a state statute. In that 1989 decision the Court did not specifically strike down the statute but instead ruled in a 5-4 vote that the statute, as applied, was unconstitutional. As a result, Congress passed a federal statute that attempted to overcome the problems of the state statute. One year later, the Court passed judgment on the federal statute and found it suffered problems similar to those of the Texas law. The vote was the same: 5-4, with Justice Brennan once again writing the majority opinion. Both decisions created considerable controversy and provided an opportunity for many politicians to criticize the Court and to campaign for a constitutional amendment to ban flag desecration. Thus far, however, Congress has not been able to muster the necessary two-thirds vote in both Houses to send a proposed amendment to the states for ratification, which requires approval of three-fourths of the state legislatures.

United States v. Eichman
and
United States v. Haggerty

Argued May 14, 1990
Decided June 11, 1990

496 U.S. 310, 110 S.Ct. 2404, 110 L.Ed.2d 287

APPEAL FROM THE DISTRICT COURT FOR THE DISTRICT
OF COLUMBIA

Syllabus

After this Court held, in *Texas v. Johnson*, 491 U.S. 397, that a Texas statute criminalizing desecration of the United States flag in a way that the actor knew would seriously offend onlookers was unconstitutional as applied to an individual who had burned a flag during a political protest, Congress passed the Flag Protection Act of 1989. The Act criminalizes the conduct of anyone who "knowingly mutilates, defaces, physically defiles, burns, maintains on the floor or ground, or tramples upon" a United States flag, except conduct related to the disposal of a "worn or soiled" flag. Subsequently, appellees were prosecuted in the District Courts for violating the Act: some for knowingly burning several flags while protesting various aspects of the Government's policies and others, in a separate incident, for knowingly burning a flag while protesting the Act's passage. In each case, appellees moved to dismiss the charges on the ground that the Act violates the First Amendment. Both District Courts, following *Johnson, supra,* held the Act unconstitutional as applied, and dismissed the charges.

Held: Appellees' prosecution for burning a flag in violation of the Act is inconsistent with the First Amendment. The Government concedes, as it must, that appellees' flag-burning constituted expressive conduct, and this Court declines to reconsider its rejection in *Johnson* of the claim that flag-burning as a mode of expression does not enjoy the First Amendment's full protection. It is true that this Act, unlike the Texas law, contains no explicit content-based limitation on the scope of prohibited conduct. Nevertheless, it is clear that the Government's asserted interest in protecting the "physical integrity" of a privately owned flag in order to preserve the flag's status as a symbol of the Nation and certain national ideals is related to the suppression, and concerned with the content, of free expression. The mere destruction or disfigurement of a symbol's physical manifestation does not diminish or otherwise affect the symbol itself. The Government's interest is implicated only when a person's treatment of the flag communicates a message to others that is inconsistent with the identified ideals. The precise language of the Act's prohibitions confirms Congress' interest in the communicative impact of flag destruction, since each of the specified terms -- with the possible exception of "burns" -- unmistakably connotes disrespectful treatment of the flag and suggests a focus on those acts likely to damage the flag's symbolic value, and since the explicit exemption for disposal of "worn or soiled" flags protects certain acts traditionally associated with patriotic respect for the flag. Thus, the Act suffers from the same fundamental flaw as the Texas law, and its restriction on expression cannot "'be justified without reference to the content of the regulated speech'" [ ]. It must therefore be subjected to "the most exacting scrutiny" [ ], and, for the reasons stated in *Johnson* [ ], the Government's interest cannot justify its infringement on First Amendment rights. This conclusion will not be reassessed in light of Congress' recent recognition of a purported "national consensus" favoring a prohibition on flag-burning, since any suggestion that the Government's interest in suppressing speech becomes more weighty as popular opposition to that speech grows is foreign to the First Amendment. While flag desecration -- like virulent ethnic and religious epithets, vulgar repudiations of the draft, and scurrilous caricatures -- is deeply offensive to many, the Government may not prohibit the expression of an idea simply because society finds the idea itself offensive or disagreeable. [ ]

No. 89-1433, 731 F.Supp. 1123 (DDC 1990); No. 89-1434, 731 F.Supp. 415, affirmed.

BRENNAN, J., delivered the opinion of the Court, in which MARSHALL, BLACKMUN, SCALIA, and KENNEDY, JJ., joined. STEVENS, J., filed a dissenting opinion, in which REHNQUIST, C.J., and WHITE and O'CONNOR, JJ., joined, [ ]

In these consolidated appeals, we consider whether appellees' prosecution for burning a United States flag in violation of the Flag Protection Act of 1989 is consistent with the First Amendment. Applying our recent decision in *Texas v. Johnson,* 491 U.S. 397 (1989), the District Courts held that the Act cannot constitutionally be applied to appellees. We affirm.

I

In No. 89-1433, the United States prosecuted certain appellees for violating the Flag Protection Act of 1989 [ ], by knowingly setting fire to several United States flags on the steps of the United States Capitol while protesting various aspects of the Government's domestic and foreign policy. In No. 89-1434, the United States prosecuted other appellees for violating the Act by knowingly setting fire to a United States flag while protesting the Act's passage. In each case, the respective appellees moved to dismiss the flag-burning charge on the ground that the Act, both on its face and as applied, violates the First Amendment. Both the United States District Court for the Western District of Washington [ ] and the United States District Court for the District of Columbia [ ], following *Johnson, supra,* held the Act unconstitutional as applied to appellees and dismissed the charges. [ ] The United States appealed both decisions directly to this Court pursuant to 18 U.S.C.A. § 700(d) (Supp. 1990). [ ] We noted probable jurisdiction and consolidated the two cases. [ ]

II

Last Term, in *Johnson,* we held that a Texas statute criminalizing the desecration of venerated objects, including the United States flag, was unconstitutional as applied to an individual who had set such a flag on fire during a political demonstration. The Texas statute provided that "[a] person commits an offense if he intentionally or knowingly desecrates . . . [a] national flag," where "desecrate" meant to "deface, damage, or otherwise physically mistreat in a way that the actor knows will seriously offend one or more persons likely to observe or discover his action." [ ] We first held that Johnson's flag-burning was "conduct `sufficiently imbued with elements of communication' to implicate the First Amendment.'" [ ] We next considered and rejected the State's contention that, under *United States v. O'Brien,* 391 U.S. 367 (1968), we ought to apply the deferential standard with which we have reviewed Government regulations of conduct containing both speech and nonspeech elements where "the governmental interest is unrelated to the suppression of free expression." [ ] We reasoned that the State's asserted interest "in preserving the flag as a symbol of nationhood and national unity" was an interest "related 'to the suppression of free expression' within the meaning of *O'Brien"* because the State's concern with protecting the flag's symbolic meaning is implicated "only when a person's treatment of the flag communicates some message." [ ]. We therefore subjected the statute to "`the most exacting scrutiny'" [ ], quoting *Boos v. Barry* [ ] (1988), and we concluded that the State's asserted interests could not justify the infringement on the demonstrator's First Amendment rights.

After our decision in Johnson, Congress passed the Flag Protection Act of 1989. [ ] The Act provides in relevant part:

> (a)(1) Whoever knowingly mutilates, defaces, physically defiles, burns, maintains on the floor or ground, or tramples upon any flag of the United States shall be fined under this title or imprisoned for not more than one year, or both.

> (2) This subsection does not prohibit any conduct consisting of the disposal of a flag when it has become worn or soiled.

> (b) As used in this section, the term "flag of the United States" means any flag of the United States, or any part thereof, made of any substance, of any size, in a form that is commonly displayed.

[ ]

The Government concedes in this case, as it must, that appellees' flag-burning constituted expressive conduct [ ], but invites us to reconsider our rejection in *Johnson* of the claim that flag-burning as a mode of expression, like obscenity or "fighting words," does not enjoy the full protection of the First Amendment. [ ]. This we decline to do. [ ] The only remaining question is whether the Flag Protection Act is sufficiently distinct from the Texas statute that it may constitutionally be applied to proscribe appellees' expressive conduct.

The Government contends that the Flag Protection Act is constitutional because, unlike the statute addressed in *Johnson,* the Act does not target expressive conduct on the basis of the content of its message. The Government asserts an interest in "protect[ing] the physical integrity of the flag under all circumstances" in order to safeguard the flag's identity "`as the unique and unalloyed symbol of the Nation.'" [ ] The Act proscribes conduct (other than disposal) that damages or mistreats a flag, without regard to the actor's motive, his intended message, or the likely effects of his conduct on onlookers. By contrast, the Texas statute expressly prohibited only those acts of physical flag desecration "that the actor knows will seriously offend" onlookers, and the former federal statute prohibited only those acts of desecration that "cas[t] contempt upon" the flag.

Although the Flag Protection Act contains no explicit content-based limitation on the scope of prohibited conduct, it is nevertheless clear that the Government's asserted interest is "related `to the suppression of free expression'" [ ], and concerned with the content of such expression. The Government's interest in protecting the "physical integrity" of a privately owned flag rests upon a perceived need to preserve the flag's status as a symbol of our Nation and certain national ideals. But the mere destruction or disfigurement of a particular physical manifestation of the symbol, without more, does not diminish or otherwise affect the symbol itself in any way. For example, the secret destruction of a flag in one's own basement would not threaten the flag's recognized meaning. Rather, the Government's desire to preserve the flag as a symbol for certain national ideals is implicated "only when a person's treatment of the flag communicates [a] message" to others that is inconsistent with those ideals. [ ]

Moreover, the precise language of the Act's prohibitions confirms Congress' interest in the communicative impact of flag destruction. The Act criminalizes the conduct of anyone who "knowingly mutilates, defaces, physically defiles, burns, maintains on the floor or ground, or tramples upon any flag." [ ] Each of the specified terms -- with the possible exception of "burns" -- unmistakably connotes disrespectful treatment of the flag and suggests a focus on those acts likely to damage the flag's symbolic value. And the explicit exemption in § 700(a)(2) for disposal of "worn or soiled" flags protects certain acts traditionally associated with patriotic respect for the flag.

As we explained in *Johnson* [ ]:

> [I]f we were to hold that a State may forbid flag-burning wherever it is likely to endanger the flag's symbolic role, but allow it wherever burning a flag promotes that role -- as where, for example, a person ceremoniously burns a dirty flag -- we would be . . . permitting a State to 'prescribe what shall be orthodox' by saying that one may burn the flag to convey one's attitude toward it and its referents only if one does not endanger the flag's representation of nationhood and national unity.

Although Congress cast the Flag Protection Act in somewhat broader terms than the Texas statute at issue in *Johnson,* the Act still suffers from the same fundamental flaw: it suppresses expression out of concern for its likely communicative impact. Despite the Act's wider scope, its restriction on expression cannot be "justified without reference to the content of the regulated speech." [ ] ... The Act therefore must be subjected to "the most exacting scrutiny" [ ], and for the reasons stated in *Johnson* [ ], the Government's interest cannot justify its infringement on First Amendment rights. We decline the Government's invitation to reassess this conclusion in light of Congress' recent recognition of a purported "national consensus" favoring a prohibition on flag-burning. [ ] Even assuming such a consensus exists, any suggestion that the Government's interest in suppressing speech becomes more weighty as popular opposition to that speech grows is foreign to the First Amendment.

III

"National unity as an end which officials may foster by persuasion and example is not in question." [ ] Government may create national symbols, promote them, and encourage their respectful treatment. But the Flag Protection Act goes well beyond this by criminally proscribing expressive conduct because of its likely communicative impact.

We are aware that desecration of the flag is deeply offensive to many. But the same might be said, for example, of virulent ethnic and religious epithets [ ], vulgar repudiations of the draft [ ], and scurrilous caricatures [ ].

> If there is a bedrock principle underlying the First Amendment, it is that the Government may not prohibit the expression of an idea simply because society finds the idea itself offensive or disagreeable.

Johnson, supra [ ]. Punishing desecration of the flag dilutes the very freedom that makes this emblem so revered, and worth revering. The judgments are

Affirmed.

STEVENS, J., dissenting

Justice STEVENS, with whom THE CHIEF JUSTICE, Justice WHITE and Justice O'CONNOR join, dissenting.

The Court's opinion ends where proper analysis of the issue should begin. Of course "the Government may not prohibit the expression of an idea simply because society finds the idea itself offensive or disagreeable." [ ] None of us disagrees with that proposition. But it is equally well settled that certain methods of expression may be prohibited if (a) the prohibition is supported by a legitimate societal interest that is unrelated to suppression of the ideas the speaker desires to express; (b) the prohibition does not entail any interference with the speaker's freedom to express those ideas by other means; and (c) the interest in allowing the speaker complete freedom of choice among alternative methods of expression is less important than the societal interest supporting the prohibition.

Contrary to the position taken by counsel for the flag burners in *Texas v. Johnson* [ ], it is now conceded that the Federal Government has a legitimate interest in protecting the symbolic value of the American flag. Obviously that value cannot be measured, or even described, with any precision. It has at least these two components: in times of national crisis, it inspires and motivates the average citizen to make personal sacrifices in order to achieve societal goals of overriding importance; at all times, it serves as a reminder of the paramount importance of pursuing the ideals that characterize our society.

The first question the Court should consider is whether the interest in preserving the value of that symbol is unrelated to suppression of the ideas that flag burners are trying to express. In my judgment, the answer depends, at least in part, on what those ideas are. A flag burner might intend various messages. The flag burner may wish simply to convey hatred, contempt, or sheer opposition directed at the United

76

States. This might be the case if the flag were burned by an enemy during time of war. A flag burner may also, or instead, seek to convey the depth of his personal conviction about some issue by willingly provoking the use of force against himself. In so doing, he says that "my disagreement with certain policies is so strong that I am prepared to risk physical harm (and perhaps imprisonment) in order to call attention to my views." This second possibility apparently describes the expressive conduct of the flag burners in these cases. Like the protesters who dramatized their opposition to our engagement in Vietnam by publicly burning their draft cards -- and who were punished for doing so -- their expressive conduct is consistent with affection for this country and respect for the ideals that the flag symbolizes. There is at least one further possibility: a flag burner may intend to make an accusation against the integrity of the American people who disagree with him. By burning the embodiment of America's collective commitment to freedom and equality, the flag burner charges that the majority has forsaken that commitment -- that continued respect for the flag is nothing more than hypocrisy. Such a charge may be made even if the flag burner loves the country and zealously pursues the ideals that the country claims to honor.

The idea expressed by a particular act of flag burning is necessarily dependent on the temporal and political context in which it occurs. In the 1960's, it may have expressed opposition to the country's Vietnam policies, or at least to the compulsory draft. In *Texas v. Johnson,* it apparently expressed opposition to the platform of the Republican Party. In these cases, the respondents have explained that it expressed their opposition to racial discrimination, to the failure to care for the homeless, and of course to statutory prohibitions of flag burning. In any of these examples, the protestors may wish both to say that their own position is the only one faithful to liberty and equality and to accuse their fellow citizens of hypocritical indifference to -- or even of a selfish departure from -- the ideals which the flag is supposed to symbolize. The ideas expressed by flag burners are thus various, and often ambiguous.

The Government's legitimate interest in preserving the symbolic value of the flag is, however, essentially the same regardless of which of many different ideas may have motivated a particular act of flag burning. As I explained in my dissent in *Johnson* [ ], the flag uniquely symbolizes the ideas of liberty, equality, and tolerance -- ideas that Americans have passionately defended and debated throughout our history. The flag embodies the spirit of our national commitment to those ideals. The message thereby transmitted does not take a stand upon our disagreements, except to say that those disagreements are best regarded as competing interpretations of shared ideals. It does not judge particular policies, except to say that they command respect when they are enlightened by the spirit of liberty and equality. To the world, the flag is our promise that we will continue to strive for these ideals. To us, the flag is a reminder both that the struggle for liberty and equality is unceasing and that our obligation of tolerance and respect for all of our fellow citizens encompasses those who disagree with us -- indeed, even those whose ideas are disagreeable or offensive.

Thus, the Government may -- indeed, it should -- protect the symbolic value of the flag without regard to the specific content of the flag burners' speech. The prosecution in this case does not depend upon the object of the defendants' protest. It is, moreover, equally clear that the prohibition does not entail any interference with the speaker's freedom to express his or her ideas by other means. It may well be true that other means of expression may be less effective in drawing attention to those ideas, but that is not itself a sufficient reason for immunizing flag burning. Presumably a gigantic fireworks display or a parade of nude models in a public park might draw even more attention to a controversial message, but such methods of expression are nevertheless subject to regulation.

This case therefore comes down to a question of judgment. Does the admittedly important interest in allowing every speaker to choose the method of expressing his or her ideas that he or she deems most effective and appropriate outweigh the societal interest in preserving the symbolic value of the flag? This question, in turn, involves three different judgments: (1) The importance of the individual interest in selecting the preferred means of communication; (2) the importance of the national symbol; and (3) the question whether tolerance of flag burning will enhance or tarnish that value. The opinions in *Texas v. Johnson* demonstrate that reasonable judges may differ with respect to each of these judgments.

The individual interest is unquestionably a matter of great importance. Indeed, it is one of the critical components of the idea of liberty that the flag itself is intended to symbolize. Moreover, it is buttressed by the societal interest in being alerted to the need for thoughtful response to voices that might otherwise go unheard. The freedom of expression protected by the First Amendment embraces not only the freedom to communicate particular ideas but also the right to communicate them effectively. That right, however, is not absolute -- the communicative value of a well-placed bomb in the Capitol does not entitle it to the protection of the First Amendment.

Burning a flag is not, of course, equivalent to burning a public building. Assuming that the protester is burning his own flag, it causes no physical harm to other persons or to their property. The impact is purely symbolic, and it is apparent that some thoughtful persons believe that impact, far from depreciating the value of the symbol, will actually enhance its meaning. I most respectfully disagree. Indeed, what makes this case particularly difficult for me is what I regard as the damage to the symbol that has already occurred as a result of this Court's decision to place its stamp of approval on the act of flag burning. A formerly dramatic expression of protest is now rather commonplace. In today's marketplace of ideas, the public burning of a Vietnam draft card is probably less provocative than lighting a cigarette. Tomorrow, flag burning may produce a similar reaction. There is surely a direct relationship between the communicative value of the act of flag burning and the symbolic value of the object being burned.

The symbolic value of the American flag is not the same today as it was yesterday. Events during the last three decades have altered the country's image in the eyes of numerous Americans, and some now have difficulty understanding the message that the flag conveyed to their parents and grandparents -- whether born abroad and naturalized or native born. Moreover, the integrity of the symbol has been compromised by those leaders who seem to advocate compulsory worship of the flag even by individuals whom it offends, or who seem to manipulate the symbol of national purpose into a pretext for partisan disputes about meaner ends. And, as I have suggested, the residual value of the symbol after this Court's decision in *Texas v. Johnson* is surely not the same as it was a year ago.

Given all these considerations, plus the fact that the Court today is really doing nothing more than reconfirming what it has already decided, it might be appropriate to defer to the judgment of the majority and merely apply the doctrine of *stare decisis* to the case at hand. That action, however, would not honestly reflect my considered judgment concerning the relative importance of the conflicting interests that are at stake. I remain persuaded that the considerations identified in my opinion in *Texas v. Johnson* are of controlling importance in this case as well.

Accordingly, I respectfully dissent.

In City of *Ladue v. Gilleo* (MCLE, page 161), the Supreme Court unanimously ruled that a city ordinance banning most residential signs violated the First Amendment. The case involved a 8.5 X 11-inch sign stating "Peace in the Gulf" that was displayed in the second story window of a private home. The opinion noted that the ordinance prohibited a "unique and important" means of communication. The First Amendment, according to the Court, is not absolute, but was clearly intended to protect this form of speech. The decision illustrates the broad protection accorded by the Constitution for individual expression.

City of Ladue v. Gilleo

Argued February 23, 1994
Decided June 13, 1994

512 U.S. 43, 114 S.Ct. 2038, 129 L.Ed.2d 36

CERTIORARI TO THE UNITED STATES COURT OF APPEALS FOR THE EIGHTH CIRCUIT

Syllabus

An ordinance of petitioner City of Ladue bans all residential signs but those falling within one of ten exemptions, for the principal purpose of minimizing the visual clutter associated with such signs. Respondent Gilleo filed this action, alleging that the ordinance violated her right to free speech by prohibiting her from displaying a sign stating, "For Peace in the Gulf," from her home. The District Court found the ordinance unconstitutional, and the Court of Appeals affirmed, holding that the ordinance was a "content-based" regulation, and that Ladue's substantial interests in enacting it were not sufficiently compelling to support such a restriction.

Held: The ordinance violates a Ladue resident's right to free speech.
[ ]

(a) While signs pose distinctive problems, and thus are subject to municipalities' police powers, measures regulating them inevitably affect communication itself. Such a regulation may be challenged on the ground that it restricts too little speech because its exemptions discriminate on the basis of signs' messages, or on the ground that it prohibits too much protected speech. For purposes of this case, the validity of Ladue's submission that its ordinance's various exemptions are free of impermissible content or viewpoint discrimination is assumed.

(b) Although Ladue has a concededly valid interest in minimizing visual clutter, it has almost completely foreclosed an important and distinct medium of expression to political, religious, or personal messages. Prohibitions foreclosing entire media may be completely free of content or viewpoint discrimination, but such measures can suppress too much speech by eliminating a common means of speaking.

(c) Ladue's attempt to justify the ordinance as a "time, place, or manner" restriction fails because alternatives such as handbills and newspaper advertisements are inadequate substitutes for the important medium that Ladue has closed off. Displaying a sign from ones' own residence carries a message quite distinct from placing the same sign someplace else, or conveying the same text or picture by other means, for it provides information about the speaker's identity, an important component of many attempts to persuade. Residential signs are also an unusually cheap and convenient form of communication. Furthermore, the audience intended to be reached by a residential sign -- neighbors -- could not be reached nearly as well by other means.

(d) A special respect for individual liberty in the home has long been part of this Nation's culture and law, and has a special resonance when the government seeks to constrain a person's ability to speak there. The decision reached here does not leave Ladue powerless to address the ills that may be associated with residential signs. In addition, residents' self-interest in maintaining their own property values and preventing "visual clutter" in their yards and neighborhoods diminishes the danger of an "unlimited" proliferation of signs. [ ]

986 F.2d 1180, affirmed.

STEVENS, J., delivered the opinion for a unanimous Court. O'CONNOR, J., filed a concurring opinion.

STEVENS, J., lead opinion

An ordinance of the City of Ladue prohibits homeowners from displaying any signs on their property except "residence identification" signs, "for sale" signs, and signs warning of safety hazards. The ordinance permits commercial establishments, churches, and nonprofit organizations to erect certain signs that are not allowed at residences. The question presented is whether the ordinance violates a Ladue resident's right to free speech.

I

Respondent Margaret P. Gilleo owns one of the 57 single-family homes in the Willow Hill subdivision of Ladue. On December 8, 1990, she placed on her front lawn a 24- by 36-inch sign printed with the words "Say No to War in the Persian Gulf, Call Congress Now." After that sign disappeared, Gilleo put up another but it was knocked to the ground. When Gilleo reported these incidents to the police, they advised her that such signs were prohibited in Ladue. The City Council denied her petition for a variance. Gilleo then filed this action under 42 U.S.C. § 1983 against the City, the Mayor, and members of the City Council, alleging that Ladue's sign ordinance violated her First Amendment right of free speech.

The District Court issued a preliminary injunction against enforcement of the ordinance. [ ] Gilleo then placed an 8.5- by 11-inch sign in the second story window of her home stating, "For Peace in the Gulf." The Ladue City Council responded to the injunction by repealing its ordinance and enacting a replacement. Like its predecessor, the new ordinance contains a general prohibition of "signs" and defines that term broadly. The ordinance prohibits all signs except those that fall within one of ten exemptions. Thus, "residential identification signs" no larger than one square foot are allowed, as are signs advertising "that the property is for sale, lease or exchange" and identifying the owner or agent. [ ] Also exempted are signs "for churches, religious institutions, and schools," "[c]ommercial signs in commercially or industrial zoned districts," and on-site signs advertising "gasoline filling stations." Unlike its predecessor, the new ordinance contains a lengthy "Declaration of Findings, Policies, Interests, and Purposes," part of which recites that the

> proliferation of an unlimited number of signs in private, residential, commercial, industrial, and public areas of the City of Ladue would create ugliness, visual blight and clutter, tarnish the natural beauty of the landscape as well as the residential and commercial architecture, impair property values, substantially impinge upon the privacy and special ambience of the community, and may cause safety and traffic hazards to motorists, pedestrians, and children[.]

[ ]

Gilleo amended her complaint to challenge the new ordinance, which explicitly prohibits window signs like hers. The District Court held the ordinance unconstitutional, and the Court of Appeals affirmed. [ ] Relying on the plurality opinion in *Metromedia, Inc. v. San Diego,* 453 U.S. 490 (1981), the Court of Appeals held the ordinance invalid as a "content based" regulation because the City treated commercial speech more favorably than noncommercial speech and favored some kinds of noncommercial speech over others. [ ]. Acknowledging that "Ladue's interests in enacting its ordinance are substantial," the Court of Appeals nevertheless concluded that those interests were "not sufficiently 'compelling' to support a content-based restriction." [ ]

We granted the City of Ladue's petition for certiorari [ ], and now affirm.

II

While signs are a form of expression protected by the Free Speech Clause, they pose distinctive problems that are subject to municipalities' police powers. Unlike oral speech, signs take up space and may obstruct views, distract motorists, displace alternative uses for land, and pose other problems that legitimately call for regulation. It is common ground that governments may regulate the physical characteristics of signs -- just as they can, within reasonable bounds and absent censorial purpose, regulate audible expression in its capacity as noise. [ ] However, because regulation of a medium inevitably affects communication itself, it is not surprising that we have had occasion to review the constitutionality of municipal ordinances prohibiting the display of certain outdoor signs.

In *Linmark Associates, Inc. v. Willingboro,* 431 U.S. 85 (1977), we addressed an ordinance that sought to maintain stable, integrated neighborhoods by prohibiting homeowners from placing "For Sale" or "Sold" signs on their property. Although we recognized the importance of Willingboro's objective, we held that the First Amendment prevented the township from "achieving its goal by restricting the free flow of truthful information." [ ] In some respects, *Linmark* is the mirror image of this case. For instead of prohibiting "For Sale" signs without banning any other signs, Ladue has exempted such signs from an otherwise virtually complete ban. Moreover, whereas, in *Linmark,* we noted that the ordinance was not concerned with the promotion of aesthetic values unrelated to the content of the prohibited speech [ ], here Ladue relies squarely on that content-neutral justification for its ordinance.

In *Metromedia,* we reviewed an ordinance imposing substantial prohibitions on outdoor advertising displays within the City of San Diego in the interest of traffic safety and aesthetics. The ordinance generally banned all except those advertising "on-site" activities. The Court concluded that the City's interest in traffic safety and its aesthetic interest in preventing "visual clutter" could justify a prohibition of off-site commercial billboards even though similar on-site signs were allowed. [ ] Nevertheless, the Court's judgment in *Metromedia,* supported by two different lines of reasoning, invalidated the San Diego ordinance in its entirety. According to Justice White's plurality opinion, the ordinance impermissibly discriminated on the basis of content by permitting on-site commercial speech while broadly prohibiting noncommercial messages. [ ] On the other hand, JUSTICE BRENNAN, joined by JUSTICE BLACKMUN, concluded "that the *practical* effect of the San Diego ordinance [was] to eliminate the billboard as an effective medium of communication" for noncommercial messages, and that the city had failed to make the strong showing needed to justify such "content-neutral prohibitions of particular media of communication." [ ] The three dissenters also viewed San Diego's ordinance as tantamount to a blanket prohibition of billboards, but would have upheld it because they did not perceive "even a hint of bias or censorship in the city's actions" nor "any reason to believe that the overall communications market in San Diego is inadequate." [ ]

In *City Council of Los Angeles v. Taxpayers for Vincent,* 466 U.S. 789 (1984), we upheld a Los Angeles ordinance that prohibited the posting of signs on public property. Noting the conclusion shared by seven Justices in *Metromedia* that San Diego's "interest in avoiding visual clutter" was sufficient to justify a prohibition of commercial billboards [ ], in *Vincent,* we upheld the Los Angeles ordinance, which was justified on the same grounds. We rejected the argument that the validity of the

City's aesthetic interest had been compromised by failing to extend the ban to private property, reasoning that the "private citizen's interest in controlling the use of his own property justifies the disparate treatment." [ ]. We also rejected as "misplaced" respondents' reliance on public forum principles, for they had

> fail[ed] to demonstrate the existence of a traditional right of access respecting such items as utility poles . . . comparable to that recognized for public streets and parks.

[ ]

These decisions identify two analytically distinct grounds for challenging the constitutionality of a municipal ordinance regulating the display of signs. One is that the measure in effect restricts too little speech because its exemptions discriminate on the basis of the signs' messages. [ ] Alternatively, such provisions are subject to attack on the ground that they simply prohibit too much protected speech. [ ] The City of Ladue contends, first, that the Court of Appeals' reliance on the former rationale was misplaced because the City's regulatory purposes are content-neutral, and, second, that those purposes justify the comprehensiveness of the sign prohibition. A comment on the former contention will help explain why we ultimately base our decision on a rejection of the latter.

III

While surprising at first glance, the notion that a regulation of speech may be impermissibly *underinclusive* is firmly grounded in basic First Amendment principles. Thus, an exemption from an otherwise permissible regulation of speech may represent a governmental "attempt to give one side of a debatable public question an advantage in expressing its views to the people." [ ] Alternatively, through the combined operation of a general speech restriction and its exemptions, the government might seek to select the "permissible subjects for public debate," and thereby to "control . . . the search for political truth." [ ]

The City argues that its sign ordinance implicates neither of these concerns, and that the Court of Appeals therefore erred in demanding a "compelling" justification for the exemptions. The mix of prohibitions and exemptions in the ordinance, Ladue maintains, reflects legitimate differences among the side effects of various kinds of signs. These differences are only adventitiously connected with content, and supply a sufficient justification, unrelated to the City's approval or disapproval of specific messages, for carving out the specified categories from the general ban. [ ] Thus, according to the Declaration of Findings, Policies, Interests, and Purposes supporting the ordinance, the permitted signs, unlike the prohibited signs, are unlikely to contribute to the dangers of "unlimited proliferation" associated with categories of signs that are not inherently limited in number. [ ] Because only a few residents will need to display "for sale" or "for rent" signs at any given time, permitting one

84

such sign per marketed house does not threaten visual clutter. [ ] Because the City has only a few businesses, churches, and schools, the same rationale explains the exemption for on-site commercial and organizational signs. [ ] Moreover, some of the exempted categories (*e.g.,* danger signs) respond to unique public needs to permit certain kinds of speech. [ ] Even if we assume the validity of these arguments, the exemptions in Ladue's ordinance nevertheless shed light on the separate question of whether the ordinance prohibits too much speech.

Exemptions from an otherwise legitimate regulation of a medium of speech may be noteworthy for a reason quite apart from the risks of viewpoint and content discrimination: they may diminish the credibility of the government's rationale for restricting speech in the first place. [ ] In this case, at the very least, the exemptions from Ladue's ordinance demonstrate that Ladue has concluded that the interest in allowing certain messages to be conveyed by means of residential signs outweighs the City's aesthetic interest in eliminating outdoor signs. Ladue has not imposed a flat ban on signs because it has determined that at least some of them are too vital to be banned.

Under the Court of Appeals' content discrimination rationale, the City might theoretically remove the defects in its ordinance by simply repealing all of the exemptions.   If, however, the ordinance is also vulnerable because it prohibits too much speech, that solution would not save it.   Moreover, if the prohibitions in Ladue's ordinance are impermissible, resting our decision on its exemptions would afford scant relief for respondent Gilleo.   She is primarily concerned not with the scope of the exemptions available in other locations, such as commercial areas and on church property.   She asserts a constitutional right to display an anti-war sign at her own home.   Therefore, we first ask whether Ladue may properly *prohibit* Gilleo from displaying her sign, and then, only if necessary, consider the separate question whether it was improper for the City simultaneously to *permit* certain other signs.   In examining the propriety of Ladue's near-total prohibition of residential signs, we will assume, *arguendo,* the validity of the City's submission that the various exemptions are free of impermissible content or viewpoint discrimination.

IV

In *Linmark* we held that the City's interest in maintaining a stable, racially integrated neighborhood was not sufficient to support a prohibition of residential "For Sale" signs. We recognized that even such a narrow sign prohibition would have a deleterious effect on residents' ability to convey important information because alternatives were "far from satisfactory." [ ] Ladue's sign ordinance is supported principally by the City's interest in minimizing the visual clutter associated with signs, an interest that is concededly valid but certainly no more compelling than the interests at stake in *Linmark*.   Moreover, whereas the ordinance in *Linmark* applied only to a form of commercial speech, Ladue's ordinance covers even such absolutely pivotal speech as a sign protesting an imminent governmental decision to go to war.

The impact on free communication of Ladue's broad sign prohibition, moreover, is manifestly greater than in *Linmark*. Gilleo and other residents of Ladue are forbidden to display virtually any "sign" on their property. The ordinance defines that term sweepingly. A prohibition is not always invalid merely because it applies to a sizeable category of speech; the sign ban we upheld in *Vincent*, for example, was quite broad. But, in *Vincent*, we specifically noted that the category of speech in question -- signs placed on public property -- was not a "uniquely valuable or important mode of communication," and that there was no evidence that "appellees' ability to communicate effectively is threatened by ever-increasing restrictions on expression." [ ]

Here, in contrast, Ladue has almost completely foreclosed a venerable means of communication that is both unique and important. It has totally foreclosed that medium to political, religious, or personal messages. Signs that react to a local happening or express a view on a controversial issue both reflect and animate change in the life of a community. Often placed on lawns or in windows, residential signs play an important part in political campaigns, during which they are displayed to signal the resident's support for particular candidates, parties, or causes. They may not afford the same opportunities for conveying complex ideas as do other media, but residential signs have long been an important and distinct medium of expression.

Our prior decisions have voiced particular concern with laws that foreclose an entire medium of expression. Thus, we have held invalid ordinances that completely banned the distribution of pamphlets within the municipality, [ ] ... Although prohibitions foreclosing entire media may be completely free of content or viewpoint discrimination, the danger they pose to the freedom of speech is readily apparent -- by eliminating a common means of speaking, such measures can suppress too much speech.

Ladue contends, however, that its ordinance is a mere regulation of the "time, place, or manner" of speech, because residents remain free to convey their desired messages by other means, such as *hand-held* signs,

> letters, handbills, flyers, telephone calls, newspaper advertisements, bumper stickers, speeches, and neighborhood or community meetings.

[ ] However, even regulations that do not foreclose an entire medium of expression, but merely shift the time, place, or manner of its use, must "leave open ample alternative channels for communication." [ ] In this case, we are not persuaded that adequate substitutes exist for the important medium of speech that Ladue has closed off.

Displaying a sign from one's own residence often carries a message quite distinct from placing the same sign someplace else, or conveying the same text or picture by other means. Precisely because of their location, such signs provide information about the identity of the "speaker." As an early and eminent student of rhetoric observed, the identity of the speaker is an important component of many attempts to persuade. A sign advocating "Peace in the Gulf" in the front lawn of a retired general or decorated war veteran may provoke a different reaction than the same sign in a 10-year-old child's bedroom window or the same message on a bumper sticker of a passing automobile. An espousal of socialism may carry different implications when displayed on the grounds of a stately mansion than when pasted on a factory wall or an ambulatory sandwich board.

Residential signs are an unusually cheap and convenient form of communication. Especially for persons of modest means or limited mobility, a yard or window sign may have no practical substitute. [ ] Even for the affluent, the added costs in money or time of taking out a newspaper advertisement, handing out leaflets on the street, or standing in front of one's house with a hand-held sign may make the difference between participating and not participating in some public debate. Furthermore, a person who puts up a sign at her residence often intends to reach *neighbors,* an audience that could not be reached nearly as well by other means.

A special respect for individual liberty in the home has long been part of our culture and our law [ ]; that principle has special resonance when the government seeks to constrain a person's ability to *speak* there. [ ] Most Americans would be understandably dismayed, given that tradition, to learn that it was illegal to display from their window an 8- by 11-inch sign expressing their political views. Whereas the government's need to mediate among various competing uses, including expressive ones, for public streets and facilities is constant and unavoidable [ ] ...

Our decision that Ladue's ban on almost all residential signs violates the First Amendment by no means leaves the City powerless to address the ills that may be associated with residential signs. It bears mentioning that individual residents themselves have strong incentives to keep their own property values up and to prevent "visual clutter" in their own yards and neighborhoods -- incentives markedly different from those of persons who erect signs on others' land, in others' neighborhoods, or on public property. Residents' self-interest diminishes the danger of the "unlimited" proliferation of residential signs that concerns the City of Ladue. We are confident that more temperate measures could in large part satisfy Ladue's stated regulatory needs without harm to the First Amendment rights of its citizens. As currently framed, however, the ordinance abridges those rights.

Accordingly, the judgment of the Court of Appeals is

Affirmed.

It is unusual for us, when faced with a regulation that, on its face, draws content distinctions, to "assume, *arguendo,* the validity of the City's submission that the various exemptions are free of impermissible content or viewpoint discrimination." [ ] With rare exceptions, content discrimination in regulations of the speech of private citizens on private property or in a traditional public forum is presumptively impermissible, and this presumption is a very strong one. [ ] The normal inquiry that our doctrine dictates is, first, to determine whether a regulation is content-based or content-neutral, and then, based on the answer to that question, to apply the proper level of scrutiny. [ ]

Over the years, some cogent criticisms have been leveled at our approach. [ ] And it is quite true that regulations are occasionally struck down because of their content-based nature, even though common sense may suggest that they are entirely reasonable. The content distinctions present in this ordinance may, to some, be a good example of this.

But though our rule has flaws, it has substantial merit, as well. It is a rule, in an area where fairly precise rules are better than more discretionary and more subjective balancing tests. [ ] On a theoretical level, it reflects important insights into the meaning of the free speech principle -- for instance, that content-based speech restrictions are especially likely to be improper attempts to value some forms of speech over others, or are particularly susceptible to being used by the government to distort public debate. [ ]. On a practical level, it has in application generally led to seemingly sensible results. And, perhaps most importantly, no better alternative has yet come to light.

I would have preferred to apply our normal analytical structure in this case, which may well have required us to examine this law with the scrutiny appropriate to content-based regulations. Perhaps this would have forced us to confront some of the difficulties with the existing doctrine; perhaps it would have shown weaknesses in the rule, and led us to modify it to take into account the special factors this case presents. But such reexamination is part of the process by which our rules evolve and improve.

Nonetheless, I join the Court's opinion, because I agree with its conclusion in Part IV that, even if the restriction were content-neutral, it would still be invalid, and because I do not think Part III casts any doubt on the propriety of our normal content discrimination inquiry.

In *National Endowment for the Arts v. Finley* (MCLE, page 169), the Supreme Court held 8-1 that a provision of a 1990 Act did not violate the First Amendment. Under the provision of the National Foundation on the Arts and Humanities Act, the chair of the National Endowment for the Arts was directed to consider "general standards of decency and respect for the diverse beliefs and values of the American public" when deciding the artistic merit of grant applications. The Act was passed after considerable controversy over NEA support for artists such as Andres Serrano, whose photos included a crucifix immersed in urine, and for an exhibit of Robert Mapplethorpe's work that included homoerotic photographs several Members of Congress condemned as pornographic. Only Justice Souter dissented, expressing concern that the provision would have a "chilling effect," even if the decency standards were not actually imposed. The majority, led by Justice O'Connor, saw no problem with the provision because it did not specifically bar the agency from funding indecent projects, and there was no evidence that it had discriminated against applicants based upon their viewpoints.

National Endowment for the Arts v. Finley

Argued March 31, 1998

Decided June 25, 1998

118 S.Ct. 2168, 141 L.Ed.2d 500

CERTIORARI TO THE UNITED STATES COURT OF APPEALS
FOR THE NINTH CIRCUIT

Syllabus

The National Foundation on the Arts and Humanities Act vests the National Endowment for the Arts (NEA) with substantial discretion to award financial grants to support the arts; it identifies only the broadest funding priorities, including "artistic and cultural significance, giving emphasis to . . . creativity and cultural diversity," "professional excellence," and the encouragement of "public . . . education . . . and appreciation of the arts." [ ] Applications for NEA funding are initially reviewed by advisory panels of experts in the relevant artistic field. The panels report to the National Council on the Arts (Council), which, in turn, advises the NEA Chairperson. In 1989, controversial photographs that appeared in two NEA-funded exhibits prompted public outcry over the agency's grantmaking procedures. Congress reacted to the controversy by inserting an amendment into the NEA's 1990 reauthorization bill. The amendment became § 954(d)(1), which directs the Chairperson to ensure that artistic excellence and artistic merit are the criteria by which [grant] applications are judged, taking into consideration general standards of decency and respect for the diverse beliefs and values of the American public.

The NEA has not promulgated an official interpretation of the provision, but the Council adopted a resolution to implement § 954(d)(1) by ensuring that advisory panel members represent geographic, ethnic, and aesthetic diversity. The four individual respondents are performance artists who applied for NEA grants before § 954(d)(1) was enacted. An advisory panel recommended approval of each of their projects, but the Council subsequently recommended disapproval, and funding was denied. They filed suit for restoration of the recommended grants or reconsideration of their applications, asserting First Amendment and statutory claims. When Congress enacted § 954(d)(1), respondents, joined by the National Association of Artists' Organizations, amended their complaint to challenge the provision as void for vagueness and impermissibly viewpoint-based. The District Court granted summary judgment in favor of respondents on their facial constitutional challenge to § 954(d)(1). The Ninth Circuit affirmed, holding that § 954(d)(1), on its face, impermissibly discriminates on the basis of viewpoint, and is void for vagueness under the First and Fifth Amendments.

Held: section 954(d)(1) is facially valid, as it neither inherently interferes with First Amendment rights nor violates constitutional vagueness principles.

(a) Respondents confront a heavy burden in advancing their facial constitutional challenge, and they have not demonstrated a substantial risk that application of § 954(d)(1) will lead to the suppression of free expression [ ]. The premise of respondents' claim is that § 954(d)(1) constrains the agency's ability to fund certain categories of artistic expression. The provision, however, simply adds "considerations" to the grantmaking process; it does not preclude awards to projects that might be deemed "indecent" or "disrespectful," nor place conditions on grants, or even specify that those factors must be given any particular weight in reviewing an application. Regardless whether the NEA's view that the formulation of diverse advisory panels is sufficient to comply with Congress' command is in fact a reasonable reading, § 954(d)(1)'s plain text clearly does not impose a categorical requirement. Furthermore, the political context surrounding the "decency and respect" clause's adoption is inconsistent with respondents' assertion. The legislation was a bipartisan proposal introduced as a counterweight to amendments that would have eliminated the NEA's funding or substantially constrained its grantmaking authority. Section 954(d)(1) merely admonishes the NEA to take "decency and respect" into consideration, and the Court does not perceive a realistic danger that it will be utilized to preclude or punish the expression of particular views. The Court typically strikes down legislation as facially unconstitutional when the dangers are both more evident and more substantial. [ ] Given the varied interpretations of the "decency and respect" criteria urged by the parties, and the provision's vague exhortation to "take them into consideration," it seems unlikely that § 954(d)(1) will significantly compromise First Amendment values.

The NEA's enabling statute contemplates a number of indisputably constitutional applications for both the "decency" and the "respect" prong of § 954(d)(1). It is well established that "decency" is a permissible factor where "educational suitability" motivates its consideration. [ ] And the statute already provides that the agency must take "cultural diversity" into account. References to permissible applications would not alone be sufficient to sustain the statute, but neither is the Court persuaded that, in other applications, the language of § 954(d)(1) itself will give rise to the suppression of protected expression. Any content-based considerations that may be taken into account are a consequence of the nature of arts funding; the NEA has limited resources to allocate among many "artistically excellent" projects, and it does so on the basis of a wide variety of subjective criteria. Respondent's reliance on *Rosenberger v. Rector and Visitors of Univ. of Va* [ ] -- in which the Court overturned a public university's objective decision denying funding to all student publications having religious editorial viewpoints -- is therefore misplaced. The NEA's mandate is to make aesthetic judgments, and the inherently content-based "excellence" threshold for NEA support sets it apart from the subsidy at issue in *Rosenberger*. Moreover, although the First Amendment applies in the subsidy context, Congress has wide latitude to set spending priorities. [ ] Unless and until § 954(d)(1) is applied in a manner that raises concern about the suppression of disfavored viewpoints, the Court will uphold it.

(b) The lower courts also erred in invalidating § 954(d)(1) as unconstitutionally vague. The First and Fifth Amendments protect speakers from arbitrary and discriminatory enforcement of vague standards [ ]. Section 954(d)(1)'s terms are undeniably opaque, and if they appeared in a criminal statute or regulatory scheme, they could raise substantial vagueness concerns. It is unlikely, however, that speakers will be compelled to steer too far clear of any forbidden area in the context of NEA grants. As a practical matter, artists may conform their speech to what they believe to be the NEA decisionmaking criteria in order to acquire funding. But, when the Government is acting as patron, rather than sovereign, the consequences of imprecision are not constitutionally severe. In the context of selective subsidies, it is not always feasible for Congress to legislate with clarity. Indeed, to accept respondents' vagueness argument would be to call into question the constitutionality of the many valuable Government programs awarding scholarships and grants on the basis of subjective criteria such as "excellence."

100 F.3d 671 reversed and remanded.

O'CONNOR, J., delivered the opinion of the Court, in which REHNQUIST, C. J., and STEVENS, KENNEDY, and BREYER, JJ., joined, and in which GINSBURG, J., joined except for Part II-B. SCALIA, J., filed an opinion concurring in the judgment, in which THOMAS, J., joined.

SOUTER, J., filed a dissenting opinion.

O'CONNOR, J., lead opinion

The National Foundation on the Arts and Humanities Act, as amended in 1990, requires the Chairperson of the National Endowment for the Arts (NEA) to ensure that

> artistic excellence and artistic merit are the criteria by which [grant] applications are judged, taking into consideration general standards of decency and respect for the diverse beliefs and values of the American public.

20 U.S.C. § 954(d)(1). In this case, we review the Court of Appeals' determination that § 954(d)(1), on its face, impermissibly discriminates on the basis of viewpoint, and is void for vagueness under the First and Fifth Amendments. We conclude that § 954(d)(1) is facially valid, as it neither inherently interferes with First Amendment rights nor violates constitutional vagueness principles.

I

A

With the establishment of the NEA in 1965, Congress embarked on a "broadly conceived national policy of support for the . . . arts in the United States," *see* § 953(b), pledging federal funds to

> help create and sustain not only a climate encouraging freedom of thought, imagination, and inquiry, but also the material conditions facilitating the release of . . . creative talent.

§ 951(7). The enabling statute vests the NEA with substantial discretion to award grants; it identifies only the broadest funding priorities, including "artistic and cultural significance, giving emphasis to American creativity and cultural diversity," "professional excellence," and the encouragement of "public knowledge, education, understanding, and appreciation of the arts." *See* §§ 954(c)(1)-(10).

Applications for NEA funding are initially reviewed by advisory panels composed of experts in the relevant field of the arts. Under the 1990 Amendments to the enabling statute, those panels must reflect "diverse artistic and cultural points of view" and include "wide geographic, ethnic, and minority representation," as well as "lay individuals who are knowledgeable about the arts." §§ 959(c)(1)-(2). The panels report to the 26-member National Council on the Arts (Council), which, in turn, advises the NEA Chairperson. The Chairperson has the ultimate authority to award grants, but may not approve an application as to which the Council has made a negative recommendation. § 955(f).

Since 1965, the NEA has distributed over three billion dollars in grants to individuals and organizations, funding that has served as a catalyst for increased state, corporate, and foundation support for the arts. Congress has recently restricted the availability of federal funding for individual artists, confining grants primarily to qualifying organizations and state arts agencies, and constraining subgranting. [ ] By far the largest portion of the grants distributed in fiscal year 1998 were awarded directly to state arts agencies. In the remaining categories, the most substantial grants were allocated to symphony orchestras, fine arts museums, dance theater foundations, and opera associations. [ ]

Throughout the NEA's history, only a handful of the agency's roughly 100,000 awards have generated formal complaints about misapplied funds or abuse of the public's trust. Two provocative works, however, prompted public controversy in 1989, and led to congressional revaluation of the NEA's funding priorities and efforts to increase oversight of its grantmaking procedures. The Institute of Contemporary Art at the University of Pennsylvania had used $30,000 of a visual arts grant it received from the NEA to fund a 1989 retrospective of photographer Robert Mapplethorpe's work. The exhibit, entitled *The Perfect Moment,* included homoerotic photographs that several Members of Congress condemned as pornographic. [ ] Members also denounced artist Andres Serrano's work Piss Christ, a photograph of a crucifix immersed in urine. [ ] Serrano had been awarded a $15,000 grant from the Southeast Center for Contemporary Art, an organization that received NEA support.

When considering the NEA's appropriations for fiscal year 1990, Congress reacted to the controversy surrounding the Mapplethorpe and Serrano photographs by eliminating $45,000 from the agency's budget, the precise amount contributed to the two exhibits by NEA grant recipients. Congress also enacted an amendment providing that no NEA funds

> may be used to promote, disseminate, or produce materials which in the judgment of [the NEA] may be considered obscene, including but not limited to, depictions of sadomasochism, homoeroticism, the sexual exploitation of children, or individuals engaged in sex acts and which, when taken as a whole, do not have serious literary, artistic, political, or scientific value.

[ ] The NEA implemented Congress' mandate by instituting a requirement that all grantees certify in writing that they would not utilize federal funding to engage in projects inconsistent with the criteria in the 1990 appropriations bill. That certification requirement was subsequently invalidated as unconstitutionally vague by a Federal District Court [ ], and the NEA did not appeal the decision.

In the 1990 appropriations bill, Congress also agreed to create an Independent Commission of constitutional law scholars to review the NEA's grantmaking procedures and assess the possibility of more focused standards for public arts funding. The Commission's report, issued in September 1990, concluded that there is no constitutional obligation to provide arts funding, but also recommended that the NEA rescind the certification requirement and cautioned against legislation setting forth any content restrictions. Instead, the Commission

93

suggested procedural changes to enhance the role of advisory panels and a statutory reaffirmation of "the high place the nation accords to the fostering of mutual respect for the disparate beliefs and values among us." [ ]

Informed by the Commission's recommendations, and cognizant of pending judicial challenges to the funding limitations in the 1990 appropriations bill, Congress debated several proposals to reform the NEA's grantmaking process when it considered the agency's reauthorization in the fall of 1990. The House rejected the Crane Amendment, which would have virtually eliminated the NEA [ ], and the Rohrabacher Amendment, which would have introduced a prohibition on awarding any grants that could be used to "promote, distribute, disseminate, or produce matter that has the purpose or effect of denigrating the beliefs, tenets, or objects of a particular religion" or "of denigrating an individual, or group of individuals, on the basis of race, sex, handicap, or national origin [ ]. Ultimately, Congress adopted the Williams Coleman Amendment, a bipartisan compromise between Members opposing any funding restrictions and those favoring some guidance to the agency. In relevant part, the Amendment became § 954(d)(1), which directs the Chairperson, in establishing procedures to judge the artistic merit of grant applications, to "tak[e] into consideration general standards of decency and respect for the diverse beliefs and values of the American public."

The NEA has not promulgated any official interpretation of the provision, but, in December, 1990, the Council unanimously adopted a resolution to implement § 954(d)(1) merely by ensuring that the members of the advisory panels that conduct the initial review of grant applications represent geographic, ethnic, and aesthetic diversity. [ ] John Frohnmayer, then Chairperson of the NEA, also declared that he would "count on [the] procedures" ensuring diverse membership on the peer review panels to fulfill Congress' mandate. [ ]

B

The four individual respondents in this case, Karen Finley, John Fleck, Holly Hughes, and Tim Miller, are performance artists who applied for NEA grants before § 954(d)(1) was enacted. An advisory panel recommended approval of respondents' projects, both initially and after receiving Frohnmayer's request to reconsider three of the applications. A majority of the Council subsequently recommended disapproval, and, in June, 1990, the NEA informed respondents that they had been denied funding. Respondents filed suit, alleging that the NEA had violated their First Amendment rights by rejecting the applications on political grounds, had failed to follow statutory procedures by basing the denial on criteria other than those set forth in the NEA's enabling statute, and had breached the confidentiality of their grant applications through the release of quotations to the press, in violation of the Privacy Act of 1974, 5 U.S.C. § 552(a). Respondents sought restoration of the recommended grants or reconsideration of their applications, as well as damages for the alleged Privacy Act violations.   When Congress enacted § 954(d)(1), respondents, now joined by the National Association of Artists' Organizations (NAAO), amended their complaint to challenge the provision as void for vagueness and impermissibly viewpoint-based. [ ]

The District Court denied the NEA's motion for judgment on the pleadings, 795 F.Supp. 1457, 1463-1468 (CD Cal. 1992), and, after discovery, the NEA agreed to settle the individual respondents' statutory and as-applied constitutional claims by paying the artists the amount of the vetoed grants, damages, and attorney's fees. [ ]

The District Court then granted summary judgment in favor of respondents on their facial constitutional challenge to § 954(d)(1), and enjoined enforcement of the provision. [ ] The court rejected the argument that the NEA could comply with § 954(d)(1) by structuring the grant selection process to provide for diverse advisory panels. [ ] The provision, the court stated, "fails adequately to notify applicants of what is required of them or to circumscribe NEA discretion." [ ] ... [ ] Drawing an analogy between arts funding and public universities, the court further ruled that the First Amendment constrains the NEA's grantmaking process, and that, because § 954(d)(1) "clearly reaches a substantial amount of protected speech," it is impermissibly overbroad on its face. 795 F.Supp. at 1476. The Government did not seek a stay of the District Court's injunction, and consequently the NEA has not applied § 954(d)(1) since June, 1992.

A divided panel of the Court of Appeals affirmed the District Court's ruling. [ ] The majority agreed with the District Court that the NEA was compelled by the adoption of § 954(d)(1) to alter its grantmaking procedures to ensure that applications are judged according to the "decency and respect" criteria. The Chairperson, the court reasoned, "has no discretion to ignore this obligation, enforce only part of it, or give it a cramped construction." [ ] Concluding that the "decency and respect" criteria are not "susceptible to objective definition," the court held that § 954(d)(1) "gives rise to the danger of arbitrary and discriminatory application," and is void for vagueness under the First and Fifth Amendments. [ ] In the alternative, the court ruled that § 954(d)(1) violates the First Amendment's prohibition on viewpoint-based restrictions on protected speech. Government funding of the arts, the court explained, is both a "traditional sphere of free expression" [ ], and an area in which the Government has stated its intention to "encourage a diversity of views from private speakers" [ ] Accordingly, finding that § 954(d)(1) "has a speech-based restriction as its sole rationale and operative principle" [ ], and noting the NEA's failure to articulate a compelling interest for the provision, the court declared it facially invalid. [ ]

The dissent asserted that the First Amendment protects artists' rights to express themselves as indecently and disrespectfully as they like, but does not compel the Government to fund that speech. [ ] The challenged provision, the dissent contended, did not prohibit the NEA from funding indecent or offensive art, but merely required the agency to consider the "decency and respect" criteria in the grant selection process. [ ] Moreover, according to the dissent's reasoning, the vagueness principles applicable to the direct regulation of speech have no bearing on the selective award of prizes, and the Government may draw distinctions based on content and viewpoint in making its funding decisions. [ ] Three judges dissented from the denial of rehearing en banc, maintaining that the panel's decision gave the statute an "implausible construction," applied the "'void for vagueness' doctrine where it does not belong," and extended "First Amendment principles to a situation that the First Amendment doesn't cover." [ ]

We granted certiorari [ ], and now reverse the judgment of the Court of Appeals.

II
A

Respondents raise a facial constitutional challenge to § 954(d)(1), and consequently they confront "a heavy burden" in advancing their claim. [ ] Facial invalidation "is, manifestly, strong medicine" that "has been employed by the Court sparingly, and only as a last resort." [ ] ... To prevail, respondents must demonstrate a substantial risk that application of the provision will lead to the suppression of speech. [ ]

Respondents argue that the provision is a paradigmatic example of viewpoint discrimination, because it rejects any artistic speech that either fails to respect mainstream values or offends standards of decency. The premise of respondents' claim is that § 954(d)(1) constrains the agency's ability to fund certain categories of artistic expression. The NEA, however, reads the provision as merely hortatory, and contends that it stops well short of an absolute restriction. Section 954(d)(1) adds "considerations" to the grantmaking process; it does not preclude awards to projects that might be deemed "indecent" or "disrespectful," nor place conditions on grants, or even specify that those factors must be given any particular weight in reviewing an application. Indeed, the agency asserts that it has adequately implemented § 954(d)(1) merely by ensuring the representation of various backgrounds and points of view on the advisory panels that analyze grant applications. [ ] ... We do not decide whether the NEA's view -- that the formulation of diverse advisory panels is sufficient to comply with Congress' command -- is in fact a reasonable reading of the statute. It is clear, however, that the text of § 954(d)(1) imposes no categorical requirement. The advisory language stands in sharp contrast to congressional efforts to prohibit the funding of certain classes of speech. When Congress has in fact intended to affirmatively constrain the NEA's grantmaking authority, it has done so in no uncertain terms. See § 954(d)(2) ("[O]bscenity is without artistic merit, is not protected speech, and shall not be funded").

Furthermore, like the plain language of § 954(d), the political context surrounding the adoption of the "decency and respect" clause is inconsistent with respondents' assertion that the provision compels the NEA to deny funding on the basis of viewpoint discriminatory criteria. The legislation was a bipartisan proposal introduced as a counterweight to amendments aimed at eliminating the NEA's funding or substantially constraining its grantmaking authority. [ ] ...

That § 954(d)(1) admonishes the NEA merely to take "decency and respect" into consideration, and that the legislation was aimed at reforming procedures, rather than precluding speech, undercut respondents' argument that the provision inevitably will be utilized as a tool for invidious viewpoint discrimination. In cases where we have struck down legislation as facially unconstitutional, the dangers were both more evident and more substantial. In *R. A. V. v. St. Paul*, 505 U.S. 377 (1992), for example, we invalidated on its face a municipal ordinance that defined as a criminal offense the placement of a symbol on public or private property

> "which one knows or has reasonable grounds to know arouses anger, alarm, or resentment in others on the basis of race, color, creed, religion, or gender."

[ ] That provision set forth a clear penalty, proscribed views on particular "disfavored subjects" [ ], and suppressed "distinctive idea[s], conveyed by a distinctive message" [ ].

In contrast, the "decency and respect" criteria do not silence speakers by expressly "threaten[ing] censorship of ideas." [ ] Thus, we do not perceive a realistic danger that § 954(d)(1) will compromise First Amendment values. As respondents' own arguments demonstrate, the considerations that the provision introduces, by their nature, do not engender the kind of directed viewpoint discrimination that would prompt this Court to invalidate a statute on its face ...

Respondents' claim that the provision is facially unconstitutional may be reduced to the argument that the criteria in § 954(d)(1) are sufficiently subjective that the agency could utilize them to engage in viewpoint discrimination. Given the varied interpretations of the criteria and the vague exhortation to "take them into consideration," it seems unlikely that this provision will introduce any greater element of selectivity than the determination of "artistic excellence" itself. And we are reluctant, in any event, to invalidate legislation "on the basis of its hypothetical application to situations not before the Court." [ ]

The NEA's enabling statute contemplates a number of indisputably constitutional applications for both the "decency" prong of § 954(d)(1) and its reference to "respect for the diverse beliefs and values of the American public." Educational programs are central to the NEA's mission [ ] ... And it is well established that "decency" is a permissible factor where "educational suitability" motivates its consideration. [ ]

Permissible applications of the mandate to consider "respect for the diverse beliefs and values of the American public" are also apparent. In setting forth the purposes of the NEA, Congress explained that "[i]t is vital to democracy to honor and preserve its multicultural artistic heritage." § 951(10). The agency expressly takes diversity into account, giving special consideration to "projects and productions . . . that reach, or reflect the culture of, a minority, inner city, rural, or tribal community," § 954(c)(4), as well as projects that generally emphasize "cultural diversity," § 954(c)(1). Respondents do not contend that the criteria in § 954(d)(1) are impermissibly applied when they may be justified, as the statute contemplates, with respect to a project's intended audience.

We recognize, of course, that reference to these permissible applications would not alone be sufficient to sustain the statute against respondents' First Amendment challenge. But neither are we persuaded that, in other applications, the language of § 954(d)(1) itself will give rise to the suppression of protected expression. Any content-based considerations that may be taken into account in the grantmaking process are a consequence of the nature of arts funding. The NEA has limited resources, and it must deny the majority of the grant applications that it receives, including many that propose "artistically excellent" projects. The agency may decide to fund particular projects for a wide variety of reasons,

> such as the technical proficiency of the artist, the creativity of the work, the anticipated public interest in or appreciation of the work, the work's contemporary relevance, its educational value, its suitability for or appeal to special audiences (such as children or the disabled), its service to a rural or isolated community, or even simply that the work could increase public knowledge of an art form.

[ ] As the dissent below noted, it would be "impossible to have a highly selective grant program without denying money to a large amount of constitutionally protected expression." [ ] The "very assumption" of the NEA is that grants will be awarded according to the "artistic worth of competing applications," and absolute neutrality is simply "inconceivable." [ ]

Respondent's reliance on our decision in *Rosenberger v. Rector and Visitors of Univ. of Va.,* 515 U.S. 819 (1995), is therefore misplaced. In *Rosenberger,* a public university declined to authorize disbursements from its Student Activities Fund to finance the printing of a Christian student newspaper. We held that, by subsidizing the Student Activities Fund, the University had created a limited public forum from which it impermissibly excluded all publications with religious editorial viewpoints. [ ] Although the scarcity of NEA funding does not distinguish this case from *Rosenberger* [ ], the competitive process according to which the grants are allocated does. In the context of arts funding, in contrast to many other subsidies, the Government does not indiscriminately "encourage a diversity of views from private speakers" *id.* [ ]. The NEA's mandate is to make aesthetic judgments, and the inherently content-based "excellence" threshold for NEA support sets it apart from the subsidy at issue in *Rosenberger* -- which was available to all student organizations that were "'related to the educational purpose of the University'" [ ] -- and from comparably objective decisions on allocating public benefits, such as access to a school auditorium or a municipal theater [ ], or the second class mailing privileges available to "'all newspapers and other periodical publications'" [ ].

Respondents do not allege discrimination in any particular funding decision. (In fact, after filing suit to challenge § 954(d)(1), two of the individual respondents received NEA grants. [ ] ... Thus, we have no occasion here to address an as-applied challenge in a situation where the denial of a grant may be shown to be the product of invidious viewpoint discrimination. If the NEA were to leverage its power to award subsidies on the basis of subjective criteria into a penalty on disfavored viewpoints, then we would confront a different case. We have stated that, even in the provision of subsidies, the Government may not "ai[m] at the suppression of dangerous ideas" [ ], and if a subsidy were "manipulated" to have a "coercive effect," then relief could be appropriate. [ ] In addition, as the NEA itself concedes, a more pressing constitutional question would arise if government funding resulted in the imposition of a disproportionate burden calculated to drive "certain ideas or viewpoints from the marketplace." [ ] Unless and until § 954(d)(1) is applied in a manner that raises concern about the suppression of disfavored viewpoints, however, we uphold the constitutionality of the provision. [ ] ...

B

Finally, although the First Amendment certainly has application in the subsidy context, we note that the Government may allocate competitive funding according to criteria that would be impermissible were direct regulation of speech or a criminal penalty at stake. So long as legislation does not infringe on other constitutionally protected rights, Congress has wide latitude to set spending priorities. [ ] In the 1990 Amendments that incorporated § 954(d)(1), Congress modified the declaration of purpose in the NEA's enabling act to provide that arts funding should "contribute to public support and confidence in the use of taxpayer funds," and that "[p]ublic funds . . . must ultimately serve public purposes the Congress defines." § 951(5). And as we held in *Rust*, Congress may

> selectively fund a program to encourage certain activities it believes to be in the public interest, without at the same time funding an alternative program which seeks to deal with the problem in another way.

[ ] In doing so, "the Government has not discriminated on the basis of viewpoint; it has merely chosen to fund one activity to the exclusion of the other." [ ] ...

III

The lower courts also erred in invalidating § 954(d)(1) as unconstitutionally vague. Under the First and Fifth Amendments, speakers are protected from arbitrary and discriminatory enforcement of vague standards. [ ] The terms of the provision are undeniably opaque, and if they appeared in a criminal statute or regulatory scheme, they could raise substantial vagueness concerns. It is unlikely, however, that speakers will be compelled to steer too far clear of any "forbidden area" in the context of grants of this nature. [ ] ... We recognize, as a practical matter, that artists may conform their speech to what they believe to be the decisionmaking criteria in order to acquire funding. [ ] But when the Government is acting as patron, rather than as sovereign, the consequences of imprecision are not constitutionally severe.

In the context of selective subsidies, it is not always feasible for Congress to legislate with clarity. Indeed, if this statute is unconstitutionally vague, then so too are all government programs awarding scholarships and grants on the basis of subjective criteria such as "excellence." [ ] ... To accept respondents' vagueness argument would be to call into question the constitutionality of these valuable government programs and countless others like them.

Section 954(d)(1) merely adds some imprecise considerations to an already subjective selection process. It does not, on its face, impermissibly infringe on First or Fifth Amendment rights. Accordingly, the judgment of the Court of Appeals is reversed, and the case is remanded for further proceedings consistent with this opinion.

It is so ordered.

In *Central Hudson Gas & Electric Corp. v. Public Service Commission of New York* (MCLE, page 200) the Supreme Court struck down as unconstitutional a state public utilities regulation prohibiting advertising by electric utilities. In an 8-1 decision the Court applied a four-prong test for determining whether a specific form of commercial speech enjoyed First Amendment protection. On the same day, the Court held that another regulation by the same agency, the Public Service Commission of New York, also violated the First Amendment. In *Consolidated Edison Company of New York v. Public Service Commission of New York,* the Court struck down an order banning consumer bill inserts on controversial issues. The four-prong *Central Hudson* analysis continues to be the test the Court applies in determining when commercial speech falls under the First Amendment umbrella.

Central Hudson Gas & Electric Corp. v. Public Service Commission of New York

Argued March 17, 1980
Decided June 20, 1980

447 U.S. 557, 100 S.Ct. 2343,
65 L.Ed.2d, 341, 6 Med.L.Rptr. 1497

APPEAL FROM THE COURT OF APPEALS OF NEW YORK

Syllabus

Held: A regulation of appellee New York Public Service Commission which completely bans an electric utility from advertising to promote the use of electricity violates the First and Fourteenth Amendments.

(a) Although the Constitution accords a lesser protection to commercial speech than to other constitutionally guaranteed expression, nevertheless the First Amendment protects commercial speech from unwarranted governmental regulation. For commercial speech to come within the First Amendment, it at least must concern lawful activity and not be misleading. Next, it must be determined whether the asserted governmental interest to be served by the restriction on commercial speech is substantial. If both inquiries yield positive answers, it must then be decided whether the regulation directly advances the governmental interest asserted, and whether it is not more extensive than is necessary to serve that interest.

(b) In this case, it is not claimed that the expression at issue is either inaccurate or relates to unlawful activity. Nor is appellant electrical utility's promotional advertising unprotected commercial speech merely because appellant holds a monopoly over the sale of electricity in its service area. Since monopoly over the supply of a product provides no protection from competition with substitutes for that product, advertising by utilities is just as valuable to consumers as advertising by unregulated firms, and there is no indication that appellant's decision to advertise was not based on the belief that consumers were interested in the advertising.

(c) The State's interest in energy conservation is clearly substantial, and is directly advanced by appellee's regulations. The State's further interest in preventing inequities in appellant's rates -- based on the assertion that successful promotion of consumption in "off-peak" periods would create extra costs that would, because of appellant's rate structure, be borne by all consumers through higher overall rates -- is also substantial. The latter interest does not, however, provide a constitutionally adequate reason for restricting protected speech because the link between the advertising prohibition and appellant's rate structure is, at most, tenuous.

(d) Appellee's regulation, which reaches all promotional advertising, regardless of the impact of the touted service on overall energy use, is more extensive than necessary to further the State's interest in energy conservation which, as important as it is, cannot justify suppressing information about electric devices or services that would cause no net increase in total energy use. In addition, no showing has been made that a more limited restriction on the content of promotional advertising would not serve adequately the State's interests.

47 N.Y.2d 94, 390 N.E.2d 749, reversed.

POWELL, J., delivered the opinion of the Court, in which BURGER, C.J., and STEWART, WHITE, and MARSHALL, JJ., joined. BRENNAN, J., filed an opinion concurring in the judgment, BLACKMUN, J., and STEVENS, J., filed opinions concurring in the judgment, in which BRENNAN, J., joined. REHNQUIST, J., filed a dissenting opinion.

POWELL, J., lead opinion

This case presents the question whether a regulation of the Public Service Commission of the State of New York violates the First and Fourteenth Amendments because it completely bans promotional advertising by an electrical utility.

I

In December, 1973, the Commission, appellee here, ordered electric utilities in New York State to cease all advertising that "promot[es] the use of electricity." [ ] The order was based on the Commission's finding that "the interconnected utility system in New York State does not have sufficient fuel stocks or sources of supply to continue furnishing all customer demands for the 1973-1974 winter." [ ]

Three years later, when the fuel shortage had eased, the Commission requested comments from the public on its proposal to continue the ban on promotional advertising. Central Hudson Gas & Electric Corp., the appellant in this case, opposed the ban on First Amendment grounds. [ ] After reviewing the public comments, the Commission extended the prohibition in a Policy Statement issued on February 25, 1977.

The Policy Statement divided advertising expenses

> into two broad categories: promotional -- advertising intended to stimulate the purchase of utility services -- and institutional and informational, a broad category inclusive of all advertising not clearly intended to promote sales.

[ ] The Commission declared all promotional advertising contrary to the national policy of conserving energy. It acknowledged that the ban is not a perfect vehicle for conserving energy. For example, the Commission's order prohibits promotional advertising to develop consumption during periods when demand for electricity is low. By limiting growth in "off-peak" consumption, the ban limits the "beneficial side effects" of such growth in terms of more efficient use of existing powerplants. [ ] And since oil dealers are not under the Commission's jurisdiction and thus remain free to advertise, it was recognized that the ban can achieve only "piecemeal conservationism." Still, the Commission adopted the restriction because it was deemed likely to "result in some dampening of unnecessary growth" in energy consumption. [ ]

The Commission's order explicitly permitted "informational" advertising designed to encourage "*shifts* of consumption" from peak demand times to periods of low electricity demand. [ ] Informational advertising would not seek to increase aggregate consumption, but would invite a leveling of demand throughout any given 24-hour period. The agency offered to review "specific proposals by the companies for specifically described [advertising] programs that meet these criteria." [ ]

When it rejected requests for rehearing on the Policy Statement, the Commission supplemented its rationale for the advertising ban. The agency observed that additional electricity probably would be more expensive to produce than existing output. Because electricity rates in New York were not then based on marginal cost, the Commission feared that additional power would be priced below the actual cost of generation. The additional electricity would be subsidized by all consumers through generally higher rates. [ ] The state agency also thought that promotional advertising would give "misleading signals" to the public by appearing to encourage energy consumption at a time when conservation is needed. [ ]

Appellant challenged the order in state court, arguing that the Commission had restrained commercial speech in violation of the First and Fourteenth Amendments.{GO>3} The Commission's order was upheld by the trial court and at the intermediate appellate level. The New York Court of Appeals affirmed. It found little value to advertising in "the

103

noncompetitive market in which electric corporations operate." [ ] Since consumers "have no choice regarding the source of their electric power," the court denied that "promotional advertising of electricity might contribute to society's interest in `informed and reliable‛ economic decisionmaking." [ ] The court also observed that, by encouraging consumption, promotional advertising would only exacerbate the current energy situation. [ ] The court concluded that the governmental interest in the prohibition outweighed the limited constitutional value of the commercial speech at issue. We noted probable jurisdiction [ ], and now reverse.

II

The Commission's order restricts only commercial speech, that is, expression related solely to the economic interests of the speaker and its audience. [ ] The First Amendment, as applied to the States through the Fourteenth Amendment, protects commercial speech from unwarranted governmental regulation. [ ] Commercial expression not only serves the economic interest of the speaker, but also assists consumers and furthers the societal interest in the fullest possible dissemination of information. In applying the First Amendment to this area, we have rejected the "highly paternalistic" view that government has complete power to suppress or regulate commercial speech …

[ ] Even when advertising communicates only an incomplete version of the relevant facts, the First Amendment presumes that some accurate information is better than no information at all. [ ] … [ ]

The Constitution therefore accords a lesser protection to commercial speech than to other constitutionally guaranteed expression. [ ] The protection available for particular commercial expression turns on the nature both of the expression and of the governmental interests served by its regulation.

The First Amendment's concern for commercial speech is based on the informational function of advertising. [ ] Consequently, there can be no constitutional objection to the suppression of commercial messages that do not accurately inform the public about lawful activity. The government may ban forms of communication more likely to deceive the public than to inform it [ ], commercial speech related to illegal activity [ ]

If the communication is neither misleading nor related to unlawful activity, the government's power is more circumscribed. The State must assert a substantial interest to be achieved by restrictions on commercial speech. Moreover, the regulatory technique must be in proportion to that interest. The limitation on expression must be designed carefully to achieve the State's goal. Compliance with this requirement may be measured by two criteria. First, the restriction must directly advance the state interest involved; the regulation may not be sustained if it provides only ineffective or remote support for the government's purpose. Second, if the governmental interest could be served as well by a more limited restriction on commercial speech, the excessive restrictions cannot survive.

Under the first criterion, the Court has declined to uphold regulations that only indirectly advance the state interest involved. In both *Bates* and *Virginia Pharmacy Board,* the Court concluded that an advertising ban could not be imposed to protect the ethical or performance standards of a profession. The Court noted in *Virginia Pharmacy Board* that "[t]he advertising ban does not directly affect professional standards one way or the other." [ ] In *Bates,* the Court overturned an advertising prohibition that was designed to protect the "quality" of a lawyer's work. "Restraints on advertising . . . are an ineffective way of deterring shoddy work." [ ]

The second criterion recognizes that the First Amendment mandates that speech restrictions be "narrowly drawn." [ ] The regulatory technique may extend only as far as the interest it serves. The State cannot regulate speech that poses no danger to the asserted state interest [ ], nor can it completely suppress information when narrower restrictions on expression would serve its interest as well. For example, in *Bates,* the Court explicitly did not "foreclose the possibility that some limited supplementation, by way of warning or disclaimer or the like, might be required" in promotional materials. [ ]. And in *Carey v. Population Services International* [ ] (1977), we held that the State's "arguments . . . do not justify the total suppression of advertising concerning contraceptives." This holding left open the possibility that the State could implement more carefully drawn restrictions. [ ]

In commercial speech cases, then, a four-part analysis has developed. At the outset, we must determine whether the expression is protected by the First Amendment. For commercial speech to come within that provision, it at least must concern lawful activity and not be misleading. Next, we ask whether the asserted governmental interest is substantial. If both inquiries yield positive answers, we must determine whether the regulation directly advances the governmental interest asserted, and whether it is not more extensive than is necessary to serve that interest.

III

We now apply this four-step analysis for commercial speech to the Commission's arguments in support of its ban on promotional advertising.

A

The Commission does not claim that the expression at issue either is inaccurate or relates to unlawful activity. Yet the New York Court of Appeals questioned whether Central Hudson's advertising is protected commercial speech. Because appellant holds a monopoly over the sale of electricity in its service area, the state court suggested that the Commission's order restricts no commercial speech of any worth. The court stated that advertising in a "noncompetitive market" could not improve the decisionmaking of consumers. [ ] The court saw no constitutional problem with barring commercial speech that it viewed as conveying little useful information.

This reasoning falls short of establishing that appellant's advertising is not commercial speech protected by the First Amendment. Monopoly over the supply of a product provides no protection from competition with substitutes for that product. Electric utilities compete with suppliers of fuel oil and natural gas in several markets, such as those for home heating and industrial power. This Court noted the existence of interfuel competition 45 years ago [ ]. Each energy source continues to offer peculiar advantages and disadvantages that may influence consumer choice. For consumers in those competitive markets, advertising by utilities is just as valuable as advertising by unregulated firms.

Even in monopoly markets, the suppression of advertising reduces the information available for consumer decisions, and thereby defeats the purpose of the First Amendment. The New York court's argument appears to assume that the providers of a monopoly service or product are willing to pay for wholly ineffective advertising. Most businesses -- even regulated monopolies -- are unlikely to underwrite promotional advertising that is of no interest or use to consumers. Indeed, a monopoly enterprise legitimately may wish to inform the public that it has developed new services or terms of doing business. A consumer may need information to aid his decision whether or not to use the monopoly service at all, or how much of the service he should purchase. In the absence of factors that would distort the decision to advertise, we may assume that the willingness of a business to promote its products reflects a belief that consumers are interested in the advertising. Since no such extraordinary conditions have been identified in this case, appellant's monopoly position does not alter the First Amendment's protection for its commercial speech.

B

The Commission offers two state interests as justifications for the ban on promotional advertising. The first concerns energy conservation. Any increase in demand for electricity -- during peak or off-peak periods -- means greater consumption of energy. The Commission argues, and the New York court agreed, that the State's interest in conserving energy is sufficient to support suppression of advertising designed to increase consumption of electricity. In view of our country's dependence on energy resources beyond our control, no one can doubt the importance of energy conservation. Plainly, therefore, the state interest asserted is substantial.

The Commission also argues that promotional advertising will aggravate inequities caused by the failure to base the utilities' rates on marginal cost. The utilities argued to the Commission that, if they could promote the use of electricity in periods of low demand, they would improve their utilization of generating capacity. The Commission responded that promotion of off-peak consumption also would increase consumption during peak periods. If peak demand were to rise, the absence of marginal cost rates would mean that the rates charged for the additional power would not reflect the true costs of expanding production. Instead, the extra costs would be borne by all consumers through higher overall rates. Without promotional advertising, the Commission stated, this inequitable turn of events would be less likely to occur. The choice among rate structures involves difficult and important questions of economic supply and distributional fairness. The State's concern that rates be fair and efficient represents a clear and substantial governmental interest.

C

Next, we focus on the relationship between the State's interests and the advertising ban. Under this criterion, the Commission's laudable concern over the equity and efficiency of appellant's rates does not provide a constitutionally adequate reason for restricting protected speech. The link between the advertising prohibition and appellant's rate structure is, at most, tenuous. The impact of promotional advertising on the equity of appellant's rates is highly speculative. Advertising to increase off-peak usage would have to increase peak usage, while other factors that directly affect the fairness and efficiency of appellant's rates remained constant. Such conditional and remote eventualities simply cannot justify silencing appellant's promotional advertising.

In contrast, the State's interest in energy conservation is directly advanced by the Commission order at issue here. There is an immediate connection between advertising and demand for electricity. Central Hudson would not contest the advertising ban unless it believed that promotion would increase its sales. Thus, we find a direct link between the state interest in conservation and the Commission's order.

D

We come finally to the critical inquiry in this case: whether the Commission's complete suppression of speech ordinarily protected by the First Amendment is no more extensive than necessary to further the State's interest in energy conservation. The Commission's order reaches all promotional advertising, regardless of the impact of the touted service on overall energy use. But the energy conservation rationale, as important as it is, cannot justify suppressing information about electric devices or services that would cause no net increase in total energy use. In addition, no showing has been made that a more limited restriction on the content of promotional advertising would not serve adequately the State's interests.

Appellant insists that, but for the ban, it would advertise products and services that use energy efficiently. These include the "heat pump," which both parties acknowledge to be a major improvement in electric heating, and the use of electric heat as a "backup" to solar and other heat sources. Although the Commission has questioned the efficiency of electric heating before this Court, neither the Commission's Policy Statement nor its order denying rehearing made findings on this issue. In the absence of authoritative findings to the contrary, we must credit as within the realm of possibility the claim that electric heat can be an efficient alternative in some circumstances.

The Commission's order prevents appellant from promoting electric services that would reduce energy use by diverting demand from less efficient sources, or that would consume roughly the same amount of energy as do alternative sources. In neither situation would the utility's advertising endanger conservation or mislead the public. To the extent that the Commission's order suppresses speech that in no way impairs the State's interest in energy conservation, the Commission's order violates the First and Fourteenth Amendments, and must be invalidated. [ ]

The Commission also has not demonstrated that its interest in conservation cannot be protected adequately by more limited regulation of appellant's commercial expression. To further its policy of conservation, the Commission could attempt to restrict the format and content of Central Hudson's advertising. It might, for example, require that the advertisements include information about the relative efficiency and expense of the offered service, both under current conditions and for the foreseeable future. [ ] In the absence of a showing that more limited speech regulation would be ineffective, we cannot approve the complete suppression of Central Hudson's advertising.

IV

Our decision today in no way disparages the national interest in energy conservation. We accept without reservation the argument that conservation, as well as the development of alternative energy sources, is an imperative national goal. Administrative bodies empowered to regulate electric utilities have the authority -- and indeed the duty -- to take appropriate action to further this goal. When, however, such action involves the suppression of speech, the First and Fourteenth Amendments require that the restriction be no more extensive than is necessary to serve the state interest. In this case, the record before us fails to show that the total ban on promotional advertising meets this requirement.

Accordingly, the judgment of the New York Court of Appeals is

Reversed.

Florida Bar v. Went For It, Inc. (MCLE, page 213) is the more recent of a series of cases handed down by the Supreme Court regarding lawyer advertising or solicitation. After issuing several decisions that generally recognized a fairly broad First Amendment right of lawyers to advertise, the Court headed in a different direction. In this 1995 case the Court ruled in a split (5-4) decision that Florida Bar Association rules prohibiting personal injury lawyers from sending targeted direct mail solicitations to victims and their relatives for 30 days after an accident or disaster did not violate the First and Fourteenth Amendments. In reaching its decision, the Court applied the four-prong *Central Hudson* test (see previous case).

Florida Bar v. Went For It, Inc.

Argued January 11, 1995
Decided June 21, 1995

515 U.S. 618, 115 S.Ct. 2371, 132 L.Ed.2d 541, 23 Med.L.Rptr. 1801

CERTIORARI TO THE UNITED STATES COURT OF APPEALS FOR THE ELEVENTH CIRCUIT

Syllabus

Respondent lawyer referral service and an individual Florida attorney filed this action for declaratory and injunctive relief challenging, as violative of the First and Fourteenth Amendments, Florida Bar rules prohibiting personal injury lawyers from sending targeted direct mail solicitations to victims and their relatives for 30 days following an accident or disaster. The District Court entered summary judgment for the plaintiffs, relying on *Bates v. State Bar of Arizona,* 433 U.S. 350, and subsequent cases. The Eleventh Circuit affirmed on similar grounds.

Held: In the circumstances presented here, the Florida Bar rules do not violate the First and Fourteenth Amendments.

(a) *Bates* and its progeny establish that lawyer advertising is commercial speech and, as such, is accorded only a limited measure of First Amendment protection. Under the "intermediate" scrutiny framework set forth in *Central Hudson Gas & Electric Corp. v. Public Service Comm'n of N.Y.* [ ], a restriction on commercial speech that, like the advertising at issue, does not concern unlawful activity and is not misleading is permissible if the government: (1) asserts a substantial interest in support of its regulation; (2) establishes that the restriction directly and materially advances that interest; and (3) demonstrates that the regulation is "'narrowly drawn'" [ ].

(b) The Florida Bar's 30-day ban on targeted direct mail solicitation withstands *Central Hudson* scrutiny. First, the Bar has substantial interest both in protecting the privacy and tranquility of personal injury victims and their loved ones against invasive, unsolicited contact by lawyers and in preventing the erosion of confidence in the profession that such repeated invasions have engendered. Second, the fact that the harms targeted by the ban are quite real is demonstrated by a Bar study, effectively unrebutted by respondents below, that contains extensive statistical and anecdotal data suggesting that the Florida public views direct mail solicitations in the immediate wake of accidents as an intrusion on privacy that reflects poorly upon the profession. [ ] Third, the ban's scope is reasonably well tailored to its stated objectives. Moreover, its duration is limited to a brief 30-day period, and there are many other ways for injured Floridians to learn about the availability of legal representation during that time.

21 F.3d 1038, reversed.

O'CONNOR, J., delivered the opinion of the Court, in which REHNQUIST, C.J., and SCALIA, THOMAS, and BREYER, JJ., joined. KENNEDY, J., filed a dissenting opinion, in which STEVENS, SOUTER, and GINSBURG, JJ., joined, *post,* p. GO>635.

O'CONNOR, J., lead opinion

Rules of the Florida Bar prohibit personal injury lawyers from sending targeted direct mail solicitations to victims and their relatives for 30 days following an accident or disaster. This case asks us to consider whether such rules violate the First and Fourteenth Amendments of the Constitution. We hold that, in the circumstances presented here, they do not.

I

In 1989, the Florida Bar completed a 2-year study of the effects of lawyer advertising on public opinion. After conducting hearings, commissioning surveys, and reviewing extensive public commentary, the Bar determined that several changes to its advertising rules were in order. In late 1990, the Florida Supreme Court adopted the Bar's proposed amendments with some modifications. [ ] Two of these amendments are at issue in this case. Rule 4-7.4(b)(1) provides that

> [a] lawyer shall not send, or knowingly permit to be sent, . . . a written communication to a prospective client for the purpose of obtaining professional employment if: (A) the written communication concerns an action for personal injury or wrongful death or otherwise relates to an accident or disaster involving the person to whom the communication is addressed or a relative of that person, unless the accident or disaster occurred more than 30 days prior to the mailing of the communication.

Rule 4-7.8(a) states that

[a] lawyer shall not accept referrals from a lawyer referral service unless the service: (1) engages in no communication with the public and in no direct contact with prospective clients in a manner that would violate the Rules of Professional Conduct if the communication or contact were made by the lawyer.

Together, these rules create a brief 30-day blackout period after an accident during which lawyers may not, directly or indirectly, single out accident victims or their relatives in order to solicit their business.

In March, 1992, G. Stewart McHenry and his wholly owned lawyer referral service, Went For It, Inc., filed this action for declaratory and injunctive relief in the United States District Court for the Middle District of Florida challenging Rules 4.7-4(b)(1) and 4.7-8 as violative of the First and Fourteenth Amendments to the Constitution. McHenry alleged that he routinely sent targeted solicitations to accident victims or their survivors within 30 days after accidents and that he wished to continue doing so in the future. Went For It, Inc. represented that it wished to contact accident victims or their survivors within 30 days of accidents and to refer potential clients to participating Florida lawyers. In October, 1992, McHenry was disbarred for reasons unrelated to this suit [　]. Another Florida lawyer, John T. Blakely, was substituted in his stead.

The District Court referred the parties' competing summary judgment motions to a Magistrate Judge, who concluded that the Florida Bar had substantial government interests, predicated on a concern for professionalism, both in protecting the personal privacy and tranquility of recent accident victims and their relatives and in ensuring that these individuals do not fall prey to undue influence or overreaching. Citing the Florida Bar's extensive study, the Magistrate Judge found that the rules directly serve those interests and sweep no further than reasonably necessary. The Magistrate recommended that the District Court grant the Florida Bar's motion for summary judgment on the ground that the rules pass constitutional muster.

The District Court rejected the Magistrate Judge's report and recommendations and entered summary judgment for the plaintiffs[　], relying on *Bates v. State Bar of Arizona* [　], and subsequent cases. The Eleventh Circuit affirmed on similar grounds [　]. The panel noted, in its conclusion, that it was "disturbed that *Bates* and its progeny require the decision" that it reached [　]. We granted certiorari, [　], and now reverse.

II

A

Constitutional protection for attorney advertising, and for commercial speech generally, is of recent vintage. Until the mid-1970s, we adhered to the broad rule laid out in *Valentine v. Chrestensen* [　] (1942), that, while the First Amendment guards against government restriction of speech in most contexts, "the Constitution imposes no such restraint on government as respects purely commercial advertising." In 1976, the Court changed course. In *Virginia State Bd. of Pharmacy v.*

111

Virginia Citizens Consumer Council, Inc., [ ], we invalidated a state statute barring pharmacists from advertising prescription drug prices. At issue was speech that involved the idea that "I will sell you the X prescription drug at the Y price." [ ] Striking the ban as unconstitutional, we rejected the argument that such speech

> is so removed from "any exposition of ideas," and from "truth, science, morality, and arts in general, in its diffusion of liberal sentiments on the administration of Government" that it lacks all protection.

[ ]

In *Virginia State Board,* the Court limited its holding to advertising by pharmacists, noting that

> [p]hysicians and lawyers . . . do not dispense standardized products; they render professional *services* of almost infinite variety and nature, with the consequent enhanced possibility for confusion and deception if they were to undertake certain kinds of advertising.

[ ] One year later, however, the Court applied the *Virginia State Board* principles to invalidate a state rule prohibiting lawyers from advertising in newspapers and other media. In *Bates v. State Bar of Arizona, supra,* the Court struck a ban on price advertising for what it deemed "routine" legal services: "the uncontested divorce, the simple adoption, the uncontested personal bankruptcy, the change of name, and the like." [ ] Expressing confidence that legal advertising would only be practicable for such simple, standardized services, the Court rejected the State's proffered justifications for regulation.

Nearly two decades of cases have built upon the foundation laid by *Bates.* It is now well established that lawyer advertising is commercial speech and, as such, is accorded a measure of First Amendment protection. [ ] Such First Amendment protection, of course, is not absolute. We have always been careful to distinguish commercial speech from speech at the First Amendment's core.

> "[C]ommercial speech [enjoys] a limited measure of protection, commensurate with its subordinate position in the scale of First Amendment values," and is subject to "modes of regulation that might be impermissible in the realm of noncommercial expression."

[ ] We have observed that

> "[t]o require a parity of constitutional protection for commercial and noncommercial speech alike could invite dilution, simply by a leveling process, of the force of the Amendment's guarantee with respect to the latter kind of speech."

[ ]

Mindful of these concerns, we engage in "intermediate" scrutiny of restrictions on commercial speech, analyzing them under the framework set forth in *Central Hudson Gas & Electric Corp. v. Public Service Comm'n of N. Y.,* [ ] (1980). Under *Central Hudson,* the government may freely regulate commercial speech that concerns unlawful activity or is misleading. [ ] Commercial speech that falls into neither of those categories, like the advertising at issue here, may be regulated if the government satisfies a test consisting of three related prongs: first, the government must assert a substantial interest in support of its regulation; second, the government must demonstrate that the restriction on commercial speech directly and materially advances that interest; and third, the regulation must be "'narrowly drawn'" [ ].

B

"Unlike rational basis review, the *Central Hudson* standard does not permit us to supplant the precise interests put forward by the State with other suppositions." [ ] The Florida Bar asserts that it has a substantial interest in protecting the privacy and tranquility of personal injury victims and their loved ones against intrusive, unsolicited contact by lawyers. [ ] This interest obviously factors into the Bar's paramount (and repeatedly professed) objective of curbing activities that "negatively affec[t] the administration of justice." [ ] ... Because direct mail solicitations in the wake of accidents are perceived by the public as intrusive, the Bar argues, the reputation of the legal profession in the eyes of Floridians has suffered commensurately. [ ] The regulation, then, is an effort to protect the flagging reputations of Florida lawyers by preventing them from engaging in conduct that, the Bar maintains,

> "is universally regarded as deplorable and beneath common decency because of its intrusion upon the special vulnerability and private grief of victims or their families."

[ ]

We have little trouble crediting the Bar's interest as substantial. On various occasions we have accepted the proposition that

> States have a compelling interest in the practice of professions within their boundaries, and . . . , as part of their power to protect the public health, safety, and other valid interests, they have broad power to establish standards for licensing practitioners and regulating the practice of professions.

[ ] Our precedents also leave no room for doubt that "the protection of potential clients' privacy is a substantial state interest." [ ] In other contexts, we have consistently recognized that

> [t]he State's interest in protecting the wellbeing, tranquility, and privacy of the home is certainly of the highest order in a free and civilized society.

[ ] Indeed, we have noted that

> a special benefit of the privacy all citizens enjoy within their own walls, which the State may legislate to protect, is an ability to avoid intrusions.

[ ]

Under *Central Hudson's* second prong, the State must demonstrate that the challenged regulation "advances the Government's interest `in a direct and material way.'" That burden, we have explained,

> "is not satisfied by mere speculation and conjecture; rather, a governmental body seeking to sustain a restriction on commercial speech must demonstrate that the harms it recites are real, and that its restriction will, in fact, alleviate them to a material degree."

[ ] In *Edenfield,* the Court invalidated a Florida ban on in-person solicitation by certified public accountants (CPAs). We observed that the State Board of Accountancy had

> present[ed] no studies that suggest personal solicitation of prospective business clients by CPAs creates the dangers of fraud, overreaching, or compromised independence that the Board claims to fear.

[ ] Moreover, "[t]he record [did] not disclose any anecdotal evidence, either from Florida or another State, that validate[d] the Board's suppositions." [ ] In fact, we concluded that the only evidence in the record tended to "contradic[t], rather than strengthe[n], the Board's submissions." [ ] Finding nothing in the record to substantiate the State's allegations of harm, we invalidated the regulation.

The direct mail solicitation regulation before us does not suffer from such infirmities. The Florida Bar submitted a 106-page summary of its 2-year study of lawyer advertising and solicitation to the District Court. That summary contains data -- both statistical and anecdotal -- supporting the Bar's contentions that the Florida public views direct mail solicitations in the immediate wake of accidents as an intrusion on privacy that reflects poorly upon the profession. As of June, 1989, lawyers mailed 700,000 direct solicitations in Florida annually, 40% of which were aimed at accident victims or their survivors. [ ] A survey of Florida adults commissioned by the Bar indicated that Floridians "have negative feelings about those attorneys who use direct mail advertising." [ ] Fifty-four percent of the general population surveyed said that contacting persons concerning accidents or similar events is a violation of privacy. [ ] A random sampling of persons who received direct mail advertising from lawyers in 1987 revealed that 45% believed that direct mail solicitation is "designed to take advantage of gullible or unstable people"; 34% found such tactics "annoying or irritating"; 26% found it "an invasion of your privacy"; and 24% reported that it "made you angry." [ ] Significantly, 27% of direct mail recipients reported that their regard for the legal profession and for the judicial process as a whole was "lower" as a result of receiving the direct mail. [ ]

The anecdotal record mustered by the Bar is noteworthy for its breadth and detail. With titles like "Scavenger Lawyers" (The Miami Herald, Sept. 29, 1987) and "Solicitors Out of Bounds" (St. Petersburg Times, Oct. 26, 1987), newspaper editorial pages in Florida have burgeoned with criticism of Florida lawyers who send targeted direct mail to victims shortly after accidents. [ ] ... The study summary also includes page upon page of excerpts from complaints of direct mail recipients. For example, a Florida citizen described how he was "appalled and angered by the brazen attempt" of a law firm to solicit him by letter shortly after he was injured and his fiancee was killed in an auto accident. [ ] Another found it "despicable and inexcusable" that a Pensacola lawyer wrote to his mother three days after his father's funeral. [ ] Another described how she was "astounded" and then "very angry" when she received a solicitation following a minor accident. [ ] Still another described as "beyond comprehension" a letter his nephew's family received the day of the nephew's funeral. [ ] One citizen wrote,

> "I consider the unsolicited contact from you after my child's accident to be
> of the rankest form of ambulance chasing and in incredibly poor taste. . . .
> I cannot begin to express with my limited vocabulary the utter contempt in
> which I hold you and your kind."

[ ]

In light of this showing -- which respondents at no time refuted, save by the conclusory assertion that the rule lacked "any factual basis" [ ] -- we conclude that the Bar has satisfied the second prong of the *Central Hudson* test. In dissent, JUSTICE KENNEDY complains that we have before us few indications of the sample size or selection procedures employed by Magid Associates (a nationally renowned consulting firm) and no copies of the actual surveys employed. [ ] As stated, we believe the evidence adduced by the Bar is sufficient to meet the standard elaborated in *Edenfield, supra.* In any event, we do not read our case law to require that empirical data come to us accompanied by a surfeit of background information. Indeed, in other First Amendment contexts, we have permitted litigants to justify speech restrictions by reference to studies and anecdotes pertaining to different locales altogether [ ]. Nothing in *Edenfield, supra,* a case in which the State offered *no* evidence or anecdotes in support of its restriction, requires more. After scouring the record, we are satisfied that the ban on direct mail solicitation in the immediate aftermath of accidents, unlike the rule at issue in *Edenfield,* targets a concrete, nonspeculative harm.

In reaching a contrary conclusion, the Court of Appeals determined that this case was governed squarely by *Shapero v. Kentucky Bar Assn.,* [ ] (1988). Making no mention of the Bar's study, the court concluded that

> "a targeted letter [does not] invade the recipient's privacy any more than
> does a substantively identical letter mailed at large. The invasion, if any,
> occurs when the lawyer discovers the recipient's legal affairs, not when he
> confronts the recipient with the discovery."

[ ] In many cases, the Court of Appeals explained, "this invasion of privacy will involve no more than reading the newspaper." [ ]

While some of *Shapero's* language might be read to support the Court of Appeals' interpretation, *Shapero* differs in several fundamental respects from the case before us. First and foremost, *Shapero's* treatment of privacy was casual. Contrary to the dissent's suggestions [ ], the State in *Shapero* did not seek to justify its regulation as a measure undertaken to prevent lawyers' invasions of privacy interests. [ ] Rather, the State focused exclusively on the special dangers of overreaching inhering in targeted solicitations. [ ] Second, in contrast to this case, *Shapero* dealt with a broad ban on *all* direct mail solicitations, whatever the time frame and whoever the recipient. Finally, the State in *Shapero* assembled no evidence attempting to demonstrate any actual harm caused by targeted direct mail. The Court rejected the State's effort to justify a prophylactic ban on the basis of blanket, untested assertions of undue influence and overreaching. [ ] Because the State did not make a privacy-based argument at all, its empirical showing on that issue was similarly infirm.

We find the Court's perfunctory treatment of privacy in *Shapero* to be of little utility in assessing this ban on targeted solicitation of victims in the immediate aftermath of accidents. While it is undoubtedly true that many people find the image of lawyers sifting through accident and police reports in pursuit of prospective clients unpalatable and invasive, this case targets a different kind of intrusion. The Florida Bar has argued, and the record reflects, that a principal purpose of the ban is

> protecting the personal privacy and tranquility of [Florida's] citizens from crass commercial intrusion by attorneys upon their personal grief in times of trauma.

[ ] ... The intrusion targeted by the Bar's regulation stems not from the fact that a lawyer has learned about an accident or disaster (as the Court of Appeals notes, in many instances a lawyer need only read the newspaper to glean this information), but from the lawyer's confrontation of victims or relatives with such information, while wounds are still open, in order to solicit their business. In this respect, an untargeted letter mailed to society at large is different in kind from a targeted solicitation; the untargeted letter involves no willful or knowing affront to or invasion of the tranquility of bereaved or injured individuals and simply does not cause the same kind of reputational harm to the profession unearthed by the Florida Bar's study.

Nor do we find *Bolger v. Youngs Drug Products Corp.* [ ] (1983), dispositive of the issue, despite any superficial resemblance. In *Bolger,* we rejected the Federal Government's paternalistic effort to ban potentially "offensive" and "intrusive" direct mail advertisements for contraceptives. Minimizing the Government's allegations of harm, we reasoned that

> [r]ecipients of objectionable mailings . . . may "effectively avoid further bombardment of their sensibilities simply by averting their eyes."

[ ] We found that the "short, though regular, journey from mail box to

trash can . . . is an acceptable burden at least so far as the Constitution is concerned." [ ] Concluding that citizens have at their disposal ample means of averting any substantial injury inhering in the delivery of objectionable contraceptive material, we deemed the State's intercession unnecessary and unduly restrictive.

Here, in contrast, the harm targeted by the Florida Bar cannot be eliminated by a brief journey to the trash can. The purpose of the 30-day targeted direct mail ban is to forestall the outrage and irritation with the state-licensed legal profession that the practice of direct solicitation only days after accidents has engendered. The Bar is concerned not with citizens' "offense" in the abstract [ ], but with the demonstrable detrimental effects that such "offense" has on the profession it regulates. [ ] Moreover, the harm posited by the Bar is as much a function of simple receipt of targeted solicitations within days of accidents as it is a function of the letters' contents. Throwing the letter away shortly after opening it may minimize the latter intrusion, but it does little to combat the former. We see no basis in *Bolger,* nor in the other, similar cases cited by the dissent [ ], for dismissing the Florida Bar's assertions of harm, particularly given the unrefuted empirical and anecdotal basis for the Bar's conclusions.

Passing to *Central Hudson's* third prong, we examine the relationship between the Florida Bar's interests and the means chosen to serve them. [ ] With respect to this prong, the differences between commercial speech and noncommercial speech are manifest. In *Fox,* we made clear that the "least restrictive means" test has no role in the commercial speech context. [ ] "What our decisions require," instead,

> is a "fit" between the legislature's ends and the means chosen to accomplish those ends, a fit that is not necessarily perfect, but reasonable; that represents not necessarily the single best disposition but one whose scope is "in proportion to the interest served," that employs not necessarily the least restrictive means but . . . a means narrowly tailored to achieve the desired objective.

[ ] Of course, we do not equate this test with the less rigorous obstacles of rational basis review; in GO>*Cincinnati v. Discovery Network, Inc.,* [ ] (1993), for example, we observed that the existence of

> numerous and obvious less-burdensome alternatives to the restriction on commercial speech . . . is certainly a relevant consideration in determining whether the "fit" between ends and means is reasonable.

Respondents levy a great deal of criticism, echoed in the dissent, [ ] at the scope of the Bar's restriction on targeted mail. "[B]y prohibiting written communications to all people, whatever their state of mind," respondents charge, the rule "keeps useful information from those accident victims who are ready, willing and able to utilize a lawyer's advice." [ ] This criticism may be parsed into two components. First, the rule does not distinguish between victims in terms of the severity of their injuries. According to respondents, the rule is unconstitutionally

117

over-inclusive insofar as it bans targeted mailings even to citizens whose injuries or grief are relatively minor. [ ] Second, the rule may prevent citizens from learning about their legal options, particularly at a time when other actors -- opposing counsel and insurance adjusters -- may be clamoring for victims' attentions. Any benefit arising from the Bar's regulation, respondents implicitly contend, is outweighed by these costs.

We are not persuaded by respondents' allegations of constitutional infirmity. We find little deficiency in the ban's failure to distinguish among injured Floridians by the severity of their pain or the intensity of their grief. Indeed, it is hard to imagine the contours of a regulation that might satisfy respondents on this score. Rather than drawing difficult lines on the basis that some injuries are "severe" and some situations appropriate (and others, presumably, inappropriate) for grief, anger, or emotion, the Florida Bar has crafted a ban applicable to all post-accident or disaster solicitations for a brief 30-day period. Unlike respondents, we do not see "numerous and obvious less-burdensome alternatives" to Florida's short temporal ban. [ ] The Bar's rule is reasonably well tailored to its stated objective of eliminating targeted mailings whose type and timing are a source of distress to Floridians, distress that has caused many of them to lose respect for the legal profession.

Respondents' second point would have force if the Bar's rule were not limited to a brief period and if there were not many other ways for injured Floridians to learn about the availability of legal representation during that time. Our lawyer advertising cases have afforded lawyers a great deal of leeway to devise innovative ways to attract new business. Florida permits lawyers to advertise on prime-time television and radio as well as in newspapers and other media. They may rent space on billboards. They may send untargeted letters to the general population, or to discrete segments thereof. There are, of course, pages upon pages devoted to lawyers in the Yellow Pages of Florida telephone directories. These listings are organized alphabetically and by area of specialty. [ ] ... These ample alternative channels for receipt of information about the availability of legal representation during the 30-day period following accidents may explain why, despite the ample evidence, testimony, and commentary submitted by those favoring (as well as opposing) unrestricted direct mail solicitation, respondents have not pointed to -- and we have not independently found -- a single example of an individual case in which immediate solicitation helped to avoid, or failure to solicit within 30 days brought about, the harms that concern the dissent [ ] In fact, the record contains considerable empirical survey information suggesting that Floridians have little difficulty finding lawyers when they need one. [ ] Finding no basis to question the commonsense conclusion that the many alternative channels for communicating necessary information about attorneys are sufficient, we see no defect in Florida's regulation.

III

Speech by professionals obviously has many dimensions. There are circumstances in which we will accord speech by attorneys on public issues and matters of legal representation the strongest protection our Constitution has to offer. [ ] This case, however, concerns pure commercial advertising, for which we have always reserved a lesser degree of protection under the First Amendment. Particularly because the standards and conduct of state-licensed lawyers have traditionally been subject to extensive regulation by the States, it is all the more appropriate that we limit our scrutiny of state regulations to a level commensurate with the "'subordinate position'" of commercial speech in the scale of First Amendment values. [ ]

We believe that the Florida Bar's 30-day restriction on targeted direct mail solicitation of accident victims and their relatives withstands scrutiny under the three-part *Central Hudson* test that we have devised for this context. The Bar has substantial interest both in protecting injured Floridians from invasive conduct by lawyers and in preventing the erosion of confidence in the profession that such repeated invasions have engendered. The Bar's proffered study, unrebutted by respondents below, provides evidence indicating that the harms it targets are far from illusory. The palliative devised by the Bar to address these harms is narrow both in scope and in duration. The Constitution, in our view, requires nothing more.

The judgment of the Court of Appeals, accordingly, is

Reversed.

KENNEDY, J., dissenting

JUSTICE KENNEDY, with whom JUSTICE STEVENS, JUSTICE SOUTER, and JUSTICE GINSBURG join, dissenting.

Attorneys who communicate their willingness to assist potential clients are engaged in speech protected by the First and Fourteenth Amendments. That principle has been understood since *Bates v. State Bar of Arizona* [ ] (1977). The Court today undercuts this guarantee in an important class of cases and unsettles leading First Amendment precedents at the expense of those victims most in need of legal assistance. With all respect for the Court, in my view, its solicitude for the privacy of victims and its concern for our profession are misplaced and self-defeating, even upon the Court's own premises.

I take it to be uncontroverted that when an accident results in death or injury, it is often urgent at once to investigate the occurrence, identify witnesses, and preserve evidence. Vital interests in speech and expression are, therefore at stake when by law an attorney cannot direct a letter to the victim or the family explaining this simple fact and offering competent legal assistance. Meanwhile, represented and better informed parties, or parties who have been solicited in ways more sophisticated and indirect, may be at work. Indeed, these parties, either themselves or by their attorneys, investigators, and adjusters, are free to contact the unrepresented persons to gather evidence or offer settlement. This scheme makes little sense. As is often true when the law makes little sense, it is not first principles but their interpretation and application that have gone awry.

Although I agree with the Court that the case can be resolved by following the three-part inquiry we have identified to assess restrictions on commercial speech [ ], a preliminary observation is in order. Speech has the capacity to convey complex substance, yielding various insights and interpretations depending upon the identity of the listener or the reader and the context of its transmission. It would oversimplify to say that what we consider here is commercial speech and nothing more, for, in many instances, the banned communications may be vital to the recipients' right to petition the courts for redress of grievances. The complex nature of expression is one reason why even so-called commercial speech has become an essential part of the public discourse the First Amendment secures. [ ] If our commercial speech rules are to control this case, then, it is imperative to apply them with exacting care and fidelity to our precedents, for what is at stake is the suppression of information and knowledge that transcends the financial self-interests of the speaker.

I

As the Court notes, the first of the *Central Hudson* factors to be considered is whether the interest the State pursues in enacting the speech restriction is a substantial one. [ ] The State says two different interests meet this standard. The first is the interest "in protecting the personal privacy and tranquility" of the victim and his or her family. [ ] As the Court notes, that interest has recognition in our decisions as a general matter; but it does not follow that the privacy interest in the cases the majority cites is applicable here. The problem the Court confronts, and cannot overcome, is our recent decision in *Shapero v. Kentucky Bar Assn.* [ ] (1988). In assessing the importance of the interest in that solicitation case, we made an explicit distinction between direct in-person solicitations and direct mail solicitations. *Shapero,* like this case, involved a direct mail solicitation, and there the State recited its fears of "overreaching and undue influence." [ ] We found, however, no such dangers presented by direct mail advertising. We reasoned that

> [a] letter, like a printed advertisement (but unlike a lawyer), can readily be put in a drawer to be considered later, ignored, or discarded.

[ ] We pointed out that

> [t]he relevant inquiry is not whether there exist potential clients whose "condition" makes them susceptible to undue influence, but whether the mode of communication poses a serious danger that lawyers will exploit any such susceptibility.

[ ] In assessing the substantiality of the evils to be prevented, we concluded that "the mode of communication makes all the difference." [ ]The direct mail in *Shapero* did not present the justification for

regulation of speech presented in *Ohralik v. Ohio State Bar Assn* [ ] ... business may be prohibited by the State). [ ] ...

To avoid the controlling effect of *Shapero* in the case before us, the Court seeks to declare that a different privacy interest is implicated. As it sees the matter, the substantial concern is that victims or their families will be offended by receiving a solicitation during their grief and trauma. But we do not allow restrictions on speech to be justified on the ground that the expression might offend the listener. On the contrary, we have said that these "are classically not justifications validating the suppression of expression protected by the First Amendment." [ ] And in *Zauderer v. Office of Disciplinary Counsel of Supreme Court of Ohio* [ ] (1985), where we struck down a ban on attorney advertising, we held that

> the mere possibility that some members of the population might find advertising . . . offensive cannot justify suppressing it. The same must hold true for advertising that some members of the bar might find beneath their dignity.

[ ]

We have applied this principle to direct mail cases as well as with respect to general advertising, noting that the right to use the mails is protected by the First Amendment. [ ] In *Bolger*, we held that a statute designed to "shiel[d] recipients of mail from materials that they are likely to find offensive" furthered an interest of "little weight," noting that "we have consistently held that the fact that protected speech may be offensive to some does not justify its suppression." [ ] It is only where an audience is captive that we will assure its protection from some offensive speech. [ ] Outside that context,

> we have never held that the Government itself can shut off the flow of mailings to protect those recipients who might potentially be offended.

[ ] The occupants of a household receiving mailings are not a captive audience [ ], and the asserted interest in preventing their offense should be no more controlling here than in our prior cases. All the recipient of objectionable mailings need do is to take "the `short, though regular, journey from mail box to trash can.'" [ ] As we have observed, this is "an acceptable burden at least so far as the Constitution is concerned." [ ] If these cases forbidding restrictions on speech that might be offensive are to be overruled, the Court should say so.

In the face of these difficulties of logic and precedent, the State and the opinion of the Court turn to a second interest: protecting the reputation and dignity of the legal profession. The argument is, it seems fair to say, that all are demeaned by the crass behavior of a few. The argument takes a further step in the *amicus* brief filed by the Association of Trial Lawyers of America. There it is said that disrespect for the profession from this sort of solicitation (but presumably from no other sort of solicitation) results in lower jury verdicts. In a sense, of course, these arguments are circular. While disrespect will arise from an unethical or improper practice, the majority begs a most critical question by assuming that direct mail solicitations constitute such a practice. The fact is, however, that direct solicitation may serve vital purposes and promote the administration of justice, and to the extent the bar seeks to protect lawyers' reputations by preventing them from engaging in speech some deem offensive, the State is doing nothing more (as *amicus* the Association of Trial Lawyers of America is at least candid enough to admit) than manipulating the public's opinion by suppressing speech that informs us how the legal system works. The disrespect argument thus proceeds from the very assumption it tries to prove, which is to say that solicitations within 30 days serve no legitimate purpose. This, of course, is censorship pure and simple; and censorship is antithetical to the first principles of free expression.

II

Even were the interests asserted substantial, the regulation here fails the second part of the *Central Hudson* test, which requires that the dangers the State seeks to eliminate be real and that a speech restriction or ban advance that asserted State interest in a direct and material way. [ ] The burden of demonstrating the reality of the asserted harm rests on the State. [ ] Slight evidence in this regard does not mean there is sufficient evidence to support the claims. Here, what the State has offered falls well short of demonstrating that the harms it is trying to redress are real, let alone that the regulation directly and materially advances the State's interests. The parties and the Court have used the term "Summary of Record" to describe a document prepared by the Florida Bar, one of the adverse parties, and submitted to the District Court in this case. [ ] This document includes no actual surveys, few indications of sample size or selection procedures, no explanations of methodology, and no discussion of excluded results. There is no description of the statistical universe or scientific framework that permits any productive use of the information the so-called Summary of Record contains. The majority describes this anecdotal matter as "noteworthy for its breadth and detail" [ ], but when examined, it is noteworthy for its incompetence. The selective synopses of unvalidated studies deal, for the most part, with television advertising and phone book listings, and not direct mail solicitations. Although there may be issues common to various kinds of attorney advertising and solicitation, it is not clear what would follow from that limited premise, unless the Court means by its decision to call into question all forms of attorney advertising. The most generous reading of this document permits identification of 34 pages on which direct mail solicitation is arguably discussed. Of these, only two are even a synopsis of a study of the attitudes of Floridians towards such solicitations. The bulk of the remaining pages include comments by lawyers about direct mail (some of them favorable), excerpts from citizen complaints about such solicitation, and a few excerpts from newspaper articles on the topic. Our cases require something more than a few pages of self-serving and unsupported statements by the State to demonstrate that a regulation directly and materially advances the elimination of a real harm when the State seeks to suppress truthful and nondeceptive speech. [ ]

It is telling that the essential thrust of all the material adduced to justify the State's interest is devoted to the reputational concerns of the Bar. It is not at all clear that this regulation advances the interest of protecting persons who are suffering trauma and grief, and we are cited to no material in the record for that claim. Indeed, when asked at oral argument what a "typical injured plaintiff get[s] in the mail," the Bar's lawyer replied: "That's not in the record. . . and I don't know the answer to that question." [ ] Having declared that the privacy interest is one both substantial and served by the regulation, the Court ought not to be excused from justifying its conclusion.

III

The insufficiency of the regulation to advance the State's interest is reinforced by the third inquiry necessary in this analysis. Were it appropriate to reach the third part of the *Central Hudson* test, it would be clear that the relationship between the Bar's interests and the means chosen to serve them is not a reasonable fit. The Bar's rule creates a flat ban that prohibits far more speech than necessary to serve the purported state interest. Even assuming that interest were legitimate, there is a wild disproportion between the harm supposed and the speech ban enforced. It is a disproportion the Court does not bother to discuss, but our speech jurisprudence requires that it do so. [ ]

To begin with, the ban applies with respect to all accidental injuries, whatever their gravity. The Court's purported justification for the excess of regulation in this respect is the difficulty of drawing lines between severe and less serious injuries [ ], but making such distinctions is not important in this analysis. Even were it significant, the Court's assertion is unconvincing. After all, the criminal law routinely distinguishes degrees of bodily harm [ ], and if that delineation is permissible and workable in the criminal context, it should not be "hard to imagine the contours of a regulation" that satisfies the reasonable fit requirement. [ ]

There is, moreover, simply no justification for assuming that, in all or most cases, an attorney's advice would be unwelcome or unnecessary when the survivors or the victim must at once begin assessing their legal and financial position in a rational manner. With regard to lesser injuries, there is little chance that, for any period, much less 30 days, the victims will become distraught upon hearing from an attorney. It is, in fact, more likely a real risk that some victims might think no attorney will be interested enough to help them. It is at this precise time that sound legal advice may be necessary and most urgent.

Even as to more serious injuries, the State's argument fails, since it must be conceded that prompt legal representation is essential where death or injury results from accidents. The only seeming justification for the State's restriction is the one the Court itself offers, which is that

123

attorneys can and do resort to other ways of communicating important legal information to potential clients. Quite aside from the latent protectionism for the established bar that the argument discloses, it fails for the more fundamental reason that it concedes the necessity for the very representation the attorneys solicit and the State seeks to ban. The accident victims who are prejudiced to vindicate the State's purported desire for more dignity in the legal profession will be the very persons who most need legal advice, for they are the victims who, because they lack education, linguistic ability, or familiarity with the legal system, are unable to seek out legal services. [ ]

The reasonableness of the State's chosen methods for redressing perceived evils can be evaluated, in part, by a commonsense consideration of other possible means of regulation that have not been tried. Here, the Court neglects the fact that this problem is largely self-policing: potential clients will not hire lawyers who offend them. And even if a person enters into a contract with an attorney and later regrets it, Florida, like some other States, allows clients to rescind certain contracts with attorneys within a stated time after they are executed. [ ] The State's restriction deprives accident victims of information which may be critical to their right to make a claim for compensation for injuries. The telephone book and general advertisements may serve this purpose in part; but the direct solicitation ban will fall on those who most need legal representation: for those with minor injuries, the victims too ill-informed to know an attorney may be interested in their cases; for those with serious injuries, the victims too ill-informed to know that time is of the essence if counsel is to assemble evidence and warn them not to enter into settlement negotiations or evidentiary discussions with investigators for opposing parties. One survey reports that over a recent 5-year period, 68% of the American population consulted a lawyer. [ ] The use of modern communication methods in a timely way is essential if clients who make up this vast demand are to be advised and informed of all of their choices and rights in selecting an attorney. The very fact that some 280,000 direct mail solicitations are sent to accident victims and their survivors in Florida each year is some indication of the efficacy of this device. Nothing in the Court's opinion demonstrates that these efforts do not serve some beneficial role. A solicitation letter is not a contract. Nothing in the record shows that these communications do not at the least serve the purpose of informing the prospective client that he or she has a number of different attorneys from whom to choose, so that the decision to select counsel, after an interview with one or more interested attorneys, can be deliberate and informed. And if these communications reveal the social costs of the tort system as a whole, then efforts can be directed to reforming the operation of that system, not to suppressing information about how the system works. The Court's approach, however, does not seem to be the proper way to begin elevating the honor of the profession.

IV

It is most ironic that, for the first time since *Bates v. State Bar of*

124

Arizona, the Court now orders a major retreat from the constitutional guarantees for commercial speech in order to shield its own profession from public criticism. Obscuring the financial aspect of the legal profession from public discussion through direct mail solicitation at the expense of the least sophisticated members of society, is not a laudable constitutional goal. There is no authority for the proposition that the Constitution permits the State to promote the public image of the legal profession by suppressing information about the profession's business aspects. If public respect for the profession erodes because solicitation distorts the idea of the law as most lawyers see it, it must be remembered that real progress begins with more rational speech, not less. I agree that if this amounts to mere "sermonizing," [ ] the attempt may be futile. The guiding principle, however, is that full and rational discussion furthers sound regulation and necessary reform. The image of the profession cannot be enhanced without improving the substance of its practice. The objective of the profession is to ensure that "the ethical standards of lawyers are linked to the service and protection of clients." [ ]

Today's opinion is a serious departure, not only from our prior decisions involving attorney advertising, but also from the principles that govern the transmission of commercial speech. The Court's opinion reflects a new-found and illegitimate confidence that it, along with the Supreme Court of Florida, knows what is best for the Bar and its clients. Self-assurance has always been the hallmark of a censor. That is why under the First Amendment the public, not the State, has the right and the power to decide what ideas and information are deserving of their adherence. "[T]he general rule is that the speaker and the audience, not the government, assess the value of the information presented." [ ] By validating Florida's rule, today's majority is complicit in the Bar's censorship. For these reasons, I dissent from the opinion of the Court and from its judgment.

In *44 Liquormart, Inc. v. Rhode Island* (MCLE, page 219) the Supreme Court held that, as applied, two state statutes and an accompanying state Liquor Control Board regulation violated the First and Fourteenth Amendments. The Court unanimously reversed a U.S. Court of Appeals decision upholding the restrictions, which (1) banned the advertising of prices of alcoholic beverages except at point of sale and (2) prohibited the publication or broadcast of any ads with prices of alcoholic beverages, even if the ads were for stores in other states. According to the Court, the state had not met its heavy burden of justifying the bans. Only a plurality of the justices could agree, however, on the appropriate test to be applied in the case to determine whether the restrictions were unconstitutional. A year earlier in *Rubin v. Coors Brewing Company,* the Court unanimously ruled that a federal statute barring the advertising of alcohol content in beer violated the First Amendment.

44 Liquormart, Inc. v. Rhode Island

Argued November 1, 1995
Decided May 13, 1996

517 U.S. 484, 116 S.Ct. 1495, 134 L.Ed.2d 711

CERTIORARI TO THE UNITED STATES COURT OF APPEALS FOR THE FIRST CIRCUIT

Syllabus

Petitioners, a licensed Rhode Island liquor retailer and a licensed Massachusetts liquor retailer patronized by Rhode Island residents, filed this action seeking a declaratory judgment that Rhode Island laws banning the advertisement of retail liquor prices except at the place of sale violate the First Amendment. In concluding that the ban was unconstitutional because it did not directly advance the State's asserted interest in the promotion of temperance and was more extensive than necessary to serve that interest, the District Court reasoned that the party seeking to uphold a restriction on commercial speech carries the burden of justifying it, and that the Twenty-first Amendment did not shift or diminish that burden. In reversing, the Court of Appeals, *inter alia,* found "inherent merit" in the State's submission that competitive price advertising would ultimately increase sales, and agreed with it that the Twenty-first Amendment gave its advertising ban an added presumption of validity.

Held: The judgment is reversed.

39 F.3d 5, reversed.

JUSTICE STEVENS delivered the opinion of the Court with respect to Parts I, II, VII, and VIII, concluding:

1. The Twenty-first Amendment cannot save Rhode Island's price advertising ban, because that Amendment does not qualify the First Amendment's prohibition against laws abridging the freedom of speech. Although the Twenty-first Amendment -- which repealed Prohibition and gave the States the power to prohibit commerce in, or the use of, alcoholic beverages -- limits the dormant Commerce Clause's effect on a State's regulatory power over the delivery or use of liquor within its borders, the Amendment does not license the States to ignore their obligations under other constitutional provisions. [ ] *California v. LaRue*, 409 U.S. 109, 118-119, disavowed. Because the First Amendment must be included among those other provisions, the Twenty-first Amendment does not shield the advertising ban from constitutional scrutiny.

2. Because Rhode Island has failed to carry its heavy burden of justifying its complete ban on price advertising, that ban is invalid.

JUSTICE STEVENS delivered the principal opinion with respect to Parts III-VI, concluding that Rhode Island's ban on advertisements that provide the public with accurate information about retail liquor prices is an unconstitutional abridgment of the freedom of speech.

(a) JUSTICE STEVENS, joined by Justice KENNEDY, JUSTICE SOUTER, and JUSTICE GINSBURG, concluded in Part III that, although the First Amendment protects the dissemination of truthful and nonmisleading commercial messages about lawful products and services in order to ensure that consumers receive accurate information [ ], the special nature of commercial speech, including its "greater objectivity" and "greater hardiness," authorizes the State to regulate potentially deceptive or overreaching advertising more freely than other forms of protected speech [ ], and requires less than strict review of such regulations. [ ] However, regulations that entirely suppress commercial speech in order to pursue a policy not related to consumer protection must be reviewed with "special care," and such blanket bans should not be approved unless the speech itself was flawed in some way, either because it was deceptive or related to unlawful activity. [ ]

(b) JUSTICE STEVENS, joined by JUSTICE KENNEDY and JUSTICE GINSBURG, concluded in Part IV that a review of the case law reveals that commercial speech regulations are not all subject to a similar form of constitutional review simply because they target a similar category of expression. When a State regulates commercial messages to protect consumers from misleading, deceptive, or aggressive sales practices, or requires the disclosure of beneficial consumer information, the regulation's purpose is consistent with the reasons for according constitutional protection to commercial speech and therefore justifies less than strict review. However, where a State entirely prohibits the dissemination of truthful, nonmisleading commercial messages for reasons unrelated to the preservation of a fair bargaining process, there

127

is far less reason to depart from the rigorous review that the First Amendment generally demands. The special dangers that attend such complete bans -- including, most obviously, the fact that they all but foreclose alternative channels of communication -- present sound reasons that justify more careful review.

(c) JUSTICE STEVENS, joined by JUSTICE KENNEDY, JUSTICE SOUTER, and JUSTICE GINSBURG, concluded in Part V that because Rhode Island's advertising ban constitutes a blanket prohibition against truthful, nonmisleading speech about a lawful product, and serves an end unrelated to consumer protection, it must be reviewed with "special care" under *Central Hudson* [ ]. It cannot survive that review, because it does not satisfy even the less than strict standard that generally applies in commercial speech cases under *Central Hudson* [ ]. First, the advertising ban does not directly advance the State's substantial interest in promoting temperance. [ ] Because a commercial speech regulation may not be sustained if it provides only ineffective or remote support for the government's purpose, *id.* at GO>564, the State bears the burden of showing not merely that its regulation will advance its interest, but also that it will do so "to a material degree." [ ] In this case, therefore, the State must show that the ban will *significantly* reduce alcohol consumption, but has presented no evidence to suggest a significant reduction. Second, the ban is more extensive than necessary to serve its stated interest [ ], since alternative forms of regulation that would not involve any speech restrictions -- *e.g.*, the maintenance of higher prices either by direct regulation or by increased taxation, the rationing of per capita purchases, or the use of educational campaigns focused on drinking problems -- would be more likely to achieve the goal of promoting temperance. Thus, the State has failed to establish the requisite "reasonable fit" between its regulation and its goal. [ ]

(d) JUSTICE STEVENS, joined by JUSTICE KENNEDY, JUSTICE THOMAS, and JUSTICE GINSBURG, concluded in Part VI that the State's arguments in support of its claim that it merely exercised appropriate "legislative judgment" in determining that a price advertising ban would best promote temperance -- *i.e.*, (1) that, because expert opinions as to the effectiveness of the ban "go both ways," the Court of Appeals correctly concluded that the ban constituted a "reasonable choice" by the legislature; (2) that precedent requires that particular deference be accorded that legislative choice, because the State could, if it chose, ban the sale of alcoholic beverages outright; and (3) that deference is appropriate because alcoholic beverages are so-called "vice" products -- must be rejected. [ ]

JUSTICE SCALIA concluded that guidance as to what the First Amendment forbids where the core offense of suppressing particular political ideas is not at issue must be taken from the long accepted practices of the American people. [ ] Since, however, the Court has before it no evidence as to state legislative practices regarding regulation of commercial speech when the First and Fourteenth Amendments were adopted, or even as to any national consensus on the subject later developed, he would simply adhere to the Court's existing jurisprudence, which renders the Rhode Island regulation invalid.

JUSTICE THOMAS concluded that, in cases such as this, in which the government's asserted interest is to keep legal users of a product or service ignorant in order to manipulate their choices in the marketplace, the *Central Hudson* balancing test should not be applied. Rather, such an "interest" is *per se* illegitimate [ ], and can no more justify regulation of "commercial" speech than it can justify regulation of "noncommercial" speech.

JUSTICE O'CONNOR, joined by THE CHIEF JUSTICE, JUSTICE SOUTER, and JUSTICE BREYER, agreed with the principal opinion that Rhode Island's prohibition on alcohol price advertising is invalid and cannot be saved by the Twenty-first Amendment, but concluded that the First Amendment question must be resolved more narrowly by applying the test established in *Central Hudson Gas & Elec. Corp. v. Public Serv. Comm'n of N.Y.* [ ]. Assuming that the prohibition satisfies the test's first three prongs -- *i.e.*, that (1) the speech at issue concerns lawful activity and is not misleading, (2) the asserted governmental interest is substantial, and (3) the regulation directly advances the governmental interest -- Rhode Island's regulation fails the final fourth prong because its ban is more extensive than necessary to serve its stated interest. Rhode Island justifies its ban on price advertising on the grounds that the ban is intended to keep alcohol prices high as a way to keep consumption low. In order for a speech restriction to pass muster under the fourth prong, there must be a reasonable fit between the legislature's goal and method. [ ] The fit here is not reasonable, since the State has other methods at its disposal -- *e.g.*, establishing minimum prices andor increasing sales taxes on alcoholic beverages -- that would more directly accomplish its stated goal without intruding on sellers' ability to provide truthful, nonmisleading information to customers. [ ] The principal opinion errs in adopting a new analysis for the evaluation of commercial speech regulation.

STEVENS, J., announced the judgment of the Court, and delivered the opinion of the Court with respects to Parts I, II, and VII, in which SCALIA, KENNEDY, SOUTER, THOMAS, and GINSBURG, JJ., joined, the opinion of the Court with respect to Part VIII, in which SCALIA, KENNEDY, SOUTER, and GINSBURG, JJ., joined, an opinion with respect to Parts III and V, in which KENNEDY, SOUTER, and GINSBURG, JJ., joined, an opinion with respect to Part VI, in which KENNEDY, THOMAS, and GINSBURG, JJ., joined, and an opinion with respect to Part IV, in which KENNEDY and GINSBURG, JJ., joined. SCALIA, J., and THOMAS, J., filed opinions concurring in part and concurring in the judgment. O'CONNOR, J., filed an opinion concurring in the judgment, in which REHNQUIST, C.J., and SOUTER and BREYER, JJ., joined,.

STEVENS, J., lead opinion

Last Term, we held that a federal law abridging a brewer's right to provide the public with accurate information about the alcoholic content of malt beverages is unconstitutional. *Rubin v. Coors Brewing Co.,* 514 U.S. 476, 491 (1995). We now hold that Rhode Island's statutory prohibition against advertisements that provide the public with accurate information about retail prices of alcoholic beverages is also invalid. Our holding rests on the conclusion that such an advertising ban is an abridgment of speech protected by the First Amendment, and that it is not shielded from constitutional scrutiny by the Twenty-first Amendment.

I

In 1956, the Rhode Island Legislature enacted two separate prohibitions against advertising the retail price of alcoholic beverages. The first applies to vendors licensed in Rhode Island as well as to out-of-state manufacturers, wholesalers, and shippers. It prohibits them from "advertising in any manner whatsoever" the price of any alcoholic beverage offered for sale in the State; the only exception is for price tags or signs displayed with the merchandise within licensed premises and not visible from the street. The second statute applies to the Rhode Island news media. It contains a categorical prohibition against the publication or broadcast of any advertisements -- even those referring to sales in other States -- that "make reference to the price of any alcoholic beverages."

In two cases decided in 1985, the Rhode Island Supreme Court reviewed the constitutionality of these two statutes. In *S&S Liquor Mart, Inc. v. Pastore* [ ], a liquor retailer located in Westerly, Rhode Island, a town that borders the State of Connecticut, having been advised that his license would be revoked if he advertised his prices in a Connecticut paper, sought to enjoin enforcement of the first statute. Over the dissent of one Justice, the court upheld the statute. It concluded that the statute served the substantial state interest in "'the promotion of temperance.'" [ ] Because the plaintiff failed to prove that the statute did not serve that interest, the court held that he had not carried his burden of establishing a violation of the First Amendment. In response to the dissent's argument that the court had placed the burden on the wrong party, the majority reasoned that the Twenty-first Amendment gave the statute "'an added presumption [of] validity.'" [ ] Although that presumption had not been overcome in that case, the State Supreme Court assumed that, in a future case, the record might "support the proposition that these advertising restrictions do not further temperance objectives." [ ].

In *Rhode Island Liquor Stores Assn. v. Evening Call Pub. Co.,* 497 A.2d 331 (R.I. 1985), the plaintiff association sought to enjoin the publisher of the local newspaper in Woonsocket, Rhode Island, from accepting advertisements disclosing the retail price of alcoholic beverages being sold across the state line in Millville, Massachusetts. In upholding the injunction, the State Supreme Court adhered to its reasoning in the

Pastore case and rejected the argument that the statute neither "directly advanced" the state interest in promoting temperance nor was "more extensive than necessary to serve that interest" as required by this Court's decision in *Central Hudson Gas & Elec. Corp. v. Public Serv. Comm'n of N.Y.* [ ] (1980). It assumed the existence of other, "perhaps more effective means" of achieving the State's "goal of temperance", but concluded that it was "not unreasonable for the State of Rhode Island to believe that price advertising will result in increased sales of alcoholic beverages generally." [ ]

II

Petitioners 44 Liquormart, Inc. (44 Liquormart), and Peoples Super Liquor Stores, Inc. (Peoples), are licensed retailers of alcoholic beverages. Petitioner 44 Liquormart operates a store in Rhode Island, and petitioner Peoples operates several stores in Massachusetts that are patronized by Rhode Island residents. Peoples uses alcohol price advertising extensively in Massachusetts, where such advertising is permitted, but Rhode Island newspapers and other media outlets have refused to accept such ads.

Complaints from competitors about an advertisement placed by 44 Liquormart in a Rhode Island newspaper in 1991 generated enforcement proceedings that, in turn, led to the initiation of this litigation. The advertisement did not state the price of any alcoholic beverages. Indeed, it noted that "State law prohibits advertising liquor prices." The ad did, however, state the low prices at which peanuts, potato chips, and Schweppes mixers were being offered, identify various brands of packaged liquor, and include the word "WOW" in large letters next to pictures of vodka and rum bottles. Based on the conclusion that the implied reference to bargain prices for liquor violated the statutory ban on price advertising, the Rhode Island Liquor Control Administrator assessed a $400 fine.

After paying the fine, 44 Liquormart, joined by Peoples, filed this action against the administrator in the Federal District Court seeking a declaratory judgment that the two statutes and the administrator's implementing regulations violate the First Amendment and other provisions of federal law. The Rhode Island Liquor Stores Association was allowed to intervene as a defendant and, in due course, the State of Rhode Island replaced the administrator as the principal defendant. The parties stipulated that the price advertising ban is vigorously enforced, that Rhode Island permits "all advertising of alcoholic beverages excepting references to price outside the licensed premises," and that petitioners' proposed ads do not concern an illegal activity, and presumably would not be false or misleading. [ ] The parties disagreed, however, about the impact of the ban on the promotion of temperance in Rhode Island. On that question, the District Court heard conflicting expert testimony and reviewed a number of studies.

In his findings of fact, the District Judge first noted that there was a pronounced lack of unanimity among researchers who have studied the impact of advertising on the level of consumption of alcoholic beverages. He referred to a 1985 Federal Trade Commission study that found no evidence that alcohol advertising significantly affects alcohol abuse. Another study indicated that Rhode Island ranks in the upper 30% of States in per capita consumption of alcoholic beverages; alcohol consumption is lower in other States that allow price advertising. After summarizing the testimony of the expert witnesses for both parties, he found

> as a fact that Rhode Island's off-premises liquor price advertising ban has no significant impact on levels of alcohol consumption in Rhode Island.

[ ]

As a matter of law, he concluded that the price advertising ban was unconstitutional because it did not "directly advance" the State's interest in reducing alcohol consumption, and was "more extensive than necessary to serve that interest." [ ] He reasoned that the party seeking to uphold a restriction on commercial speech carries the burden of justifying it, and that the Twenty-first Amendment did not shift or diminish that burden. Acknowledging that it might have been reasonable for the state legislature to "assume a correlation between the price advertising ban and reduced consumption," he held that more than a rational basis was required to justify the speech restriction, and that the State had failed to demonstrate a reasonable "'fit" between its policy objectives and its chosen means. [ ]

The Court of Appeals reversed. It found "inherent merit" in the State's submission that competitive price advertising would lower prices and that lower prices would produce more sales. [ ] Moreover, it agreed with the reasoning of the Rhode Island Supreme Court that the Twenty-first Amendment gave the statutes an added presumption of validity. [ ] Alternatively, it concluded that reversal was compelled by this Court's summary action in *Queensgate Investment Co. v. Liquor Control Comm'n of Ohio* [ ]. In that case, the Court dismissed the appeal from a decision of the Ohio Supreme Court upholding a prohibition against off-premises advertising of the prices of alcoholic beverages sold by the drink. [ ]

Queensgate has been both followed and distinguished in subsequent cases reviewing the validity of similar advertising bans. We are now persuaded that the importance of the First Amendment issue, as well the suggested relevance of the Twenty-first Amendment, merits more thorough analysis than it received when we refused to accept jurisdiction of the *Queensgate* appeal. We therefore granted certiorari. [ ]

III

Advertising has been a part of our culture throughout our history. Even in colonial days, the public relied on "commercial speech" for vital information about the market. Early newspapers displayed advertisements for goods and services on their front pages, and town criers called out prices in public squares. [ ] Indeed, commercial messages played such a central role in public life prior to the Founding that Benjamin Franklin authored his early defense of a free press in support of his decision to print, of all things, an advertisement for voyages to Barbados. [ ]

In accord with the role that commercial messages have long played, the law has developed to ensure that advertising provides consumers with accurate information about the availability of goods and services. In the early years, the common law, and later, statutes, served the consumers' interest in the receipt of accurate information in the commercial market by prohibiting fraudulent and misleading advertising. It was not until the 1970's, however, that this Court held that the First Amendment protected the dissemination of truthful and nonmisleading commercial messages about lawful products and services. [ ]

In *Bigelow v. Virginia*, 421 U.S. 809 (1975), we held that it was error to assume that commercial speech was entitled to no First Amendment protection or that it was without value in the marketplace of ideas. *Id.* at GO>825-826. The following Term, in *Virginia Bd. of Pharmacy v. Virginia Citizens Consumer Council, Inc.*, 425 U.S. 748 (1976), we expanded on our holding in *Bigelow* and held that the State's blanket ban on advertising the price of prescription drugs violated the First Amendment.

Virginia Pharmacy Bd. reflected the conclusion that the same interest that supports regulation of potentially misleading advertising, namely the public's interest in receiving accurate commercial information, also supports an interpretation of the First Amendment that provides constitutional protection for the dissemination of accurate and nonmisleading commercial messages. We explained:

> Advertising, however tasteless and excessive it sometimes may seem, is nonetheless dissemination of information as to who is producing and selling what product, for what reason, and at what price. So long as we preserve a predominantly free enterprise economy, the allocation of our resources in large measure will be made through numerous private economic decisions. It is a matter of public interest that those decisions, in the aggregate, be intelligent and well informed. To this end, the free flow of commercial information is indispensable.

[ ] The opinion further explained that a State's paternalistic assumption that the public will use truthful, nonmisleading commercial information unwisely cannot justify a decision to suppress it:

> There is, of course, an alternative to this highly paternalistic approach. That alternative is to assume that this information is not in itself harmful, that people will perceive their own best interests if only they are well enough informed, and that the best means to that end is to open the channels of communication, rather than to close them. If they are truly open, nothing prevents the "professional" pharmacist from marketing his own assertedly superior product, and contrasting it with that of the low-cost, high-volume prescription drug retailer. But the choice among these

133

alternative approaches is not ours to make, or the Virginia General Assembly's. It is precisely this kind of choice, between the dangers of suppressing information and the dangers of its misuse if it is freely available, that the First Amendment makes for us.

[ ]

On the basis of these principles, our early cases uniformly struck down several broadly based bans on truthful, nonmisleading commercial speech, each of which served ends unrelated to consumer protection. Indeed, one of those cases expressly likened the rationale that *Virginia Pharmacy Bd.* employed to the one that Justice Brandeis adopted in his concurrence in *Whitney v. California*, 274 U.S. 357 (1927). [ ] There, Justice Brandeis wrote, in explaining his objection to a prohibition of *political* speech, that "the remedy to be applied is more speech, not enforced silence. Only an emergency can justify repression." [ ] ...

At the same time, our early cases recognized that the State may regulate some types of commercial advertising more freely than other forms of protected speech. Specifically, we explained that the State may require commercial messages to "appear in such a form, or include such additional information, warnings, and disclaimers, as are necessary to prevent its being deceptive" [ ], and that it may restrict some forms of aggressive sales practices that have the potential to exert "undue influence" over consumers. [ ]

Virginia Pharmacy Bd. attributed the State's authority to impose these regulations in part to certain "common sense differences" that exist between commercial messages and other types of protected expression. [ ] Our opinion noted that the greater "objectivity" of commercial speech justifies affording the State more freedom to distinguish false commercial advertisements from true ones [ ], and that the greater "hardiness" of commercial speech, inspired as it is by the profit motive, likely diminishes the chilling effect that may attend its regulation [ ].

Subsequent cases explained that the State's power to regulate commercial transactions justifies its concomitant power to regulate commercial speech that is "linked inextricably" to those transactions. [ ] ...

Nevertheless, as we explained in *Linmark,* the State retains less regulatory authority when its commercial speech restrictions strike at "the substance of the information communicated," rather than the "commercial aspect of [it] -- with offerors communicating offers to offerees." [ ]

In *Central Hudson Gas & Elec. Corp. v. Public Serv. Comm'n of N.Y.* [ ] (1980), we took stock of our developing commercial speech jurisprudence. In that case, we considered a regulation "completely" banning all promotional advertising by electric utilities. [ ] Our decision acknowledged the special features of commercial speech, but identified the serious First Amendment concerns that attend blanket advertising prohibitions that do not protect consumers from commercial harms.

Five Members of the Court recognized that the state interest in the conservation of energy was substantial, and that there was "an immediate connection between advertising and demand for electricity." [ ] Nevertheless, they concluded that the regulation was invalid because the Commission had failed to make a showing that a more limited speech regulation would not have adequately served the State's interest. [ ]

In reaching its conclusion, the majority explained that, although the special nature of commercial speech may require less than strict review of its regulation, special concerns arise from "regulations that entirely suppress commercial speech in order to pursue a nonspeech-related policy." [ ] In those circumstances, "a ban on speech could screen from public view the underlying governmental policy." [ ] As a result, the Court concluded that "special care" should attend the review of such blanket bans, and it pointedly remarked that,

> in recent years, this Court has not approved a blanket ban on commercial speech unless the speech itself was flawed in some way, either because it was deceptive or related to unlawful activity.

[ ]

IV

As our review of the case law reveals, Rhode Island errs in concluding that *all* commercial speech regulations are subject to a similar form of constitutional review simply because they target a similar category of expression. The mere fact that messages propose commercial transactions does not, in and of itself, dictate the constitutional analysis that should apply to decisions to suppress them. [ ]

When a State regulates commercial messages to protect consumers from misleading, deceptive, or aggressive sales practices, or requires the disclosure of beneficial consumer information, the purpose of its regulation is consistent with the reasons for according constitutional protection to commercial speech and therefore justifies less than strict review. However, when a State entirely prohibits the dissemination of truthful, nonmisleading commercial messages for reasons unrelated to the preservation of a fair bargaining process, there is far less reason to depart from the rigorous review that the First Amendment generally demands.

Sound reasons justify reviewing the latter type of commercial speech regulation more carefully. Most obviously, complete speech bans, unlike content-neutral restrictions on the time, place, or manner of expression [ ], are particularly dangerous because they all but foreclose alternative means of disseminating certain information.

Our commercial speech cases have recognized the dangers that attend governmental attempts to single out certain messages for

135

suppression. For example, in *Linmark,* 431 U.S. at 92-94, we concluded that a ban on "For Sale" signs was "content-based" and failed to leave open "satisfactory" alternative channels of communication [ ]. Moreover, last Term, we upheld a 30-day prohibition against a certain form of legal solicitation largely because it left so many channels of communication open to Florida lawyers. [ ]

The special dangers that attend complete bans on truthful, nonmisleading commercial speech cannot be explained away by appeals to the "commonsense distinctions" that exist between commercial and noncommercial speech. [ ] Regulations that suppress the truth are no less troubling because they target objectively verifiable information, nor are they less effective because they aim at durable messages. As a result, neither the "greater objectivity" nor the "greater hardiness" of truthful, nonmisleading commercial speech justifies reviewing its complete suppression with added deference. [ ]

It is the State's interest in protecting consumers from "commercial harms" that provides "the typical reason why commercial speech can be subject to greater governmental regulation than noncommercial speech." [ ] Yet bans that target truthful, nonmisleading commercial messages rarely protect consumers from such harms.{GO>12} Instead, such bans often serve only to obscure an "underlying governmental policy" that could be implemented without regulating speech. [ ] In this way, these commercial speech bans not only hinder consumer choice, but also impede debate over central issues of public policy. [ ]

Precisely because bans against truthful, nonmisleading commercial speech rarely seek to protect consumers from either deception or overreaching, they usually rest solely on the offensive assumption that the public will respond "irrationally" to the truth. [ ] The First Amendment directs us to be especially skeptical of regulations that seek to keep people in the dark for what the government perceives to be their own good. That teaching applies equally to state attempts to deprive consumers of accurate information about their chosen products ...

V

In this case, there is no question that Rhode Island's price advertising ban constitutes a blanket prohibition against truthful, nonmisleading speech about a lawful product. There is also no question that the ban serves an end unrelated to consumer protection. Accordingly, we must review the price advertising ban with "special care" [ ], mindful that speech prohibitions of this type rarely survive constitutional review. [ ]

The State argues that the price advertising prohibition should nevertheless be upheld because it directly advances the State's substantial interest in promoting temperance, and because it is no more extensive than necessary. [ ]. Although there is some confusion as to what Rhode Island means by temperance, we assume that the State asserts an interest in reducing alcohol consumption.

In evaluating the ban's effectiveness in advancing the State's interest, we note that a commercial speech regulation "may not be sustained if it provides only ineffective or remote support for the government's purpose." [ ]. For that reason, the State bears the burden of showing not merely that its regulation will advance its interest, but also that it will do so "to a material degree." [ ] The need for the State to make such a showing is particularly great given the drastic nature of its chosen means -- the wholesale suppression of truthful, nonmisleading information. Accordingly, we must determine whether the State has shown that the price advertising ban will *significantly* reduce alcohol consumption.

We can agree that common sense supports the conclusion that a prohibition against price advertising, like a collusive agreement among competitors to refrain from such advertising, will tend to mitigate competition and maintain prices at a higher level than would prevail in a completely free market. Despite the absence of proof on the point, we can even agree with the State's contention that it is reasonable to assume that demand, and hence consumption throughout the market, is somewhat lower whenever a higher, noncompetitive price level prevails. However, without any findings of fact, or indeed any evidentiary support whatsoever, we cannot agree with the assertion that the price advertising ban will significantly advance the State's interest in promoting temperance.

Although the record suggests that the price advertising ban may have some impact on the purchasing patterns of temperate drinkers of modest means [ ], the State has presented no evidence to suggest that its speech prohibition will *significantly* reduce marketwide consumption. Indeed, the District Court's considered and uncontradicted finding on this point is directly to the contrary. [ ] Moreover, the evidence suggests that the abusive drinker will probably not be deterred by a marginal price increase, and that the true alcoholic may simply reduce his purchases of other necessities.

In addition, as the District Court noted, the State has not identified what price level would lead to a significant reduction in alcohol consumption, nor has it identified the amount that it believes prices would decrease without the ban. [ ] Thus, the State's own showing reveals that any connection between the ban and a significant change in alcohol consumption would be purely fortuitous.

As is evident, any conclusion that elimination of the ban would significantly increase alcohol consumption would require us to engage in the sort of "speculation or conjecture" that is an unacceptable means of demonstrating that a restriction on commercial speech directly advances the State's asserted interest. [ ] Such speculation certainly does not suffice when the State takes aim at accurate commercial information for paternalistic ends.

The State also cannot satisfy the requirement that its restriction on speech be no more extensive than necessary. It is perfectly obvious that alternative forms of regulation that would not involve any restriction on speech would be more likely to achieve the State's goal of promoting temperance. As the State's own expert conceded, higher prices can be maintained either by direct regulation or by increased taxation. [ ]. Per capita purchases could be limited as is the case with prescription drugs. Even educational campaigns focused on the problems of excessive, or even moderate, drinking might prove to be more effective.

As a result, even under the less than strict standard that generally applies in commercial speech cases, the State has failed to establish a "reasonable fit" between its abridgment of speech and its temperance goal. [ ] ... It necessarily follows that the price advertising ban cannot survive the more stringent constitutional review that *Central Hudson* itself concluded was appropriate for the complete suppression of truthful, nonmisleading commercial speech. [ ]

VI

The State responds by arguing that it merely exercised appropriate "legislative judgment" in determining that a price advertising ban would best promote temperance. Relying on the *Central Hudson* analysis set forth in *Posadas de Puerto Rico Associates v. Tourism Co. of P.R.,* 478 U.S. 328 (1986), and *United States v. Edge Broadcasting Co.,* 509 U.S. 418 (1993), Rhode Island first argues that, because expert opinions as to the effectiveness of the price advertising ban "go both ways," the Court of Appeals correctly concluded that the ban constituted a "reasonable choice" by the legislature. [ ] The State next contends that precedent requires us to give particular deference to that legislative choice, because the State could, if it chose, ban the sale of alcoholic beverages outright. [ ] Finally, the State argues that deference is appropriate because alcoholic beverages are so-called "vice" products. [ ] We consider each of these contentions in turn.

The State's first argument fails to justify the speech prohibition at issue. Our commercial speech cases recognize some room for the exercise of legislative judgment. [ ] However, Rhode Island errs in concluding that *Edge* and *Posadas* establish the degree of deference that its decision to impose a price advertising ban warrants.

In *Edge,* we upheld a federal statute that permitted only those broadcasters located in States that had legalized lotteries to air lottery advertising. The statute was designed to regulate advertising about an activity that had been deemed illegal in the jurisdiction in which the broadcaster was located. [ ] Here, by contrast, the commercial speech ban targets information about entirely lawful behavior.

Posadas is more directly relevant. There, a five-Member majority held that, under the *Central Hudson* test, it was "up to the legislature" to choose to reduce gambling by suppressing in-state casino advertising, rather than engaging in educational speech. [ ] Rhode Island argues that this logic demonstrates the constitutionality of its own decision to ban price advertising in lieu of raising taxes or employing some other less speech-restrictive means of promoting temperance.

The reasoning in *Posadas* does support the State's argument, but, on reflection, we are now persuaded that *Posadas* erroneously performed the First Amendment analysis. The casino advertising ban was designed to keep truthful, nonmisleading speech from members of the public for fear that they would be more likely to gamble if they received it. As a result, the advertising ban served to shield the State's anti-gambling policy from the public scrutiny that more direct, nonspeech regulation would draw. [ ]

Given our longstanding hostility to commercial speech regulation of this type, *Posadas* clearly erred in concluding that it was "up to the legislature" to choose suppression over a less speech-restrictive policy. The *Posadas* majority's conclusion on that point cannot be reconciled with the unbroken line of prior cases striking down similarly broad regulations on truthful, nonmisleading advertising when nonspeech-related alternatives were available. [ ]

Because the 5-to-4 decision in *Posadas* marked such a sharp break from our prior precedent, and because it concerned a constitutional question about which this Court is the final arbiter, we decline to give force to its highly deferential approach. Instead, in keeping with our prior holdings, we conclude that a state legislature does not have the broad discretion to suppress truthful, nonmisleading information for paternalistic purposes that the *Posadas* majority was willing to tolerate. ...

We also cannot accept the State's second contention, which is premised entirely on the "greater includes the lesser" reasoning endorsed toward the end of the majority's opinion in *Posadas*. There, the majority stated that "the greater power to completely ban casino gambling necessarily includes the lesser power to ban advertising of casino gambling." [ ] ... [ ] ...

[ ] On the basis of these statements, the State reasons that its undisputed authority to ban alcoholic beverages must include the power to restrict advertisements offering them for sale.

In *Rubin v. Coors Brewing Co.* [ ], the United States advanced a similar argument as a basis for supporting a statutory prohibition against revealing the alcoholic content of malt beverages on product labels. We rejected the argument, noting that the statement in the *Posadas* opinion was made only after the majority had concluded that the Puerto Rican regulation "survived the *Central Hudson* test." [ ] Further consideration persuades us that the "greater includes the lesser" argument should be rejected for the additional and more important reason that it is inconsistent with both logic and well settled doctrine.

Although we do not dispute the proposition that greater powers include lesser ones, we fail to see how that syllogism requires the

139

conclusion that the State's power to regulate commercial *activity* is "greater" than its power to ban truthful, nonmisleading commercial *speech.* Contrary to the assumption made in *Posadas,* we think it quite clear that banning speech may sometimes prove far more intrusive than banning conduct. As a venerable proverb teaches, it may prove more injurious to prevent people from teaching others how to fish than to prevent fish from being sold. Similarly, a local ordinance banning bicycle lessons may curtail freedom far more than one that prohibits bicycle riding within city limits. In short, we reject the assumption that words are necessarily less vital to freedom than actions, or that logic somehow proves that the power to prohibit an activity is necessarily "greater" than the power to suppress speech about it.

As a matter of First Amendment doctrine, the *Posadas* syllogism is even less defensible. The text of the First Amendment makes clear that the Constitution presumes that attempts to regulate speech are more dangerous than attempts to regulate conduct. That presumption accords with the essential role that the free flow of information plays in a democratic society. As a result, the First Amendment directs that government may not suppress speech as easily as it may suppress conduct, and that speech restrictions cannot be treated as simply another means that the government may use to achieve its ends.

These basic First Amendment principles clearly apply to commercial speech; indeed, the *Posadas* majority impliedly conceded as much by applying the *Central Hudson* test. Thus, it is no answer that commercial speech concerns products and services that the government may freely regulate. Our decisions from *Virginia Pharmacy Bd.* on have made plain that a State's regulation of the sale of goods differs in kind from a State's regulation of accurate information about those goods. The distinction that our cases have consistently drawn between these two types of governmental action is fundamentally incompatible with the absolutist view that the State may ban commercial speech simply because it may constitutionally prohibit the underlying conduct.

That the State has chosen to license its liquor retailers does not change the analysis. Even though government is under no obligation to provide a person, or the public, a particular benefit, it does not follow that conferral of the benefit may be conditioned on the surrender of a constitutional right. [ ]. In *Perry v. Sindermann* [ ], relying on a host of cases applying that principle during the preceding quarter-century, the Court explained that government

> may not deny a benefit to a person on a basis that infringes his constitutionally protected interests -- especially his interest in freedom of speech.

[ ] That teaching clearly applies to state attempts to regulate commercial speech, as our cases striking down bans on truthful, nonmisleading speech by licensed professionals attest. [ ]

Thus, just as it is perfectly clear that Rhode Island could not ban all

140

obscene liquor ads except those that advocated temperance, we think it equally clear that its power to ban the sale of liquor entirely does not include a power to censor all advertisements that contain accurate and nonmisleading information about the price of the product. As the entire Court apparently now agrees, the statements in the *Posadas* opinion on which Rhode Island relies are no longer persuasive.

Finally, we find unpersuasive the State's contention that, under *Posadas* and *Edge,* the price advertising ban should be upheld because it targets commercial speech that pertains to a "vice" activity. The appellees premise their request for a so-called "vice" exception to our commercial speech doctrine on language in *Edge* which characterized gambling as a "vice". [ ] The respondents misread our precedent. Our decision last Term striking down an alcohol-related advertising restriction effectively rejected the very contention respondents now make. [ ]

Moreover, the scope of any "vice" exception to the protection afforded by the First Amendment would be difficult, if not impossible, to define. Almost any product that poses some threat to public health or public morals might reasonably be characterized by a state legislature as relating to "vice activity". Such characterization, however, is anomalous when applied to products such as alcoholic beverages, lottery tickets, or playing cards, that may be lawfully purchased on the open market. The recognition of such an exception would also have the unfortunate consequence of either allowing state legislatures to justify censorship by the simple expedient of placing the "vice" label on selected lawful activities, or requiring the federal courts to establish a federal common law of vice. [ ] For these reasons, a "vice" label that is unaccompanied by a corresponding prohibition against the commercial behavior at issue fails to provide a principled justification for the regulation of commercial speech about that activity.

VII

From 1919 until 1933, the Eighteenth Amendment to the Constitution totally prohibited "the manufacture, sale, or transportation of intoxicating liquors" in the United States and its territories. Section 1 of the Twenty-first Amendment repealed that prohibition, and § 2 delegated to the several States the power to prohibit commerce in, or the use of, alcoholic beverages.{GO>21} The States' regulatory power over this segment of commerce is therefore largely "unfettered by the Commerce Clause." [ ]

As is clear, the text of the Twenty-first Amendment supports the view that, while it grants the States authority over commerce that might otherwise be reserved to the Federal Government, it places no limit whatsoever on other constitutional provisions. Nevertheless, Rhode Island argues, and the Court of Appeals agreed, that in this case the Twenty-first Amendment tilts the First Amendment analysis in the State's favor. [ ]

141

In reaching its conclusion, the Court of Appeals relied on our decision in *California v. LaRue,* 409 U.S. 109 (1972). In *LaRue,* five Members of the Court relied on the Twenty-first Amendment to buttress the conclusion that the First Amendment did not invalidate California's prohibition of certain grossly sexual exhibitions in premises licensed to serve alcoholic beverages. Specifically, the opinion stated that the Twenty-first Amendment required that the prohibition be given an added presumption in favor of its validity. [ ] We are now persuaded that the Court's analysis in *LaRue* would have led to precisely the same result if it had placed no reliance on the Twenty-first Amendment.

Entirely apart from the Twenty-first Amendment, the State has ample power to prohibit the sale of alcoholic beverages in inappropriate locations. Moreover, in subsequent cases, the Court has recognized that the States' inherent police powers provide ample authority to restrict the kind of "bacchanalian revelries" described in the *LaRue* opinion, regardless of whether alcoholic beverages are involved. [ ] ...

Without questioning the holding in *LaRue,* we now disavow its reasoning insofar as it relied on the Twenty-first Amendment. As we explained in a case decided more than a decade after *LaRue,* although the Twenty-first Amendment limits the effect of the dormant Commerce Clause on a State's regulatory power over the delivery or use of intoxicating beverages within its borders, "the Amendment does not license the States to ignore their obligations under other provisions of the Constitution." [ ] That general conclusion reflects our specific holdings that the Twenty-first Amendment does not in any way diminish the force of the Supremacy Clause [ ], the Establishment Clause, [ ], or the Equal Protection Clause [ ]. We see no reason why the First Amendment should not also be included in that list. Accordingly, we now hold that the Twenty-first Amendment does not qualify the constitutional prohibition against laws abridging the freedom of speech embodied in the First Amendment. The Twenty-first Amendment, therefore, cannot save Rhode Island's ban on liquor price advertising.

VIII

Because Rhode Island has failed to carry its heavy burden of justifying its complete ban on price advertising, we conclude that R.I.Gen.Laws §§ 3-8-7 and 3-8-8.1, as well as Regulation 32 of the Rhode Island Liquor Control Administration, abridge speech in violation of the First Amendment as made applicable to the States by the Due Process Clause of the Fourteenth Amendment. The judgment of the Court of Appeals is therefore reversed.

It is so ordered.

In *Red Lion Broadcasting Co., Inc. v. Federal Communications Commission* (MCLE, page 281), the Supreme Court unanimously ruled that the FCC's Fairness Doctrine and its personal attack and political editorial provisions did not violate the First Amendment. The Court based its decision on the scarcity rationale -- *i.e.,* that broadcasting is a limited public resource. The government, therefore, can require broadcasters to operate in the public interest. This includes the authority to establish rules under which stations must air programming encompassing debate on controversial issues and providing free airtime for individuals to respond who have been attacked in political editorials. The Court continues to cite *Red Lion* as precedent for regulating broadcasting in spite of the pervasiveness of newer technologies such as cable and satellite television.

Red Lion Broadcasting Co., Inc. v. Federal Communications Commission

Argued April 2-3, 1969
Decided June 9, 1969

395 U.S. 367, 89 S.Ct. 1794, 23 L.Ed.2d 371, 1 Med.L.Rptr. 2053

CERTIORARI TO THE UNITED STATES COURT OF APPEALS FOR THE DISTRICT OF COLUMBIA CIRCUIT

Syllabus

The Federal Communications Commission (FCC) has for many years imposed on broadcasters a "fairness doctrine," requiring that public issues be presented by broadcasters and that each side of those issues be given fair coverage. In No. 2, the FCC declared that petitioner Red Lion Broadcasting Co. had failed to meet its obligation under the fairness doctrine when it carried a program which constituted a personal attack on one Cook, and ordered it to send a transcript of the broadcast to Cook and provide reply time, whether or not Cook would pay for it. The Court of Appeals upheld the FCC's position. After the commencement of the *Red Lion* litigation, the FCC began a rulemaking proceeding to make the personal attack aspect of the fairness doctrine more precise and more readily enforceable, and to specify its rules relating to political editorials. The rules, as adopted and amended, were held unconstitutional by the Court of Appeals in *RTNDA* (No. 717) as abridging the freedoms of speech and press.

Held:

1. The history of the fairness doctrine and of related legislation shows that the FCC's action in the *Red Lion* case did not exceed its

authority, and that, in adopting the new regulations, the FCC was implementing congressional policy.

(a) The fairness doctrine began shortly after the Federal Radio Commission was established to allocate frequencies among competing applicants in the public interest, and insofar as there is an affirmative obligation of the broadcaster to see that both sides are presented, the personal attack doctrine and regulations do not differ from the fairness doctrine.

(b) The FCC's statutory mandate to see that broadcasters operate in the public interest and Congress' reaffirmation, in the 1959 amendment to § 315 of the Communications Act, of the FCC's view that the fairness doctrine inhered in the public interest standard, support the conclusion that the doctrine and its component personal attack and political editorializing' regulations are a legitimate exercise of congressionally delegated authority.

2. The fairness doctrine and its specific manifestations in the personal attack and political editorial rules do not violate the First Amendment.

(a) The First Amendment is relevant to public broadcasting, but it is the right of the viewing and listening public, and not the right of the broadcasters, which is paramount.

(b) The First Amendment does not protect private censorship by broadcasters who are licensed by the Government to use a scarce resource which is denied to others.

(c) The danger that licensees will eliminate coverage of controversial issues as a result of the personal attack and political editorial rules is, at best, speculative, and, in any event, the FCC has authority to guard against this danger.

(d) There was nothing vague about the FCC's specific ruling in the *Red Lion* case, and the regulations at issue in No. 717 could be employed in precisely the same way as the fairness doctrine in *Red Lion*. It is not necessary to decide every aspect of the fairness doctrine to decide these cases. Problems involving more extreme applications or more difficult constitutional questions will be dealt with if and when they arise.

(e) It has not been shown that the scarcity of broadcast frequencies, which impelled governmental regulation, is entirely a thing of the past, as new uses for the frequency spectrum have kept pace with improved technology and more efficient utilization of that spectrum.

No. 2, 127 U.S.App.D.C. 129, 381 F.2d 908, affirmed; No. 717, 400 F.2d 1002, reversed and remanded.

WHITE, J., lead opinion

The Federal Communications Commission has for many years

imposed on radio and television broadcasters the requirement that discussion of public issues be presented on broadcast stations, and that each side of those issues must be given fair coverage. This is known as the fairness doctrine, which originated very early in the history of broadcasting and has maintained its present outlines for some time. It is an obligation whose content has been defined in a long series of FCC rulings in particular cases, and which is distinct from the statutory requirement of § 315 of the Communications Act that equal time be allotted all qualified candidates for public office. Two aspects of the fairness doctrine, relating to personal attacks in the context of controversial public issues and to political editorializing, were codified more precisely in the form of FCC regulations in 1967. The two cases before us now, which were decided separately below, challenge the constitutional and statutory bases of the doctrine and component rules. *Red Lion* involves the application of the fairness doctrine to a particular broadcast, and *RTNDA* arises as an action to review the FCC's 1967 promulgation of the personal attack and political editorializing regulations, which were laid down after the *Red Lion* litigation had begun.

I

A

The Red Lion Broadcasting Company is licensed to operate a Pennsylvania radio station, WGCB. On November 27, 1964, WGCB carried a 15-minute broadcast by the Reverend Billy James Hargis as part of a "Christian Crusade" series. A book by Fred J. Cook entitled "Goldwater -- Extremist on the Right" was discussed by Hargis, who said that Cook had been fired by a newspaper for making false charges against city officials; that Cook had then worked for a Communist-affiliated publication; that he had defended Alger Hiss and attacked J. Edgar Hoover and the Central Intelligence Agency, and that he had now written a "book to smear and destroy Barry Goldwater." When Cook heard of the broadcast, he concluded that he had been personally attacked and demanded free reply time, which the station refused. After an exchange of letters among Cook, Red Lion, and the FCC, the FCC declared that the Hargis broadcast constituted a personal attack on Cook; that Red Lion had failed to meet its obligation under the fairness doctrine as expressed in *Times-Mirror Broadcasting Co.* [ ], to send a tape, transcript, or summary of the broadcast to Cook and offer him reply time, and that the station must provide reply time whether or not Cook would pay for it. On review in the Court of Appeals for the District of Columbia Circuit, the FCC's position was upheld as constitutional and otherwise proper.

B

Not long after the *Red Lion* litigation was begun, the FCC issued a Notice of Proposed Rule Making [ ], with an eye to making the personal attack aspect of the fairness doctrine more precise and more readily enforceable, and to specifying its rules relating to political editorials.

145

After considering written comments supporting and opposing the rules, the FCC adopted them substantially as proposed [ ]. Twice amended [ ], the rules were held unconstitutional in the *RTNDA* litigation by the Court of Appeals for the Seventh Circuit, on review of the rulemaking proceeding, as abridging the freedoms of speech and press. [ ]

As they now stand amended, the regulations read as follows:

Personal attacks; political editorials.

(a) When, during the presentation of views on a controversial issue of public importance, an attack is made upon the honesty, character, integrity or like personal qualities of an identified person or group, the licensee shall, within a reasonable time and in no event later than 1 week after the attack, transmit to the person or group attacked (1) notification of the date, time and identification of the broadcast; (2) a script or tape (or an accurate summary if a script or tape is not available) of the attack, and (3) an offer of a reasonable opportunity to respond over the licensee's facilities.

(b) The provisions of paragraph (a) of this section shall not be applicable (1) to attacks on foreign groups or foreign public figures; (2) to personal attacks which are made by legally qualified candidates, their authorized spokesmen, or those associated with them in the campaign, on other such candidates, their authorized spokesmen, or persons associated with the candidates in the campaign, and (3) to bona fide newscasts, bona fide news interviews, and on-the-spot coverage of a bona fide news event (including commentary or analysis contained in the foregoing programs, but the provisions of paragraph (a) of this section shall be applicable to editorials of the licensee).

NOTE: The fairness doctrine is applicable to situations coming within [(3)], above, and, in a specific factual situation, may be applicable in the general area of political broadcasts [(2)], above. [ ] ...

(c) Where a licensee, in an editorial, (i) endorses or (ii) opposes a legally qualified candidate or candidates, the licensee shall, within 24 hours after the editorial, transmit to respectively (i) the other qualified candidate or candidates for the same office or (ii) the candidate opposed in the editorial (1) notification of the date and the time of the editorial; (2) a script or tape of the editorial, and (3) an offer of a reasonable opportunity for a candidate or a spokesman of the candidate to respond over the licensee's facilities: *Provided, however,* That where such editorials are broadcast within 72 hours prior to the day of the election, the licensee shall comply with the provisions of this paragraph sufficiently far in advance of the broadcast to enable the candidate or candidates to have a reasonable opportunity to prepare a response and to present it in a timely fashion.

[ ]

C

Believing that the specific application of the fairness doctrine in *Red Lion,* and the promulgation of the regulations in *RTNDA,* are both authorized by Congress and enhance, rather than abridge, the freedoms of speech and press protected by the First Amendment, we hold them valid and constitutional, reversing the judgment below in *RTNDA* and affirming the judgment below in *Red Lion.*

II

The history of the emergence of the fairness doctrine and of the related legislation shows that the Commission's action in the *Red Lion* case did not exceed its authority, and that, in adopting the new regulations, the Commission was implementing congressional policy, rather than embarking on a frolic of its own.

A

Before 1927, the allocation of frequencies was left entirely to the private sector, and the result was chaos. It quickly became apparent that broadcast frequencies constituted a scarce resource whose use could be regulated and rationalized only by the Government. Without government control, the medium would be of little use because of the cacaphony of competing voices, none of which could be clearly and predictably heard. Consequently, the Federal Radio Commission was established to allocate frequencies among competing applicants in a manner responsive to the public "convenience, interest, or necessity."

Very shortly thereafter, the Commission expressed its view that the

> public interest requires ample play for the free and fair competition of
> opposing views, and the commission believes that the principle applies . . .
> to all discussions of issues of importance to the public.

[ ] This doctrine was applied through denial of license renewals or construction permits, both by the FRC [ ]. After an extended period during which the licensee was obliged not only to cover and to cover fairly the views of others but also to refrain from expressing his own personal views [ ], the latter limitation on the licensee was abandoned, and the doctrine developed into its present form.

There is a twofold duty laid down by the FCC's decisions and described by the 1949 Report on Editorializing by Broadcast Licensees [ ]. The broadcaster must give adequate coverage to public issues [ ], and coverage must be fair in that it accurately reflects the opposing views. [ ] This must be done at the broadcaster's own expense if sponsorship is unavailable. [ ] Moreover, the duty must be met by programming obtained at the licensee's own initiative if available from no other source. [ ] The Federal Radio Commission had imposed these two basic duties on broadcasters since the outset [ ], and in particular respects the personal attack rules and regulations at issue here have spelled them out in greater detail.

When a personal attack has been made on a figure involved in a public issue, both the doctrine of cases such as *Red Lion* and *Times-Mirror Broadcasting Co.* [ ], and also the 1967 regulations at issue in

147

RTNDA, require that the individual attacked himself be offered an opportunity to respond. Likewise, where one candidate is endorsed in a political editorial, the other candidates must themselves be offered reply time to use personally or through a spokesman. These obligations differ from the general fairness requirement that issues be presented, and presented with coverage of competing views, in that the broadcaster does not have the option of presenting the attacked party's side himself or choosing a third party to represent that side. But insofar as there is an obligation of the broadcaster to see that both sides are presented, and insofar as that is an affirmative obligation, the personal attack doctrine and regulations do not differ from the preceding fairness doctrine. The simple fact that the attacked men or unendorsed candidates may respond themselves or through agents is not a critical distinction, and, indeed, it is not unreasonable for the FCC to conclude that the objective of adequate presentation of all sides may best be served by allowing those most closely affected to make the response, rather than leaving the response in the hands of the station which has attacked their candidacies, endorsed their opponents, or carried a personal attack upon them.

B

The statutory authority of the FCC to promulgate these regulations derives from the mandate to the "Commission from time to time, as public convenience, interest, or necessity requires" to promulgate

> such rules and regulations and prescribe such restrictions and conditions . . . as may be necessary to carry out the provisions of this chapter. . . .

[ ] The Commission is specifically directed to consider the demands of the public interest in the course of granting licenses [ ], renewing them [ ], and modifying them. [ ] Moreover, the FCC has included among the conditions of the Red Lion license itself the requirement that operation of the station be carried out in the public interest [ ]. This mandate to the FCC to assure that broadcasters operate in the public interest is a broad one, a power "not niggardly but expansive" [ ], whose validity we have long upheld. [ ] It is broad enough to encompass these regulations.

The fairness doctrine finds specific recognition in statutory form, is in part modeled on explicit statutory provisions relating to political candidates, and is approvingly reflected in legislative history.

In 1959, the Congress amended the statutory requirement of § 315 that equal time be accorded each political candidate to except certain appearances on news programs, but added that this constituted no exception

> *from the obligation imposed upon them under this Act to operate in the public interest and to afford reasonable opportunity for the discussion of conflicting views on issues of public importance.*

[ ] This language makes it very plain that Congress, in 1959, announced

148

that the phrase "public interest," which had been in the Act since 1927, imposed a duty on broadcasters to discuss both sides of controversial public issues. In other words, the amendment vindicated the FCC's general view that the fairness doctrine inhered in the public interest standard. Subsequent legislation declaring the intent of an earlier statute is entitled to great weight in statutory construction. And here this principle is given special force by the equally venerable principle that the construction of a statute by those charged with its execution should be followed unless there are compelling indications that it is wrong, especially when Congress has refused to alter the administrative construction. Here, the Congress has not just kept its silence by refusing to overturn the administrative construction, but has ratified it with positive legislation. Thirty years of consistent administrative construction left undisturbed by Congress until 1959, when that construction was expressly accepted, reinforce the natural conclusion that the public interest language of the Act authorized the Commission to require licensees to use their stations for discussion of public issues, and that the FCC is free to implement this requirement by reasonable rules and regulations which fall short of abridgment of the freedom of speech and press, and of the censorship proscribed by § 326 of the Act.

The objectives of § 315 themselves could readily be circumvented but for the complementary fairness doctrine ratified by § 315. The section applies only to campaign appearances by candidates, and not by family, friends, campaign managers, or other supporters. Without the fairness doctrine, then, a licensee could ban all campaign appearances by candidates themselves from the air and proceed to deliver over his station entirely to the supporters of one slate of candidates, to the exclusion of all others. In this way, the broadcaster could have a far greater impact on the favored candidacy than he could by simply allowing a spot appearance by the candidate himself. It is the fairness doctrine as an aspect of the obligation to operate in the public interest, rather than § 315, which prohibits the broadcaster from taking such a step.

The legislative history reinforces this view of the effect of the 1959 amendment. Even before the language relevant here was added, the Senate report on amending § 315 noted that

> broadcast frequencies are limited, and, therefore, they have been necessarily considered a public trust. Every licensee who is fortunate in obtaining a license is mandated to operate in the public interest, and has assumed the obligation of presenting important public questions fairly and without bias. [ ] ...

Rather than leave this approval solely in the legislative history, Senator Proxmire suggested an amendment to make it part of the Act. [ ] This amendment, which Senator Pastore, a manager of the bill and a ranking member of the Senate Committee, considered "rather surplusage" [ ], constituted a positive statement of doctrine, and was altered to the present merely approving language in the conference committee. In explaining the language to the Senate after the committee changes, Senator Pastore said:

> We insisted that that provision remain in the bill, to be a continuing reminder and admonition to the Federal Communications Commission and to the broadcasters alike that we were not abandoning the philosophy that gave birth to section 316, in giving the people the right to have a full and complete disclosure of conflicting views on news of interest to the people of the country.

[ ] Senator Scott, another Senate manager, added that: "It is intended to encompass all legitimate areas of public importance which are controversial," not just politics. [ ]

It is true that the personal attack aspect of the fairness doctrine was not actually adjudicated until after 1959, so that Congress then did not have those rules specifically before it. However, the obligation to offer time to reply to a personal attack was presaged by the FCC's 1949 Report on Editorializing, which the FCC views as the principal summary of its *ratio decidendi* in cases in this area:

> In determining whether to honor specific requests for time, the station will inevitably be confronted with such questions as . . . whether there may not be other available groups or individuals who might be more appropriate spokesmen for the particular point of view than the person making the request. The latter's personal involvement in the controversy may also be a factor which must be considered, for elementary considerations of fairness may dictate that time be allocated to a person or group which has been specifically attacked over the station, where otherwise no such obligation would exist.

[ ] When the Congress ratified the FCC's implication of a fairness doctrine in 1959, it did not, of course, approve every past decision or pronouncement by the Commission on this subject, or give it a completely free hand for the future. The statutory authority does not go so far. But we cannot say that, when a station publishes personal attacks or endorses political candidates, it is a misconstruction of the public interest standard to require the station to offer time for a response, rather than to leave the response entirely within the control of the station which has attacked either the candidacies or the men who wish to reply in their own defense. When a broadcaster grants time to a political candidate, Congress itself requires that equal time be offered to his opponents. It would exceed our competence to hold that the Commission is unauthorized by the statute to employ a similar device where personal attacks or political editorials are broadcast by a radio or television station.

In light of the fact that the "public interest" in broadcasting clearly encompasses the presentation of vigorous debate of controversial issues of importance and concern to the public, the fact that the FCC has rested upon that language from its very inception a doctrine that these issues must be discussed, and fairly, and the fact that Congress has acknowledged that the analogous provisions of § 315 are not preclusive in this area, and knowingly preserved the FCC's complementary efforts, we think the fairness doctrine and its component personal attack and political editorializing regulations are a legitimate exercise of congressionally delegated authority. The Communications Act is not notable for the precision of its substantive standards, and, in this respect the explicit provisions of § 315, and the doctrine and rules at issue here which are closely modeled upon that section, are far more explicit than the generalized "public interest" standard in which the Commission ordinarily finds its sole guidance, and which we have held a broad but adequate standard before. [ ] We cannot say that the FCC's declaratory ruling in *Red Lion,* or the regulations at issue in *RTNDA,* are beyond the scope of the congressionally conferred power to assure that stations are operated by those whose possession of a license serves "the public interest."

III

The broadcasters challenge the fairness doctrine and its specific manifestations in the personal attack and political editorial rules on conventional First Amendment grounds, alleging that the rules abridge their freedom of speech and press. Their contention is that the First Amendment protects their desire to use their allotted frequencies continuously to broadcast whatever they choose, and to exclude whomever they choose from ever using that frequency. No man may be prevented from saying or publishing what he thinks, or from refusing in his speech or other utterances to give equal weight to the views of his opponents. This right, they say, applies equally to broadcasters.

A

Although broadcasting is clearly a medium affected by a First Amendment interest [ ], differences in the characteristics of new media justify differences in the First Amendment standards applied to them. [ ] For example, the ability of new technology to produce sounds more raucous than those of the human voice justifies restrictions on the sound level, and on the hours and places of use, of sound trucks so long as the restrictions are reasonable and applied without discrimination. [ ]

Just as the Government may limit the use of sound-amplifying equipment potentially so noisy that it drowns out civilized private speech, so may the Government limit the use of broadcast equipment. The right of free speech of a broadcaster, the user of a sound truck, or any other individual does not embrace a right to snuff out the free speech of others. [ ]

When two people converse face to face, both should not speak at once if either is to be clearly understood. But the range of the human voice is so limited that there could be meaningful communications if half the people in the United States were talking and the other half listening. Just as clearly, half the people might publish and the other half read. But the reach of radio signals is incomparably greater than the range of the human voice, and the problem of interference is a massive reality. The lack of know-how and equipment may keep many from the air, but only a tiny fraction of those with resources and intelligence can hope to communicate by radio at the same time if intelligible communication is to be had, even if the entire radio spectrum is utilized in the present state of commercially acceptable technology.

It was this fact, and the chaos which ensued from permitting anyone to use any frequency at whatever power level he wished, which made necessary the enactment of the Radio Act of 1927 and the Communications Act of 1934, as the Court has noted at length before. [ ] It was this reality which, at the very least, necessitated first the division of the radio spectrum into portions reserved respectively for public broadcasting and for other important radio uses such as amateur operation, aircraft, police, defense, and navigation, and then the subdivision of each portion, and assignment of specific frequencies to individual users or groups of users. Beyond this, however, because the frequencies reserved for public broadcasting were limited in number, it was essential for the Government to tell some applicants that they could not broadcast at all, because there was room for only a few.

Where there are substantially more individuals who want to broadcast than there are frequencies to allocate, it is idle to posit an unabridgeable First Amendment right to broadcast comparable to the right of every individual to speak, write, or publish. If 100 persons want broadcast licenses, but there are only 10 frequencies to allocate, all of them may have the same "right" to a license, but, if there is to be any effective communication by radio, only a few can be licensed, and the rest must be barred from the airwaves. It would be strange if the First Amendment, aimed at protecting and furthering communications, prevented the Government from making radio communication possible by requiring licenses to broadcast and by limiting the number of licenses so as not to overcrowd the spectrum.

This has been the consistent view of the Court. Congress unquestionably has the power to grant and deny licenses and to eliminate existing stations. [ ] No one has a First Amendment right to a license or to monopolize a radio frequency; to deny a station license because "the public interest" requires it "is not a denial of free speech." [ ]

By the same token, as far as the First Amendment is concerned, those who are licensed stand no better than those to whom licenses are refused. A license permits broadcasting, but the licensee has no constitutional right to be the one who holds the license or to monopolize a radio frequency to the exclusion of his fellow citizens. There is nothing in the First Amendment which prevents the Government from requiring a licensee to share his frequency with others and to conduct himself as a proxy or fiduciary with obligations to present those views and voices which are representative of his community and which would otherwise, by necessity, be barred from the airwaves.

This is not to say that the First Amendment is irrelevant to public broadcasting. On the contrary, it has a major role to play, as the Congress itself recognized in § 326, which forbids FCC interference with "the right of free speech by means of radio communication." Because of the scarcity of radio frequencies, the Government is permitted to put restraints on licensees in favor of others whose views should be expressed on this unique medium. But the people as a whole retain their interest in free speech by radio and their collective right to have the medium function consistently with the ends and purposes of the First Amendment. It is the right of the viewers and listeners, not the right of the broadcasters, which is paramount. [ ] It is the purpose of the First Amendment to preserve an uninhibited marketplace of ideas in which truth will ultimately prevail, rather than to countenance monopolization of that market, whether it be by the Government itself or a private licensee. [   ] "[S]peech concerning public affairs is more than self-expression; it is the essence of self-government." [ ] It is the right of the public to receive suitable access to social, political, esthetic, moral, and other ideas and experiences which is crucial here. That right may not constitutionally be abridged either by Congress or by the FCC.

B

Rather than confer frequency monopolies on a relatively small number of licensees, in a Nation of 200,000,000, the Government could surely have decreed that each frequency should be shared among all or some of those who wish to use it, each being assigned a portion of the broadcast day or the broadcast week. The ruling and regulations at issue here do not go quite so far. They assert that, under specified circumstances, a licensee must offer to make available a reasonable amount of broadcast time to those who have a view different from that which has already been expressed on his station. The expression of a political endorsement, or of a personal attack while dealing with a controversial public issue, simply triggers this time-sharing. As we have said, the First Amendment confers no right on licensees to prevent others from broadcasting on "their" frequencies, and no right to an unconditional monopoly of a scarce resource which the Government has denied others the right to use.

In terms of constitutional principle, and as enforced sharing of a scarce resource, the personal attack and political editorial rules are indistinguishable from the equal time provision of § 315, a specific enactment of Congress requiring stations to set aside reply time under specified circumstances and to which the fairness doctrine and these constituent regulations are important complements. That provision, which has been part of the law since 1927, Radio Act of 1927, § 18, 44 Stat. 1170, has been held valid by this Court as an obligation of the licensee relieving him of any power in any way to prevent or censor the broadcast, and thus insulating him from liability for defamation. The constitutionality of the statute under the First Amendment was unquestioned. [ ]

153

Nor can we say that it is inconsistent with the First Amendment goal of producing an informed public capable of conducting its own affairs to require a broadcaster to permit answers to personal attacks occurring in the course of discussing controversial issues, or to require that the political opponents of those endorsed by the station be given a chance to communicate with the public. Otherwise, station owners and a few networks would have unfettered power to make time available only to the highest bidders, to communicate only their own views on public issues, people and candidates, and to permit on the air only those with whom they agreed. There is no sanctuary in the First Amendment for unlimited private censorship operating in a medium not open to all.

> Freedom of the press from governmental interference under the First Amendment does not sanction repression of that freedom by private interests. [ ]

C

It is strenuously argued, however, that, if political editorials or personal attacks will trigger an obligation in broadcasters to afford the opportunity for expression to speakers who need not pay for time and whose views are unpalatable to the licensees, then broadcasters will be irresistibly forced to self-censorship, and their coverage of controversial public issues will be eliminated, or at least rendered wholly ineffective. Such a result would indeed be a serious matter, for, should licensees actually eliminate their coverage of controversial issues, the purposes of the doctrine would be stifled.

At this point, however, as the Federal Communications Commission has indicated, that possibility is, at best, speculative. The communications industry, and, in particular, the networks, have taken pains to present controversial issues in the past, and even now they do not assert that they intend to abandon their efforts in this regard. It would be better if the FCC's encouragement were never necessary to induce the broadcasters to meet their responsibility. And if experience with the administration of these doctrines indicates that they have the net effect of reducing, rather than enhancing, the volume and quality of coverage, there will be time enough to reconsider the constitutional implications. The fairness doctrine in the past has had no such overall effect.

That this will occur now seems unlikely, however, since, if present licensees should suddenly prove timorous, the Commission is not powerless to insist that they give adequate and fair attention to public issues. It does not violate the First Amendment to treat licensees given the privilege of using scarce radio frequencies as proxies for the entire community, obligated to give suitable time and attention to matters of great public concern. To condition the granting or renewal of licenses on a willingness to present representative community views on controversial issues is consistent with the ends and purposes of those constitutional provisions forbidding the abridgment of freedom of speech and freedom of the press. Congress need not stand idly by and permit those with licenses to ignore the problems which beset the people or to exclude from the airways anything but their own views of fundamental questions. The statute, long administrative practice, and cases are to this effect.

Licenses to broadcast do not confer ownership of designated frequencies, but only the temporary privilege of using them. [ ] Unless renewed, they expire within three years. [ ] The statute mandates the issuance of licenses if the "public convenience, interest, or necessity will be served thereby." [ ] In applying this standard, the Commission for 40 years has been choosing licensees based in part on their program proposals. In *FRC v. Nelson Bros. Bond & Mortgage Co* [ ], the Court noted that, in "view of the limited number of available broadcasting frequencies, the Congress has authorized allocation and licenses." In determining how best to allocate frequencies, the Federal Radio Commission considered the needs of competing communities and the programs offered by competing stations to meet those needs; moreover, if needs or programs shifted, the Commission could alter its allocations to reflect those shifts. [ ] In the same vein, in *FCC v. Pottsville Broadcasting Co.* [ ], the Court noted that the statutory standard was a supple instrument to effect congressional desires "to maintain . . . a grip on the dynamic aspects of radio transmission" and allay fears that, "in the absence of governmental control, the public interest might be subordinated to monopolistic domination in the broadcasting field." Three years later, the Court considered the validity of the Commission's chain broadcasting regulations, which, among other things, forbade stations from devoting too much time to network programs in order that there be suitable opportunity for local programs serving local needs. The Court upheld the regulations, unequivocally recognizing that the Commission was more than a traffic policeman concerned with the technical aspects of broadcasting and that it neither exceeded its powers under the statute nor transgressed the First Amendment in interesting itself in general program format and the kinds of programs broadcast by licensees. [ ]

D

The litigants embellish their First Amendment arguments with the contention that the regulations are so vague that their duties are impossible to discern. Of this point it is enough to say that, judging the validity of the regulations on their face as they are presented here, we cannot conclude that the FCC has been left a free hand to vindicate its own idiosyncratic conception of the public interest or of the requirements of free speech. Past adjudications by the FCC give added precision to the regulations; there was nothing vague about the FCC's specific ruling in *Red Lion* that Fred Cook should be provided an opportunity to reply. The regulations at issue in *RTNDA* could be employed in precisely the same way as the fairness doctrine was in *Red Lion*. Moreover, the FCC itself has recognized that the applicability of its regulations to situations beyond the scope of past cases may be questionable [ ], and will not impose sanctions in such cases without warning. We need not approve every aspect of the fairness doctrine to decide these cases, and we will not now pass upon the constitutionality of these regulations by envisioning the most extreme applications conceivable [ ], but will deal with those problems if and when they arise.

We need not and do not now ratify every past and future decision by the FCC with regard to programming. There is no question here of the Commission's refusal to permit the broadcaster to carry a particular program or to publish his own views; of a discriminatory refusal to require the licensee to broadcast certain views which have been denied access to the airwaves; of government censorship of a particular program contrary to § 326; or of the official government view dominating public broadcasting. Such questions would raise more serious First Amendment issues. But we do hold that the Congress and the Commission do not violate the First Amendment when they require a radio or television station to give reply time to answer personal attacks and political editorials.

E

It is argued that, even if, at one time, the lack of available frequencies for all who wished to use them justified the Government's choice of those who would best serve the public interest by acting as proxy for those who would present differing views, or by giving the latter access directly to broadcast facilities, this condition no longer prevails, so that continuing control is not justified. To this there are several answers.

Scarcity is not entirely a thing of the past. Advances in technology, such as microwave transmission, have led to more efficient utilization of the frequency spectrum, but uses for that spectrum have also gown apace. Portions of the spectrum must be reserved for vital uses unconnected with human communication, such as radionavigational aids used by aircraft and vessels. Conflicts have even emerged between such vital functions as defense preparedness and experimentation in methods of averting mid-air collisions through radio warning devices. "Land mobile services" such as police, ambulance, fire department, public utility, and other communications systems have been occupying an increasingly crowded portion of the frequency spectrum,{GO>22} and there are, apart from licensed amateur radio operators' equipment, 5,000,000 transmitters operated on the "citizens' band," which is also increasingly congested. Among the various uses for radio frequency space, including marine, aviation, amateur, military, and common carrier users, there are easily enough claimants to permit use of the whole with an even smaller allocation to broadcast radio and television uses than now exists.

Comparative hearings between competing applicants for broadcast spectrum space are by no means a thing of the past. The radio spectrum has become so congested that, at times, it has been necessary to suspend new applications. The very high frequency television spectrum is, in the country's major markets, almost entirely occupied, although space reserved for ultra high frequency television transmission, which is a relatively recent development as a commercially viable alternative, has not yet been completely filled.

The rapidity with which technological advances succeed one another to create more efficient use of spectrum space, on the one hand, and to create new uses for that space by ever-growing numbers of people, on the other, makes it unwise to speculate on the future allocation of that space. It is enough to say that the resource is one of considerable and growing importance whose scarcity impelled its regulation by an agency authorized by Congress. Nothing in this record, or in our own researches, convinces us that the resource is no longer one for which there are more immediate and potential uses than can be accommodated, and for which wise planning is essential. This does not mean, of course, that every possible wavelength must be occupied at every hour by some vital use in order to sustain the congressional judgment. The substantial capital investment required for many uses, in addition to the potentiality for confusion and interference inherent in any scheme for continuous kaleidoscopic reallocation of all available space may make this unfeasible. The allocation need not be made at such a breakneck pace that the objectives of the allocation are themselves imperiled.

Even where there are gaps in spectrum utilization, the fact remains that existing broadcasters have often attained their present position because of their initial government selection in competition with others before new technological advances opened new opportunities for further uses. Long experience in broadcasting, confirmed habits of listeners and viewers, network affiliation, and other advantages in program procurement give existing broadcasters a substantial advantage over new entrants, even where new entry is technologically possible. These advantages are the fruit of a preferred position conferred by the Government. Some present possibility for new entry by competing stations is not enough, in itself, to render unconstitutional the Government's effort to assure that a broadcaster's programming ranges widely enough to serve the public interest.

In view of the scarcity of broadcast frequencies, the Government's role in allocating those frequencies, and the legitimate claims of those unable without governmental assistance to gain access to those frequencies for expression of their views, we hold the regulations and ruling at issue here are both authorized by statute and constitutional. The judgment of the Court of Appeals in *Red Lion* is affirmed and that in *RTNDA* reversed, and the causes remanded for proceedings consistent with this opinion.

It is so ordered.

Not having heard oral argument in these cases, MR. JUSTICE DOUGLAS took no part in the Court's decision.

Turner Broadcasting System, Inc. v. Federal Communications Commission

Argued October 7, 1996
Decided March 31, 1997

520 U.S. 180, 117 S.Ct. 1174, 137 L.Ed.2d 369, 25 Med.L.Rptr. 1449

APPEAL FROM THE UNITED STATES DISTRICT COURT
FOR THE DISTRICT OF COLUMBIA

Syllabus

Sections 4 and 5 of the Cable Television Consumer Protection and Competition Act of 1992 (Cable Act) require cable television systems to dedicate some of their channels to local broadcast television stations. In *Turner Broadcasting System, Inc. v. FCC*, 512 U.S. 622 (*Turner*), this Court held these so-called "must-carry" provisions to be subject to intermediate First Amendment scrutiny under *United States v. O'Brien*, 391 U.S. 367, 377, whereby a content-neutral regulation will be sustained if it advances important governmental interests unrelated to the suppression of free speech and does not burden substantially more speech than necessary to further those interests. However, because a plurality considered the record, as then developed, insufficient to determine whether the provisions would in fact alleviate real harms in a direct and material way, and would not burden substantially more speech than necessary, the Court remanded the case. After 18 months of additional factfinding, the District Court granted summary judgment for the Government and other appellees, concluding that the expanded record contained substantial evidence supporting Congress' predictive judgment that the must-carry provisions further important governmental interests in preserving cable carriage of local broadcast stations, and that the provisions are narrowly tailored to promote those interests. This direct appeal followed.

Held: the judgment is affirmed.

910 F.Supp. 734 affirmed.

JUSTICE KENNEDY delivered the opinion of the Court with respect to all but a portion of Part II-A-1, concluding that the must-carry provisions are consistent with the First Amendment:

1. The record as it now stands supports Congress' predictive judgment that the must-carry provisions further important governmental interests.

(a) This Court decided in *Turner* [ ], and now reaffirms, that must-carry was designed to serve three interrelated, important governmental interests: (1) preserving the benefits of free, over-the-air local broadcast television, (2) promoting the widespread dissemination of information from a multiplicity of sources, and (3) promoting fair competition in the television programming market. Protecting non-cable households from loss of regular broadcasting service due to competition from cable systems is important because 40 percent of American households still rely on over-the-air signals for television programming. [ ] Moreover, there is a corresponding governmental purpose of the highest order in ensuring public access to a multiplicity of information sources [ ], and the Government has an interest in eliminating restraints on fair competition even when the regulated parties are engaged in protected expressive activity [ ]. The parties' attempts to recast these interests in forms more readily proved -- *i.e.,* the Government's claim that the loss of even a few broadcast stations is critically important and appellants' assertions that Congress' interest in preserving broadcasting is not implicated absent a showing that the entire industry would fail, and that its interest in assuring a multiplicity of information sources extends only as far as preserving a minimum amount of broadcast service -- are inconsistent with Congress' stated interests in enacting must-carry.

(b) Even in the realm of First Amendment questions, where Congress must base its conclusions upon substantial evidence, courts must accord deference to its findings as to the harm to be avoided and to the remedial measures adopted for that end, lest the traditional legislative authority to make predictive judgments when enacting nationwide regulatory policy be infringed. [ ] The courts' sole obligation is to assure that, in formulating its judgments, Congress has drawn reasonable inferences based on substantial evidence. [ ]

(c) The must-carry provisions serve important governmental interests "in a direct and effective way." [ ] Congress could reasonably conclude

159

from the substantial body of evidence before it that attaining cable carriage would be of increasing importance to ensuring broadcasters' economic viability, and that, absent legislative action, the free local off-air broadcast system was endangered. Such evidence amply indicated that: a broadcast station's viability depends to a material extent on its ability to secure cable carriage, and thereby to increase its audience size and revenues; broadcast stations had fallen into bankruptcy, curtailed their operations, and suffered serious reductions in operating revenues as a result of adverse carriage decisions by cable systems; stations without carriage encountered severe difficulties obtaining financing for operations; and the potentially adverse impact of losing carriage was increasing as the growth of "clustering" -- *i.e.,* the acquisition of as many cable systems in a given market as possible -- gave multiple system operators centralized control over more local markets. The reasonableness of the congressional judgment is confirmed by evidence assembled on remand that clearly establishes the importance of cable to broadcast stations and suggests that expansion in the cable industry was harming broadcasting. Although the record also contains evidence to support a contrary conclusion, the question is not whether Congress was correct as an objective matter, but whether the legislative conclusion was reasonable and supported by substantial evidence [ ]. Where, as here, that standard is satisfied, summary judgment is appropriate regardless of whether the evidence is in conflict. [ ]

2. The must-carry provisions do not burden substantially more speech than is necessary to further the governmental interests they promote [ ]. Appellants say must-carry's burden is great, but significant evidence adduced on remand indicates the vast majority of cable operators have not been affected in a significant manner. This includes evidence that: such operators have satisfied their must-carry obligations 87 percent of the time using previously unused channel capacity; 94.5 percent of the cable systems nationwide have not had to drop any programming; the remaining 5.5 percent have had to drop an average of only 1.22 services from their programming; operators nationwide carry 99.8 percent of the programming they carried before must-carry; and broadcast stations gained carriage on only 5,880 cable channels as a result of must-carry. The burden imposed by must-carry is congruent to the benefits it affords, because, as appellants concede, most of those 5,880 stations would be dropped in its absence. Must-carry therefore is narrowly tailored to preserve a multiplicity of broadcast stations for the 40 percent of American households without cable. [ ] The possibilities that must-carry will prohibit dropping a broadcaster even if the cable operator has no anticompetitive motives or if the broadcaster would survive without cable access are not so prevalent that they render must-carry substantially overbroad. This Court's precedents establish that it will not invalidate the preferred remedial scheme merely because some alternative solution is marginally less intrusive on a speaker's First Amendment interests. In any event, a careful examination of each of appellants' suggestions -- a more limited set of must-carry obligations modeled on those earlier used by the Federal Communications

Commission; use of so-called AB switches, giving consumers a choice of both cable and broadcast signals; a leased-access regime requiring cable operators to set aside channels for both broadcasters and cable programmers to use at a regulated price; subsidies for broadcasters; and a system of antitrust enforcement or an administrative complaint procedure -- reveals that none of them is an adequate alternative to must-carry for achieving the Government's aims. Because it has received only the most glancing attention from the District Court and the parties, prudence dictates that this Court not reach appellants' challenge to the Cable Act provision requiring carriage of low-power stations in certain circumstances.

JUSTICE KENNEDY, joined by The Chief JUSTICE, JUSTICE STEVENS, and JUSTICE SOUTER, and by JUSTICE BREYER in part, concluded in Part II-A-1 that the expanded record contains substantial evidence to support Congress' conclusion that enactment of must-carry was justified by a real threat to local broadcasting's economic health. The harm Congress feared was that broadcast stations dropped or denied cable carriage would be at a serious risk of financial difficulty [ ], and would deteriorate to a substantial degree or fail altogether [ ]. The evidence before Congress, as supplemented on remand, indicated, *inter alia,* that: cable operators had considerable and growing market power over local video programming markets in 1992; the industry's expanding horizontal and vertical integration would give cable operators increasing ability and incentive to drop, or reposition to less-viewed channels, independent local broadcast stations, which competed with the operators for audiences and advertisers; significant numbers of local broadcasters had already been dropped; and, absent must-carry, additional stations would be deleted, repositioned, or not carried in an attempt to capture their local advertising revenues to offset waning cable subscription growth. The reasonableness of Congress' predictive judgment is also supported by additional evidence, developed on remand, indicating that the percentage of local broadcasters not carried on the typical cable system is increasing, and that the growth of cable systems' market power has proceeded apace, better enabling them to sell their own reach to potential advertisers, and to deny broadcast competitors access to all or substantially all the cable homes in a market area.

JUSTICE BREYER, although agreeing that the statute satisfies the intermediate scrutiny standard set forth in *United States v. O'Brien,* 391 U.S. 367, rested his conclusion not upon the principal opinion's analysis of the statute's efforts to promote fair competition, but rather upon its discussion of the statute's other two objectives. He therefore joined the opinion of the Court except insofar as Part II-A-1 relies on an anticompetitive rationale.

KENNEDY, J., announced the judgment of the Court and delivered the opinion of the Court, except as to a portion of Part II-A-1. REHNQUIST, C.J., and STEVENS and SOUTER, JJ., joined that opinion in full, and BREYER, J., joined except insofar as Part II-A-1 relied on an anticompetitive rationale. STEVENS, J., filed a concurring opinion.

161

BREYER, J., filed an opinion concurring in part. O'CONNOR, J., filed a dissenting opinion, in which SCALIA, THOMAS, and GINSBURG, JJ., joined.

KENNEDY, J., lead opinion

Sections 4 and 5 of the Cable Television Consumer Protection and Competition Act of 1992 require cable television systems to dedicate some of their channels to local broadcast television stations. Earlier in this case, we held the so-called "must-carry" provisions to be content-neutral restrictions on speech, subject to intermediate First Amendment scrutiny under *United States v. O'Brien* [ ] (1968). A plurality of the Court considered the record as then developed insufficient to determine whether the provisions were narrowly tailored to further important governmental interests, and we remanded the case to the District Court for the District of Columbia for additional factfinding.

On appeal from the District Court's grant of summary judgment for appellees, the case now presents the two questions left open during the first appeal: first, whether the record as it now stands supports Congress' predictive judgment that the must-carry provisions further important governmental interests; and second, whether the provisions do not burden substantially more speech than necessary to further those interests. We answer both questions in the affirmative, and conclude the must-carry provisions are consistent with the First Amendment.

I

An outline of the Cable Act, Congress' purposes in adopting it, and the facts of the case are set out in detail in our first opinion [ ] (*Turner*), and a more abbreviated summary will suffice here. Soon after Congress enacted the Cable Television Consumer Protection and Competition Act of 1992 [ ] (Cable Act), appellants brought suit against the United States and the Federal Communications Commission (both referred to here as the Government) in the United States District Court for the District of Columbia, challenging the constitutionality of the must-carry provisions under the First Amendment. The three-judge District Court, in a divided opinion, granted summary judgment for the Government and intervenor-defendants. A majority of the court sustained the must-carry provisions under the intermediate standard of scrutiny set forth in *United States v. O'Brien, supra,* concluding the must-carry provisions were content-neutral "industry-specific antitrust and fair trade" legislation narrowly tailored to preserve local broadcasting beset by monopoly power in most cable systems, growing concentration in the cable industry, and concomitant risks of programming decisions driven by anticompetitive policies. [ ]

On appeal, we agreed with the District Court that must-carry does not "distinguish favored speech from disfavored speech on the basis of the ideas or views expressed," [ ], but is a content-neutral regulation designed "to prevent cable operators from exploiting their economic

162

power to the detriment of broadcasters," and

> to ensure that all Americans, especially those unable to subscribe to cable, have access to free television programming -- whatever its content.

[ ] We held that, under the intermediate level of scrutiny applicable to content-neutral regulations, must-carry would be sustained if it were shown to further an important or substantial governmental interest unrelated to the suppression of free speech, provided the incidental restrictions did not "burden substantially more speech than is necessary to further" those interests. [ ]. Although we "ha[d] no difficulty concluding" the interests must-carry was designed to serve were important in the abstract [ ], a four-Justice plurality concluded genuine issues of material fact remained regarding whether "the economic health of local broadcasting is in genuine jeopardy and need of the protections afforded by must-carry," and whether must-carry "`burden[s] substantially more speech than is necessary to further the government's legitimate interests.'" [ ] JUSTICE STEVENS would have found the statute valid on the record then before us; he agreed to remand the case to ensure a judgment of the Court, and the case was returned to the District Court for further proceedings. [ ]

The District Court oversaw another 18 months of factual development on remand "yielding a record of tens of thousands of pages" of evidence [ ], comprised of materials acquired during Congress' three years of pre-enactment hearings [ ], as well as additional expert submissions, sworn declarations and testimony, and industry documents obtained on remand. Upon consideration of the expanded record, a divided panel of the District Court again granted summary judgment to appellees. [ ] The majority determined "Congress drew reasonable inferences" from substantial evidence before it to conclude that "in the absence of must-carry rules, `significant' numbers of broadcast stations would be refused carriage." [ ] The court found Congress drew on studies and anecdotal evidence indicating "cable operators had already dropped, refused to carry, or adversely repositioned significant numbers of local broadcasters," and suggesting that, in the vast majority of cases, the broadcasters were not restored to carriage in their prior position. [ ] Noting evidence in the record before Congress and the testimony of experts on remand [ ], the court decided the noncarriage problem would grow worse without must-carry because cable operators had refrained from dropping broadcast stations during Congress' investigation and the pendency of this litigation [ ], and possessed increasing incentives to use their growing economic power to capture broadcasters' advertising revenues and promote affiliated cable programmers. [ ] The court concluded "substantial evidence before Congress" supported the predictive judgment that a local broadcaster denied carriage "would suffer financial harm and possible ruin." [ ] It cited evidence that adverse carriage actions decrease broadcasters' revenues by reducing audience levels, *id.* at 744-745, and evidence that the invalidation of the FCC's prior must-carry regulations had contributed to declining growth in the broadcast industry. [ ]

The court held must-carry to be narrowly tailored to promote the Government's legitimate interests. It found the effects of must-carry on cable operators to be minimal, noting evidence that: most cable systems had not been required to add any broadcast stations since the rules were adopted; only 1.2 percent of all cable channels had been devoted to broadcast stations added because of must-carry; and the burden was likely to diminish as channel capacity expanded in the future. [ ] The court proceeded to consider a number of alternatives to must-carry that appellants had proposed, including: a leased-access regime, under which cable operators would be required to set aside channels for both broadcasters and cable programmers to use at a regulated price; use of so-called AB switches, giving consumers a choice of both cable and broadcast signals; a more limited set of must-carry obligations modeled on those earlier used by the FCC; and subsidies for broadcasters. The court rejected each in turn, concluding that, "even assuming that [the alternatives] would be less burdensome" on cable operators' First Amendment interests, they "are not in any respect as effective in achieving the government's [interests]." [ ] Judge Jackson would have preferred a trial to summary judgment, but concurred in the judgment of the court. [ ]

Judge Williams dissented. His review of the record, and particularly evidence concerning growth in the number of broadcasters, industry advertising revenues, and per-station profits during the period without must-carry, led him to conclude the broadcast industry as a whole would not be "'seriously jeopardized'" in the absence of must-carry. [ ] Judge Williams acknowledged the Government had a legitimate interest in preventing anticompetitive behavior, and accepted that cable operators have incentives to discriminate against broadcasters in favor of their own vertically integrated cable programming. [ ] He would have granted summary judgment for appellants nonetheless on the ground must-carry is not narrowly tailored. In his view, must-carry constitutes a significant (though "diminish[ing]" [ ] burden on cable operators' and programmers' rights [ ], and the Cable Act's must-carry provisions suppress more speech than necessary because "less restrictive" alternatives exist to accomplish the Government's legitimate objectives. [ ]

This direct appeal followed. [ ] We noted probable jurisdiction [ ], and we now affirm.

II

We begin where the plurality ended in *Turner,* applying the standards for intermediate scrutiny enunciated in *O'Brien.* A content-neutral regulation will be sustained under the First Amendment if it advances important governmental interests unrelated to the suppression of free speech and does not burden substantially more speech than necessary to further those interests. [ ] As noted in *Turner,* must-carry was designed to serve "three interrelated interests: (1) preserving the benefits of free, over-the-air local broadcast television, (2) promoting the widespread dissemination of information from a multiplicity of sources, and (3) promoting fair competition in the market for television programming." [ ] We decided then, and now reaffirm, that each of those is an important governmental interest. We have been most explicit in holding that

> "protecting non-cable households from loss of regular television broadcasting service due to competition from cable systems" is an important federal interest.

[ ] Forty percent of American households continue to rely on over-the-air signals for television programming. Despite the growing importance of cable television and alternative technologies, "`broadcasting is demonstrably a principal source of information and entertainment for a great part of the Nation's population.'" [ ] We have identified a corresponding "governmental purpose of the highest order" in ensuring public access to "a multiplicity of information sources" [ ]. And it is undisputed the Government has an interest in

> eliminating restraints on fair competition . . . , even when the individuals or entities subject to particular regulations are engaged in expressive activity protected by the First Amendment.

[ ]

On remand, and again before this Court, both sides have advanced new interpretations of these interests in an attempt to recast them in forms "more readily proven." [ ] The Government downplays the importance of showing a risk to the broadcast industry as a whole and suggests the loss of even a few broadcast stations "is a matter of critical importance." [ ] Taking the opposite approach, appellants argue Congress' interest in preserving broadcasting is not implicated unless it is shown the industry as a whole would fail without must-carry [ ], and suggest Congress' legitimate interest in "assuring that the public has access to a multiplicity of information sources" [ ], extends only as far as preserving "a minimum amount of television broadcast service." [ ]

These alternative formulations are inconsistent with Congress' stated interests in enacting must-carry. The congressional findings do not reflect concern that, absent must-carry, "a few voices" [ ], would be lost from the television marketplace. In explicit factual findings, Congress expressed clear concern that the "marked shift in market share from broadcast television to cable television services" [ ], resulting from increasing market penetration by cable services, as well as the expanding horizontal concentration and vertical integration of cable operators, combined to give cable systems the incentive and ability to delete, reposition, or decline carriage to local broadcasters in an attempt to favor affiliated cable programmers. [ ] Congress predicted that "absent the reimposition of [must-carry], additional local broadcast signals will be deleted, repositioned, or not carried" [ ], with the end result that "the economic viability of free local broadcast television and its ability to originate quality local programming will be seriously jeopardized." [ ]

165

At the same time, Congress was under no illusion that there would be a complete disappearance of broadcast television nationwide in the absence of must-carry. Congress recognized broadcast programming (and network programming in particular) "remains the most popular programming on cable systems" [ ]. Indeed, reflecting the popularity and strength of some broadcasters, Congress included in the Cable Act a provision permitting broadcasters to charge cable systems for carriage of the broadcasters' signals. [ ] Congress was concerned not that broadcast television would disappear in its entirety without must-carry, but that, without it, "significant numbers of broadcast stations will be refused carriage on cable systems," and those "broadcast stations denied carriage will either deteriorate to a substantial degree or fail altogether." 512 U.S. at GO>666. [ ] ... Nor do the congressional findings support appellants' suggestion that legitimate legislative goals would be satisfied by the preservation of a rump broadcasting industry providing a minimum of broadcast service to Americans without cable. We have noted that

> "it has long been a basic tenet of national communications policy that 'the widest possible dissemination of information from diverse and antagonistic sources is essential to the welfare of the public.'"

[ ] Consistent with this objective, the Cable Act's findings reflect a concern that congressional action was necessary to prevent "a reduction in the number of media voices available to consumers." [ ] Congress identified a specific interest in "ensuring [the] continuation" of "the local origination of [broadcast] programming" [ ], an interest consistent with its larger purpose of promoting multiple types of media [ ], and found must-carry necessary "to serve the goals" of the original Communications Act of 1934 of "providing a fair, efficient, and equitable distribution of broadcast services" [ ]. In short, Congress enacted must-carry to

> preserve the existing structure of the Nation's broadcast television medium while permitting the concomitant expansion and development of cable television.

[ ]

Although Congress set no definite number of broadcast stations sufficient for these purposes, the Cable Act's requirement that all cable operators with more than 12 channels set aside one-third of their channel capacity for local broadcasters [ ], refutes the notion that Congress contemplated preserving only a bare minimum of stations. Congress' evident interest in "preserv[ing] the existing structure" [ ] of the broadcast industry discloses a purpose to prevent any significant reduction in the multiplicity of broadcast programming sources available to non-cable households. To the extent the appellants question the substantiality of the Government's interest in preserving something more than a minimum number of stations in each community, their position is meritless. It is for Congress to decide how much local broadcast television should be preserved for non-cable households, and the validity of its determination

166

"does not turn on a judge's agreement with the responsible decisionmaker concerning" . . . the degree to which [the Government's] interests should be promoted.

[ ] ... The dissent proceeds on the assumption that must-carry is designed solely to be (and can only be justified as) a measure to protect broadcasters from cable operators' anticompetitive behavior. [ ] Federal policy, however, has long favored preserving a multiplicity of broadcast outlets regardless of whether the conduct that threatens it is motivated by anticompetitive animus or rises to the level of an antitrust violation. [ ] ... Broadcast television is an important source of information to many Americans. Though it is but one of many means for communication, by tradition and use for decades now it has been an essential part of the national discourse on subjects across the whole broad spectrum of speech, thought, and expression. [ ] Congress has an independent interest in preserving a multiplicity of broadcasters to ensure that all households have access to information and entertainment on an equal footing with those who subscribe to cable.

A

On our earlier review, we were constrained by the state of the record to assessing the importance of the Government's asserted interests when "viewed in the abstract" [ ]. The expanded record now permits us to consider whether the must-carry provisions were designed to address a real harm, and whether those provisions will alleviate it in a material way. [ ] We turn first to the harm or risk which prompted Congress to act. The Government's assertion that "the economic health of local broadcasting is in genuine jeopardy and in need of the protections afforded by must-carry" [ ], rests on two component propositions: first, "significant numbers of broadcast stations will be refused carriage on cable systems" absent must-carry [ ]. Second, "the broadcast stations denied carriage will either deteriorate to a substantial degree or fail altogether." [ ]

In reviewing the constitutionality of a statute, "courts must accord substantial deference to the predictive judgments of Congress." [ ] Our sole obligation is "to assure that, in formulating its judgments, Congress has drawn reasonable inferences based on substantial evidence." [ ] As noted in the first appeal, substantiality is to be measured in this context by a standard more deferential than we accord to judgments of an administrative agency. [ ] We owe Congress' findings deference in part because the institution "is far better equipped than the judiciary to `amass and evaluate the vast amounts of data' bearing upon" legislative questions. [ ] ... This principle has special significance in cases, like this one, involving congressional judgments concerning regulatory schemes of inherent complexity and assessments about the likely interaction of industries undergoing rapid economic and technological change. Though different in degree, the deference to Congress is in one respect akin to deference owed to administrative agencies because of their expertise. [ ] ... This is not the sum of the matter, however. We owe Congress' findings

167

an additional measure of deference out of respect for its authority to exercise the legislative power. Even in the realm of First Amendment questions where Congress must base its conclusions upon substantial evidence, deference must be accorded to its findings as to the harm to be avoided and to the remedial measures adopted for that end, lest we infringe on traditional legislative authority to make predictive judgments when enacting nationwide regulatory policy.

1

We have no difficulty in finding a substantial basis to support Congress' conclusion that a real threat justified enactment of the must-carry provisions. We examine first the evidence before Congress and then the further evidence presented to the District Court on remand to supplement the congressional determination.

As to the evidence before Congress, there was specific support for its conclusion that cable operators had considerable and growing market power over local video programming markets. Cable served at least 60 percent of American households in 1992 [   ], and evidence indicated cable market penetration was projected to grow beyond 70 percent. [   ] As Congress noted [   ], cable operators possess a local monopoly over cable households. Only one percent of communities are served by more than one cable system [   ]. Even in communities with two or more cable systems, in the typical case each system has a local monopoly over its subscribers. [   ] Cable operators thus exercise

> control over most (if not all) of the television programming that is channeled into the subscriber's home . . . , [and] can thus silence the voice of competing speakers with a mere flick of the switch.

[   ]

Evidence indicated the structure of the cable industry would give cable operators increasing ability and incentive to drop local broadcast stations from their systems, or reposition them to a less-viewed channel. Horizontal concentration was increasing as a small number of multiple system operators (MSO's) acquired large numbers of cable systems nationwide. [   ] The trend was accelerating, giving the MSO's increasing market power. In 1985, the 10 largest MSO's controlled cable systems serving slightly less than 42 percent of all cable subscribers; by 1989, the figure was nearly 54 percent [   ] Vertical integration in the industry also was increasing. As Congress was aware, many MSO's owned or had affiliation agreements with cable programmers. [   ] Evidence indicated that before 1984 cable operators had equity interests in 38 percent of cable programming networks. In the late 1980's, 64 percent of new cable programmers were held in vertical ownership. [   ] Congress concluded that "vertical integration gives cable operators the incentive and ability to favor their affiliated programming services" [   ]; a conclusion that even Judge Williams' dissent conceded to be reasonable. [   ] Extensive testimony indicated that cable operators would have an incentive to drop local broadcasters and to favor affiliated programmers ... Though the dissent criticizes our reliance on evidence provided to Congress by parties that are private appellees here, [ ], that argument displays a lack of regard for Congress' factfinding function. It is the nature of the legislative process to consider the submissions of the parties most affected by legislation. Appellants too sent representatives before Congress to try to persuade them of their side of the debate. [ ] After hearing years of testimony, and reviewing volumes of documentary evidence and studies offered by both sides, Congress concluded that the cable industry posed a threat to broadcast television. The Constitution gives to Congress the role of weighing conflicting evidence in the legislative process. Even when the resulting regulation touches on First Amendment concerns, we must give considerable deference, in examining the evidence, to Congress' findings and conclusions, including its findings and conclusions with respect to conflicting economic predictions. [ ] Furthermore, much of the testimony, though offered by interested parties, was supported by verifiable information and citation to independent sources. [ ]

The reasonableness of Congress' conclusion was borne out by the evidence on remand, which also reflected cable industry favoritism for integrated programmers ... In addition, evidence before Congress, supplemented on remand, indicated that cable systems would have incentives to drop local broadcasters in favor of other programmers less likely to compete with them for audience and advertisers. Independent local broadcasters tend to be the closest substitutes for cable programs, because their programming tends to be similar, [ ], and because both primarily target the same type of advertiser: those interested in cheaper (and more frequent) ad spots than are typically available on network affiliates. [ ] With expanded viewership, broadcast presents a more competitive medium for television advertising. Empirical studies indicate that cable-carried broadcasters so enhance competition for advertising that even modest increases in the numbers of broadcast stations carried on cable are correlated with significant decreases in advertising revenue to cable systems. [ ] Empirical evidence also indicates that demand for premium cable services (such as pay-per-view) is reduced when a cable system carries more independent broadcasters. [ ] Thus, operators stand to benefit by dropping broadcast stations. [ ]

Cable systems also have more systemic reasons for seeking to disadvantage broadcast stations: simply stated, cable has little interest in assisting, through carriage, a competing medium of communication. As one cable industry executive put it, "our job is to promote cable television, not broadcast television." [ ] ... Evidence adduced on remand indicated cable systems have little incentive to carry, and a significant incentive to drop, broadcast stations that will only be strengthened by access to the 60% of the television market that cable typically controls. [ ] Congress could therefore reasonably conclude that cable systems would drop broadcasters in favor of programmers -- even unaffiliated ones -- less likely to compete with them for audience and advertisers. The cap on carriage of affiliates included in the Cable Act [ ], and relied on by the dissent [ ], is of limited utility in protecting broadcasters.

169

The dissent contends Congress could not reasonably conclude cable systems would engage in such predation because cable operators, whose primary source of revenue is subscriptions, would not risk dropping a widely viewed broadcast station in order to capture advertising revenues. [ ] However, if viewers are faced with the choice of sacrificing a handful of broadcast stations to gain access to dozens of cable channels (plus network affiliates), it is likely they would still subscribe to cable even if they would prefer the dropped television stations to the cable programming that replaced them. Substantial evidence introduced on remand bears this out: With the exception of a handful of very popular broadcast stations (typically network affiliates), a cable system's choice between carrying a cable programmer or broadcast station has little or no effect on cable subscriptions, and subscribership thus typically does not bear on carriage decisions. [ ]

It was more than a theoretical possibility in 1992 that cable operators would take actions adverse to local broadcasters; indeed, significant numbers of broadcasters had already been dropped. The record before Congress contained extensive anecdotal evidence about scores of adverse carriage decisions against broadcast stations. [ ] Congress considered an FCC-sponsored study detailing cable system carriage practices in the wake of decisions by the United States Court of Appeals for the District of Columbia Circuit striking down prior must-carry regulations. [ ] It indicated that, in 1988, 280 out of 912 responding broadcast stations had been dropped or denied carriage in 1,533 instances. [ ] Even assuming that every station dropped or denied coverage responded to the survey, it would indicate that nearly a quarter (21 percent) of the approximately 1,356 broadcast stations then in existence [ ], had been denied carriage. The same study reported 869 of 4,303 reporting cable systems had denied carriage to 704 broadcast stations in 1,820 instances, id. at 48, and 279 of those stations had qualified for carriage under the prior must-carry rules. [ ] A contemporaneous study of public television stations indicated that, in the vast majority of cases, dropped stations were not restored to the cable service. [ ]

Substantial evidence demonstrated that absent must-carry the already "serious" [ ], problem of noncarriage would grow worse because "additional local broadcast signals will be deleted, repositioned, or not carried" [ ]. The record included anecdotal evidence showing the cable industry was acting with restraint in dropping broadcast stations in an effort to discourage reregulation. [ ] There was also substantial evidence that advertising revenue would be of increasing importance to cable operators as subscribership growth began to flatten, providing a steady, increasing incentive to deny carriage to local broadcasters in an effort to capture their advertising revenue. [ ] A contemporaneous FCC report noted that "[c]able operators' incentive to deny carriage . . . appears to be particularly great as against local broadcasters." [ ]. Then-FCC Commissioner James Quello warned Congress that the carriage problems

occurring today are just the "tip of the iceberg." These activities come at a time when the cable industry is just beginning to recognize the importance of local advertising.

[ ] Quello continued:

As [cable] systems mature and penetration levels off, systems will turn increasingly to advertising for revenues. The incentive to deny carriage to local stations is a logical, rational, and, without must carry, a legal business strategy.

[ ] The FCC advised Congress the "diversity in broadcast television service . . . will be jeopardized if this situation continues unredressed."
[ ]

Additional evidence developed on remand supports the reasonableness of Congress' predictive judgment. Approximately 11 percent of local broadcasters were not carried on the typical cable system in 1989. [ ] The figure had grown to even more significant proportions by 1992. According to one of appellants' own experts, between 19 and 31 percent of all local broadcast stations, including network affiliates, were not carried by the typical cable system. [ ] Based on the same data, another expert concluded that 47 percent of local independent commercial stations, and 36 percent of noncommercial stations, were not carried by the typical cable system. The rate of noncarriage was even higher for new stations. [ ] Appellees introduced evidence drawn from an empirical study concluding the 1988 FCC survey substantially underestimated the actual number of drops [ ], and the noncarriage problem grew steadily worse during the period without must-carry. By the time the Cable Act was passed, 1,261 broadcast stations had been dropped for at least one year, in a total of 7,945 incidents. [ ]

The dissent cites evidence indicating that many dropped broadcasters were stations few viewers watch, [ ], and it suggests that must-carry thwarts non-cable viewers' preferences. [ ] Undoubtedly, viewers without cable -- the immediate, though not sole, beneficiaries of efforts to preserve broadcast television -- would have a strong preference for carriage of any broadcast program over any cable program, for the simple reason that it helps to preserve a medium to which they have access. The methodological flaws in the cited evidence are of concern. [ ] Even aside from that, the evidence overlooks that the broadcasters added by must-carry had ratings greater than or equal to the cable programs they replaced. [ ] ... On average, even the lowest-rated station added pursuant to must-carry had ratings better than or equal to at least nine basic cable program services carried on the system. [ ] If cable systems refused to carry certain local broadcast stations because of their subscribers' preferences for the cable services carried in their place, one would expect that all cable programming services would have ratings exceeding those of broadcasters not carried. That is simply not the case.

The evidence on remand also indicated that the growth of cable systems' market power proceeded apace. The trend towards greater horizontal concentration continued, driven by "[e]nhanced growth prospects for advertising sales." [ ] Paul Kagan Assocs., Inc, Cable TV Advertising 1 (Sept. 30, 1994) (App. 301). MSO's began to gain control of as many cable systems in a given market as they could, in a trend known as "clustering." [ ] Cable systems looked increasingly to advertising (and especially local advertising) for revenue growth [ ] ... The vertical integration of the cable industry also continued, so by 1994, MSO's serving about 70 percent of the Nation's cable subscribers held equity interests in cable programmers. [ ] The FTC study the dissent cites [ ], takes a skeptical view of the potential for cable systems to engage in anticompetitive behavior, but concedes the risk of anticompetitive carriage denials is "most plausible" when "the cable system's franchise area is large relative to the local area served by the affected broadcast station" [ ], and when "a system's penetration rate is both high and relatively unresponsive to the system's carriage decisions," *id.* at 18 (App. 175). That describes "precisely what is happening" as large cable operators expand their control over individual markets through clustering. [ ] As they do so, they are better able to sell their own reach to potential advertisers, and to limit the access of broadcast competitors by denying them access to all or substantially all the cable homes in the market area. [ ]

This is not a case in which we are called upon to give our best judgment as to the likely economic consequences of certain financial arrangements or business structures, or to assess competing economic theories and predictive judgments, as we would in a case arising, say, under the antitrust laws.

> Statutes frequently require courts to make policy judgments. The Sherman Act, for example, requires courts to delve deeply into the theory of economic organization.

[ ] The issue before us is whether, given conflicting views of the probable development of the television industry, Congress had substantial evidence for making the judgment that it did. We need not put our imprimatur on Congress' economic theory in order to validate the reasonableness of its judgment.

2

The harm Congress feared was that stations dropped or denied carriage would be at a "serious risk of financial difficulty" [ ], and would "deteriorate to a substantial degree or fail altogether." [ ] Congress had before it substantial evidence to support its conclusion. Congress was advised the viability of a broadcast station depends to a material extent on its ability to secure cable carriage. [ ] One broadcast industry executive explained it this way:

> Simply put, a television station's audience size directly translates into revenue -- large audiences attract larger revenues, through the sale of advertising time. If a station is not carried on cable, and thereby loses a substantial portion of its audience, it will lose revenue. With less revenue, the station can not serve its community as well. The station will have less

money to invest in equipment and programming. The attractiveness of its programming will lessen, as will its audience. Revenues will continue to decline, and the cycle will repeat.

[   ] Empirical research in the record before Congress confirmed the "`direct correlation [between] size in audience and station [advertising] revenues" [   ], and that viewership was in turn heavily dependent on cable carriage. [   ]

Considerable evidence, consisting of statements compiled from dozens of broadcasters who testified before Congress and the FCC, confirmed that broadcast stations had fallen into bankruptcy [   ], curtailed their broadcast operations [   ], and suffered serious reductions in operating revenues as a result of adverse carriage decisions by cable systems. [   ] The record also reflected substantial evidence that stations without cable carriage encountered severe difficulties obtaining financing for operations, reflecting the financial markets' judgment that the prospects are poor for broadcasters unable to secure carriage. [   ] Evidence before Congress suggested the potential adverse impact of losing carriage was increasing as the growth of clustering gave MSO's centralized control over more local markets. [   ] Congress thus had ample basis to conclude that attaining cable carriage would be of increasing importance to ensuring a station's viability. We hold Congress could conclude from the substantial body of evidence before it that, "absent legislative action, the free local off-air broadcast system is endangered." [   ]

The evidence assembled on remand confirms the reasonableness of the congressional judgment. Documents produced on remand reflect that internal cable industry studies

> clearly establis[h] the importance of cable television to broadcast television stations. Because viewership equates to ratings and in turn ratings equate to revenues, it is unlikely that broadcast stations could afford to be off the cable system's lineup for any extended period of time.

[   ] Another study prepared by a large MSO in 1993 concluded that

> [w]ith cable penetration now exceeding 70% in many markets, the ability of a broadcast television station to easily reach its audience through cable television is crucial.

[   ] The study acknowledged that, even in a market with significantly below-average cable penetration, "[t]he loss of cable carriage could cause a significant decrease in a station's ratings and a resulting loss in advertising revenues." [   ] For an average market, "the impact would be even greater." [   ] The study determined that for a popular station in a major television market, even modest reductions in carriage could result in sizeable reductions in revenue. A 5 percent reduction in cable viewers, for example, would result in a $1.48 million reduction in gross revenue for the station. [   ]

173

To be sure, the record also contains evidence to support a contrary conclusion. Appellants (and the dissent in the District Court) make much of the fact that the number of broadcast stations and their advertising revenue continued to grow during the period without must-carry, albeit at a diminished rate. Evidence introduced on remand indicated that only 31 broadcast stations actually went dark during the period without must-carry (one of which failed after a tornado destroyed its transmitter), and during the same period some 263 new stations signed on the air. [ ] New evidence appellants produced on remand indicates the average cable system voluntarily carried local broadcast stations accounting for about 97 percent of television ratings in non-cable households. [ ] Appellants, as well as the dissent in the District Court, contend that in light of such evidence, it is clear "the must-carry law is not necessary to assure the economic viability of the broadcast system as a whole." [ ]

This assertion misapprehends the relevant inquiry. The question is not whether Congress, as an objective matter, was correct to determine must-carry is necessary to prevent a substantial number of broadcast stations from losing cable carriage and suffering significant financial hardship. Rather, the question is whether the legislative conclusion was reasonable and supported by substantial evidence in the record before Congress. [ ] In making that determination, we are not to "reweigh the evidence *de novo,* or to replace Congress' factual predictions with our own." [ ] Rather, we are simply to determine if the standard is satisfied. If it is, summary judgment for defendants-appellees is appropriate regardless of whether the evidence is in conflict. We have noted in another context, involving less deferential review than is at issue here, that

> "the possibility of drawing two inconsistent conclusions from the evidence does not prevent . . . [a] finding from being supported by substantial evidence."

[ ] Although evidence of continuing growth in broadcast could have supported the opposite conclusion, a reasonable interpretation is that expansion in the cable industry was causing harm to broadcasting. Growth continued, but the rate of growth fell to a considerable extent during the period without must-carry (from 4.5 percent in 1986 to 1.7 percent by 1992), and appeared to be tapering off further. [ ] At the same time, "in an almost unprecedented development" [ ], stations began to fail in increasing numbers. [ ] Broadcast advertising revenues declined in real terms by 11 percent between 1986 and 1991, during a period in which cable's real advertising revenues nearly doubled. [ ] While these phenomena could be thought to stem from factors quite separate from the increasing market power of cable (for example, a recession in 1990-1992), it was for Congress to determine the better explanation. We are not at liberty to substitute our judgment for the reasonable conclusion of a legislative body. [ ] It is true the number of bankruptcies among local broadcasters was small; but Congress could forecast continuance of the "unprecedented" five-year downward trend

and conclude the station failures of 1985-1992 were, as Commissioner Quello warned, the tip of the iceberg. A fundamental principle of legislation is that Congress is under no obligation to wait until the entire harm occurs but may act to prevent it. "An industry need not be in its death throes before Congress may act to protect it from economic harm threatened by a monopoly." [ ] As a Senate Committee noted in a Report on the Cable Act,

> we need not wait until widespread further harm has occurred to the system of local broadcasting or to competition in the video market before taking action to forestall such consequences. Congress is allowed to make a rational predication of the consequences of inaction and of the effects of regulation in furthering governmental interests.

[ ]

Despite the considerable evidence before Congress and adduced on remand indicating that the significant numbers of broadcast stations are at risk, the dissent believes yet more is required before Congress could act. It demands more information about which of the dropped broadcast stations still qualify for mandatory carriage [ ]; about the broadcast markets in which adverse decisions take place [ ]; and about the features of the markets in which bankrupt broadcast stations were located prior to their demise. [ ] The level of detail in factfinding required by the dissent would be an improper burden for courts to impose on the Legislative Branch. That amount of detail is as unreasonable in the legislative context as it is constitutionally unwarranted.

> Congress is not obligated, when enacting its statutes, to make a record of the type that an administrative agency or court does to accommodate judicial review.

[ ]

We think it apparent must-carry serves the Government's interests "in a direct and effective way." [ ] Must-carry ensures that a number of local broadcasters retain cable carriage, with the concomitant audience access and advertising revenues needed to support a multiplicity of stations. Appellants contend that even were this so, must-carry is broader than necessary to accomplish its goals. We turn to this question.

B

The second portion of the *O'Brien* inquiry concerns the fit between the asserted interests and the means chosen to advance them. Content-neutral regulations do not pose the same "inherent dangers to free expression" [ ], that content-based regulations do, and thus are subject to a less rigorous analysis, which affords the Government latitude in designing a regulatory solution. [ ] Under intermediate scrutiny, the Government may employ the means of its choosing "so long as the . . .

175

regulation promotes a substantial governmental interest that would be achieved less effectively absent the regulation," and does not "burden substantially more speech than is necessary to further" that interest. [ ]

The must-carry provisions have the potential to interfere with protected speech in two ways. First, the provisions restrain cable operators' editorial discretion in creating programming packages by "reduc[ing] the number of channels over which [they] exercise unfettered control." [ ] Second, the rules "render it more difficult for cable programmers to compete for carriage on the limited channels remaining." [ ]

Appellants say the burden of must-carry is great, but the evidence adduced on remand indicates the actual effects are modest. Significant evidence indicates the vast majority of cable operators have not been affected in a significant manner by must-carry. Cable operators have been able to satisfy their must-carry obligations 87 percent of the time using previously unused channel capacity [ ]; 94.5 percent of the 11,628 cable systems nationwide have not had to drop any programming in order to fulfill their must-carry obligations; the remaining 5.5 percent have had to drop an average of only 1.22 services from their programming [ ]; and cable operators nationwide carry 99.8 percent of the programming they carried before enactment of must-carry. [ ] Appellees note that only 1.18 percent of the approximately 500,000 cable channels nationwide is devoted to channels added because of must-carry [ ]; weighted for subscribership, the figure is 2.4 percent. [ ] Appellees contend the burdens of must-carry will soon diminish as cable channel capacity increases, as is occurring nationwide. [ ]

We do not understand appellants to dispute in any fundamental way the accuracy of those figures, only their significance. [ ] They note national averages fail to account for greater crowding on certain (especially urban) cable systems [ ], and contend that half of all cable systems, serving two-thirds of all cable subscribers, have no available capacity [ ]. Appellants argue that the rate of growth in cable programming outstrips cable operators' creation of new channel space, that the rate of cable growth is lower than claimed [ ], and that must-carry infringes First Amendment rights now irrespective of future growth. [ ] Finally, they say that, regardless of the percentage of channels occupied, must-carry still represents "thousands of real and individual infringements of speech." [ ]

While the parties' evidence is susceptible of varying interpretations, a few definite conclusions can be drawn about the burdens of must-carry. It is undisputed that broadcast stations gained carriage on 5,880 channels as a result of must-carry. While broadcast stations occupy another 30,006 cable channels nationwide, this carriage does not represent a significant First Amendment harm to either system operators or cable programmers, because those stations were carried voluntarily before 1992, and even appellants represent [ ] that the vast majority of those channels would continue to be carried in the absence of any legal obligation to do so. [ ] The 5,880 channels occupied by added broadcasters represent the actual burden of the regulatory scheme. Appellants concede most of those stations would be dropped in the absence of must-carry [ ], so the figure approximates the benefits of must-carry as well.

Because the burden imposed by must-carry is congruent to the benefits it affords, we conclude must-carry is narrowly tailored to preserve a multiplicity of broadcast stations for the 40 percent of American households without cable. [ ] ... Congress took steps to confine the breadth and burden of the regulatory scheme. For example, the more popular stations (which appellants concede would be carried anyway) will likely opt to be paid for cable carriage under the "retransmission consent" provision of the Cable Act; those stations will nonetheless be counted towards systems' must-carry obligations. Congress exempted systems of 12 or fewer channels, and limited the must-carry obligation of larger systems to one-third of capacity [ ]; allowed cable operators discretion in choosing which competing and qualified signals would be carried [ ]; and permitted operators to carry public stations on unused public, educational, and governmental channels in some circumstances [ ].

Appellants say the must-carry provisions are overbroad because they require carriage in some instances when the Government's interests are not implicated: the must-carry rules prohibit a cable system operator from dropping a broadcaster

> even if the operator has no anticompetitive motives, and even if the broadcaster that would have to be dropped . . . would survive without cable access.

[ ] We are not persuaded that either possibility is so prevalent that must-carry is substantially overbroad. As discussed [ ], cable systems serving 70 percent of subscribers are vertically integrated with cable programmers, so anticompetitive motives may be implicated in a majority of systems' decisions not to carry broadcasters. Some broadcasters will opt for must-carry although they would not suffer serious financial harm in its absence. [ ] Broadcasters with stronger finances tend, however, to be popular ones that ordinarily seek payment from cable systems for transmission, so their reliance on must-carry should be minimal. It appears, for example, that no more than a few hundred of the 500,000 cable channels nationwide are occupied by network affiliates opting for must-carry [ ], a number insufficient to render must-carry "substantially broader than necessary to achieve the government's interest." [ ] Even on the doubtful assumption that a narrower but still practicable must-carry rule could be drafted to exclude all instances in which the Government's interests are not implicated, our cases establish that content-neutral regulations are not "invalid simply because there is some imaginable alternative that might be less burdensome on speech." [ ]

Appellants posit a number of alternatives in an effort to demonstrate a less restrictive means to achieve the Government's aims. They ask us, in effect, to

> sif[t] through all the available or imagined alternative means of regulating [cable television] in order to determine whether the [Government's] solution was "the least intrusive means" of achieving the desired end,

an approach we rejected in *Ward v. Rock Against Racism* [ ]. This "less restrictive alternative analysis . . . has never been a part of the inquiry into the validity" of content-neutral regulations on speech. [ ] Our precedents establish that, when evaluating a content-neutral regulation which incidentally burdens speech, we will not invalidate the preferred remedial scheme because some alternative solution is marginally less intrusive on a speaker's First Amendment interests.

> So long as the means chosen are not substantially broader than necessary to achieve the government's interest, . . . the regulation will not be invalid simply because a court concludes that the government's interest could be adequately served by some less-speech-restrictive alternative.

[ ] ... It is well established a regulation's validity

> does not turn on a judge's agreement with the responsible decisionmaker concerning the most appropriate method for promoting significant government interests.

[ ]

In any event, after careful examination of each of the alternatives suggested by appellants, we cannot conclude that any of them is an adequate alternative to must-carry for promoting the Government's legitimate interests. First among appellants' suggested alternatives is a proposal to revive a more limited set of must-carry rules, known as the "*Century* rules" after the 1987 court decision striking them down [ ] Those rules included a minimum viewership standard for eligibility and limited the must-carry obligation to 25 percent of channel capacity. The parties agree only 14 percent of broadcasters added to cable systems under the Cable Act would be eligible for carriage under the *Century* rules. [ ] The *Century* rules, for the most part, would require carriage of the same stations a system would carry without statutory compulsion. While we acknowledge appellants' criticism of any rationale that more is better, the scheme in question does not place limitless must-carry obligations on cable system operators. In the final analysis, this alternative represents nothing more than appellants'

> "[dis]agreement with the responsible decisionmaker concerning" . . . the degree to which [the Government's] interests should be promoted.

[ ] Congress legislated in the shadow of *Quincy* and *Century Communications*. Its deliberations reflect awareness of the must-carry rules at issue in those cases [ ]; indeed, in drafting the must-carry provisions of the Cable Act, Congress made specific comparisons to the rules struck down in *Quincy Cable TV, Inc v. FCC* [ ]. The record reflects

a deliberate congressional choice to adopt the present levels of protection, to which this Court must defer.

The second alternative appellants urge is the use of input selector or "AB" switches, which, in combination with antennas, would permit viewers to switch between cable and broadcast input, allowing cable subscribers to watch broadcast programs not carried on cable. Congress examined the use of AB switches as an alternative to must-carry, and concluded it was "not an enduring or feasible method of distribution and . . . not in the public interest." [ ] The data showed that: many households lacked adequate antennas to receive broadcast signals [ ]; AB switches suffered from technical flaws [ ]; viewers might be required to reset channel settings repeatedly in order to view both UHF and cable channels [ ]; and installation and use of the switch with other common video equipment (such as videocassette recorders) could be "cumbersome or impossible." [ ] Even the cable industry trade association (one of appellants here) determined that "the AB switch is not a workable solution to the carriage problem." [ ] The group's engineering committee likewise concluded the switches suffered from technical problems, and that no solution "appear[ed] imminent." [ ] Congress also had before it "considerable evidence," including two empirical studies, that "it is rare for [cable subscribers] ever to switch to receive an over-the-air signal" [ ]. A 1991 study demonstrated that, even

> after several years of a government mandated program of providing A-B switches [to] consumers and a simultaneous education program on their use,

[ ], only 11.7 percent of all cable-connected television sets were attached to an antenna and had an AB switch. [ ] Of the small number of households possessing the switch, an even smaller number (only 38 percent) had ever used it. [ ] Congress' decision that use of AB switches was not a real alternative to must-carry was a reasonable one based on substantial evidence of technical shortcomings and lack of consumer acceptance. The reasonableness of its judgment was confirmed by additional evidence on remand that AB switches can create signal interference and add complexity to video systems, factors discouraging their use. [ ] ... Appellants also suggest a leased-access regime, under which both broadcasters and cable programmers would have equal access to cable channels at regulated rates. [ ] Appellants do not specify what kind of regime they would propose, or how it would operate, making this alternative difficult to compare to the must-carry rules. Whatever virtues the proposal might otherwise have, it would reduce the number of cable channels under cable systems' control in the same manner as must-carry. Because this alternative is aimed solely at addressing the bottleneck control of cable operators, it would not be as effective in achieving Congress' further goal of ensuring that significant programming remains available for the 40 percent of American households without cable. Indeed, unless the number of channels set aside for local broadcast stations were to decrease (sacrificing Congress' interest in preserving a multiplicity of broadcasters), additional channels

would have to be set aside for cable programmers, further reducing the channels under the systems' control. Furthermore, Congress was specific in noting that requiring payment for cable carriage was inimical to the interests it was pursuing, because of the burden it would impose on small broadcasters. [ ] Congress specifically prohibited such payments under the Cable Act. [ ]

Appellants next suggest a system of subsidies for financially weak stations. Appellants have not proposed any particular subsidy scheme, so it is difficult to determine whether this option presents a feasible means of achieving the Government's interests, let alone one preferable to must-carry under the First Amendment. To begin with, a system of subsidies would serve a very different purpose than must-carry. Must-carry is intended not to guarantee the financial health of all broadcasters, but to ensure a base number of broadcasters survive to provide service to non-cable households. Must-carry is simpler to administer and less likely to involve the Government in making content-based determinations about programming. The must-carry rules distinguish between categories of speakers based solely on the technology used to communicate. The rules acknowledge cable systems' expertise by according them discretion to determine which broadcasters to carry on reserved channels, and (within the Cable Act's strictures) allow them to choose broadcasters with a view to offering program choices appealing to local subscribers. Appellants' proposal would require the Government to develop other criteria for giving subsidies and to establish a potentially elaborate administrative structure to make subsidy determinations.

Appellants also suggest a system of antitrust enforcement or an administrative complaint procedure to protect broadcasters from cable operators' anticompetitive conduct. [ ] Congress could conclude, however, that the considerable expense and delay inherent in antitrust litigation, and the great disparities in wealth and sophistication between the average independent broadcast station and average cable system operator, would make these remedies inadequate substitutes for guaranteed carriage. The record suggests independent broadcasters simply are not in a position to engage in complex antitrust litigation, which involves extensive discovery, significant motions practice, appeals, and the payment of high legal fees throughout. [ ] An administrative complaint procedure, although less burdensome, would still require stations to incur considerable expense and delay before enforcing their rights. As it is, some public stations have been forced by limited resources to forgo pursuing administrative complaints under the Cable Act to obtain carriage. [ ] Those problems would be compounded if instead of proving entitlement under must-carry, the station instead had to prove facts establishing an antitrust violation.

There is a final argument made by appellants that we do not reach. Appellant Time Warner Entertainment raises in its brief a separate First Amendment challenge to a subsection of the Cable Act [ ] that requires carriage on unfilled must-carry channels of low power broadcast stations if the FCC determines that the station's programming

> would address local news and informational needs which are not being
> adequately served by full power television broadcast stations because of
> the geographic distance of such full power stations from the low power
> station's community of license.

[ ] We earlier reserved this question and invited the District Court to address it on remand. [ ] Because this question has received "only the most glancing" attention [ ], from the District Court and the parties, we have no more information about "the operation of, and justifications for, the low-power broadcast provisions," [ ] on which to base an informed determination than we did on the earlier appeal. The District Court's primary opinion disposed of the question in a perfunctory discussion [ ]; and the dissent explicitly declined to reach the question. [ ] The issue has received even less attention from the parties. It was not addressed in the jurisdictional statement, the motions to affirm, or the appellants' oppositions to the motions to affirm. In over 400 pages of merits briefs, the parties devoted a total of four paragraphs (two of which were relegated to footnotes) to conclusory argumentation on this subject, largely concerning not the merits of the question but whether it was even properly before us. On this state of the record, we have insufficient basis to make an informed judgment on this discrete issue. Even if the issue is "fairly included" in the broadly worded question presented, it is tangential to the main issue, and prudence dictates that we not decide this question based on such scant argumentation. [ ]

III

Judgments about how competing economic interests are to be reconciled in the complex and fast-changing field of television are for Congress to make. Those judgments "cannot be ignored or undervalued simply because [appellants] cas[t] [their] claims under the umbrella of the First Amendment." [ ] Appellants' challenges to must-carry reflect little more than disagreement over the level of protection broadcast stations are to be afforded and how protection is to be attained. We cannot displace Congress' judgment respecting content-neutral regulations with our own, so long as its policy is grounded on reasonable factual findings supported by evidence that is substantial for a legislative determination. Those requirements were met in this case, and in these circumstances the First Amendment requires nothing more. The judgment of the District Court is affirmed.

It is so ordered.

New York Times Co. v. Sullivan (MCLE, page 344) is considered by many legal scholars one of the most important media law decision rendered by the U.S. Supreme Court. This landmark decision established a new defense to libel known as *constitutional privilege*. According to the Court, the First Amendment requires public officials (later extended to public figures) to demonstrate that defamatory information was disseminated by a media defendant with *actual malice* -- that is, knowledge that the information was false or with reckless disregard for whether it was false or true. Although the Court has narrowed the application of the actual malice rule, as illustrated in the next case (*Gertz v. Welch*), it continues to affirm the *Sullivan* decision almost four decades later.

New York Times Co. v. Sullivan

Argued January 6, 1964
Decided March 9, 1964

376 U.S. 254, 11 L.Ed.2d 686, 84 S.Ct. 710, 1 Med.L.Rptr. 1527

CERTIORARI TO THE SUPREME COURT OF ALABAMA

Syllabus

Respondent, an elected official in Montgomery, Alabama, brought suit in a state court alleging that he had been libeled by an advertisement in corporate petitioner's newspaper, the text of which appeared over the names of the four individual petitioners and many others. The advertisement included statements, some of which were false, about police action allegedly directed against students who participated in a civil rights demonstration and against a leader of the civil rights movement; respondent claimed the statements referred to him because his duties included supervision of the police department. The trial judge instructed the jury that such statements were "libelous *per se*," legal injury being implied without proof of actual damages, and that, for the purpose of compensatory damages, malice was presumed, so that such damages could be awarded against petitioners if the statements were found to have been published by them and to have related to respondent. As to punitive damages, the judge instructed that mere negligence was not evidence of actual malice, and would not justify an award of punitive damages; he refused to instruct that actual intent to harm or recklessness had to be found before punitive damages could be awarded, or that a verdict for respondent should differentiate between compensatory and punitive damages. The jury found for respondent, and the State Supreme Court affirmed.

Held: A State cannot, under the First and Fourteenth Amendments, award damages to a public official for defamatory falsehood relating to his official conduct unless he proves "actual malice" -- that the statement was made with knowledge of its falsity or with reckless disregard of whether it was true or false.

(a) Application by state courts of a rule of law, whether statutory or not, to award a judgment in a civil action, is "state action" under the Fourteenth Amendment.

(b) Expression does not lose constitutional protection to which it would otherwise be entitled because it appears in the form of a paid advertisement.

(c) Factual error, content defamatory of official reputation, or both, are insufficient to warrant an award of damages for false statements unless "actual malice" -- knowledge that statements are false or in reckless disregard of the truth -- is alleged and proved.

(d) State court judgment entered upon a general verdict which does not differentiate between punitive damages, as to which, under state law, actual malice must be proved, and general damages, as to which it is "presumed," precludes any determination as to the basis of the verdict, and requires reversal, where presumption of malice is inconsistent with federal constitutional requirements.

(e) The evidence was constitutionally insufficient to support the judgment for respondent, since it failed to support a finding that the statements were made with actual malice or that they related to respondent.

273 Ala. 656, 144 So.2d 25, reversed and remanded.

BRENNAN, J., lead opinion

We are required in this case to determine for the first time the extent to which the constitutional protections for speech and press limit a State's power to award damages in a libel action brought by a public official against critics of his official conduct.

Respondent L. B. Sullivan is one of the three elected Commissioners of the City of Montgomery, Alabama. He testified that he was

> Commissioner of Public Affairs, and the duties are supervision of the Police Department, Fire Department, Department of Cemetery and Department of Scales.

He brought this civil libel action against the four individual petitioners, who are Negroes and Alabama clergymen, and against petitioner the New York Times Company, a New York corporation which publishes the New York Times, a daily newspaper. A jury in the Circuit Court of Montgomery County awarded him damages of $500,000, the full amount claimed, against all the petitioners, and the Supreme Court of Alabama affirmed. [ ]

Respondent's complaint alleged that he had been libeled by statements in a full-page advertisement that was carried in the New York Times on March 29, 1960. Entitled "Heed Their Rising Voices," the advertisement began by stating that,

> As the whole world knows by now, thousands of Southern Negro students are engaged in widespread nonviolent demonstrations in positive affirmation of the right to live in human dignity as guaranteed by the U.S. Constitution and the Bill of Rights.

It went on to charge that,

> in their efforts to uphold these guarantees, they are being met by an unprecedented wave of terror by those who would deny and negate that document which the whole world looks upon as setting the pattern for modern freedom. . . .

Succeeding paragraphs purported to illustrate the "wave of terror" by describing certain alleged events. The text concluded with an appeal for funds for three purposes: support of the student movement, "the struggle for the right to vote," and the legal defense of Dr. Martin Luther King, Jr., leader of the movement, against a perjury indictment then pending in Montgomery.

The text appeared over the names of 64 persons, many widely known for their activities in public affairs, religion, trade unions, and the performing arts. Below these names, and under a line reading "We in the south who are struggling daily for dignity and freedom warmly endorse this appeal," appeared the names of the four individual petitioners and of 16 other persons, all but two of whom were identified as clergymen in various Southern cities. The advertisement was signed at the bottom of the page by the "Committee to Defend Martin Luther King and the Struggle for Freedom in the South," and the officers of the Committee were listed.

Of the 10 paragraphs of text in the advertisement, the third and a portion of the sixth were the basis of respondent's claim of libel. They read as follows:

Third paragraph:

> In Montgomery, Alabama, after students sang "My Country, 'Tis of Thee" on the State Capitol steps, their leaders were expelled from school, and truckloads of police armed with shotguns and tear-gas ringed the Alabama State College Campus. When the entire student body protested to state authorities by refusing to reregister, their dining hall was padlocked in an attempt to starve them into submission.

Sixth paragraph:

> Again and again, the Southern violators have answered Dr. King's peaceful protests with intimidation and violence. They have bombed his home, almost killing his wife and child. They have assaulted his person.

They have arrested him seven times -- for "speeding," "loitering" and similar "offenses." And now they have charged him with "perjury" -- a *felony* under which they could imprison him for *ten years*. . . .

Although neither of these statements mentions respondent by name, he contended that the word "police" in the third paragraph referred to him as the Montgomery Commissioner who supervised the Police Department, so that he was being accused of "ringing" the campus with police. He further claimed that the paragraph would be read as imputing to the police, and hence to him, the padlocking of the dining hall in order to starve the students into submission. As to the sixth paragraph, he contended that, since arrests are ordinarily made by the police, the statement "They have arrested [Dr. King] seven times" would be read as referring to him; he further contended that the "They" who did the arresting would be equated with the "They" who committed the other described acts and with the "Southern violators." Thus, he argued, the paragraph would be read as accusing the Montgomery police, and hence him, of answering Dr. King's protests with "intimidation and violence," bombing his home, assaulting his person, and charging him with perjury. Respondent and six other Montgomery residents testified that they read some or all of the statements as referring to him in his capacity as Commissioner.

It is uncontroverted that some of the statements contained in the two paragraphs were not accurate descriptions of events which occurred in Montgomery. Although Negro students staged a demonstration on the State Capitol steps, they sang the National Anthem and not "My Country, 'Tis of Thee." Although nine students were expelled by the State Board of Education, this was not for leading the demonstration at the Capitol, but for demanding service at a lunch counter in the Montgomery County Courthouse on another day. Not the entire student body, but most of it, had protested the expulsion, not by refusing to register, but by boycotting classes on a single day; virtually all the students did register for the ensuing semester. The campus dining hall was not padlocked on any occasion, and the only students who may have been barred from eating there were the few who had neither signed a preregistration application nor requested temporary meal tickets. Although the police were deployed near the campus in large numbers on three occasions, they did not at any time "ring" the campus, and they were not called to the campus in connection with the demonstration on the State Capitol steps, as the third paragraph implied. Dr. King had not been arrested seven times, but only four, and although he claimed to have been assaulted some years earlier in connection with his arrest for loitering outside a courtroom, one of the officers who made the arrest denied that there was such an assault.

On the premise that the charges in the sixth paragraph could be read as referring to him, respondent was allowed to prove that he had not participated in the events described. Although Dr. King's home had, in fact, been bombed twice when his wife and child were there, both of these occasions antedated respondent's tenure as Commissioner, and

185

the police were not only not implicated in the bombings, but had made every effort to apprehend those who were. Three of Dr. King's four arrests took place before respondent became Commissioner. Although Dr. King had, in fact, been indicted (he was subsequently acquitted) on two counts of perjury, each of which carried a possible five-year sentence, respondent had nothing to do with procuring the indictment.

Respondent made no effort to prove that he suffered actual pecuniary loss as a result of the alleged libel. One of his witnesses, a former employer, testified that, if he had believed the statements, he doubted whether he "would want to be associated with anybody who would be a party to such things that are stated in that ad," and that he would not reemploy respondent if he believed "that he allowed the Police Department to do the things that the paper say he did." But neither this witness nor any of the others testified that he had actually believed the statements in their supposed reference to respondent. The cost of the advertisement was approximately $4800, and it was published by the Times upon an order from a New York advertising agency acting for the signatory Committee. The agency submitted the advertisement with a letter from A. Philip Randolph, Chairman of the Committee, certifying that the persons whose names appeared on the advertisement had given their permission. Mr. Randolph was known to the Times' Advertising Acceptability Department as a responsible person, and, in accepting the letter as sufficient proof of authorization, it followed its established practice. There was testimony that the copy of the advertisement which accompanied the letter listed only the 64 names appearing under the text, and that the statement, "We in the south . . . warmly endorse this appeal," and the list of names thereunder, which included those of the individual petitioners, were subsequently added when the first proof of the advertisement was received. Each of the individual petitioners testified that he had not authorized the use of his name, and that he had been unaware of its use until receipt of respondent's demand for a retraction. The manager of the Advertising Acceptability Department testified that he had approved the advertisement for publication because he knew nothing to cause him to believe that anything in it was false, and because it bore the endorsement of "a number of people who are well known and whose reputation" he "had no reason to question." Neither he nor anyone else at the Times made an effort to confirm the accuracy of the advertisement, either by checking it against recent Times news stories relating to some of the described events or by any other means.

Alabama law denies a public officer recovery of punitive damages in a libel action brought on account of a publication concerning his official conduct unless he first makes a written demand for a public retraction and the defendant fails or refuses to comply. [ ] Respondent served such a demand upon each of the petitioners. None of the individual petitioners responded to the demand, primarily because each took the position that he had not authorized the use of his name on the advertisement, and therefore had not published the statements that respondent alleged had libeled him. The Times did not publish a retraction in response to the demand, but wrote respondent a letter

186

stating, among other things, that "we . . . are somewhat puzzled as to how you think the statements in any way reflect on you," and "you might, if you desire, let us know in what respect you claim that the statements in the advertisement reflect on you." Respondent filed this suit a few days later without answering the letter. The Times did, however, subsequently publish a retraction of the advertisement upon the demand of Governor John Patterson of Alabama, who asserted that the publication charged him with

> grave misconduct and . . . improper actions and omissions as Governor of Alabama and Ex-Officio Chairman of the State Board of Education of Alabama.

When asked to explain why there had been a retraction for the Governor but not for respondent, the Secretary of the Times testified:

> We did that because we didn't want anything that was published by The Times to be a reflection on the State of Alabama, and the Governor was, as far as we could see, the embodiment of the State of Alabama and the proper representative of the State, and, furthermore, we had by that time learned more of the actual facts which the and purported to recite and, finally, the ad did refer to the action of the State authorities and the Board of Education, presumably of which the Governor is the ex-officio chairman. . . .

On the other hand, he testified that he did not think that "any of the language in there referred to Mr. Sullivan."

The trial judge submitted the case to the jury under instructions that the statements in the advertisement were "libelous *per se*," and were not privileged, so that petitioners might be held liable if the jury found that they had published the advertisement and that the statements were made "of and concerning" respondent. The jury was instructed that, because the statements were libelous *per se*, "the law . . . implies legal injury from the bare fact of publication itself," "falsity and malice are presumed," "general damages need not be alleged or proved, but are presumed," and "punitive damages may be awarded by the jury even though the amount of actual damages is neither found nor shown." An award of punitive damages -- as distinguished from "general" damages, which are compensatory in nature -- apparently requires proof of actual malice under Alabama law, and the judge charged that

> mere negligence or carelessness is not evidence of actual malice or malice
> in fact, and does not justify an award of exemplary or punitive damages.

He refused to charge, however, that the jury must be "convinced" of malice, in the sense of "actual intent" to harm or "gross negligence and recklessness," to make such an award, and he also refused to require that a verdict for respondent differentiate between compensatory and punitive damages. The judge rejected petitioners' contention that his rulings abridged the freedoms of speech and of the press that are guaranteed by the First and Fourteenth Amendments.

In affirming the judgment, the Supreme Court of Alabama sustained the trial judge's rulings and instructions in all respects. [ ] It held that,

> where the words published tend to injure a person libeled by them in his reputation, profession, trade or business, or charge him with an indictable offense, or tend to bring the individual into public contempt,

they are "libelous *per se*"; that "the matter complained of is, under the above doctrine, libelous *per se*, if it was published of and concerning the plaintiff", and that it was actionable without "proof of pecuniary injury . . . . such injury being implied." [ ] It approved the trial court's ruling that the jury could find the statements to have been made "of and concerning" respondent, stating:

> We think it common knowledge that the average person knows that municipal agents, such as police and firemen, and others, are under the control and direction of the city governing body, and, more particularly, under the direction and control of a single commissioner. In measuring the performance or deficiencies of such groups, praise or criticism is usually attached to the official in complete control of the body.

[ ] In sustaining the trial court's determination that the verdict was not excessive, the court said that malice could be inferred from the Times' "irresponsibility" in printing the advertisement while

> the Times, in its own files, had articles already published which would have demonstrated the falsity of the allegations in the advertisement;

from the Times' failure to retract for respondent while retracting for the Governor, whereas the falsity of some of the allegations was then known to the Times and "the matter contained in the advertisement was equally false as to both parties", and from the testimony of the Times' Secretary that, apart from the statement that the dining hall was padlocked, he thought the two paragraphs were "substantially correct." [ ] The court reaffirmed a statement in an earlier opinion that "There is no legal measure of damages in cases of this character."   [   ] It rejected petitioners' constitutional contentions with the brief statements that "The First Amendment of the U.S. Constitution does not protect libelous publications," and "The Fourteenth Amendment is directed against State action, and not private action." [ ]

Because of the importance of the constitutional issues involved, we granted the separate petitions for certiorari of the individual petitioners and of the Times. [ ] We reverse the judgment. We hold that the rule of law applied by the Alabama courts is constitutionally deficient for failure to provide the safeguards for freedom of speech and of the press that are required by the First and Fourteenth Amendments in a libel action brought by a public official against critics of his official conduct. We further hold that, under the proper safeguards, the evidence presented in this case is constitutionally insufficient to support the judgment for respondent.

I.

We may dispose at the outset of two grounds asserted to insulate the judgment of the Alabama courts from constitutional scrutiny. The first is the proposition relied on by the State Supreme Court -- that "The Fourteenth Amendment is directed against State action, and not private action." That proposition has no application to this case. Although this is a civil lawsuit between private parties, the Alabama courts have applied a state rule of law which petitioners claim to impose invalid restrictions on their constitutional freedoms of speech and press. It matters not that that law has been applied in a civil action and that it is common law only, though supplemented by statute. [ ] The test is not the form in which state power has been applied but, whatever the form, whether such power has, in fact, been exercised. [ ]

The second contention is that the constitutional guarantees of freedom of speech and of the press are inapplicable here, at least so far as the Times is concerned, because the allegedly libelous statements were published as part of a paid, "commercial" advertisement. The argument relies on *Valentine v. Chrestensen,* 316 U.S. 52, where the Court held that a city ordinance forbidding street distribution of commercial and business advertising matter did not abridge the First Amendment freedoms, even as applied to a handbill having a commercial message on one side but a protest against certain official action, on the other. The reliance is wholly misplaced. The Court in *Chrestensen* reaffirmed the constitutional protection for "the freedom of communicating information and disseminating opinion"; its holding was based upon the factual conclusions that the handbill was "purely commercial advertising" and that the protest against official action had been added only to evade the ordinance.

The publication here was not a "commercial" advertisement in the sense in which the word was used in *Chrestensen.* It communicated information, expressed opinion, recited grievances, protested claimed abuses, and sought financial support on behalf of a movement whose existence and objectives are matters of the highest public interest and concern. [ ] That the Times was paid for publishing the advertisement is as immaterial in this connection as is the fact that newspapers and books are sold. [ ] Any other conclusion would discourage newspapers from carrying "editorial advertisements" of this type, and so might shut off an important outlet for the promulgation of information and ideas by persons who do not themselves have access to publishing facilities -- who wish to exercise their freedom of speech even though they are not members of the press. [ ] The effect would be to shackle the First Amendment in its attempt to secure "the widest possible dissemination of information from diverse and antagonistic sources." [ ] To avoid placing such a handicap upon the freedoms of expression, we hold that, if the allegedly libelous statements would otherwise be constitutionally protected from the present judgment, they do not forfeit that protection because they were published in the form of a paid advertisement.

II

Under Alabama law, as applied in this case, a publication is "libelous *per se*" if the words "tend to injure a person . . . in his reputation" or to "bring [him] into public contempt"; the trial court stated that the standard was met if the words are such as to "injure him in his public office, or impute misconduct to him in his office, or want of official integrity, or want of fidelity to a public trust. . . ." The jury must find that the words were published "of and concerning" the plaintiff, but, where the plaintiff is a public official, his place in the governmental hierarchy is sufficient evidence to support a finding that his reputation has been affected by statements that reflect upon the agency of which he is in charge. Once "libel *per se*" has been established, the defendant has no defense as to stated facts unless he can persuade the jury that they were true in all their particulars. [ ] His privilege of "fair comment" for expressions of opinion depends on the truth of the facts upon which the comment is based. [ ] Unless he can discharge the burden of proving truth, general damages are presumed, and may be awarded without proof of pecuniary injury. A showing of actual malice is apparently a prerequisite to recovery of punitive damages, and the defendant may, in any event, forestall a punitive award by a retraction meeting the statutory requirements. Good motives and belief in truth do not negate an inference of malice, but are relevant only in mitigation of punitive damages if the jury chooses to accord them weight. [ ]

The question before us is whether this rule of liability, as applied to an action brought by a public official against critics of his official conduct, abridges the freedom of speech and of the press that is guaranteed by the First and Fourteenth Amendments.

Respondent relies heavily, as did the Alabama courts, on statements of this Court to the effect that the Constitution does not protect libelous publications. Those statements do not foreclose our inquiry here. None of the cases sustained the use of libel laws to impose sanctions upon expression critical of the official conduct of public officials. The dictum in *Pennekamp v. Florida* [ ] that "when the statements amount to defamation, a judge has such remedy in damages for libel as do other public servants," implied no view as to what remedy might constitutionally be afforded to public officials. In *Beauharnais v. Illinois* [ ], the Court sustained an Illinois criminal libel statute as applied to a publication held to be both defamatory of a racial group and "liable to cause violence and disorder." But the Court was careful to note that it "retains and exercises authority to nullify action which encroaches on freedom of utterance under the guise of punishing libel"; for "public men are, as it were, public property," and "discussion cannot be denied, and the right, as well as the duty, of criticism must not be stifled." [ ] In the only previous case that did present the question of constitutional limitations upon the power to award damages for libel of a public official, the Court was equally divided and the question was not decided. [ ] In deciding the question now, we are compelled by neither precedent nor policy to give any more weight to the epithet "libel" than we have to other

190

"mere labels" of state law. [ ] Like insurrection, contempt, advocacy of unlawful acts, breach of the peace, obscenity, solicitation of legal business, and the various other formulae for the repression of expression that have been challenged in this Court, libel can claim no talismanic immunity from constitutional limitations. It must be measured by standards that satisfy the First Amendment.

The general proposition that freedom of expression upon public questions is secured by the First Amendment has long been settled by our decisions. The constitutional safeguard, we have said, "was fashioned to assure unfettered interchange of ideas for the bringing about of political and social changes desired by the people." [ ]

> The maintenance of the opportunity for free political discussion to the end that government may be responsive to the will of the people and that changes may be obtained by lawful means, an opportunity essential to the security of the Republic, is a fundamental principle of our constitutional system.

[ ] "[I]t is a prized American privilege to speak one's mind, although not always with perfect good taste, on all public institutions" [ ], and this opportunity is to be afforded for "vigorous advocacy" no less than "abstract discussion." [ ] The First Amendment, said Judge Learned Hand,

> presupposes that right conclusions are more likely to be gathered out of a multitude of tongues than through any kind of authoritative selection. To many, this is, and always will be, folly, but we have staked upon it our all.

[ ] Mr. Justice Brandeis, in his concurring opinion in *Whitney v. California* [ ], gave the principle its classic formulation:

> Those who won our independence believed . . . that public discussion is a political duty, and that this should be a fundamental principle of the American government. They recognized the risks to which all human institutions are subject. But they knew that order cannot be secured merely through fear of punishment for its infraction; that it is hazardous to discourage thought, hope and imagination; that fear breeds repression; that repression breeds hate; that hate menaces stable government; that the path of safety lies in the opportunity to discuss freely supposed grievances and proposed remedies, and that the fitting remedy for evil counsels is good ones. Believing in the power of reason as applied through public discussion, they eschewed silence coerced by law -- the argument of force in its worst form. Recognizing the occasional tyrannies of governing majorities, they amended the Constitution so that free speech and assembly should be guaranteed.

Thus, we consider this case against the background of a profound national commitment to the principle that debate on public issues should be uninhibited, robust, and wide-open, and that it may well include vehement, caustic, and sometimes unpleasantly sharp attacks on government and public officials. [ ] The present advertisement, as an expression of grievance and protest on one of the major public issues of our time, would seem clearly to qualify for the constitutional protection. The question is whether it forfeits that protection by the falsity of some of its factual statements and by its alleged defamation of respondent.

Authoritative interpretations of the First Amendment guarantees have consistently refused to recognize an exception for any test of truth -- whether administered by judges, juries, or administrative officials -- and especially one that puts the burden of proving truth on the speaker. [ ] The constitutional protection does not turn upon "the truth, popularity, or social utility of the ideas and beliefs which are offered." [ ] As Madison said, "Some degree of abuse is inseparable from the proper use of every thing, and in no instance is this more true than in that of the press." [ ] In *Cantwell v. Connecticut* [ ], the Court declared:

> In the realm of religious faith, and in that of political belief, sharp differences arise. In both fields, the tenets of one man may seem the rankest error to his neighbor. To persuade others to his own point of view, the pleader, as we know, at times resorts to exaggeration, to vilification of men who have been, or are, prominent in church or state, and even to false statement. But the people of this nation have ordained, in the light of history, that, in spite of the probability of excesses and abuses, these liberties are, in the long view, essential to enlightened opinion and right conduct on the part of the citizens of a democracy.

That erroneous statement is inevitable in free debate, and that it must be protected if the freedoms of expression are to have the "breathing space" that they "need . . . to survive" [ ] also recognized by the Court of Appeals for the District of Columbia Circuit in *Sweeney v. Patterson* [ ]. Judge Edgerton spoke for a unanimous court which affirmed the dismissal of a Congressman's libel suit based upon a newspaper article charging him with anti-Semitism in opposing a judicial appointment. He said:

> Cases which impose liability for erroneous reports of the political conduct of officials reflect the obsolete doctrine that the governed must not criticize their governors. . . . The interest of the public here outweighs the interest of appellant or any other individual. The protection of the public requires not merely discussion, but information. Political conduct and views which some respectable people approve, and others condemn, are constantly imputed to Congressmen. Errors of fact, particularly in regard to a man's mental states and processes, are inevitable. . . . Whatever is added to the field of libel is taken from the field of free debate.

Injury to official reputation affords no more warrant for repressing speech that would otherwise be free than does factual error. Where judicial officers are involved, this Court has held that concern for the dignity and reputation of the courts does not justify the punishment as criminal contempt of criticism of the judge or his decision. [ ] This is true even though the utterance contains "half-truths" and "misinformation." [ ] Such repression can be justified, if at all, only by a clear and present danger of the obstruction of justice. [ ] If judges are

192

to be treated as "men of fortitude, able to thrive in a hardy climate" [ ], surely the same must be true of other government officials, such as elected city commissioners. Criticism of their official conduct does not lose its constitutional protection merely because it is effective criticism, and hence diminishes their official reputations.

If neither factual error nor defamatory content suffices to remove the constitutional shield from criticism of official conduct, the combination of the two elements is no less inadequate. This is the lesson to be drawn from the great controversy over the Sedition Act of 1798 [ ], which first crystallized a national awareness of the central meaning of the First Amendment. [ ] That statute made it a crime, punishable by a $5,000 fine and five years in prison,

> if any person shall write, print, utter or publish . . . any false, scandalous and malicious writing or writings against the government of the United States, or either house of the Congress . . . or the President . . . with intent to defame . . . or to bring them, or either of them, into contempt or disrepute; or to excite against them, or either or any of them, the hatred of the good people of the United States.

The Act allowed the defendant the defense of truth, and provided that the jury were to be judges both of the law and the facts. Despite these qualifications, the Act was vigorously condemned as unconstitutional in an attack joined in by Jefferson and Madison. In the famous Virginia Resolutions of 1798, the General Assembly of Virginia resolved that it

> doth particularly protest against the palpable and alarming infractions of the Constitution in the two late cases of the "Alien and Sedition Acts," passed at the last session of Congress. . . . [The Sedition Act] exercises . . . a power not delegated by the Constitution, but, on the contrary, expressly and positively forbidden by one of the amendments thereto -- a power which, more than any other, ought to produce universal alarm because it is leveled against the right of freely examining public characters and measures, and of free communication among the people thereon, which has ever been justly deemed the only effectual guardian of every other right.

[ ] Madison prepared the Report in support of the protest. His premise was that the Constitution created a form of government under which "The people, not the government, possess the absolute sovereignty." The structure of the government dispersed power in reflection of the people's distrust of concentrated power, and of power itself at all levels. This form of government was "altogether different" from the British form, under which the Crown was sovereign and the people were subjects. "Is it not natural and necessary, under such different circumstances," he asked, "that a different degree of freedom in the use of the press should be contemplated?" [ ] Earlier, in a debate in the House of Representatives, Madison had said:

> If we advert to the nature of Republican Government, we shall find that the censorial power is in the people over the Government, and not in the Government over the people.

[ ] Of the exercise of that power by the press, his Report said:

> In every state, probably, in the Union, the press has exerted a freedom in canvassing the merits and measures of public men, of every description, which has not been confined to the strict limits of the common law. On this footing, the freedom of the press has stood; on this foundation it yet stands. . . .

[ ]. The right of free public discussion of the stewardship of public officials was thus, in Madison's view, a fundamental principle of the American form of government.

Although the Sedition Act was never tested in this Court, the attack upon its validity has carried the day in the court of history. Fines levied in its prosecution were repaid by Act of Congress on the ground that it was unconstitutional. [ ] Calhoun, reporting to the Senate on February 4, 1836, assumed that its invalidity was a matter "which no one now doubts." [ ] Jefferson, as President, pardoned those who had been convicted and sentenced under the Act and remitted their fines, stating:

> I discharged every person under punishment or prosecution under the sedition law because I considered, and now consider, that law to be a nullity, as absolute and as palpable as if Congress had ordered us to fall down and worship a golden image.

[ ] The invalidity of the Act has also been assumed by Justices of this Court. [ ] These views reflect a broad consensus that the Act, because of the restraint it imposed upon criticism of government and public officials, was inconsistent with the First Amendment.

There is no force in respondent's argument that the constitutional limitations implicit in the history of the Sedition Act apply only to Congress, and not to the States. It is true that the First Amendment was originally addressed only to action by the Federal Government, and that Jefferson, for one, while denying the power of Congress "to controul the freedom of the press," recognized such a power in the States. [ ] But this distinction was eliminated with the adoption of the Fourteenth Amendment and the application to the States of the First Amendment's restrictions. [ ] What a State may not constitutionally bring about by means of a criminal statute is likewise beyond the reach of its civil law of libel. The fear of damage awards under a rule such as that invoked by the Alabama courts here may be markedly more inhibiting than the fear of prosecution under a criminal statute. [ ] Alabama, for example, has a criminal libel law which subjects to prosecution "any person who speaks, writes, or prints of and concerning another any accusation falsely and maliciously importing the commission by such person of a felony, or any other indictable offense involving moral turpitude," and which allows as punishment upon conviction a fine not exceeding $500 and a prison sentence of six months. [ ] Presumably, a person charged with violation of this statute enjoys ordinary criminal law safeguards such as the requirements of an indictment and of proof beyond a reasonable doubt. These safeguards are not available to the defendant in a civil action. The judgment awarded in this case -- without the need for any proof of actual pecuniary loss -- was one thousand times greater than the maximum fine provided by the Alabama criminal statute, and one hundred times greater than that provided by the Sedition Act. And since there is no double jeopardy limitation applicable to civil lawsuits, this is not the only judgment that may be awarded against petitioners for the same publication. Whether or not a newspaper can survive a succession of such judgments, the pall of fear and timidity imposed upon those who would give voice to public criticism is an atmosphere in which the First Amendment freedoms cannot survive. Plainly the Alabama law of civil libel is

> a form of regulation that creates hazards to protected freedoms markedly greater than those that attend reliance upon the criminal law.

[ ]

The state rule of law is not saved by its allowance of the defense of truth. A defense for erroneous statements honestly made is no less essential here than was the requirement of proof of guilty knowledge which, in *Smith v. California* [   ], we held indispensable to a valid conviction of a bookseller for possessing obscene writings for sale. We said:

> For, if the bookseller is criminally liable without knowledge of the contents, . . . He will tend to restrict the books he sells to those he has inspected, and thus the State will have imposed a restriction upon the distribution of constitutionally protected, as well as obscene, literature. . . . And the bookseller's burden would become the public's burden, for, by restricting him, the public's access to reading matter would be restricted. . . . [H]is timidity in the face of his absolute criminal liability thus would tend to restrict the public's access to forms of the printed word which the State could not constitutionally suppress directly. The bookseller's self-censorship, compelled by the State, would be a censorship affecting the whole public, hardly less virulent for being privately administered. Through it, the distribution of all books, both obscene and not obscene, would be impeded.

[ ] A rule compelling the critic of official conduct to guarantee the truth of all his factual assertions -- and to do so on pain of libel judgments virtually unlimited in amount -- leads to a comparable "self-censorship." Allowance of the defense of truth, with the burden of proving it on the defendant, does not mean that only false speech will be deterred. Even courts accepting this defense as an adequate safeguard have recognized the difficulties of adducing legal proofs that the alleged libel was true in all its factual particulars. [ ] Under such a rule, would-be critics of official conduct may be deterred from voicing their criticism, even though it is believed to be true and even though it is, in fact, true, because of doubt whether it can be proved in court or fear of the expense of having to do so. They tend to make only statements which "steer far wider of the unlawful zone." [ ] The rule thus dampens the vigor and limits the variety of public debate. It is inconsistent with the First and Fourteenth

Amendments. The constitutional guarantees require, we think, a federal rule that prohibits a public official from recovering damages for a defamatory falsehood relating to his official conduct unless he proves that the statement was made with "actual malice" -- that is, with knowledge that it was false or with reckless disregard of whether it was false or not. An oft-cited statement of a like rule, which has been adopted by a number of state courts, is found in the Kansas case of *Coleman v. MacLennan* [ ]. The State Attorney General, a candidate for reelection and a member of the commission charged with the management and control of the state school fund, sued a newspaper publisher for alleged libel in an article purporting to state facts relating to his official conduct in connection with a school-fund transaction. The defendant pleaded privilege and the trial judge, over the plaintiff's objection, instructed the jury that

> where an article is published and circulated among voters for the sole purpose of giving what the defendant believes to be truthful information concerning a candidate for public office and for the purpose of enabling such voters to cast their ballot more intelligently, and the whole thing is done in good faith and without malice, the article is privileged, although the principal matters contained in the article may be untrue, in fact, and derogatory to the character of the plaintiff, and in such a case the burden is on the plaintiff to show actual malice in the publication of the article.

In answer to a special question, the jury found that the plaintiff had not proved actual malice, and a general verdict was returned for the defendant. On appeal, the Supreme Court of Kansas, in an opinion by Justice Burch, reasoned as follows [ ]:

> It is of the utmost consequence that the people should discuss the character and qualifications of candidates for their suffrages. The importance to the state and to society of such discussions is so vast, and the advantages derived are so great, that they more than counterbalance the inconvenience of private persons whose conduct may be involved, and occasional injury to the reputations of individuals must yield to the public welfare, although at times such injury may be great. The public benefit from publicity is so great, and the chance of injury to private character so small, that such discussion must be privileged.

The court thus sustained the trial court's instruction as a correct statement of the law, saying:

> In such a case the occasion gives rise to a privilege, qualified to this extent: any one claiming to be defamed by the communication must show actual malice or go remediless. This privilege extends to a great variety of subjects, and includes matters of public concern, public men, and candidates for office.

[ ]

Such a privilege for criticism of official conduct is appropriately analogous to the protection accorded a public official when he is sued for libel by a private citizen. In *Barr v. Matteo* [ ], this Court held the utterance of a federal official to be absolutely privileged if made "within the outer perimeter" of his duties. The States accord the same immunity to statements of their highest officers, although some differentiate their lesser officials and qualify the privilege they enjoy. But all hold that all officials are protected unless actual malice can be proved. The reason for the official privilege is said to be that the threat of damage suits would otherwise "inhibit the fearless, vigorous, and effective administration of policies of government" and "dampen the ardor of all but the most resolute, or the most irresponsible, in the unflinching discharge of their duties." [ ] Analogous considerations support the privilege for the citizen-critic of government. It is as much his duty to criticize as it is the official's duty to administer. [ ] As Madison said [ ], "the censorial power is in the people over the Government, and not in the Government over the people." It would give public servants an unjustified preference over the public they serve, if critics of official conduct did not have a fair equivalent of the immunity granted to the officials themselves.

We conclude that such a privilege is required by the First and Fourteenth Amendments.

III

We hold today that the Constitution delimits a State's power to award damages for libel in actions brought by public officials against critics of their official conduct. Since this is such an action,{GO>23} the rule requiring proof of actual malice is applicable. While Alabama law apparently requires proof of actual malice for an award of punitive damages, where general damages are concerned malice is "presumed." Such a presumption is inconsistent with the federal rule. "The power to create presumptions is not a means of escape from constitutional restrictions" [ ], "the showing of malice required for the forfeiture of the privilege is not presumed but is a matter for proof by the plaintiff. . . ." [ ] Since the trial judge did not instruct the jury to differentiate between general and punitive damages, it may be that the verdict was wholly an award of one or the other. But it is impossible to know, in view of the general verdict returned. Because of this uncertainty, the judgment must be reversed and the case remanded. [ ]

Since respondent may seek a new trial, we deem that considerations of effective judicial administration require us to review the evidence in the present record to determine whether it could constitutionally support a judgment for respondent. This Court's duty is not limited to the elaboration of constitutional principles; we must also in proper cases review the evidence to make certain that those principles have been constitutionally applied. This is such a case, particularly since the question is one of alleged trespass across "the line between speech unconditionally guaranteed and speech which may legitimately be regulated." [ ] In cases where that line must be drawn, the rule is that we examine for ourselves the statements in issue and the circumstances under which they were made to see . . . whether they are of a character which the principles of the First Amendment, as adopted by the Due Process Clause of the Fourteenth Amendment, protect.

[ ] We must "make an independent examination of the whole record" [ ], so as to assure ourselves that the judgment does not constitute a forbidden intrusion on the field of free expression.

Applying these standards, we consider that the proof presented to show actual malice lacks the convincing clarity which the constitutional standard demands, and hence that it would not constitutionally sustain the judgment for respondent under the proper rule of law. The case of the individual petitioners requires little discussion. Even assuming that they could constitutionally be found to have authorized the use of their names on the advertisement, there was no evidence whatever that they were aware of any erroneous statements or were in any way reckless in that regard. The judgment against them is thus without constitutional support.

As to the Times, we similarly conclude that the facts do not support a finding of actual malice. The statement by the Times' Secretary that, apart from the padlocking allegation, he thought the advertisement was "substantially correct," affords no constitutional warrant for the Alabama Supreme Court's conclusion that it was a

> cavalier ignoring of the falsity of the advertisement [from which] the jury could not have but been impressed with the bad faith of The Times, and its maliciousness inferable therefrom.

The statement does not indicate malice at the time of the publication; even if the advertisement was not "substantially correct" -- although respondent's own proofs tend to show that it was -- that opinion was at least a reasonable one, and there was no evidence to impeach the witness' good faith in holding it. The Times' failure to retract upon respondent's demand, although it later retracted upon the demand of Governor Patterson, is likewise not adequate evidence of malice for constitutional purposes. Whether or not a failure to retract may ever constitute such evidence, there are two reasons why it does not here. First, the letter written by the Times reflected a reasonable doubt on its part as to whether the advertisement could reasonably be taken to refer to respondent at all. Second, it was not a final refusal, since it asked for an explanation on this point -- a request that respondent chose to ignore. Nor does the retraction upon the demand of the Governor supply the necessary proof. It may be doubted that a failure to retract, which is not itself evidence of malice, can retroactively become such by virtue of a retraction subsequently made to another party. But, in any event, that did not happen here, since the explanation given by the Times' Secretary for the distinction drawn between respondent and the Governor was a reasonable one, the good faith of which was not impeached.

Finally, there is evidence that the Times published the advertisement without checking its accuracy against the news stories in the Times' own files. The mere presence of the stories in the files does not, of course, establish that the Times "knew" the advertisement was false, since the state of mind required for actual malice would have to be brought home to the persons in the Times' organization having responsibility for the publication of the advertisement. With respect to the failure of those persons to make the check, the record shows that they relied upon their knowledge of the good reputation of many of those whose names were listed as sponsors of the advertisement, and upon the letter from A. Philip Randolph, known to them as a responsible individual, certifying that the use of the names was authorized. There was testimony that the persons handling the advertisement saw nothing in it that would render it unacceptable under the Times' policy of rejecting advertisements containing "attacks of a personal character"; their failure to reject it on this ground was not unreasonable. We think the evidence against the Times supports, at most, a finding of negligence in failing to discover the misstatements, and is constitutionally insufficient to show the recklessness that is required for a finding of actual malice. [ ]

We also think the evidence was constitutionally defective in another respect: it was incapable of supporting the jury's finding that the allegedly libelous statements were made "of and concerning" respondent. Respondent relies on the words of the advertisement and the testimony of six witnesses to establish a connection between it and himself. Thus, in his brief to this Court, he states:

> The reference to respondent as police commissioner is clear from the ad. In addition, the jury heard the testimony of a newspaper editor . . . ; a real estate and insurance man . . . ; the sales manager of a men's clothing store . . . ; a food equipment man . . . ; a service station operator . . . , and the operator of a truck line for whom respondent had formerly worked. . . . Each of these witnesses stated that he associated the statements with respondent. . . .

(Citations to record omitted.) There was no reference to respondent in the advertisement, either by name or official position. A number of the allegedly libelous statements -- the charges that the dining hall was padlocked and that Dr. King's home was bombed, his person assaulted, and a perjury prosecution instituted against him -- did not even concern the police; despite the ingenuity of the arguments which would attach this significance to the word "They," it is plain that these statements could not reasonably be read as accusing respondent of personal involvement in the acts in question. The statements upon which respondent principally relies as referring to him are the two allegations that did concern the police or police functions: that "truckloads of police . . . ringed the Alabama State College Campus" after the demonstration on the State Capitol steps, and that Dr. King had been "arrested . . . seven times." These statements were false only in that the police had been "deployed near" the campus, but had not actually "ringed" it, and had not gone there in connection with the State Capitol demonstration, and in that Dr. King had been arrested only four times. The ruling that

199

these discrepancies between what was true and what was asserted were sufficient to injure respondent's reputation may itself raise constitutional problems, but we need not consider them here. Although the statements may be taken as referring to the police, they did not, on their face, make even an oblique reference to respondent as an individual. Support for the asserted reference must, therefore, be sought in the testimony of respondent's witnesses. But none of them suggested any basis for the belief that respondent himself was attacked in the advertisement beyond the bare fact that he was in overall charge of the Police Department and thus bore official responsibility for police conduct; to the extent that some of the witnesses thought respondent to have been charged with ordering or approving the conduct or otherwise being personally involved in it, they based this notion not on any statements in the advertisement, and not on any evidence that he had, in fact, been so involved, but solely on the unsupported assumption that, because of his official position, he must have been.{GO>28} This reliance on the bare fact of respondent's official position{GO>29} was made explicit by the Supreme Court of Alabama. That court, in holding that the trial court "did not err in overruling the demurrer [of the Times] in the aspect that the libelous matter was not of and concerning the [plaintiff,]" based its ruling on the proposition that:

> We think it common knowledge that the average person knows that municipal agents, such as police and firemen, and others, are under the control and direction of the city governing body, and more particularly under the direction and control of a single commissioner. In measuring the performance or deficiencies of such groups, praise or criticism is usually attached to the official in complete control of the body.

[ ]

This proposition has disquieting implications for criticism of governmental conduct. For good reason,

> no court of last resort in this country has ever held, or even suggested, that prosecutions for libel on government have any place in the American system of jurisprudence.

[ ] The present proposition would sidestep this obstacle by transmuting criticism of government, however impersonal it may seem on its face, into personal criticism, and hence potential libel, of the officials of whom the government is composed. There is no legal alchemy by which a State may thus create the cause of action that would otherwise be denied for a publication which, as respondent himself said of the advertisement, "reflects not only on me but on the other Commissioners and the community." Raising as it does the possibility that a good faith critic of government will be penalized for his criticism, the proposition relied on by the Alabama courts strikes at the very center of the constitutionally protected area of free expression. We hold that such a proposition may not constitutionally be utilized to establish that an otherwise impersonal attack on governmental operations was a libel of an official responsible for those operations. Since it was relied on exclusively here, and there

was no other evidence to connect the statements with respondent, the evidence was constitutionally insufficient to support a finding that the statements referred to respondent.

The judgment of the Supreme Court of Alabama is reversed, and the case is remanded to that court for further proceedings not inconsistent with this opinion.

Reversed and remanded.

Gertz v. Robert Welch, Inc. (MCLE, page 352) was handed down by the Supreme Court 10 years after *New York Times v. Sullivan*. For the first time the Court considered the standard of care to be applied in the case of a private figure. In a split (5-4) decision, the justices ruled that each state may set its own standard so long as it is not liability without fault ("strict liability"). According to the Court, there are two types of public figures -- "all-purpose" and "limited." For purposes of libel, the former are treated the same as public officials -- *i.e.*, they must demonstrate actual malice to recover damages for defamation. The latter need to demonstrate actual malice only when the defamatory information concerns a public controversy in which the individual has voluntarily become involved. The Court also held that all individuals -- public officials, public figures and private figures -- must demonstrate actual malice in order to recover punitive damages. Most communication law scholars consider the *Gertz* decision second in importance in libel law only to *New York Times v. Sullivan*.

Gertz v. Robert Welch, Inc.

Argued November 14, 1973
Decided June 25, 1974

418 U.S. 323, 94 S.Ct. 2997, 41 L.Ed.2d 789, 1 Med.L.Rptr. 1633

CERTIORARI TO THE UNITED STATES COURT OF APPEALS FOR THE SEVENTH CIRCUIT

Syllabus

A Chicago policeman named Nuccio was convicted of murder. The victim's family retained petitioner, a reputable attorney, to represent them in civil litigation against Nuccio. An article appearing in respondent's magazine alleged that Nuccio's murder trial was part of a Communist conspiracy to discredit the local police, and it falsely stated that petitioner had arranged Nuccio's "frameup," implied that petitioner had a criminal record, and labeled him a "Communist-fronter." Petitioner brought this diversity libel action against respondent. After the jury returned a verdict for petitioner, the District Court decided that the standard enunciated in *New York Times Co. v. Sullivan,* 376 U.S. 254, which bars media liability for defamation of a public official absent proof that the defamatory statements were published with knowledge of their falsity or in reckless disregard of the truth, should apply to this suit. The court concluded that that standard protects media discussion of a public issue without regard to whether the person defamed is a public official as in *New York Times Co. v. Sullivan, supra,* or a public figure, as in *Curtis Publishing Co. v. Butts,* 388 U.S. 130. The court found that petitioner had failed to prove knowledge of falsity or reckless disregard for the truth, and therefore entered judgment *n.o.v.* for respondent. The Court of Appeals affirmed.

Held:

1. A publisher or broadcaster of defamatory falsehoods about an individual who is neither a public official nor a public figure may not claim the *New York Times* protection against liability for defamation on the ground that the defamatory statements concern an issue of public or general interest.

(a) Because private individuals characteristically have less effective opportunities for rebuttal than do public officials and public figures, they are more vulnerable to injury from defamation. Because they have not voluntarily exposed themselves to increased risk of injury from defamatory falsehoods, they are also more deserving of recovery. The state interest in compensating injury to the reputation of private individuals is therefore greater than for public officials and public figures.

(b) To extend the *New York Times* standard to media defamation of private persons whenever an issue of general or public interest is involved would abridge to an unacceptable degree the legitimate state interest in compensating private individuals for injury to reputation and would occasion the additional difficulty of forcing courts to decide on an *ad hoc* basis which publications and broadcasts address issues of general or public interest and which do not.

(c) So long as they do not impose liability without fault, the States may define for themselves the appropriate standard of liability for a publisher or broadcaster of defamatory falsehood which injures a private individual and whose substance makes substantial danger to reputation apparent.

2. The States, however, may not permit recovery of presumed or punitive damages when liability is not based on knowledge of falsity or reckless disregard for the truth, and the private defamation plaintiff who establishes liability under a less demanding standard than the *New York Times* test may recover compensation only for actual injury.

3. Petitioner was neither a public official nor a public figure.

(a) Neither petitioner's past service on certain city committees nor his appearance as an attorney at the coroner's inquest into the death of the murder victim made him a public official.

(b) Petitioner was also not a public figure. Absent clear evidence of general fame or notoriety in the community and pervasive involvement in ordering the affairs of society, an individual should not be deemed a public figure for all aspects of his life. Rather, the public figure question should be determined by reference to the individual's participation in the particular controversy giving rise to the defamation. Petitioner's role in the Nuccio affair did not make him a public figure.

471 F.2d 801, reversed and remanded.

POWELL, J., delivered the opinion of the Court, in which WHITE, MARSHALL, BLACKMUN, and REHNQUIST, JJ., joined. BLACKMUN, J., filed a concurring opinion, BURGER, C.J., DOUGLAS, J., BRENNAN, J., and WHITE, J., filed dissenting opinions.

POWELL, J., lead opinion

MR. JUSTICE POWELL delivered the opinion of the Court.

This Court has struggled for nearly a decade to define the proper accommodation between the law of defamation and the freedoms of speech and press protected by the First Amendment. With this decision we return to that effort. We granted certiorari to reconsider the extent of a publisher's constitutional privilege against liability for defamation of a private citizen. [ ]

I

In 1968, a Chicago policeman named Nuccio shot and killed a youth named Nelson. The state authorities prosecuted Nuccio for the homicide and ultimately obtained a conviction for murder in the second degree. The Nelson family retained petitioner Elmer Gertz, a reputable attorney, to represent them in civil litigation against Nuccio.

Respondent publishes American Opinion, a monthly outlet for the views of the John Birch Society. Early in the 1960's, the magazine began to warn of a nationwide conspiracy to discredit local law enforcement agencies and create in their stead a national police force capable of supporting a Communist dictatorship. As part of the continuing effort to alert the public to this assumed danger, the managing editor of American Opinion commissioned an article on the murder trial of Officer Nuccio. For this purpose, he engaged a regular contributor to the magazine. In March, 1969, respondent published the resulting article under the title "FRAME-UP: Richard Nuccio And The War On Police." The article purports to demonstrate that the testimony against Nuccio at his criminal trial was false, and that his prosecution was part of the Communist campaign against the police.

In his capacity as counsel for the Nelson family in the civil litigation, petitioner attended the coroner's inquest into the boy's death and initiated actions for damages, but he neither discussed Officer Nuccio with the press nor played any part in the criminal proceeding. Notwithstanding petitioner's remote connection with the prosecution of Nuccio, respondent's magazine portrayed him as an architect of the "frame-up." According to the article, the police file on petitioner took "a big, Irish cop to lift." The article stated that petitioner had been an official of the

204

Marxist League for Industrial Democracy, originally known as the Intercollegiate Socialist Society, which has advocated the violent seizure of our government.

It labeled Gertz a "Leninist" and a "Communist-fronter." It also stated that Gertz had been an officer of the National Lawyers Guild, described as a Communist organization that "probably did more than any other outfit to plan the Communist attack on the Chicago police during the 1968 Democratic Convention."

These statements contained serious inaccuracies. The implication that petitioner had a criminal record was false. Petitioner had been a member and officer of the National Lawyers Guild some 15 years earlier, but there was no evidence that he or that organization had taken any part in planning the 1968 demonstrations in Chicago. There was also no basis for the charge that petitioner was a "Leninist" or a "Communist-fronter." And he had never been a member of the "Marxist League for Industrial Democracy" or the "Intercollegiate Socialist Society."

The managing editor of American Opinion made no effort to verify or substantiate the charges against petitioner. Instead, he appended an editorial introduction stating that the author had "conducted extensive research into the Richard Nuccio Case." And he included in the article a photograph of petitioner and wrote the caption that appeared under it: "Elmer Gertz of Red Guild harasses Nuccio." Respondent placed the issue of American Opinion containing the article on sale at newsstands throughout the country and distributed reprints of the article on the streets of Chicago.

Petitioner filed a diversity action for libel in the United States District Court for the Northern District of Illinois. He claimed that the falsehoods published by respondent injured his reputation as a lawyer and a citizen. Before filing an answer, respondent moved to dismiss the complaint for failure to state a claim upon which relief could be granted, apparently on the ground that petitioner failed to allege special damages. But the court ruled that statements contained in the article constituted libel *per se* under Illinois law, and that, consequently, petitioner need not plead special damages. [ ]

After answering the complaint, respondent filed a pretrial motion for summary judgment, claiming a constitutional privilege against liability for defamation. It asserted that petitioner was a public official or a public figure, and that the article concerned an issue of public interest and concern. For these reasons, respondent argued, it was entitled to invoke the privilege enunciated in *New York Times Co. v. Sullivan* [ ]. Under this rule, respondent would escape liability unless petitioner could prove publication of defamatory falsehood "with `actual malice' -- that is, with knowledge that it was false or with reckless disregard of whether it was false or not." [ ] Respondent claimed that petitioner could not make such a showing, and submitted a supporting affidavit by the magazine's managing editor. The editor denied any knowledge of the falsity of the statements concerning petitioner, and stated that he had relied on the author's reputation and on his prior experience with the accuracy and authenticity of the author's contributions to American Opinion.

The District Court denied respondent's motion for summary judgment in a memorandum opinion of September 16, 1970. The court

did not dispute respondent's claim to the protection of the *New York Times* standard. Rather, it concluded that petitioner might overcome the constitutional privilege by making a factual showing sufficient to prove publication of defamatory falsehood in reckless disregard of the truth. During the course of the trial, however, it became clear that the trial court had not accepted all of respondent's asserted grounds for applying the *New York Times* rule to this case. It thought that respondent's claim to the protection of the constitutional privilege depended on the contention that petitioner was either a public official under the *New York Times* decision or a public figure under *Curtis Publishing Co. v. Butts* [ ], apparently discounting the argument that a privilege would arise from the presence of a public issue. After all the evidence had been presented but before submission of the case to the jury, the court ruled, in effect, that petitioner was neither a public official nor a public figure. It added that, if he were, the resulting application of the *New York Times* standard would require a directed verdict for respondent. Because some statements in the article constituted libel *per se* under Illinois law, the court submitted the case to the jury under instructions that withdrew from its consideration all issues save the measure of damages. The jury awarded $50,000 to petitioner.

Following the jury verdict and on further reflection, the District Court concluded that the *New York Times* standard should govern this case even though petitioner was not a public official or public figure. It accepted respondent's contention that that privilege protected discussion of any public issue without regard to the status of a person defamed therein. Accordingly, the court entered judgment for respondent notwithstanding the jury's verdict.{GO>2} This conclusion anticipated the reasoning of a plurality of this Court in *Rosenbloom v. Metromedia, Inc.* [ ].

Petitioner appealed to contest the applicability of the *New York Times* standard to this case. Although the Court of Appeals for the Seventh Circuit doubted the correctness of the District Court's determination that petitioner was not a public figure, it did not overturn that finding. It agreed with the District Court that respondent could assert the constitutional privilege because the article concerned a matter of public interest, citing this Court's intervening decision in *Rosenbloom v. Metromedia, Inc., supra*. The Court of Appeals read Rosenbloom to require application of the *New York Times* standard to any publication or broadcast about an issue of significant public interest, without regard to the position, fame, or anonymity of the person defamed, and it concluded that respondent's statements concerned such an issue. After reviewing the record, the Court of Appeals endorsed the District Court's conclusion that petitioner had failed to show by clear and convincing evidence that respondent had acted with "actual malice" as defined by *New York Times*. There was no evidence that the managing editor of American Opinion knew of the falsity of the accusations made in the article. In fact, he knew nothing about petitioner except what he learned from the article. The court correctly noted that mere proof of failure to investigate, without more, cannot establish reckless disregard for the truth. Rather, the publisher must act with a "high degree of awareness of . . . probable falsity." [ ] The evidence in this case did not reveal that respondent had cause for such an awareness. The Court of Appeals therefore affirmed [ ]. For the reasons stated below, we reverse.

II

The principal issue in this case is whether a newspaper or broadcaster that publishes defamatory falsehoods about an individual who is neither a public official nor a public figure may claim a constitutional privilege against liability for the injury inflicted by those statements. The Court considered this question on the rather different set of facts presented in *Rosenbloom v. Metromedia, Inc.* [ ]. Rosenbloom, a distributor of nudist magazines, was arrested for selling allegedly obscene material while making a delivery to a retail dealer. The police obtained a warrant and seized his entire inventory of 3,000 books and magazines. He sought and obtained an injunction prohibiting further police interference with his business. He then sued a local radio station for failing to note in two of its newscasts that the 3,000 items seized were only "reportedly" or "allegedly" obscene and for broadcasting references to "the smut literature racket" and to "girlie book peddlers" in its coverage of the court proceeding for injunctive relief. He obtained a judgment against the radio station, but the Court of Appeals for the Third Circuit held the *New York Times* privilege applicable to the broadcast, and reversed. [ ]

This Court affirmed the decision below, but no majority could agree on a controlling rationale. The eight Justices who participated in *Rosenbloom* announced their views in five separate opinions, none of which commanded more than three votes. The several statements not only reveal disagreement about the appropriate result in that case, they also reflect divergent traditions of thought about the general problem of reconciling the law of defamation with the First Amendment. One approach has been to extend the *New York Times* test to an expanding variety of situations. Another has been to vary the level of constitutional privilege for defamatory falsehood with the status of the person defamed. And a third view would grant to the press and broadcast media absolute immunity from liability for defamation. To place our holding in the proper context, we preface our discussion of this case with a review of the several *Rosenbloom* opinions and their antecedents.

In affirming the trial court's judgment in the instant case, the Court of Appeals relied on MR. JUSTICE BRENNAN's conclusion for the *Rosenbloom* plurality that "all discussion and communication involving matters of public or general concern" [ ], warrant the protection from liability for defamation accorded by the rule originally enunciated in *New York Times Co. v. Sullivan* [ ]. There, this Court defined a constitutional privilege intended to free criticism of public officials from the restraints imposed by the common law of defamation. The Times ran a political advertisement endorsing civil rights demonstrations by black students in Alabama and impliedly condemning the performance of local law enforcement officials. A police commissioner established in state court that certain misstatements in the advertisement referred to him, and that they constituted libel *per se* under Alabama law. This showing left the Times with the single defense of truth, for, under Alabama law, neither good faith nor reasonable care would protect the newspaper from liability. This Court concluded that a "rule compelling the critic of official conduct to guarantee the truth of all his factual assertions" would deter protected speech [ ], and announced the constitutional privilege designed to counter that effect:

> The constitutional guarantees require, we think, a federal rule that prohibits a public official from recovering damages for a defamatory falsehood relating to his official conduct unless he proves that the statement was made with "actual malice" -- that is, with knowledge that it was false or with reckless disregard of whether it was false or not. [ ]

Three years after *New York Times,* a majority of the Court agreed to extend the constitutional privilege to defamatory criticism of "public figures." This extension was announced in *Curtis Publishing Co. v. Butts* and its companion [ ]. The first case involved the Saturday Evening Post's charge that Coach Wally Butts of the University of Georgia had conspired with Coach "Bear" Bryant of the University of Alabama to fix a football game between their respective schools. *Walker* involved an erroneous Associated Press account of former Major General Edwin Waler's participation in a University of Mississippi campus riot. Because Butts was paid by a private alumni association and Walker had resigned from the Army, neither could be classified as a "public official" under *New York Times.* Although Mr. Justice Harlan announced the result in both cases, a majority of the Court agreed with Mr. Chief Justice Warren's conclusion that the *New York Times* test should apply to criticism of "public figures" as well as "public officials." The Court extended the constitutional privilege announced in that case to protect defamatory criticism of nonpublic persons who

> are nevertheless intimately involved in the resolution of important public questions or, by reason of their fame, shape events in areas of concern to society at large.

[ ]

In his opinion for the plurality in *Rosenbloom v. Metromedia, Inc.* [ ], MR. JUSTICE BRENNAN took the *New York Times* privilege one step further. He concluded that its protection should extend to defamatory

208

falsehoods relating to private persons if the statements concerned matters of general or public interest. He abjured the suggested distinction between public officials and public figures, on the one hand, and private individuals, on the other. He focused instead on society's interest in learning about certain issues:

> If a matter is a subject of public or general interest, it cannot suddenly become less so merely because a private individual is involved, or because in some sense the individual did not "voluntarily" choose to become involved.

[ ] Thus, under the plurality opinion, a private citizen involuntarily associated with a matter of general interest has no recourse for injury to his reputation unless he can satisfy the demanding requirements of the *New York Times* test.

Two Members of the Court concurred in the result in *Rosenbloom,* but departed from the reasoning of the plurality. Mr. Justice Black restated his view, long shared by MR. JUSTICE DOUGLAS, that the First Amendment cloaks the news media with an absolute and indefeasible immunity from liability for defamation. [ ] MR JUSTICE WHITE concurred on a narrower ground. [ ] He concluded that

> the First Amendment gives the press and the broadcast media a privilege to report and comment upon the official actions of public servants in full detail, with no requirement that the reputation or the privacy of an individual involved in or affected by the official action be spared from public view.

[ ] He therefore declined to reach the broader questions addressed by the other Justices.

Mr. Justice Harlan dissented. Although he had joined the opinion of the Court in *New York Times,* in *Curtis Publishing Co.,* he had contested the extension of the privilege to public figures. There, he had argued that a public figure who held no governmental office should be allowed to recover damages for defamation

> on a showing of highly unreasonable conduct constituting an extreme departure from the standards of investigation and reporting ordinarily adhered to by responsible publishers.

[ ] In his *Curtis Publishing Co.* opinion, Mr. Justice Harlan had distinguished *New York Times* primarily on the ground that defamation actions by public officials "lay close to seditious libel. . . ." [ ] Recovery of damages by one who held no public office, however, could not "be viewed as a vindication of governmental policy." [ ] Additionally, he had intimated that, because most public officials enjoyed absolute immunity from liability for their own defamatory utterances under [ ], they lacked a strong claim to the protection of the courts.

In *Rosenbloom,* Mr. Justice Harlan modified these views.   He acquiesced in the application of the privilege to defamation of public figures, but argued that a different rule should obtain where defamatory falsehood harmed a private individual.   He noted that a private person has less likelihood "of securing access to channels of communication sufficient to rebut falsehoods concerning him" than do public officials and public figures [   ], and has not voluntarily placed himself in the public spotlight.   Mr. Justice Harlan concluded that the States could constitutionally allow private individuals to recover damages for defamation on the basis of any standard of care except liability without fault.

MR. JUSTICE MARSHALL dissented in *Rosenbloom* in an opinion joined by MR. JUSTICE STEWART. [   ] He thought that the plurality's "public or general interest" test for determining the applicability of the *New York Times* privilege would involve the courts in the dangerous business of deciding "what information is relevant to self-government." [   ] He also contended that the plurality's position inadequately served "society's interest in protecting private individuals from being thrust into the public eye by the distorting light of defamation." [ ] MR. JUSTICE MARSHALL therefore reached the conclusion, also reached by Mr. Justice Harlan, that the States should be "essentially free to continue the evolution of the common law of defamation and to articulate whatever fault standard best suits the State's need," so long as the States did not impose liability without fault. [   ] The principal point of disagreement among the three dissenters concerned punitive damages.   Whereas Mr. Justice Harlan thought that the States could allow punitive damages in amounts bearing "a reasonable and purposeful relationship to the actual harm done . . ." [   ], MR. JUSTICE MARSHALL concluded that the size and unpredictability of jury awards of exemplary damages unnecessarily exacerbated the problems of media self-censorship, and that such damages should therefore be forbidden.

III

We begin with the common ground.   Under the First Amendment, there is no such thing as a false idea.   However pernicious an opinion may seem, we depend for its correction not on the conscience of judges and juries, but on the competition of other ideas. But there is no constitutional value in false statements of fact.   Neither the intentional lie nor the careless error materially advances society's interest in "uninhibited, robust? and wide-open" debate on public issues. [   ] They belong to that category of utterances which

> are no essential part of any exposition of ideas, and are of such slight social value as a step to truth that any benefit that may be derived from them is clearly outweighed by the social interest in order and morality.

[   ]

Although the erroneous statement of fact is not worthy of constitutional protection, it is nevertheless inevitable in free debate.   As

210

James Madison pointed out in the Report on the Virginia Resolutions of 1798: "Some degree of abuse is inseparable from the proper use of every thing; and in no instance is this more true than in that of the press." [ ] And punishment of error runs the risk of inducing a cautious and restrictive exercise of the constitutionally guaranteed freedoms of speech and press. Our decisions recognize that a rule of strict liability that compels a publisher or broadcaster to guarantee the accuracy of his factual assertions may lead to intolerable self-censorship. Allowing the media to avoid liability only by proving the truth of all injurious statements does not accord adequate protection to First Amendment liberties. As the Court stated in *New York Times Co. v. Sullivan* [ ]:

> Allowance of the defense of truth, with the burden of proving it on the defendant, does not mean that only false speech will be deterred.

The First Amendment requires that we protect some falsehood in order to protect speech that matters.

The need to avoid self-censorship by the news media is, however, not the only societal value at issue. If it were, this Court would have embraced long ago the view that publishers and broadcasters enjoy an unconditional and indefeasible immunity from liability for defamation. [ ] Such a rule would, indeed, obviate the fear that the prospect of civil liability for injurious falsehood might dissuade a timorous press from the effective exercise of First Amendment freedoms. Yet absolute protection for the communications media requires a total sacrifice of the competing value served by the law of defamation.

The legitimate state interest underlying the law of libel is the compensation of individuals for the harm inflicted on them by defamatory falsehood. We would not lightly require the State to abandon this purpose, for, as MR. JUSTICE STEWART has reminded us, the individual's right to the protection of his own good name

> reflects no more than our basic concept of the essential dignity and worth of every human being -- a concept at the root of any decent system of ordered liberty. The protection of private personality, like the protection of life itself, is left primarily to the individual States under the Ninth and Tenth Amendments. But this does not mean that the right is entitled to any less recognition by this Court as a basic of our constitutional system.

[ ]

Some tension necessarily exists between the need for a vigorous and uninhibited press and the legitimate interest in redressing wrongful injury. As Mr. Justice Harlan stated,

> some antithesis between freedom of speech and press and libel actions persists, for libel remains premised on the content of speech and limits the freedom of the publisher to express certain sentiments, at least without guaranteeing legal proof of their substantial accuracy.

[ ] In our continuing effort to define the proper accommodation between

these competing concerns, we have been especially anxious to assure to the freedoms of speech and press that "breathing space" essential to their fruitful exercise. [ ] To that end, this Court has extended a measure of strategic protection to defamatory falsehood.

The *New York Times* standard defines the level of constitutional protection appropriate to the context of defamation of a public person. Those who, by reason of the notoriety of their achievements or the vigor and success with which they seek the public's attention, are properly classed as public figures and those who hold governmental office may recover for injury to reputation only on clear and convincing proof that the defamatory falsehood was made with knowledge of its falsity or with reckless disregard for the truth. This standard administers an extremely powerful antidote to the inducement to media self-censorship of the common law rule of strict liability for libel and slander. And it exacts a correspondingly high price from the victims of defamatory falsehood. Plainly, many deserving plaintiffs, including some intentionally subjected to injury, will be unable to surmount the barrier of the *New York Times* test. Despite this substantial abridgment of the state law right to compensation for wrongful hurt to one's reputation, the Court has concluded that the protection of the *New York Times* privilege should be available to publishers and broadcasters of defamatory falsehood concerning public officials and public figures. [ ] We think that these decisions are correct, but we do not find their holdings justified solely by reference to the interest of the press and broadcast media in immunity from liability. Rather, we believe that the *New York Times* rule states an accommodation between this concern and the limited state interest present in the context of libel actions brought by public persons. For the reasons stated below, we conclude that the state interest in compensating injury to the reputation of private individuals requires that a different rule should obtain with respect to them.

Theoretically, of course, the balance between the needs of the press and the individual's claim to compensation for wrongful injury might be struck on a case-by-case basis. As Mr. Justice Harlan hypothesized,

> it might seem, purely as an abstract matter, that the most utilitarian approach would be to scrutinize carefully every jury verdict in every libel case, in order to ascertain whether the final judgment leaves fully protected whatever First Amendment values transcend the legitimate state interest in protecting the particular plaintiff who prevailed.

[ ] But this approach would lead to unpredictable results and uncertain expectations, and it could render our duty to supervise the lower courts unmanageable. Because an *ad hoc* resolution of the competing interests at stake in each particular case is not feasible, we must lay down broad rules of general application: such rules necessarily treat alike various cases involving differences as well as similarities. Thus, it is often true that not all of the considerations which justify adoption of a given rule will obtain in each particular case decided under its authority.

With that caveat, we have no difficulty in distinguishing among defamation plaintiffs. The first remedy of any victim of defamation is self-help -- using available opportunities to contradict the lie or correct the error, and thereby to minimize its adverse impact on reputation. Public officials and public figures usually enjoy significantly greater access to the channels of effective communication, and hence have a more realistic opportunity to counteract false statements than private individuals normally enjoy. Private individuals are therefore more vulnerable to injury, and the state interest in protecting them is correspondingly greater.

More important than the likelihood that private individuals will lack effective opportunities for rebuttal, there is a compelling normative consideration underlying the distinction between public and private defamation plaintiffs. An individual who decides to seek governmental office must accept certain necessary consequences of that involvement in public affairs. He runs the risk of closer public scrutiny than might otherwise be the case. And society's interest in the officers of government is not strictly limited to the formal discharge of official duties. As the Court pointed out in *Garrison v. Louisiana* [ ], the public's interest extends to

> anything which might touch on an official's fitness for office. . . . Few personal attributes are more germane to fitness for office than dishonesty, malfeasance, or improper motivation, even though these characteristics may also affect the official's private character.

Those classed as public figures stand in a similar position. Hypothetically, it may be possible for someone to become a public figure through no purposeful action of his own, but the instances of truly involuntary public figures must be exceedingly rare. For the most part, those who attain this status have assumed roles of especial prominence in the affairs of society. Some occupy positions of such persuasive power and influence that they are deemed public figures for all purposes. More commonly, those classed as public figures have thrust themselves to the forefront of particular public controversies in order to influence the resolution of the issues involved. In either event, they invite attention and comment.

Even if the foregoing generalities do not obtain in every instance, the communications media are entitled to act on the assumption that public officials and public figures have voluntarily exposed themselves to increased risk of injury from defamatory falsehood concerning them. No such assumption is justified with respect to a private individual. He has not accepted public office or assumed an "influential role in ordering society." [ ] He has relinquished no part of his interest in the protection of his own good name, and consequently he has a more compelling call on the courts for redress of injury inflicted by defamatory falsehood. Thus, private individuals are not only more vulnerable to injury than public officials and public figures; they are also more deserving of recovery.

For these reasons, we conclude that the States should retain
213

substantial latitude in their efforts to enforce a legal remedy for defamatory falsehood injurious to the reputation of a private individual. The extension of the *New York Times* test proposed by the *Rosenbloom* plurality would abridge this legitimate state interest to a degree that we find unacceptable. And it would occasion the additional difficulty of forcing state and federal judges to decide on an *ad hoc* basis which publications address issues of "general or public interest" and which do not -- to determine, in the words of MR. JUSTICE MARSHALL, "what information is relevant to self-government." [ ] We doubt the wisdom of committing this task to the conscience of judges. Nor does the Constitution require us to draw so thin a line between the drastic alternatives of the *New York Times* privilege and the common law of strict liability for defamatory error. The "public or general interest" test for determining the applicability of the *New York Times* standard to private defamation actions inadequately serves both of the competing values at stake. On the one hand, a private individual whose reputation is injured by defamatory falsehood that does concern an issue of public or general interest has no recourse unless he can meet the rigorous requirements of *New York Times*. This is true despite the factors that distinguish the state interest in compensating private individuals from the analogous interest involved in the context of public persons. On the other hand, a publisher or broadcaster of a defamatory error which a court deems unrelated to an issue of public or general interest may be held liable in damages even if it took every reasonable precaution to ensure the accuracy of its assertions. And liability may far exceed compensation for any actual injury to the plaintiff, for the jury may be permitted to presume damages without proof of loss and even to award punitive damages.

We hold that, so long as they do not impose liability without fault, the States may define for themselves the appropriate standard of liability for a publisher or broadcaster of defamatory falsehood injurious to a private individual. This approach provides a more equitable boundary between the competing concerns involved here. It recognizes the strength of the legitimate state interest in compensating private individuals for wrongful injury to reputation, yet shields the press and broadcast media from the rigors of strict liability for defamation. At least this conclusion obtains where, as here, the substance of the defamatory statement "makes substantial danger to reputation apparent." This phrase places in perspective the conclusion we announce today. Our inquiry would involve considerations somewhat different from those discussed above if a State purported to condition civil liability on a factual misstatement whose content did not warn a reasonably prudent editor or broadcaster of its defamatory potential. [ ] Such a case is not now before us, and we intimate no view as to its proper resolution.

IV

Our accommodation of the competing values at stake in defamation suits by private individuals allows the States to impose liability on the publisher or broadcaster of defamatory falsehood on a less demanding showing than that required by *New York Times*. This conclusion is not based on a belief that the considerations which prompted the adoption of the *New York Times* privilege for defamation of public officials and its extension to public figures are wholly inapplicable to the context of private individuals. Rather, we endorse this approach in recognition of the strong and legitimate state interest in compensating private individuals for injury to reputation. But this countervailing state interest extends no further than compensation for actual injury. For the reasons stated below, we hold that the States may not permit recovery of presumed or punitive damages, at least when liability is not based on a showing of knowledge of falsity or reckless disregard for the truth.

The common law of defamation is an oddity of tort law, for it allows recovery of purportedly compensatory damages without evidence of actual loss. Under the traditional rules pertaining to actions for libel, the existence of injury is presumed from the fact of publication. Juries may award substantial sums as compensation for supposed damage to reputation without any proof that such harm actually occurred. The largely uncontrolled discretion of juries to award damages where there is no loss unnecessarily compounds the potential of any system of liability for defamatory falsehood to inhibit the vigorous exercise of First Amendment freedoms. Additionally, the doctrine of presumed damages invites juries to punish unpopular opinion, rather than to compensate individuals for injury sustained by the publication of a false fact. More to the point, the States have no substantial interest in securing for plaintiffs such as this petitioner gratuitous awards of money damages far in excess of any actual injury.

We would not, of course, invalidate state law simply because we doubt its wisdom, but here we are attempting to reconcile state law with a competing interest grounded in the constitutional command of the First Amendment. It is therefore appropriate to require that state remedies for defamatory falsehood reach no farther than is necessary to protect the legitimate interest involved. It is necessary to restrict defamation plaintiffs who do not prove knowledge of falsity or reckless disregard for the truth to compensation for actual injury. We need not define "actual injury," as trial courts have wide experience in framing appropriate jury instructions in tort actions. Suffice it to say that actual injury is not limited to out-of-pocket loss. Indeed, the more customary types of actual harm inflicted by defamatory falsehood include impairment of reputation and standing in the community, personal humiliation, and mental anguish and suffering. Of course, juries must be limited by appropriate instructions, and all awards must be supported by competent evidence concerning the injury, although there need be no evidence which assigns an actual dollar value to the injury.

We also find no justification for allowing awards of punitive damages against publishers and broadcasters held liable under state-defined standards of liability for defamation. In most jurisdictions jury discretion over the amounts awarded is limited only by the gentle rule that they not be excessive. Consequently, juries assess punitive damages in wholly unpredictable amounts bearing no necessary relation to the actual harm caused. And they remain free to use their discretion selectively to punish expressions of unpopular views. Like the doctrine of presumed damages, jury discretion to award punitive damages unnecessarily exacerbates the danger of media self-censorship, but, unlike the former rule, punitive damages are wholly irrelevant to the state interest that justifies a negligence standard for private defamation actions. They are not compensation for injury. Instead, they are private fines levied by civil juries to punish reprehensible conduct and to deter its future occurrence. In short, the private defamation plaintiff who establishes liability under a less demanding standard than that stated by *New York Times* may recover only such damages as are sufficient to compensate him for actual injury.

V

Notwithstanding our refusal to extend the *New York Times* privilege to defamation of private individuals, respondent contends that we should affirm the judgment below on the ground that petitioner is either a public official or a public figure. There is little basis for the former assertion. Several years prior to the present incident, petitioner had served briefly on housing committees appointed by the mayor of Chicago, but, at the time of publication, he had never held any remunerative governmental position. Respondent admits this, but argues that petitioner's appearance at the coroner's inquest rendered him a "*de facto* public official." Our cases recognize no such concept. Respondent's suggestion would sweep all lawyers under the *New York Times* rule as officers of the court, and distort the plain meaning of the "public official" category beyond all recognition. We decline to follow it.

Respondent's characterization of petitioner as a public figure raises a different question. That designation may rest on either of two alternative bases. In some instances an individual may achieve such pervasive fame or notoriety that he becomes a public figure for all purposes and in all contexts. More commonly, an individual voluntarily injects himself or is drawn into a particular public controversy, and thereby becomes a public figure for a limited range of issues. In either case, such persons assume special prominence in the resolution of public questions.

Petitioner has long been active in community and professional affairs. He has served as an officer of local civic groups and of various professional organizations, and he has published several books and articles on legal subjects. Although petitioner was consequently well known in some circles, he had achieved no general fame or notoriety in the community. None of the prospective jurors called at the trial had ever heard of petitioner prior to this litigation, and respondent offered no proof that this response was atypical of the local population. We would not lightly assume that a citizen's participation in community and professional affairs rendered him a public figure for all purposes. Absent clear evidence of general fame or notoriety in the community, and pervasive involvement in the affairs of society, an individual should not be deemed a public personality for all aspects of his life. It is preferable to reduce the public figure question to a more meaningful context by looking to the nature and extent of an individual's participation in the particular controversy giving rise to the defamation.

In this context, it is plain that petitioner was not a public figure. He played a minimal role at the coroner's inquest, and his participation related solely to his representation of a private client. He took no part in the criminal prosecution of Officer Nuccio. Moreover, he never discussed either the criminal or civil litigation with the press, and was never quoted as having done so. He plainly did not thrust himself into the vortex of this public issue, nor did he engage the public's attention in an attempt to influence its outcome. We are persuaded that the trial court did not err in refusing to characterize petitioner as a public figure for the purpose of this litigation.

We therefore conclude that the *New York Times* standard is inapplicable to this case, and that the trial court erred in entering judgment for respondent. Because the jury was allowed to impose liability without fault and was permitted to presume damages without proof of injury, a new trial is necessary. We reverse and remand for further proceedings in accord with this opinion.

It is so ordered.

Hustler Magazine, Inc. v. Falwell (MCLE, page 361) concerned a parody published in *Hustler* magazine in which Rev. Jerry Falwell related in a fictional interview that he had lost his virginity when he had sex with his mother in an outhouse. The Court unanimously ruled that because the jury had determined that Falwell had not been libeled, he was not entitled to the damages the jury had awarded him for intentional infliction of emotional distress. To recover damages, according to the Court, the plaintiff had to demonstrate that the publication included false statements of fact and the information was published with actual malice. In other words, the statements had to be represented as facts and perceived as such by the public.

Hustler Magazine, Inc. v. Falwell

Argued December 2, 1987
Decided February 24, 1988

485 U.S. 46, 108 S.Ct. 876, 99 L.Ed.2d 41, 14 Med.L.Rptr. 2281

CERTIORARI TO THE UNITED STATES COURT OF APPEALS
FOR
THE FOURTH CIRCUIT

Syllabus

Respondent, a nationally known minister and commentator on politics and public affairs, filed a diversity action in Federal District Court against petitioners, a nationally circulated magazine and its publisher, to recover damages for, *inter alia,* libel and intentional infliction of emotional distress arising from the publication of an advertisement "parody" which, among other things, portrayed respondent as having engaged in a drunken incestuous rendezvous with his mother in an outhouse. The jury found against respondent on the libel claim, specifically finding that the parody could not "reasonably be understood as describing actual facts . . . or events," but ruled in his favor on the emotional distress claim, stating that he should be awarded compensatory and punitive damages. The Court of Appeals affirmed, rejecting petitioners' contention that the "actual malice" standard of *New York Times Co. v. Sullivan* [ ], must be met before respondent can recover for emotional distress. Rejecting as irrelevant the contention that, because the jury found that the parody did not describe actual facts, the ad was an opinion protected by the First Amendment to the Federal Constitution, the court ruled that the issue was whether the ad's publication was sufficiently outrageous to constitute intentional infliction of emotional distress.

Held: In order to protect the free flow of ideas and opinions on matters of public interest and concern, the First and Fourteenth Amendments prohibit public figures and public officials from recovering damages for the tort of intentional infliction of emotional distress by reason of the publication of a caricature such as the ad parody at issue without showing in addition that the publication contains a false statement of fact which was made with "actual malice," *i.e.,* with knowledge that the statement was false or with reckless disregard as to whether or not it was true. The State's interest in protecting public figures from emotional distress is not sufficient to deny First Amendment protection to speech that is patently offensive and is intended to inflict emotional injury when that speech could not reasonably have been interpreted as stating actual facts about the public figure involved. Here, respondent is clearly a "public figure" for First Amendment purposes, and the lower courts' finding that the ad parody was not reasonably believable must be accepted. "Outrageousness" in the area of political and social discourse has an inherent subjectiveness about it which would allow a jury to impose liability on the basis of the jurors' tastes or views, or perhaps on the basis of their dislike of a particular expression, and cannot, consistently with the First Amendment, form a basis for the award of damages for conduct such as that involved here.

797 F.2d 1270, reversed.

REHNQUIST, C.J., delivered the opinion of the Court, in which BRENNAN, MARSHALL, BLACKMUN, STEVENS, O'CONNOR, and SCALIA, JJ., joined. WHITE, J., filed an opinion concurring in the judgment. KENNEDY, J., took no part in the consideration or decision of the case.

REHNQUIST, J., lead opinion

Petitioner Hustler Magazine, Inc., is a magazine of nationwide circulation. Respondent Jerry Falwell, a nationally known minister who has been active as a commentator on politics and public affairs, sued petitioner and its publisher, petitioner Larry Flynt, to recover damages for invasion of privacy, libel, and intentional infliction of emotional distress. The District Court directed a verdict against respondent on the privacy claim, and submitted the other two claims to a jury. The jury found for petitioners on the defamation claim, but found for respondent on the claim for intentional infliction of emotional distress and awarded damages. We now consider whether this award is consistent with the First and Fourteenth Amendments of the United States Constitution.

The inside front cover of the November, 1983, issue of Hustler Magazine featured a "parody" of an advertisement for Campari Liqueur that contained the name and picture of respondent and was entitled "Jerry Falwell talks about his first time." This parody was modeled after actual Campari ads that included interviews with various celebrities about their "first times." Although it was apparent by the end of each interview that this meant the first time they sampled Campari, the ads clearly played on the sexual double entendre of the general subject of "first times." Copying the form and layout of these Campari ads, Hustler's editors chose respondent as the featured celebrity and drafted an alleged "interview" with him in which he states that his "first time" was during a drunken incestuous rendezvous with his mother in an outhouse. The Hustler parody portrays respondent and his mother as drunk and immoral, and suggests that respondent is a hypocrite who preaches only when he is drunk. In small print at the bottom of the page, the ad contains the disclaimer, "ad parody -- not to be taken seriously." The magazine's table of contents also lists the ad as "Fiction; Ad and Personality Parody."

Soon after the November issue of Hustler became available to the public, respondent brought this diversity action in the United States District Court for the Western District of Virginia against Hustler Magazine, Inc., Larry C. Flynt, and Flynt Distributing Co., Inc. Respondent stated in his complaint that publication of the ad parody in Hustler entitled him to recover damages for libel, invasion of privacy, and intentional infliction of emotional distress. The case proceeded to trial. At the close of the evidence, the District Court granted a directed verdict for petitioners on the invasion of privacy claim. The jury then found against respondent on the libel claim, specifically finding that the ad parody could not "reasonably be understood as describing actual facts about [respondent] or actual events in which [he] participated." [ ] The jury ruled for respondent on the intentional infliction of emotional distress claim, however, and stated that he should be awarded $100,000 in compensatory damages, as well as $50,000 each in punitive damages from petitioners. Petitioners' motion for judgment notwithstanding the verdict was denied.

On appeal, the United States Court of Appeals for the Fourth Circuit affirmed the judgment against petitioners. [ ] The court rejected petitioners' argument that the "actual malice" standard of New York Times Co. v. Sullivan [ ], must be met before respondent can recover for emotional distress. The court agreed that, because respondent is concededly a public figure, petitioners are "entitled to the same level of first amendment protection in the claim for intentional infliction of emotional distress that they received in [respondent's] claim for libel." [ ] But this does not mean that a literal application of the actual malice rule is appropriate in the context of an emotional distress claim. In the court's view, the New York Times decision emphasized the constitutional importance not of the falsity of the statement or the defendant's disregard for the truth, but of the heightened level of culpability embodied in the requirement of "knowing . . . or reckless" conduct. Here, the New York Times standard is satisfied by the state law requirement, and the jury's finding, that the defendants have acted intentionally or recklessly. The Court of Appeals then went on to reject the contention that, because the jury found that the ad parody did not describe actual facts about respondent, the ad was an opinion that is protected by the

220

First Amendment. As the court put it, this was "irrelevant," as the issue is "whether [the ad's] publication was sufficiently outrageous to constitute intentional infliction of emotional distress." [ ] Petitioners then filed a petition for rehearing en banc, but this was denied by a divided court. Given the importance of the constitutional issues involved, we granted certiorari. [ ]

This case presents us with a novel question involving First Amendment limitations upon a State's authority to protect its citizens from the intentional infliction of emotional distress. We must decide whether a public figure may recover damages for emotional harm caused by the publication of an ad parody offensive to him, and doubtless gross and repugnant in the eyes of most. Respondent would have us find that a State's interest in protecting public figures from emotional distress is sufficient to deny First Amendment protection to speech that is patently offensive and is intended to inflict emotional injury, even when that speech could not reasonably have been interpreted as stating actual facts about the public figure involved. This we decline to do.

At the heart of the First Amendment is the recognition of the fundamental importance of the free flow of ideas and opinions on matters of public interest and concern.

> [T]he freedom to speak one's mind is not only an aspect of individual liberty -- and thus a good unto itself -- but also is essential to the common quest for truth and the vitality of society as a whole.

[ ] We have therefore been particularly vigilant to ensure that individual expressions of ideas remain free from governmentally imposed sanctions. The First Amendment recognizes no such thing as a "false" idea. [ ] As Justice Holmes wrote,

> when men have realized that time has upset many fighting faiths, they may come to believe even more than they believe the very foundations of their own conduct that the ultimate good desired is better reached by free trade in ideas -- that the best test of truth is the power of the thought to get itself accepted in the competition of the market. . . .

[ ]

The sort of robust political debate encouraged by the First Amendment is bound to produce speech that is critical of those who hold public office or those public figures who are

> intimately involved in the resolution of important public questions or, by reason of their fame, shape events in areas of concern to society at large.

[ ] Justice Frankfurter put it succinctly in *Baumgartner v. United States* [ ], when he said that "[o]ne of the prerogatives of American citizenship is the right to criticize public men and measures." Such criticism, inevitably, will not always be reasoned or moderate; public figures as well as public officials will be subject to "vehement, caustic, and sometimes unpleasantly sharp attacks" [ ].

[T]he candidate who vaunts his spotless record and sterling integrity cannot convincingly cry "Foul!" when an opponent or an industrious reporter attempts to demonstrate the contrary.

[ ]

Of course, this does not mean that any speech about a public figure is immune from sanction in the form of damages. Since *New York Times Co. v. Sullivan* [ ], we have consistently ruled that a public figure may hold a speaker liable for the damage to reputation caused by publication of a defamatory falsehood, but only if the statement was made "with knowledge that it was false or with reckless disregard of whether it was false or not." [ ] False statements of fact are particularly valueless; they interfere with the truthseeking function of the marketplace of ideas, and they cause damage to an individual's reputation that cannot easily be repaired by counterspeech, however persuasive or effective. [ ] But even though falsehoods have little value in and of themselves, they are "nevertheless inevitable in free debate" [ ], and a rule that would impose strict liability on a publisher for false factual assertions would have an undoubted "chilling" effect on speech relating to public figures that does have constitutional value. "'Freedoms of expression require "breathing space."'" [ ] ... This breathing space is provided by a constitutional rule that allows public figures to recover for libel or defamation only when they can prove both that the statement was false and that the statement was made with the requisite level of culpability.

Respondent argues, however, that a different standard should apply in this case because, here, the State seeks to prevent not reputational damage, but the severe emotional distress suffered by the person who is the subject of an offensive publication. [ ] ... In respondent's view, and in the view of the Court of Appeals, so long as the utterance was intended to inflict emotional distress, was outrageous, and did in fact inflict serious emotional distress, it is of no constitutional import whether the statement was a fact or an opinion, or whether it was true or false. It is the intent to cause injury that is the gravamen of the tort, and the State's interest in preventing emotional harm simply outweighs whatever interest a speaker may have in speech of this type.

Generally speaking, the law does not regard the intent to inflict emotional distress as one which should receive much solicitude, and it is quite understandable that most, if not all, jurisdictions have chosen to make it civilly culpable where the conduct in question is sufficiently "outrageous." But in the world of debate about public affairs, many things done with motives that are less than admirable are protected by the First Amendment. In *Garrison v. Louisiana* [ ], we held that, even when a speaker or writer is motivated by hatred or ill-will, his expression was protected by the First Amendment:

> Debate on public issues will not be uninhibited if the speaker must run the risk that it will be proved in court that he spoke out of hatred; even if he did speak out of hatred, utterances honestly believed contribute to the free interchange of ideas and the ascertainment of truth.

222

[ ] Thus, while such a bad motive may be deemed controlling for purposes of tort liability in other areas of the law, we think the First Amendment prohibits such a result in the area of public debate about public figures.

Were we to hold otherwise, there can be little doubt that political cartoonists and satirists would be subjected to damages awards without any showing that their work falsely defamed its subject. Webster's defines a caricature as "the deliberately distorted picturing or imitating of a person, literary style, etc. by exaggerating features or mannerisms for satirical effect." Webster's New Unabridged Twentieth [ ] The appeal of the political cartoon or caricature is often based on exploitation of unfortunate physical traits or politically embarrassing events -- an exploitation often calculated to injure the feelings of the subject of the portrayal. The art of the cartoonist is often not reasoned or evenhanded, but slashing and one-sided. One cartoonist expressed the nature of the art in these words:

> The political cartoon is a weapon of attack, of scorn and ridicule and satire; it is least effective when it tries to pat some politician on the back. It is usually as welcome as a bee sting, and is always controversial in some quarters.

[ ] Several famous examples of this type of intentionally injurious speech were drawn by Thomas Nast, probably the greatest American cartoonist to date, who was associated for many years during the post-Civil War era with Harper's Weekly. In the pages of that publication Nast conducted a graphic vendetta against William M. "Boss" Tweed and his corrupt associates in New York City's "Tweed Ring." It has been described by one historian of the subject as "a sustained attack which in its passion and effectiveness stands alone in the history of American graphic art." [ ] Another writer explains that the success of the Nast cartoon was achieved "because of the emotional impact of its presentation. It continuously goes beyond the bounds of good taste and conventional manners." [ ]

Despite their sometimes caustic nature, from the early cartoon portraying George Washington as an ass down to the present day, graphic depictions and satirical cartoons have played a prominent role in public and political debate. Nast's castigation of the Tweed Ring, Walt McDougall's characterization of Presidential candidate James G. Blaine's banquet with the millionaires at Delmonico's as "The Royal Feast of Belshazzar," and numerous other efforts have undoubtedly had an effect on the course and outcome of contemporaneous debate. Lincoln's tall, gangling posture, Teddy Roosevelt's glasses and teeth, and Franklin D. Roosevelt's jutting jaw and cigarette holder have been memorialized by political cartoons with an effect that could not have been obtained by the photographer or the portrait artist. From the viewpoint of history, it is clear that our political discourse would have been considerably poorer without them.

Respondent contends, however, that the caricature in question here
223

was so "outrageous" as to distinguish it from more traditional political cartoons. There is no doubt that the caricature of respondent and his mother published in Hustler is at best a distant cousin of the political cartoons described above, and a rather poor relation at that. If it were possible by laying down a principled standard to separate the one from the other, public discourse would probably suffer little or no harm. But we doubt that there is any such standard, and we are quite sure that the pejorative description "outrageous" does not supply one. "Outrageousness" in the area of political and social discourse has an inherent subjectiveness about it which would allow a jury to impose liability on the basis of the jurors' tastes or views, or perhaps on the basis of their dislike of a particular expression. An "outrageousness" standard thus runs afoul of our longstanding refusal to allow damages to be awarded because the speech in question may have an adverse emotional impact on the audience. [ ] … And, as we stated in *FCC v. Pacifica Foundation* [ ]:

> [T]he fact that society may find speech offensive is not a sufficient reason for suppressing it. Indeed, if it is the speaker's opinion that gives offense, that consequence is a reason for according it constitutional protection. For it is a central tenet of the First Amendment that the government must remain neutral in the marketplace of ideas.

[ ] Admittedly, these oft-repeated First Amendment principles, like other principles, are subject to limitations. We recognized in *Pacifica Foundation* that speech that is "'vulgar,' 'offensive,' and 'shocking'" is "not entitled to absolute constitutional protection under all circumstances." [ ] In *Chaplinsky v. New Hampshire* [ ], we held that a State could lawfully punish an individual for the use of insulting "'fighting' words -- those which by their very utterance inflict injury or tend to incite an immediate breach of the peace." [ ] These limitations are but recognition of the observation in [ ], that this Court has "long recognized that not all speech is of equal First Amendment importance." But the sort of expression involved in this case does not seem to us to be governed by any exception to the general First Amendment principles stated above.

We conclude that public figures and public officials may not recover for the tort of intentional infliction of emotional distress by reason of publications such as the one here at issue without showing, in addition, that the publication contains a false statement of fact which was made with "actual malice," *i.e.,* with knowledge that the statement was false or with reckless disregard as to whether or not it was true. This is not merely a "blind application" of the *New York Times* standard [ ]; it reflects our considered judgment that such a standard is necessary to give adequate "breathing space" to the freedoms protected by the First Amendment.

Here it is clear that respondent Falwell is a "public figure" for purposes of First Amendment law. The jury found against respondent on his libel claim when it decided that the Hustler ad parody could not "reasonably be understood as describing actual facts about [respondent] or actual events in which [he] participated." [ ] The Court of Appeals interpreted the jury's finding to be that the ad parody "was not reasonably believable," [   ], and, in accordance with our custom, we accept this finding. Respondent is thus relegated to his claim for damages awarded by the jury for the intentional infliction of emotional distress by "outrageous" conduct. But, for reasons heretofore stated, this claim cannot, consistently with the First Amendment, form a basis for the award of damages when the conduct in question is the publication of a caricature such as the ad parody involved here. The judgment of the Court of Appeals is accordingly

Reversed.

JUSTICE KENNEDY took no part in the consideration or decision of this case.

In *Zacchini v. Scripps-Howard Broadcasting Co.* (MCLE, page 391), the Supreme Court held in a split (5-4) decision that a television station could be held liable for invasion of privacy for broadcasting in a newscast the entire act (15 seconds) of a performer without his consent. According to the Court, newsworthiness had not been demonstrated, and thus the performer enjoyed a right of publicity as recognized under state law. The justices were particularly concerned that broadcast of the human cannonball's entire act could deprive him of potential revenue. The impact of the decision on the tort of appropriation is still not entirely clear, although mass media obviously need to be concerned when they show a performer's entire act without consent.

Zacchini v. Scripps-Howard Broadcasting Co.

Argued April 25, 1977
Decided June 28, 1977

433 U.S. 562, 97 S.Ct. 2849, 53 L.Ed.2d 965, 2 Med.L.Rptr. 1199

CERTIORARI TO THE SUPREME COURT OF OHIO

Syllabus

Petitioner's 15-second "human cannonball" act, in which he is shot from a cannon into a net some 200 feet away, was, without his consent, videotaped in its entirety at a county fair in Ohio by a reporter for respondent broadcasting company and shown on a television news program later the same day. Petitioner then brought a damages action in state court against respondent, alleging an "unlawful appropriation" of his "professional property." The trial court's summary judgment for respondent was reversed by the Ohio Court of Appeals on the ground that the complaint stated a cause of action. The Ohio Supreme Court, while recognizing that petitioner had a cause of action under state law on his "right to the publicity value of his performance," nevertheless, relying on *Time, Inc. v. Hill* [ ], rendered judgment for respondent on the ground that it is constitutionally privileged to include in its newscasts matters of public interest that would otherwise be protected by the right of publicity, absent an intent to injure or to appropriate for some nonprivileged purpose.

Held:

1. It appears from the Ohio Supreme Court's opinion syllabus (which is to be looked to for the rule of law in the case), as clarified by the opinion itself, that the judgment below did not rest on an adequate and independent state ground, but rested solely on federal grounds, in that

the court considered the source of respondent's privilege to be the First and Fourteenth Amendments, and therefore this Court has jurisdiction to decide the federal issue.

2. The First and Fourteenth Amendments do not immunize the news media when they broadcast a performer's entire act without his consent, and the Constitution no more prevents a State from requiring respondent to compensate petitioner for broadcasting his act on television than it would privilege respondent to film and broadcast a copyrighted dramatic work without liability to the copyright owner, or to film or broadcast a prize fight or a baseball game, where the promoters or participants had other plans for publicizing the event. *Time, Inc. v. Hill, supra,* distinguished.

(a) The broadcast of a film of petitioner's entire act poses a substantial threat to the economic value of that performance, since (1) if the public can see the act free on television it will be less willing to pay to see it at the fair, and (2) the broadcast goes to the heart of petitioner's ability to earn a living as an entertainer.

(b) The protection of petitioner's right of publicity provides an economic incentive for him to make the investment required to produce a performance of interest to the public.

(c) While entertainment, as well as news, enjoys First Amendment protection, and entertainment itself can be important news, neither the public nor respondent will be deprived of the benefit of petitioner's performance as long as his commercial stake in his act is appropriately recognized.

(d) Although the State may, as a matter of its own law, privilege the press in the circumstances of this case, the First and Fourteenth Amendments do not require it to do so.

47 Ohio St.2d 224, 351 N.E.2d 454, reversed.

WHITE, J., delivered the opinion of the Court, in which BURGER, C.J., and STEWART, BLACKMUN, and REHNQUIST, JJ., joined. POWELL, J., filed a dissenting opinion, in which BRENNAN and MARSHALL, JJ., joined. STEVENS, J., filed a dissenting opinion.

WHITE, J., lead opinion

MR. JUSTICE WHITE delivered the opinion of the Court.

Petitioner, Hugo Zacchini, is an entertainer. He performs a "human cannonball" act in which he is shot from a cannon into a net some 200 feet away. Each performance occupies some 15 seconds. In August and September, 1972, petitioner was engaged to perform his act on a regular basis at the Geauga County Fair in Burton, Ohio. He performed in a fenced area, surrounded by grandstands, at the fair grounds. Members of the public attending the fair were not charged a separate admission fee to observe his act.

On August 30, a freelance reporter for Scripps-Howard Broadcasting Co., the operator of a television broadcasting station and respondent in this case, attended the fair. He carried a small movie camera. Petitioner noticed the reporter and asked him not to film the performance. The reporter did not do so on that day; but on the instructions of the producer of respondent's daily newscast, he returned the following day and videotaped the entire act. This film clip, approximately 15 seconds in length, was shown on the 11 o'clock news program that night, together with favorable commentary.

Petitioner then brought this action for damages, alleging that he is "engaged in the entertainment business," that the act he performs is one "invented by his father and . . . performed only by his family for the last fifty years," that respondent "showed and commercialized the film of his act without his consent," and that such conduct was an "unlawful appropriation of plaintiff's professional property." [ ] Respondent answered and moved for summary judgment, which was granted by the trial court.

The Court of Appeals of Ohio reversed. The majority held that petitioner's complaint stated a cause of action for conversion and for infringement of a common law copyright, and one judge concurred in the judgment on the ground that the complaint stated a cause of action for appropriation of petitioner's "right of publicity" in the film of his act. All three judges agreed that the First Amendment did not privilege the press to show the entire performance on a news program without compensating petitioner for any financial injury he could prove at trial.

Like the concurring judge in the Court of Appeals, the Supreme Court of Ohio rested petitioner's cause of action under state law on his "right to publicity value of his performance." [ ] The opinion syllabus, to which we are to look for the rule of law used to decide the case, declared first that one may not use for his own benefit the name or likeness of another, whether or not the use or benefit is a commercial one, and second that respondent would be liable for the appropriation, over petitioner's objection and in the absence of license or privilege, of petitioner's right to the publicity value of his performance. [ ] The court nevertheless gave judgment for respondent because, in the words of the syllabus:

> A TV station has a privilege to report in its newscasts matters of legitimate public interest which would otherwise be protected by an individual's right of publicity, unless the actual intent of the TV station was to appropriate the benefit of the publicity for some nonprivileged private use, or unless the actual intent was to injure the individual.

Ibid.

We granted certiorari [ ] to consider an issue unresolved by this Court: whether the First and Fourteenth Amendments immunized respondent from damages for its alleged infringement of petitioner's state law "right of publicity." [ ] Insofar as the Ohio Supreme Court held that

228

the First and Fourteenth Amendments of the United States Constitution required judgment for respondent, we reverse the judgment of that court.

I

If the judgment below rested on an independent and adequate state ground, the writ of certiorari should be dismissed as improvidently granted [ ], for

> [o]ur only power over state judgments is to correct them to the extent that they incorrectly adjudge federal rights. And our power is to correct wrong judgments, not to revise opinions. We are not permitted to render an advisory opinion, and if the same judgment would be rendered by the state court after we corrected its views of federal laws, our review could amount to nothing more than an advisory opinion.

[ ] We are confident, however, that the judgment below did not rest on an adequate and independent state ground and that we have jurisdiction to decide the federal issue presented in this case.

There is no doubt that petitioner's complaint was grounded in state law and that the right of publicity which petitioner was held to possess was a right arising under Ohio law. It is also clear that respondent's claim of constitutional privilege was sustained. The source of this privilege was not identified in the syllabus. It is clear enough from the opinion of the Ohio Supreme Court, which we are permitted to consult for understanding of the syllabus [ ], that in adjudicating the crucial question of whether respondent had a privilege to film and televise petitioner's performance, the court placed principal reliance on *Time, Inc. v. Hill* [ ], a case involving First Amendment limitations on state tort actions. It construed the principle of that case, along with that of *New York Times Co. v. Sullivan* [ ], to be that "the press has a privilege to report matters of legitimate public interest even though such reports might intrude on matters otherwise private," and concluded, therefore, that the press is also "privileged when an individual seeks to publicly exploit his talents while keeping the benefits private." [ ] The privilege thus exists in cases "where appropriation of a right of publicity's claimed." The court's opinion also referred to Draft 21 of the relevant portion of Restatement (Second) of Torts (1975), which was understood to make room for reasonable press appropriations by limiting the reach of the right of privacy, rather than by creating a privileged invasion. The court preferred the notion of privilege over the Restatement's formulation, however, reasoning that,

> since the gravamen of the issue in this case is not whether the degree of intrusion is reasonable, but whether *First Amendment* principles require that the right of privacy give way to the public right to be informed of matters of public interest and concern, the concept of privilege seems the more useful and appropriate one.[ ]

Had the Ohio court rested its decision on both state and federal grounds, either of which would have been dispositive, we would have had no jurisdiction. [ ] But the opinion, like the syllabus, did not mention the Ohio Constitution, citing instead this Court's First Amendment cases as controlling. It appears to us that the decision rested solely on federal grounds. That the Ohio court might have, but did not, invoke state law does not foreclose jurisdiction here. [ ]

Even if the judgment in favor of respondent must nevertheless be understood as ultimately resting on Ohio law, it appears that, at the very least, the Ohio court felt compelled by what it understood to be federal constitutional considerations to construe and apply its own law in the manner it did. In this event, we have jurisdiction, and should decide the federal issue; for if the state court erred in its understanding of our cases and of the First and Fourteenth Amendments, we should so declare, leaving the state court free to decide the privilege issue solely as a matter of Ohio law. [ ] If the Supreme Court of Ohio

> held as it did because it felt under compulsion of federal law as enunciated by this Court so to hold, it should be relieved of that compulsion. It should be freed to decide . . . these suits according to its own local law.

[ ]

II

The Ohio Supreme Court held that respondent is constitutionally privileged to include in its newscasts matters of public interest that would otherwise be protected by the right of publicity, absent an intent to injure or to appropriate for some nonprivileged purpose. If, under this standard, respondent had merely reported that petitioner was performing at the fair and described or commented on his act, with or without showing his picture on television, we would have a very different case. But petitioner is not contending that his appearance at the fair and his performance could not be reported by the press as newsworthy items. His complaint is that respondent filmed his entire act and displayed that film on television for the public to see and enjoy. This, he claimed, was an appropriation of his professional property. The Ohio Supreme Court agreed that petitioner had "a right of publicity" that gave him "personal control over commercial display and exploitation of his personality and the exercise of his talents."{GO>4} This right of "exclusive control over the publicity given to his performances" was said to be such a "valuable part of the benefit which may be attained by his talents and efforts" that it was entitled to legal protection. It was also observed, or at least expressly assumed, that petitioner had not abandoned his rights by performing under the circumstances present at the Geauga County Far Grounds.

The Ohio Supreme Court nevertheless held that the challenged invasion was privileged, saying that the press

> must be accorded broad latitude in its choice of how much it presents of each story or incident, and of the emphasis to be given to such presentation. No fixed standard which would bar the press from reporting

or depicting either an entire occurrence or an entire discrete part of a public performance can be formulated which would not unduly restrict the "breathing room" in reporting which freedom of the press requires.

[ ] Under this view, respondent was thus constitutionally free to film and display petitioner's entire act.

The Ohio Supreme Court relied heavily on *Time, Inc. v. Hill* [ ], but that case does not mandate a media privilege to televise a performer's entire act without his consent. Involved in *Time, Inc. v. Hill* was a claim under the New York "Right of Privacy" statute that Life Magazine, in the course of reviewing a new play, had connected the play with a long-past incident involving petitioner and his family, and had falsely described their experience and conduct at that time. The complaint sought damages for humiliation and suffering flowing from these nondefamatory falsehoods that allegedly invaded Hill's privacy. The Court held, however, that the opening of a new play linked to an actual incident was a matter of public interest, and that Hill could not recover without showing that the Life report was knowingly false or was published with reckless disregard for the truth -- the same rigorous standard that had been applied in *New York Times Co. v. Sullivan* [ ].

Time, Inc. v. Hill, which was hotly contested and decided by a divided Court, involved an entirely different tort from the "right of publicity" recognized by the Ohio Supreme Court. As the opinion reveals in *Time, Inc. v. Hill,* the Court was steeped in the literature of privacy law, and was aware of the developing distinctions and nuances in this branch of the law. The Court, for example, cited W. Prosser, Law of Torts 831-832 (3d ed.1964), and the same author's well known article, Privacy, 48 Calif.L.Rev. 383 (1960), both of which divided privacy into four distinct branches. The Court was aware that it was adjudicating a "false light" privacy case involving a matter of public interest, not a case involving "intrusion" [ ], "appropriation" of a name or likeness for the purposes of trade [ ], or "private details" about a non-newsworthy person or event [ ]. It is also abundantly clear that *Time, Inc. v. Hill* did not involve a performer, a person with a name having commercial value, or any claim to a "right of publicity." This discrete kind of "appropriation" case was plainly identified in the literature cited by the Court, and had been adjudicated in the reported cases.

The differences between these two torts are important. First, the State's interests in providing a cause of action in each instance are different. "The interest protected" in permitting recovery for placing the plaintiff in a false light "is clearly that of reputation, with the same overtones of mental distress as in defamation." [ ] By contrast, the State's interest in permitting a "right of publicity" is in protecting the proprietary interest of the individual in his act in part to encourage such entertainment. As we later note, the State's interest is closely analogous to the goals of patent and copyright law, focusing on the right of the individual to reap the reward of his endeavors and having little to do with protecting feelings or reputation. Second, the two torts differ in the degree to which they intrude on dissemination of information to the public. In "false light" cases, the only way to protect the interests involved is to attempt to minimize publication of the damaging matter, while in "right of publicity" cases, the only question is who gets to do the publishing. An entertainer such as petitioner usually has no objection to the widespread publication of his act as long as he gets the commercial benefit of such publication. Indeed, in the present case, petitioner did not seek to enjoin the broadcast of his act; he simply sought compensation for the broadcast in the form of damages.

Nor does it appear that our later cases, such as *Rosenbloom v. Metromedia, Inc.* [ ]; *Gertz v. Robert Welch, Inc.* [ ]; and *Time, Inc. v. Firestone* [ ], require or furnish substantial support for the Ohio court's privilege ruling. These cases, like *New York Times,* emphasize the protection extended to the press by the First Amendment in defamation cases, particularly when suit is brought by a public official or a public figure. None of them involves an alleged appropriation by the press of a right of publicity existing under state law.

Moreover, *Time, Inc. v. Hill, New York Times, Metromedia, Gertz,* and *Firestone* all involved the reporting of events; in none of them was there an attempt to broadcast or publish an entire act for which the performer ordinarily gets paid. It is evident, and there is no claim here to the contrary, that petitioner's state law right of publicity would not serve to prevent respondent from reporting the newsworthy facts about petitioner's act. Wherever the line in particular situations is to be drawn between media reports that are protected and those that are not, we are quite sure that the First and Fourteenth Amendments do not immunize the media when they broadcast a performer's entire act without his consent. The Constitution no more prevents a State from requiring respondent to compensate petitioner for broadcasting his act on television than it would privilege respondent to film and broadcast a copyrighted dramatic work without liability to the copyright owner [ ]; [ ] or to film and broadcast a prize fight, [ ]; or a baseball game [ ] where the promoters or the participants had other plans for publicizing the event. There are ample reasons for reaching this conclusion.

The broadcast of a film of petitioner's entire act poses a substantial threat to the economic value of that performance. As the Ohio court recognized, this act is the product of petitioner's own talents and energy, the end result of much time, effort, and expense. Much of its economic value lies in the "right of exclusive control over the publicity given to his performance"; if the public can see the act free on television, it will be less willing to pay to see it at the fair. The effect of a public broadcast of the performance is similar to preventing petitioner from charging an admission fee.

> The rationale for [protecting the right of publicity] is the straightforward one of preventing unjust enrichment by the theft of good will. No social purpose is served by having the defendant get free some aspect of the plaintiff that would have market value and for which he would normally

pay.

[ ] Moreover, the broadcast of petitioner's entire performance, unlike the unauthorized use of another's name for purposes of trade or the incidental use of a name or picture by the press, goes to the heart of petitioner's ability to earn a living as an entertainer. Thus, in this case, Ohio has recognized what may be the strongest case for a "right of publicity" -- involving, not the appropriation of an entertainer's reputation to enhance the attractiveness of a commercial product, but the appropriation of the very activity by which the entertainer acquired his reputation in the first place.

Of course, Ohio's decision to protect petitioner's right of publicity here rests on more than a desire to compensate the performer for the time and effort invested in his act; the protection provides an economic incentive for him to make the investment required to produce a performance of interest to the public. This same consideration underlies the patent and copyright laws long enforced by this Court. As the Court stated in *Mazer v. Stein* [ ]:

> The economic philosophy behind the clause empowering Congress to grant patents and copyrights is the conviction that encouragement of individual effort by personal gain is the best way to advance public welfare through the talents of authors and inventors in "science and useful Arts." Sacrificial days devoted to such creative activities deserve rewards commensurate with the services rendered. These laws perhaps regard the "reward to the owner [as] a secondary consideration" [ ], but they were "intended definitely to grant valuable, enforceable rights" in order to afford greater encouragement to the production of works of benefit to the public. [ ] The Constitution does not prevent Ohio from making a similar choice here in deciding to protect the entertainer's incentive in order to encourage the production of this type of work. [ ]

There is no doubt that entertainment, as well as news, enjoys First Amendment protection. It is also true that entertainment itself can be important news. *Time, Inc. v. Hill.* But it is important to note that neither the public nor respondent will be deprived of the benefit of petitioner's performance as long as his commercial stake in his act is appropriately recognized. Petitioner does not seek to enjoin the broadcast of his performance; he simply wants to be paid for it. Nor do we think that a state law damages remedy against respondent would represent a species of liability without fault contrary to the letter or spirit of *Gertz v. Robert Welch, Inc.* [ ]. Respondent knew that petitioner objected to televising his act, but nevertheless displayed the entire film.

We conclude that, although the State of Ohio may, as a matter of its own law, privilege the press in the circumstances of this case, the First and Fourteenth Amendments do not require it to do so.

Reversed.

POWELL, J., dissenting

MR. JUSTICE POWELL, with whom MR. JUSTICE BRENNAN and MR. JUSTICE MARSHALL join, dissenting.

Disclaiming any attempt to do more than decide the narrow case before us, the Court reverses the decision of the Supreme Court of Ohio based on repeated incantation of a single formula: "a performer's entire act." The holding today is summed up in one sentence:

> Wherever the line in particular situations is to be drawn between media reports that are protected and those that are not, we are quite sure that the First and Fourteenth Amendments do not immunize the media when they broadcast a performer's entire act without his consent.

[ ] I doubt that this formula provides a standard clear enough even for resolution of this case. In any event, I am not persuaded that the Court's opinion is appropriately sensitive to the First Amendment values at stake, and I therefore dissent.

Although the Court would draw no distinction [ ], I do not view respondent's action as comparable to unauthorized commercial broadcasts of sporting events, theatrical performances, and the like, where the broadcaster keeps the profits. There is no suggestion here that respondent made any such use of the film. Instead, it simply reported on what petitioner concedes to be a newsworthy event, in a way hardly surprising for a television station -- by means of film coverage. The report was part of an ordinary daily news program, consuming a total of 15 seconds. It is a routine example of the press' fulfilling the informing function so vital to our system.

The Court's holding that the station's ordinary news report may give rise to substantial liability has disturbing implications, for the decision could lead to a degree of media self-censorship. [ ] Hereafter, whenever a television news editor is unsure whether certain film footage received from a camera crew might be held to portray an "entire act,"{GO>3} he may decline coverage -- even of clearly newsworthy events -- or confine the broadcast to watered-down verbal reporting, perhaps with an occasional still picture. The public is then the loser. This is hardly the kind of news reportage that the First Amendment is meant to foster. [ ] In my view, the First Amendment commands a different analytical starting point from the one selected by the Court. Rather than begin with a quantitative analysis of the performer's behavior -- is this or is this not his entire act. -- we should direct initial attention to the actions of the news media: what use did the station make of the film footage? When a film is used, as here, for a routine portion of a regular news program, I would hold that the First Amendment protects the station from a "right of publicity" or "appropriation" suit, absent a strong showing by the plaintiff that the news broadcast was a subterfuge or cover for private or commercial exploitation.

I emphasize that this is a "reappropriation" suit, rather than one of the other varieties of "right of privacy" tort suits identified by Dean Prosser in his classic article. [ ] In those other causes of action, the competing interests are considerably different. The plaintiff generally seeks to avoid any sort of public exposure, and the existence of constitutional privilege is therefore less likely to turn on whether the publication occurred in a news broadcast or in some other fashion. In a suit like the one before us, however, the plaintiff does not complain about the fact of exposure to the public, but rather about its timing or manner. He welcomes some publicity, but seeks to retain control over means and manner as a way to maximize for himself the monetary benefits that flow from such publication. But having made the matter public -- having chosen, in essence, to make it newsworthy -- he cannot, consistent with the First Amendment, complain of routine news reportage. [ ] ...

Since the film clip here was undeniably treated as news, and since there is no claim that the use was subterfuge, respondent's actions were constitutionally privileged. I would affirm.

STEVENS, J., dissenting

MR. JUSTICE STEVENS, dissenting.

The Ohio Supreme Court held that respondent's telecast of the "human cannonball" was a privileged invasion of petitioner's common law "right of publicity" because respondent's actual intent was neither (a) to appropriate the benefit of the publicity for a private use nor (b) to injure petitioner.

As I read the state court's explanation of the limits on the concept of privilege, they define the substantive reach of a common law tort, rather than anything I recognize as a limit on a federal constitutional right. The decision was unquestionably influenced by the Ohio court's proper sensitivity to First Amendment principles, and to this Court's cases construing the First Amendment; indeed, I must confess that the opinion can be read as resting entirely on federal constitutional grounds. Nevertheless, the basis of the state court's action is sufficiently doubtful that I would remand the case to that court for clarification of its holding before deciding the federal constitutional issue.

In *Florida Star v. B.J.F.* (MCLE, page 422), the Supreme Court held in a 5-4 decision that a newspaper enjoyed First Amendment protection in publishing the name of a rape victim that had been lawfully obtained and, therefore, could not be successfully sued for damages. According to the Court, a newspaper could be punished, if at all, for publishing truthful information that had been lawfully obtained only when the government has demonstrated such punishment was narrowly tailored to serve "a state interest of the highest order." The newspaper had accidentally published the name in violation of its own internal policy after the name was inadvertently disclosed in a police report. The Court made it clear that it was not extending First Amendment protection to all truthful publication but that such protection was warranted under the circumstances in this case.

Florida Star v. B.J.F.

Argued March 21, 1989
Decided June 21, 1989

491 U.S. 524, 109 S.Ct. 2603, 105 L.Ed.2d 443, 16 Med.L.Rptr. 1801

APPEAL FROM THE DISTRICT COURT OF APPEAL OF FLORIDA,
FIRST DISTRICT

Syllabus

Appellant, The Florida Star, is a newspaper which publishes a "Police Reports" section containing brief articles describing local criminal incidents under police investigation. After appellee B.J.F. reported to the Sheriff's Department (Department) that she had been robbed and sexually assaulted, the Department prepared a report, which identified B.J.F. by her full name, and placed it in the Department's pressroom. The Department does not restrict access to the room or to the reports available there. A Star reporter-trainee sent to the pressroom copied the police report verbatim, including B.J.F.'s full name. Consequently, her name was included in a "Police Reports" story in the paper, in violation of the Star's internal policy. Florida Stat. § 794.03 makes it unlawful to "print, publish, or broadcast . . . in any instrument of mass communication" the name of the victim of a sexual offense. B.J.F. filed suit in a Florida court alleging, *inter alia,* that the Star had negligently violated § 794.03. The trial court denied the Star's motion to dismiss, which claimed, among other things, that imposing civil sanctions on the newspaper pursuant to § 794.03 violated the First Amendment. However, it granted B.J.F.'s motion for a directed verdict on the issue of negligence, finding the Star *per se* negligent based on its violation of §

794.03. The jury then awarded B.J.F. both compensatory and punitive damages. The verdict was upheld on appeal.

Held: Imposing damages on the Star for publishing B.J.F.'s name violates the First Amendment.

(a) The sensitivity and significance of the interests presented in clashes between First Amendment and privacy rights counsels the Court to rely on limited principles that sweep no more broadly than the appropriate context of the instant case, rather than to accept invitations to hold broadly that truthful publication may never be punished consistent with the First Amendment or that publication of a rape victim's name never enjoys constitutional protection. One such principle is that,

> if a newspaper lawfully obtains truthful information about a matter of public significance, then state officials may not constitutionally punish publication of the information, absent a need to further a state interest of the highest order.

[ ] Applied to the instant case, the *Daily Mail* principle commands reversal.

(b) The Star "lawfully obtain[ed] truthful information." The actual news article was accurate, and the Star lawfully obtained B.J.F.'s name from the government. The fact that state officials are not required to disclose such reports or that the Sheriff's Department apparently failed to fulfill its § 794.03 obligation not to cause or allow B.J.F.'s name to be published does not make it unlawful for the Star to have received the information, and Florida has taken no steps to proscribe such receipt. The government has ample means to safeguard the information that are less drastic than punishing truthful publication. Furthermore, it is clear that the news article generally, as opposed to the specific identity contained in it, involved "a matter of public significance": the commission, and investigation, of a violent crime that had been reported to authorities.

(c) Imposing liability on the Star does not serve "a need to further a state interest of the highest order." Although the interests in protecting the privacy and safety of sexual assault victims and in encouraging them to report offenses without fear of exposure are highly significant, imposing liability on the Star in this case is too precipitous a means of advancing those interests. Since the Star obtained the information because the Sheriff's Department failed to abide by § 794.03's policy, the imposition of damages can hardly be said to be a narrowly tailored means of safeguarding anonymity. Self-censorship is especially likely to result from imposition of liability when a newspaper gains access to the information from a government news release. Moreover, the negligence *per se* standard adopted by the courts below does not permit case-by-case findings that the disclosure was one a reasonable person would find offensive, and does not have a scienter requirement of any kind. In addition, § 794.03's facial underinclusiveness -- which prohibits publication only by an "instrument of mass communication" and does not prohibit the spread of victims' names by other means -- raises serious doubts about whether Florida is serving the interests specified by B.J.F. A State must demonstrate its commitment to the extraordinary measure of punishing truthful publication in the name of privacy by applying its prohibition evenhandedly to both the small-time disseminator and the media giant.

499 So.2d 883, reversed.

MARSHALL, J., delivered the opinion of the Court, in which BRENNAN, BLACKMUN, STEVENS, and KENNEDY, JJ., joined. SCALIA, J., filed an opinion concurring in part and concurring in the judgment. WHITE, J., filed a dissenting opinion, in which REHNQUIST, C.J., and O'CONNOR, J., joined.

MARSHALL, J., lead opinion

Florida Stat. § 794.03 (1987) makes it unlawful to "print, publish, or broadcast . . . in any instrument of mass communication" the name of the victim of a sexual offense. Pursuant to this statute, appellant The Florida Star was found civilly liable for publishing the name of a rape victim which it had obtained from a publicly released police report. The issue presented here is whether this result comports with the First Amendment. We hold that it does not.

I

The Florida Star is a weekly newspaper which serves the community of Jacksonville, Florida, and which has an average circulation of approximately 18,000 copies. A regular feature of the newspaper is its "Police Reports" section. That section, typically two to three pages in length, contains brief articles describing local criminal incidents under police investigation.

On October 20, 1983, appellee B.J.F. reported to the Duval County, Florida, Sheriff's Department (the Department) that she had been robbed and sexually assaulted by an unknown assailant. The Department prepared a report on the incident which identified B.J.F. by her full name. The Department then placed the report in its pressroom. The Department does not restrict access either to the pressroom or to the reports made available therein.

A Florida Star reporter-trainee sent to the pressroom copied the police report verbatim, including B.J.F.'s full name, on a blank duplicate of the Department's forms. A Florida Star reporter then prepared a one-paragraph article about the crime, derived entirely from the trainee's copy of the police report. The article included B.J.F.'s full name. It appeared in the "Robberies" subsection of the "Police Reports" section on October 29, 1983, one of fifty-four police blotter stories in that day's edition. The article read:

238

[B.J.F.] reported on Thursday, October 20, she was crossing Brentwood Park, which is in the 500 block of Golfair Boulevard, enroute to her bus stop, when an unknown black man ran up behind the lady and placed a knife to her neck and told her not to yell. The suspect then undressed the lady and had sexual intercourse with her before fleeing the scene with her 60 cents, Timex watch and gold necklace. Patrol efforts have been suspended concerning this incident because of a lack of evidence. In printing B.J.F.'s full name, The Florida Star violated its internal policy of not publishing the names of sexual offense victims.

On September 26, 1984, B.J.F. filed suit in the Circuit Court of Duval County against the Department and The Florida Star, alleging that these parties negligently violated § 794.03. [ ] Before trial, the Department settled with B.J.F. for $2,500. The Florida Star moved to dismiss, claiming, *inter alia,* that imposing civil sanctions on the newspaper pursuant to § 794.03 violated the First Amendment. The trial judge rejected the motion. [ ]

At the ensuing day-long trial, B.J.F. testified that she had suffered emotional distress from the publication of her name. She stated that she had heard about the article from fellow workers and acquaintances; that her mother had received several threatening phone calls from a man who stated that he would rape B.J.F. again; and that these events had forced B.J.F. to change her phone number and residence, to seek police protection, and to obtain mental health counseling. In defense, The Florida Star put forth evidence indicating that the newspaper had learned B.J.F.'s name from the incident report released by the Department, and that the newspaper's violation of its internal rule against publishing the names of sexual offense victims was inadvertent.

At the close of B.J.F.'s case, and again at the close of its defense, The Florida Star moved for a directed verdict. On both occasions, the trial judge denied these motions. He ruled from the bench that § 794.03 was constitutional because it reflected a proper balance between the First Amendment and privacy rights, as it applied only to a narrow set of "rather sensitive . . . criminal offenses." [ ] At the close of the newspaper's defense, the judge granted B.J.F.'s motion for a directed verdict on the issue of negligence, finding the newspaper *per se* negligent based upon its violation of § 794.03. [ ] This ruling left the jury to consider only the questions of causation and damages. The judge instructed the jury that it could award B.J.F. punitive damages if it found that the newspaper had "acted with reckless indifference to the rights of others." [ ] The jury awarded B.J.F. $75,000 in compensatory damages and $25,000 in punitive damages. Against the actual damages award, the judge set off B.J.F.'s settlement with the Department.

The First District Court of Appeal affirmed in a three-paragraph per curiam opinion. [ ] In the paragraph devoted to The Florida Star's First Amendment claim, the court stated that the directed verdict for B.J.F. had been properly entered because, under § 794.03, a rape victim's name is "of a private nature and not to be published as a matter of law." [ ]

239

The Supreme Court of Florida denied discretionary review.

The Florida Star appealed to this Court. We noted probable jurisdiction [ ] and now reverse.

II

The tension between the right which the First Amendment accords to a free press, on the one hand, and the protections which various statutes and common law doctrines accord to personal privacy against the publication of truthful information, on the other, is a subject we have addressed several times in recent years. Our decisions in cases involving government attempts to sanction the accurate dissemination of information as invasive of privacy have not, however, exhaustively considered this conflict. On the contrary, although our decisions have without exception upheld the press' right to publish, we have emphasized each time that we were resolving this conflict only as it arose in a discrete factual context.

The parties to this case frame their contentions in light of a trilogy of cases which have presented, in different contexts, the conflict between truthful reporting and state-protected privacy interests. In *Cox Broadcasting Corp. v. Cohn* [ ], we found unconstitutional a civil damages award entered against a television station for broadcasting the name of a rape-murder victim which the station had obtained from courthouse records. In *Oklahoma Publishing Co. v. Oklahoma County District Court* [ ], we found unconstitutional a state court's pretrial order enjoining the media from publishing the name or photograph of an 11-year-old boy in connection with a juvenile proceeding involving that child which reporters had attended. Finally, in *Smith v. Daily Mail Publishing Co.* [ ], we found unconstitutional the indictment of two newspapers for violating a state statute forbidding newspapers to publish, without written approval of the juvenile court, the name of any youth charged as a juvenile offender. The papers had learned about a shooting by monitoring a police band radio frequency, and had obtained the name of the alleged juvenile assailant from witnesses, the police, and a local prosecutor.

Appellant takes the position that this case is indistinguishable from *Cox Broadcasting.* [ ] Alternatively, it urges that our decisions in the above trilogy, and in other cases in which we have held that the right of the press to publish truth overcame asserted interests other than personal privacy, can be distilled to yield a broader First Amendment principle that the press may never be punished, civilly or criminally, for publishing the truth. [ ] Appellee counters that the privacy trilogy is inapposite, because in each case the private information already appeared on a "public record" [ ], and because the privacy interests at stake were far less profound than in the present case. [ ] In the alternative, appellee urges that *Cox Broadcasting* be overruled and replaced with a categorical rule that publication of the name of a rape victim never enjoys constitutional protection. [ ]

240

We conclude that imposing damages on appellant for publishing B.J.F.'s name violates the First Amendment, although not for either of the reasons appellant urges. Despite the strong resemblance this case bears to *Cox Broadcasting,* that case cannot fairly be read as controlling here. The name of the rape victim in that case was obtained from courthouse records that were open to public inspection, a fact which JUSTICE WHITE'S opinion for the Court repeatedly noted. [ ] ... Significantly, one of the reasons we gave in *Cox Broadcasting* for invalidating the challenged damages award was the important role the press plays in subjecting trials to public scrutiny and thereby helping guarantee their fairness. [ ] That role is not directly compromised where, as here, the information in question comes from a police report prepared and disseminated at a time at which not only had no adversarial criminal proceedings begun, but no suspect had been identified.

Nor need we accept appellant's invitation to hold broadly that truthful publication may never be punished consistent with the First Amendment. Our cases have carefully eschewed reaching this ultimate question, mindful that the future may bring scenarios which prudence counsels our not resolving anticipatorily. [ ] ... Indeed, in *Cox Broadcasting,* we pointedly refused to answer even the less sweeping question "whether truthful publications may ever be subjected to civil or criminal liability" for invading "an area of privacy" defined by the State. [ ] Respecting the fact that press freedom and privacy rights are both "plainly rooted in the traditions and significant concerns of our society," we instead focused on the less sweeping issue

> whether the State may impose sanctions on the accurate publication of the name of a rape victim obtained from public records -- more specifically, from judicial records which are maintained in connection with a public prosecution and which themselves are open to public inspection.

[ ] We continue to believe that the sensitivity and significance of the interests presented in clashes between First Amendment and privacy rights counsel relying on limited principles that sweep no more broadly than the appropriate context of the instant case.

In our view, this case is appropriately analyzed with reference to such a limited First Amendment principle. It is the one, in fact, which we articulated in *Daily Mail* in our synthesis of prior cases involving attempts to punish truthful publication:

> [I]f a newspaper lawfully obtains truthful information about a matter of public significance, then state officials may not constitutionally punish publication of the information, absent a need to further a state interest of the highest order.

[ ] According the press the ample protection provided by that principle is supported by at least three separate considerations, in addition to, of course, the overarching "public interest, secured by the Constitution, in the dissemination of truth.'" [ ] The cases on which the *Daily Mail*

241

synthesis relied demonstrate these considerations.

First, because the *Daily Mail* formulation only protects the publication of information which a newspaper has "lawfully obtain[ed]" [ ], the government retains ample means of safeguarding significant interests upon which publication may impinge, including protecting a rape victim's anonymity. To the extent sensitive information rests in private hands, the government may under some circumstances forbid its nonconsensual acquisition, thereby bringing outside of the *Daily Mail* principle the publication of any information so acquired. To the extent sensitive information is in the government's custody, it has even greater power to forestall or mitigate the injury caused by its release. The government may classify certain information, establish and enforce procedures ensuring its redacted release, and extend a damages remedy against the government or its officials where the government's mishandling of sensitive information leads to its dissemination. Where information is entrusted to the government, a less drastic means than punishing truthful publication almost always exists for guarding against the dissemination of private facts. [ ] ... A second consideration undergirding the *Daily Mail* principle is the fact that punishing the press for its dissemination of information which is already publicly available is relatively unlikely to advance the interests in the service of which the State seeks to act. It is not, of course, always the case that information lawfully acquired by the press is known, or accessible, to others. But where the government has made certain information publicly available, it is highly anomalous to sanction persons other than the source of its release. We noted this anomaly in *Cox Broadcasting*:

> By placing the information in the public domain on official court records, the State must be presumed to have concluded that the public interest was thereby being served.

[ ] The *Daily Mail* formulation reflects the fact that it is a limited set of cases indeed where, despite the accessibility of the public to certain information, a meaningful public interest is served by restricting its further release by other entities, like the press. As *Daily Mail* observed in its summary of *Oklahoma Publishing*,

> once the truthful information was "publicly revealed" or "in the public domain," the court could not constitutionally restrain its dissemination.

[ ]

A third and final consideration is the "timidity and self-censorship" which may result from allowing the media to be punished for publishing certain truthful information. [ ] *Cox Broadcasting* noted this concern with overdeterrence in the context of information made public through official court records, but the fear of excessive media self-suppression is applicable as well to other information released, without qualification, by the government. A contrary rule, depriving protection to those who rely on the government's implied representations of the lawfulness of dissemination, would force upon the media the onerous obligation of

242

sifting through government press releases, reports, and pronouncements to prune out material arguably unlawful for publication. This situation could inhere even where the newspaper's sole object was to reproduce, with no substantial change, the government's rendition of the event in question.

Applied to the instant case, the *Daily Mail* principle clearly commands reversal. The first inquiry is whether the newspaper "lawfully obtain[ed] truthful information about a matter of public significance." [ ] It is undisputed that the news article describing the assault on B.J.F. was accurate. In addition, appellant lawfully obtained B.J.F.'s name. Appellee's argument to the contrary is based on the fact that under Florida law, police reports which reveal the identity of the victim of a sexual offense are not among the matters of "public record" which the public, by law, is entitled to inspect. [ ] But the fact that state officials are not required to disclose such reports does not make it unlawful for a newspaper to receive them when furnished by the government. Nor does the fact that the Department apparently failed to fulfill its obligation under § 794.03 not to "cause or allow to be . . . published" the name of a sexual offense victim make the newspaper's ensuing receipt of this information unlawful. Even assuming the Constitution permitted a State to proscribe *receipt* of information, Florida has not taken this step. It is, clear, furthermore, that the news article concerned "a matter of public significance" [ ], in the sense in which the *Daily Mail* synthesis of prior cases used that term. That is, the article generally, as opposed to the specific identity contained within it, involved a matter of paramount public import: the commission, and investigation, of a violent crime which had been reported to authorities. [ ] ... The second inquiry is whether imposing liability on appellant pursuant to § 794.03 serves "a need to further a state interest of the highest order." [ ] Appellee argues that a rule punishing publication furthers three closely related interests: the privacy of victims of sexual offenses; the physical safety of such victims, who may be targeted for retaliation if their names become known to their assailants; and the goal of encouraging victims of such crimes to report these offenses without fear of exposure. [ ]

At a time in which we are daily reminded of the tragic reality of rape, it is undeniable that these are highly significant interests, a fact underscored by the Florida Legislature's explicit attempt to protect these interests by enacting a criminal statute prohibiting much dissemination of victim identities. We accordingly do not rule out the possibility that, in a proper case, imposing civil sanctions for publication of the name of a rape victim might be so overwhelmingly necessary to advance these interests as to satisfy the *Daily Mail* standard. For three independent reasons, however, imposing liability for publication under the circumstances of this case is too precipitous a means of advancing these interests to convince us that there is a "need" within the meaning of the *Daily Mail* formulation for Florida to take this extreme step. [ ] ... First is the manner in which appellant obtained the identifying information in question. As we have noted, where the government itself provides information to the media, it is most appropriate to assume that the government had, but failed to utilize, far more limited means of guarding against dissemination than the extreme step of punishing truthful speech. That assumption is richly borne out in this case. B.J.F.'s identity would never have come to light were it not for the erroneous, if inadvertent, inclusion by the Department of her full name in an incident report made available in a pressroom open to the public. Florida's policy against disclosure of rape victims' identities, reflected in § 794.03, was undercut by the Department's failure to abide by this policy. Where, as here, the government has failed to police itself in disseminating information, it is clear under *Cox Broadcasting, Oklahoma Publishing,* and *Landmark Communications* that the imposition of damages against the press for its subsequent publication can hardly be said to be a narrowly tailored means of safeguarding anonymity. [ ] Once the government has placed such information in the public domain, "reliance must rest upon the judgment of those who decide what to publish or broadcast" [ ], and hopes for restitution must rest upon the willingness of the government to compensate victims for their loss of privacy and to protect them from the other consequences of its mishandling of the information which these victims provided in confidence.

That appellant gained access to the information in question through a government news release makes it especially likely that, if liability were to be imposed, self-censorship would result. Reliance on a news release "is a paradigmatically routine newspaper reporting techniqu[e]." [ ] The government's issuance of such a release, without qualification, can only convey to recipients that the government considered dissemination lawful, and indeed expected the recipients to disseminate the information further. Had appellant merely reproduced the news release prepared and released by the Department, imposing civil damages would surely violate the First Amendment. The fact that appellant converted the police report into a news story by adding the linguistic connecting tissue necessary to transform the report's facts into full sentences cannot change this result.

A second problem with Florida's imposition of liability for publication is the broad sweep of the negligence *per se* standard applied under the civil cause of action implied from § 794.03. Unlike claims based on the common law tort of invasion of privacy [ ], civil actions based on § 794.03 require no case-by-case findings that the disclosure of a fact about a person's private life was one that a reasonable person would find highly offensive. On the contrary, under the *per se* theory of negligence adopted by the courts below, liability follows automatically from publication. This is so regardless of whether the identity of the victim is already known throughout the community; whether the victim has voluntarily called public attention to the offense; or whether the identity of the victim has otherwise become a reasonable subject of public concern -- because, perhaps, questions have arisen whether the victim fabricated an assault by a particular person. Nor is there a scienter requirement of any kind under § 794.03, engendering the perverse result that truthful publications challenged pursuant to this cause of action are less protected by the First Amendment than even the least protected defamatory falsehoods: those involving purely private figures, where

244

liability is evaluated under a standard, usually applied by a jury, of ordinary negligence. [ ] We have previously noted the impermissibility of categorical prohibitions upon media access where important First Amendment interests are at stake. [   ] ... More individualized adjudication is no less indispensable where the State, seeking to safeguard the anonymity of crime victims, sets its face against publication of their names.

Third, and finally, the facial underinclusiveness of § 794.03 raises serious doubts about whether Florida is, in fact, serving, with this statute, the significant interests which appellee invokes in support of affirmance. Section 794.03 prohibits the publication of identifying information only if this information appears in an "instrument of mass communication," a term the statute does not define. Section 794.03 does not prohibit the spread by other means of the identities of victims of sexual offenses. An individual who maliciously spreads word of the identity of a rape victim is thus not covered, despite the fact that the communication of such information to persons who live near, or work with, the victim may have consequences as devastating as the exposure of her name to large numbers of strangers. [ ] ...

When a State attempts the extraordinary measure of punishing truthful publication in the name of privacy, it must demonstrate its commitment to advancing this interest by applying its prohibition evenhandedly, to the small-time disseminator as well as the media giant. Where important First Amendment interests are at stake, the mass scope of disclosure is not an acceptable surrogate for injury. A ban on disclosures effected by "instrument[s] of mass communication" simply cannot be defended on the ground that partial prohibitions may effect partial relief. [ ] ... Without more careful and inclusive precautions against alternative forms of dissemination, we cannot conclude that Florida's selective ban on publication by the mass media satisfactorily accomplishes its stated purpose.

III

Our holding today is limited. We do not hold that truthful publication is automatically constitutionally protected, or that there is no zone of personal privacy within which the State may protect the individual from intrusion by the press, or even that a State may never punish publication of the name of a victim of a sexual offense. We hold only that, where a newspaper publishes truthful information which it has lawfully obtained, punishment may lawfully be imposed, if at all, only when narrowly tailored to a state interest of the highest order, and that no such interest is satisfactorily served by imposing liability under § 794.03 to appellant under the facts of this case. The decision below is therefore

Reversed.

In *Richmond Newspapers, Inc. v. Virginia* (MCLE, page 446), the Supreme Court ruled in a 7-1 decision that the 1st and 14th Amendments to the U.S. Constitution guarantee press and public access to criminal trials. Although the right is not absolute, the Court said, criminal trials must be open to the public unless the government has demonstrated an "overriding interest." This is the first time the Court had specifically recognized such a right, but the Court has subsequently extended it to include the jury selection process and certain types of pretrial criminal proceedings. The Court, however, has not, as of yet, broadened the right to include civil trials, although most states now open both civil and criminal trials to the press and the public.

Richmond Newspapers, Inc. v. Virginia

Argued February 19, 1980
Decided July 2, 1980

448 U.S. 555, 100 S.Ct. 2814, 65 L.Ed.2d 973, 6 Med.L.Rptr. 1833

APPEAL FROM THE SUPREME COURT OF VIRGINIA

Syllabus

At the commencement of a fourth trial on a murder charge (the defendant's conviction after the first trial having been reversed on appeal, and two subsequent retrials having ended in mistrials), the Virginia trial court granted defense counsel's motion that the trial be closed to the public without any objections having been made by the prosecutor or by appellants, a newspaper and two of its reporters who were present in the courtroom, defense counsel having stated that he did not "want any information being shuffled back and forth when we have a recess as to . . who testified to what." Later that same day, however, the trial judge granted appellants' request for a hearing on a motion to vacate the closure order, and appellants' counsel contended that constitutional considerations mandated that, before ordering closure, the court should first decide that the defendant's rights could be protected in no other way. But the trial judge denied the motion, saying that, if he felt that the defendant's rights were infringed in any way and others' rights were not overridden, he was inclined to order closure, and ordered the trial to continue "with the press and public excluded." The next day, the court granted defendant's motion to strike the prosecution's evidence, excused the jury, and found the defendant not guilty. Thereafter, the court granted appellants' motion to intervene *nunc pro tunc* in the case, and the Virginia Supreme Court dismissed their mandamus and prohibition petitions and, finding no reversible error, denied their petition for appeal from the closure order.

Held: The judgment is reversed.

Reversed.

MR. CHIEF JUSTICE BURGER, joined by MR JUSTICE WHITE and MR. JUSTICE STEVENS, concluded that the right of the public and press to attend criminal trials is guaranteed under the First and Fourteenth Amendments. Absent an overriding interest articulated in findings, the trial of a criminal case must be open to the public. [ ]

(a) The historical evidence of the evolution of the criminal trial in Anglo-American justice demonstrates conclusively that, at the time this Nation's organic laws were adopted, criminal trials both here and in England had long been presumptively open, thus giving assurance that the proceedings were conducted fairly to all concerned and discouraging perjury, the misconduct of participants, or decisions based on secret bias or partiality. In addition, the significant community therapeutic value of public trials was recognized: when a shocking crime occurs, a community reaction of outrage and public protest often follows, and thereafter the open processes of justice serve an important prophylactic purpose, providing an outlet for community concern, hostility, and emotion. To work effectively, it is important that society's criminal process "satisfy the appearance of justice" [ ], which can best be provided by allowing people to observe such process. From this unbroken, uncontradicted history, supported by reasons as valid today as in centuries past, it must be concluded that a presumption of openness inheres in the very nature of a criminal trial under this Nation's system of justice. [ ]

(b) The freedoms of speech, press, and assembly, expressly guaranteed by the First Amendment, share a common core purpose of assuring freedom of communication on matters relating to the functioning of government. In guaranteeing freedoms such as those of speech and press, the First Amendment can be read as protecting the right of everyone to attend trials so as to give meaning to those explicit guarantees; the First Amendment right to receive information and ideas means, in the context of trials, that the guarantees of speech and press, standing alone, prohibit government from summarily closing courtroom doors which had long been open to the public at the time the First Amendment was adopted. Moreover, the right of assembly is also relevant, having been regarded not only as an independent right, but also as a catalyst to augment the free exercise of the other First Amendment rights with which it was deliberately linked by the draftsmen. A trial courtroom is a public place where the people generally -- and representatives of the media -- have a right to be present, and where their presence historically has been thought to enhance the integrity and quality of what takes place.

(c) Even though the Constitution contains no provision which, by its terms, guarantees to the public the right to attend criminal trials, various fundamental rights, not expressly guaranteed, have been recognized as indispensable to the enjoyment of enumerated rights. The right to attend criminal trials is implicit in the guarantees of the First Amendment; without the freedom to attend such trials, which people have exercised for centuries, important aspects of freedom of speech and of the press could be eviscerated.

(d) With respect to the closure order in this case, despite the fact that this was the accused's fourth trial, the trial judge made no findings to support closure; no inquiry was made as to whether alternative solutions would have met the need to ensure fairness; there was no recognition of any right under the Constitution for the public or press to attend the trial; and there was no suggestion that any problems with witnesses could not have been dealt with by exclusion from the courtroom or sequestration during the trial, or that sequestration of the jurors would not have guarded against their being subjected to any improper information.

MR. JUSTICE BRENNAN, joined by MR. JUSTICE MARSHALL, concluded that the First Amendment -- of itself and as applied to the States through the Fourteenth Amendment -- secures the public a right of access to trial proceedings, and that, without more, agreement of the trial judge and the parties cannot constitutionally close a trial to the public. Historically and functionally, open trials have been closely associated with the development of the fundamental procedure of trial by jury, and trial access assumes structural importance in this Nation's government of laws by assuring the public that procedural rights are respected and that justice is afforded equally, by serving as an effective restraint on possible abuse of judicial power, and by aiding the accuracy of the trial factfinding process. It was further concluded that it was not necessary to consider in this case what countervailing interests might be sufficiently compelling to reverse the presumption of openness of trials, since the Virginia statute involved -- authorizing trial closures at the unfettered discretion of the judge and parties -- violated the First and Fourteenth Amendments.

MR. JUSTICE STEWART concluded that the First and Fourteenth Amendments clearly give the press and the public a right of access to trials, civil as well as criminal; that such right is not absolute, since various considerations may sometimes justify limitations upon the unrestricted presence of spectators in the courtroom; but that, in the present case, the trial judge apparently gave no recognition to the right of representatives of the press and members of the public to be present at the trial.

MR. JUSTICE BLACKMUN, while being of the view that *Gannett Co. v. DePasquale, supra,* was in error, both in its interpretation of the Sixth Amendment generally and in its application to the suppression hearing involved there, and that the right to a public trial is to be found in the Sixth Amendment, concluded, as a secondary position, that the First Amendment must provide some measure of protection for public access

248

to the trial, and that here, by closing the trial, the trial judge abridged these First Amendment interests of the public.

BURGER, C J., announced the Court's judgment and delivered an opinion, in which WHITE and STEVENS, JJ., joined. WHITE, J., and STEVENS, J., filed concurring opinions. BRENNAN, J., filed an opinion concurring in the judgment, in which MARSHALL, J., joined. STEWART, J., and BLACKMUN, J., filed opinions concurring in the judgment. REHNQUIST, J., filed a dissenting opinion. POWELL, J., took no part in the consideration or decision of the case.

BURGER, J., lead opinion

The narrow question presented in this case is whether the right of the public and press to attend criminal trials is guaranteed under the United States Constitution.

I

In March, 1976, one Stevenson was indicted for the murder of a hotel manager who had been found stabbed to death on December 2, 1975. Tried promptly in July, 1976, Stevenson was convicted of second-degree murder in the Circuit Court of Hanover County, Va. The Virginia Supreme Court reversed the conviction in October, 1977, holding that a bloodstained shirt purportedly belonging to Stevenson had been improperly admitted into evidence. [ ]

Stevenson was retried in the same court. This second trial ended in a mistrial on May 30, 1978, when a juror asked to be excused after trial had begun and no alternate was available.

A third trial, which began in the same court on June 6, 1978, also ended in a mistrial. It appears that the mistrial may have been declared because a prospective juror had read about Stevenson's previous trials in a newspaper and had told other prospective jurors about the case before the retrial began. [ ]

Stevenson was tried in the same court for a fourth time beginning on September 11, 1978. Present in the courtroom when the case was called were appellants Wheeler and McCarthy, reporters for appellant Richmond Newspapers, Inc. Before the trial began, counsel for the defendant moved that it be closed to the public:

> [T]here was this woman that was with the family of the deceased when we were here before. She had sat in the Courtroom. I would like to ask that everybody be excluded from the Courtroom because I don't want any information being shuffled back and forth when we have a recess as to what -- who testified to what.

[ ]

The trial judge, who had presided over two of the three previous trials, asked if the prosecution had any objection to clearing the

249

courtroom. The prosecutor stated he had no objection, and would leave it to the discretion of the court. [ ] Presumably referring to Va.Code § 19.2-266 (Supp. 1980), the trial judge then announced: "[T]he statute gives me that power specifically, and the defendant has made the motion." He then ordered "that the Courtroom be kept clear of all parties except the witnesses when they testify." [ ] The record does not show that any objections to the closure order were made by anyone present at the time, including appellants Wheeler and McCarthy.

Later that same day, however, appellants sought a hearing on a motion to vacate the closure order. The trial judge granted the request and scheduled a hearing to follow the close of the day's proceedings. When the hearing began, the court ruled that the hearing was to be treated as part of the trial; accordingly, he again ordered the reporters to leave the courtroom, and they complied.

At the closed hearing, counsel for appellants observed that no evidentiary findings had been made by the court prior to the entry of its closure order, and pointed out that the court had failed to consider any other less drastic measures within its power to ensure a fair trial. [ ] Counsel for appellants argued that constitutional considerations mandated that, before ordering closure, the court should first decide that the rights of the defendant could be protected in no other way.

Counsel for defendant Stevenson pointed out that this was the fourth time he was standing trial. He also referred to "difficulty with information between the Jurors," and stated that he "didn't want information to leak out," be published by the media, perhaps inaccurately, and then be seen by the jurors. Defense counsel argued that these things, plus the fact that "this is a small community," made this a proper case for closure. [ ]

The trial judge noted that counsel for the defendant had made similar statements at the morning hearing. The court also stated:

> [O]ne of the other points that we take into consideration in this particular Courtroom is layout of the Courtroom. I think that having people in the Courtroom is distracting to the jury. Now, we have to have certain people in here, and maybe that's not a very good reason. When we get into our new Court Building, people can sit in the audience so the jury can't see them. The rule of the Court may be different under those circumstances. . . .

[ ] The prosecutor again declined comment, and the court summed up by saying:

> I'm inclined to agree with [defense counsel] that, if I feel that the rights of the defendant are infringed in any way, [when] he makes the motion to do something and it doesn't completely override all rights of everyone else, then I'm inclined to go along with the defendant's motion.

[ ] The court denied the motion to vacate, and ordered the trial to

continue the following morning "with the press and public excluded." [ ]

What transpired when the closed trial resumed the next day was disclosed in the following manner by an order of the court entered September 12, 1978:

> [I]n the absence of the jury, the defendant, by counsel, made a Motion that a mistrial be declared, which motion was taken under advisement.
>
> At the conclusion of the Commonwealth's evidence, the attorney for the defendant moved the Court to strike the Commonwealth's evidence on grounds stated to the record, which Motion was sustained by the Court.
>
> And the jury having been excused, the Court doth find the accused NOT GUILTY of Murder, as charged in the Indictment, and he was allowed to depart.

[ ]

On September 27, 1978, the trial court granted appellants' motion to intervene *nunc pro tunc* in the Stevenson case. Appellants then petitioned the Virginia Supreme Court for writs of mandamus and prohibition, and filed an appeal from the trial court's closure order. On July 9, 1979, the Virginia Supreme Court dismissed the mandamus and prohibition petitions and, finding no reversible error, denied the petition for appeal. [ ]

Appellants then sought review in this Court, invoking both our appellate [ ] and certiorari jurisdiction. [ ] We postponed further consideration of the question of our jurisdiction to the hearing of the case on the merits. [ ] We conclude that jurisdiction by appeal does not lie; however, treating the filed papers as a petition for a writ of certiorari pursuant to 28 U.S.C. § 2103, we grant the petition.

The criminal trial which appellants sought to attend has long since ended, and there is thus some suggestion that the case is moot. This Court has frequently recognized, however, that its jurisdiction is not necessarily defeated by the practical termination of a contest which is short-lived by nature. [ ] If the underlying dispute is "capable of repetition, yet evading review" [ ], it is not moot.

Since the Virginia Supreme Court declined plenary review, it is reasonably foreseeable that other trials may be closed by other judges without any more showing of need than is presented on this record. More often than not, criminal trials will be of sufficiently short duration that a closure order "will evade review, or at least considered plenary review in this Court." [ ] Accordingly, we turn to the merits.

II

We begin consideration of this case by noting that the precise issue presented here has not previously been before this Court for decision. In *Gannett Co. v. DePasquale, supra,* the Court was not required to decide whether a right of access to *trials,* as distinguished from hearings on pretrial motions, was constitutionally guaranteed. The Court held that the Sixth Amendment's guarantee to the accused of a public trial gave neither the public nor the press an enforceable right of access to a pretrial suppression hearing. One concurring opinion specifically emphasized that "a hearing on a motion before trial to suppress evidence is not a trial. . . ." [ ] Moreover, the Court did not decide whether the First and Fourteenth Amendments guarantee a right of the public to attend trials [ ]; nor did the dissenting opinion reach this issue. [ ]

In prior cases, the Court has treated questions involving conflicts between publicity and a defendant's right to a fair trial; as we observed in *Nebraska Press Assn. v. Stuart* [ ], "[t]he problems presented by this [conflict] are almost as old as the Republic." [ ] But here, for the first time, the Court is asked to decide whether a criminal trial itself may be closed to the public upon the unopposed request of a defendant, without any demonstration that closure is required to protect the defendant's superior right to a fair trial, or that some other overriding consideration requires closure.

A

The origins of the proceeding which has become the modern criminal trial in Anglo-American justice can be traced back beyond reliable historical records. We need not here review all details of its development, but a summary of that history is instructive. What is significant for present purposes is that, throughout its evolution, the trial has been open to all who cared to observe.

In the days before the Norman conquest, cases in England were generally brought before moots, such as the local court of the hundred or the county court, which were attended by the freemen of the community. [ ] Somewhat like modern jury duty, attendance at these early meetings was compulsory on the part of the freemen, who were called upon to render judgment. [ ]

With the gradual evolution of the jury system in the years after the Norman Conquest [ ], the duty of all freemen to attend trials to render judgment was relaxed, but there is no indication that criminal trials did not remain public. When certain groups were excused from compelled attendance [ ], the statutory exemption did not prevent them from attending; Lord Coke observed that those excused "are not compellable to come, but left to their own liberty." [ ]

Although there appear to be few contemporary statements on the subject, reports of the Eyre of Kent, a general court held in 1313-1314, evince a recognition of the importance of public attendance apart from the "jury duty" aspect. It was explained that

> the King's will was that all evil doers should be punished after their deserts, and that justice should be ministered indifferently to rich as to poor; *and for the better accomplishing of this,* he prayed the community of the

county *by their attendance* there to lend him their aid in the establishing of a happy and certain peace that should be both for the honour of the realm and for their own welfare.

[ ]

From these early times, although great changes in courts and procedure took place, one thing remained constant: the public character of the trial at which guilt or innocence was decided. Sir Thomas Smith, writing in 1565 about "the definitive proceedinges in causes criminall," explained that, while the indictment was put in writing as in civil law countries:

> All the rest is doone openlie in the presence of the Judges, the Justices, the enquest, the prisoner, *and so manie as will or can come so neare as to heare it*, and all depositions and witnesses given aloude, *that all men may heare from the mouth of the depositors and witnesses what is saide.*

> [ ] Three centuries later, Sir Frederick Pollock was able to state of the "rule of publicity" that, "[h]ere we have one tradition, at any rate, which has persisted through all changes."

We have found nothing to suggest that the presumptive openness of the trial which English courts were later to call "one of the essential qualities of a court of justice" [ ], was not also an attribute of the judicial systems of colonial America. In Virginia, for example, such records as there are of early criminal trials indicate that they were open, and nothing to the contrary has been cited. [ ] Indeed, when in the mid-1600's the Virginia Assembly felt that the respect due the courts was

> by the clamorous unmannerlynes of the people lost, and order, gravity and decoram which should manifest the authority of a court in the court it selfe neglected,

the response was not to restrict the openness of the trials to the public, but, instead, to prescribe rules for the conduct of those attending them. [ ]

In some instances, the openness of trials was explicitly recognized as part of the fundamental law of the Colony. The 1677 Concessions and Agreements of West New Jersey, for example, provided:

> That in all publick courts of justice for tryals of causes, civil or criminal, any person or persons, inhabitants of the said Province may freely come into, and attend the said courts, and hear and be present, at all or any such tryals as shall be there had or passed, that justice may not be done in a corner nor in any covert manner.

[ ] ... Other contemporary writings confirm the recognition that part of the very nature of a criminal trial was its openness to those who wished to attend. Perhaps the best indication of this is found in an address to the inhabitants of Quebec which was drafted by a committee consisting

of Thomas Cushing, Richard Henry Lee, and John Dickinson and approved by the First Continental Congress on October 26, 1774. [ ] This address, written to explain the position of the Colonies and to gain the support of the people of Quebec, is an "exposition of the fundamental rights of the colonists, as they were understood by a representative assembly chosen from all the colonies." [ ] Because it was intended for the inhabitants of Quebec, who had been "educated under another form of government" and had only recently become English subjects, it was thought desirable for the Continental Congress to explain "the inestimable advantages of a free English constitution of government, which it is the privilege of all English subjects to enjoy." [ ]

> [One] great right is that of trial by jury. This provides that neither life, liberty nor property can be taken from the possessor until twelve of his unexceptionable countrymen and peers of his vicinage, who from that neighbourhood may reasonably be supposed to be acquainted with his character and the characters of the witnesses, upon a fair trial, and full enquiry, face to face, *in open Court, before as many of the people as chuse to attend,* shall pass their sentence upon oath against him. . . .

[ ]

B

As we have shown, and as was shown in both the Court's opinion and the dissent in *Gannett* [ ], the historical evidence demonstrate conclusively that, at the time when our organic laws were adopted, criminal trials both here and in England had long been presumptively open. This is no quirk of history; rather, it has long been recognized as an indispensable attribute of an Anglo-American trial. Both Hale in the 17th century and Blackstone in the 18th saw the importance of openness to the proper functioning of a trial; it gave assurance that the proceedings were conducted fairly to all concerned, and it discouraged perjury, the misconduct of participants, and decisions based on secret bias or partiality. [ ] Jeremy Bentham not only recognized the therapeutic value of open justice but regarded it as the keystone:

> Without publicity, all other checks are insufficient: in comparison of publicity, all other checks are of small account. Recordation, appeal, whatever other institutions might present themselves in the character of checks, would be found to operate rather as cloaks than checks; as cloaks in reality, as checks only in appearance.

[ ] Panegyrics on the values of openness were by no means confined to self-praise by the English. Foreign observers of English criminal procedure in the 18th and early 19th centuries came away impressed by the very fact that they had been freely admitted to the courts, as many were not in their own homelands. [ ] They marveled that "the whole juridical procedure passes in public" [ ], and one commentator declared:

> The main excellence of the English judicature consists in publicity, in the free trial by jury, and in the extraordinary despatch with which business is

transacted. The publicity of their proceedings is indeed astonishing. *Free access to the courts is universally granted.*

[ ] The nexus between openness, fairness, and the perception of fairness was not lost on them:

> [T]he judge, the counsel, and the jury, are constantly exposed to public animadversion, and this greatly tends to augment the extraordinary confidence which the English repose in the administration of justice.

[ ]

This observation raises the important point that "[t]he publicity of a judicial proceeding is a requirement of much broader bearing than its mere effect upon the quality of testimony." [ ] The early history of open trials in part reflects the widespread acknowledgment, long before there were behavioral scientists, that public trials had significant community therapeutic value. Even without such experts to frame the concept in words, people sensed from experience and observation that, especially in the administration of criminal justice, the means used to achieve justice must have the support derived from public acceptance of both the process and its results.

When a shocking crime occurs, a community reaction of outrage and public protest often follows. [ ] Thereafter the open processes of justice serve an important prophylactic purpose, providing an outlet for community concern, hostility, and emotion. Without an awareness that society's responses to criminal conduct are underway, natural human reactions of outrage and protest are frustrated, and may manifest themselves in some form of vengeful "self-help," as indeed they did regularly in the activities of vigilante "committees" on our frontiers.

> The accusation and conviction or acquittal, as much perhaps as the execution of punishment, operat[e] to restore the imbalance which was created by the offense or public charge, to reaffirm the temporarily lost feeling of security and, perhaps, to satisfy that latent "urge to punish."

[ ]

Civilized societies withdraw both from the victim and the vigilante the enforcement of criminal laws, but they cannot erase from people's consciousness the fundamental, natural yearning to see justice done -- or even the urge for retribution. The crucial prophylactic aspects of the administration of justice cannot function in the dark; no community catharsis can occur if justice is "done in a corner [or] in any covert manner." [ ] It is not enough to say that results alone will satiate the natural community desire for "satisfaction." A result considered untoward may undermine public confidence, and where the trial has been concealed from public view, an unexpected outcome can cause a reaction that the system, at best, has failed, and, at worst, has been corrupted. To work effectively, it is important that society's criminal process "satisfy the appearance of justice" [ ], and the appearance of justice can best be provided by allowing people to observe it.

Looking back, we see that, when the ancient "town meeting" form of trial became too cumbersome, 12 members of the community were delegated to act as its surrogates, but the community did not surrender its right to observe the conduct of trials. The people retained a "right of visitation" which enabled them to satisfy themselves that justice was, in fact, being done.

People in an open society do not demand infallibility from their institutions, but it is difficult for them to accept what they are prohibited from observing. When a criminal trial is conducted in the open, there is at least an opportunity both for understanding the system in general and its workings in a particular case:

> The educative effect of public attendance is a material advantage. Not only is respect for the law increased and intelligent acquaintance acquired with the methods of government, but a strong confidence in judicial remedies is secured which could never be inspired by a system of secrecy.

[ ]

In earlier times, both in England and America, attendance at court was a common mode of "passing the time." [ ] With the press, cinema, and electronic media now supplying the representations or reality of the real life drama once available only in the courtroom, attendance at court is no longer a widespread pastime. Yet

> [i]t is not unrealistic, even in this day, to believe that public inclusion affords citizens a form of legal education, and hopefully promotes confidence in the fair administration of justice.

[ ] Instead of acquiring information about trials by firsthand observation or by word of mouth from those who attended, people now acquire it chiefly through the print and electronic media. In a sense, this validates the media claim of functioning as surrogates for the public. While media representatives enjoy the same right of access as the public, they often are provided special seating and priority of entry so that they may report what people in attendance have seen and heard. This

> contribute[s] to public understanding of the rule of law and to comprehension of the functioning of the entire criminal justice system. . . .

[ ]

C

From this unbroken, uncontradicted history, supported by reasons as valid today as in centuries past, we are bound to conclude that a presumption of openness inheres in the very nature of a criminal trial under our system of justice. This conclusion is hardly novel; without a direct holding on the issue, the Court has voiced its recognition of it in a variety of contexts over the years. Even while holding, in *Levine v. United*

States [   ], that a criminal contempt proceeding was not a "criminal prosecution" within the meaning of the Sixth Amendment, the Court was careful to note that more than the Sixth Amendment was involved:

> [W]hile the right to a "public trial" is explicitly guaranteed by the Sixth Amendment only for "criminal prosecutions," that provision is a reflection of the notion, deeply rooted in the common law, that "justice must satisfy the appearance of justice." . . . [D]ue process demands appropriate regard for the requirements of a public proceeding in cases of criminal contempt . . . as it does for all adjudications through the exercise of the judicial power, barring narrowly limited categories of exceptions. . . .

[   ] And recently, in *Gannett Co. v. DePasquale* [   ], both the majority [   ], and dissenting opinion [   ], agreed that open trials were part of the common law tradition.

Despite the history of criminal trials being presumptively open since long before the Constitution, the State presses its contention that neither the Constitution nor the Bill of Rights contains any provision which, by its terms, guarantees to the public the right to attend criminal trials. Standing alone, this is correct, but there remains the question whether, absent an explicit provision, the Constitution affords protection against exclusion of the public from criminal trials.

III

A

The First Amendment, in conjunction with the Fourteenth, prohibits governments from

> abridging the freedom of speech, or of the press; or the right of the people peaceably to assemble, and to petition the Government for a redress of grievances.

These expressly guaranteed freedoms share a common core purpose of assuring freedom of communication on matters relating to the functioning of government. Plainly it would be difficult to single out any aspect of government of higher concern and importance to the people than the manner in which criminal trials are conducted; as we have shown, recognition of this pervades the centuries-old history of open trials and the opinions of this Court. [   ]

The Bill of Rights was enacted against the backdrop of the long history of trials being presumptively open. Public access to trials was then regarded as an important aspect of the process itself; the conduct of trials "before as many of the people as chuse to attend" was regarded as one of "the inestimable advantages of a free English constitution of government." [   ] In guaranteeing freedoms such as those of speech and press, the First Amendment can be read as protecting the right of everyone to attend trials so as to give meaning to those explicit guarantees.

[T]he First Amendment goes beyond protection of the press and the self-

257

expression of individuals to prohibit government from limiting the stock of information from which members of the public may draw.

[ ] Free speech carries with it some freedom to listen. "In a variety of contexts, this Court has referred to a First Amendment right to `receive information and ideas.'" [ ] What this means in the context of trials is that the First Amendment guarantees of speech and press, standing alone, prohibit government from summarily closing courtroom doors which had long been open to the public at the time that Amendment was adopted.

> For the First Amendment does not speak equivocally. . . . It must be taken as a command of the broadest scope that explicit language, read in the context of a liberty-loving society, will allow.

[ ] It is not crucial whether we describe this right to attend criminal trials to hear, see, and communicate observations concerning them as a "right of access" [ ] or a "right to gather information," for we have recognized that, "without some protection for seeking out the news, freedom of the press could be eviscerated." [ ] The explicit, guaranteed rights to speak and to publish concerning what takes place at a trial would lose much meaning if access to observe the trial could, as it was here, be foreclosed arbitrarily.

B

The right of access to places traditionally open to the public, as criminal trials have long been, may be seen as assured by the amalgam of the First Amendment guarantees of speech and press; and their affinity to the right of assembly is not without relevance. From the outset, the right of assembly was regarded not only as an independent right, but also as a catalyst to augment the free exercise of the other First Amendment rights with which it was deliberately linked by the draftsmen. "The right of peaceable assembly is a right cognate to those of free speech and free press, and is equally fundamental." [ ] People assemble in public places not only to speak or to take action, but also to listen, observe, and learn; indeed, they may "assembl[e] for any lawful purpose" [ ] Subject to the traditional time, place, and manner restrictions [ ], streets, sidewalks, and parks are places traditionally open, where First Amendment rights may be exercised [ ]; a trial courtroom also is a public place where the people generally -- and representatives of the media -- have a right to be present, and where their presence historically has been thought to enhance the integrity and quality of what takes place.

C

The State argues that the Constitution nowhere spells out a guarantee for the right of the public to attend trials, and that, accordingly, no such right is protected. The possibility that such a contention could be made did not escape the notice of the Constitution's draftsmen; they were concerned that some important rights might be thought disparaged because not specifically guaranteed. It was even argued that, because of this danger, no Bill of Rights should be adopted. [ ] In a letter to Thomas Jefferson in October, 1788, James Madison explained why he, although "in favor of a bill of rights," had "not viewed it in an important light" up to that time: "I conceive that, in a certain degree . . . , the rights in question are reserved by the manner in which the federal powers are granted." He went on to state that "there is great reason to fear that a positive declaration of some of the most essential rights could not be obtained in the requisite latitude." [ ]

But arguments such as the State makes have not precluded recognition of important rights not enumerated. Notwithstanding the appropriate caution against reading into the Constitution rights not explicitly defined, the Court has acknowledged that certain unarticulated rights are implicit in enumerated guarantees. For example, the rights of association and of privacy, the right to be presumed innocent, and the right to be judged by a standard of proof beyond a reasonable doubt in a criminal trial, as well as the right to travel, appear nowhere in the Constitution or Bill of Rights. Yet these important but unarticulated rights have nonetheless been found to share constitutional protection in common with explicit guarantees. The concerns expressed by Madison and others have thus been resolved; fundamental rights, even though not expressly guaranteed, have been recognized by the Court as indispensable to the enjoyment of rights explicitly defined.

We hold that the right to attend criminal trials is implicit in the guarantees of the First Amendment; without the freedom to attend such trials, which people have exercised for centuries, important aspects of freedom of speech and "of the press could be eviscerated." [ ]

D

Having concluded there was a guaranteed right of the public under the First and Fourteenth Amendments to attend the trial of Stevenson's case, we return to the closure order challenged by appellants. The Court in *Gannett* made clear that, although the Sixth Amendment guarantees the accused a right to a public trial, it does not give a right to a private trial. [ ] Despite the fact that this was the fourth trial of the accused, the trial judge made no findings to support closure; no inquiry was made as to whether alternative solutions would have met the need to ensure fairness; there was no recognition of any right under the Constitution for the public or press to attend the trial. In contrast to the pretrial proceeding dealt with in *Gannett,* there exist in the context of the trial itself various tested alternatives to satisfy the constitutional demands of fairness. [ ] There was no suggestion that any problems with witnesses could not have been dealt with by their exclusion from the courtroom or their sequestration during the trial. [ ] Nor is there anything to indicate that sequestration of the jurors would not have guarded against their being subjected to any improper information. All of the alternatives admittedly present difficulties for trial courts, but none of the factors relied on here was beyond the realm of the manageable. Absent an

259

overriding interest articulated in findings, the trial of a criminal case must be open to the public. Accordingly, the judgment under review is

Reversed.

MR. JUSTICE POWELL took no part in the consideration or decision of this case.

In *Chandler v. Florida* (MCLE, page 451), the Supreme Court unanimously held that state rules permitting broadcast and still camera presence in criminal proceedings did not inherently violate a defendant's 6th Amendment right to a trial by an impartial jury nor the defendant's 4th Amendment right to due process. The ruling was in sharp contrast to the decision by the Court 16 years earlier in *Estes v. Texas*. As a result of the decision, nearly all states and some federal courts now allow microphones, recorders and cameras in the courtroom. Undoubtedly, the positive shift in public attitudes toward such coverage and the lack of intrusiveness of new media technologies contributed to the Court's own change in attitude.

Chandler v. Florida

Argued November 12, 1980
Decided January 26, 1981

449 U.S. 560, 101 S.Ct. 802, 66 L.Ed.2d 740, 7 Med.L.Rptr. 1041

APPEAL FROM THE SUPREME COURT OF FLORIDA

Syllabus

The Florida Supreme Court, following a pilot program for televising judicial proceedings in the State, promulgated a revised Canon 3A (7) of the Florida Code of Judicial Conduct. The Canon permits electronic media and still photography coverage of judicial proceedings, subject to the control of the presiding judge and to implementing guidelines placing on trial judges obligations to protect the fundamental right of the accused in a criminal case to a fair trial. Appellants, who were charged with a crime that attracted media attention, were convicted after a jury trial in a Florida trial court over objections that the televising and broadcast of parts of their trial denied them a fair and impartial trial. The Florida District Court of Appeal affirmed, finding no evidence that the presence of a television camera hampered appellants in presenting their case, deprived them of an impartial jury, or impaired the fairness of the trial. The Florida Supreme Court denied review. The Florida courts did not construe *Estes v. Texas* [ ], as laying down a *per se* constitutional rule barring broadcast coverage under all circumstances.

Held: The Constitution does not prohibit a state from experimenting with a program such as is authorized by Florida's Canon 3A(7).

(a) This Court has no supervisory jurisdiction over state courts, and, in reviewing a state court judgment, is confined to evaluating it in relation to the Federal Constitution.

(b) *Estes v. Texas, supra,* did not announce a constitutional rule that all photographic, radio, and television coverage of criminal trials is inherently a denial of due process. It does not stand as an absolute ban on state experimentation with an evolving technology, which, in terms of modes of mass communication, was in its relative infancy in 1964 when *Estes* was decided, and is, even now, in a state of continuing change.

(c) An absolute constitutional ban on broadcast coverage of trials cannot be justified simply because there is a danger that, in some cases, conduct of the broadcasting process or prejudicial broadcast accounts of pretrial and trial events may impair the ability of jurors to decide the issue of guilt or innocence uninfluenced by extraneous matter. The appropriate safeguard against juror prejudice is the defendant's right to demonstrate that the media's coverage of his case -- be it printed or broadcast compromised the ability of the particular jury that heard the case to adjudicate fairly.

(d) Whatever may be the "mischievous potentialities [of broadcast coverage] for intruding upon the detached atmosphere which should always surround the judicial process" [ ], at present no one has presented empirical data sufficient to establish that the mere presence of the broadcast media in the courtroom inherently has an adverse effect on that process under all circumstances. Here, appellants have offered nothing to demonstrate that their trial was subtly tainted by broadcast coverage -- let alone that all broadcast trials would be so tainted.

(e) Nor have appellants shown either that the media's coverage of their trial -- printed or broadcast -- compromised the jury's ability to judge them fairly, or that the broadcast coverage of their particular trial had an adverse impact on the trial participants sufficient to constitute a denial of due process.

(f) Absent a showing of prejudice of constitutional dimensions to these appellants, there is no reason for this Court either to endorse or to invalidate Florida's experiment.

376 So.2d 1157, affirmed.

BURGER, C.J., delivered the opinion of the Court, in which BRENNAN, MARSHALL, BLACKMUN, POWELL, and REHNQUIST, JJ., joined. STEWART, J., filed an opinion concurring in the result, WHITE, J., filed an opinion concurring in the judgment. STEVENS, J., took no part in the decision of the case.

BURGER, J., lead opinion

The question presented on this appeal is whether, consistent with constitutional guarantees, a state may provide for radio, television, and still photographic coverage of a criminal trial for public broadcast, notwithstanding the objection of the accused.

I

Background. Over the past 50 years, some criminal cases characterized as "sensational" have been subjected to extensive coverage by news media, sometimes seriously interfering with the conduct of the proceedings and creating a setting wholly inappropriate for the administration of justice. Judges, lawyers, and others soon became concerned, and in 1937, after study, the American Bar Association House of Delegates adopted Judicial Canon 35, declaring that all photographic and broadcast coverage of courtroom proceedings should be prohibited. In 1962, the House of Delegates amended Canon 35 to proscribe television coverage as well. [ ] The Canon's proscription was reaffirmed in 1972, when the Code of Judicial Conduct replaced the Canons of Judicial Ethics and Canon 3A(7) superseded Canon 35. [ ] A majority of the states, including Florida, adopted the substance of the ABA provision and its amendments. In Florida, the rule was embodied in Canon 3A(7) of the Florida Code of Judicial Conduct.

In February, 1978, the American Bar Association Committee on Fair Trial-Free Press proposed revised standards. These included a provision permitting courtroom coverage by the electronic media under conditions to be established by local rule and under the control of the trial judge, but only if such coverage was carried out unobtrusively and without affecting the conduct of the trial. The revision was endorsed by the ABA's Standing Committee on Standards for Criminal Justice and by its Committee on Criminal Justice and the Media, but it was rejected by the House of Delegates on February 12, 1979. [ ]

In 1978, based upon its own study of the matter, the Conference of State Chief Justices, by a vote of 94 to 1, approved a resolution to allow the highest court of each state to promulgate standards and guidelines regulating radio, television, and other photographic coverage of court proceedings.

The Florida Program. In January, 1975, while these developments were unfolding, the Post-Newsweek Stations of Florida petitioned the Supreme Court of Florida urging a change in Florida's Canon 3A(7). In April, 1975, the court invited presentations in the nature of a rulemaking proceeding, and, in January, 1976, announced an experimental program for televising one civil and one criminal trial under specific guidelines. [ ] These initial guidelines required the consent of all parties. It developed, however, that, in practice, such consent could not be obtained. The Florida Supreme Court then supplemented its order and established a new 1-year pilot program during which the electronic media were permitted to cover all judicial proceedings in Florida without reference to the consent of participants, subject to detailed standards with respect to technology and the conduct of operators. [ ] The experiment began in July, 1977, and continued through June, 1978.

When the pilot program ended, the Florida Supreme Court received and reviewed briefs, reports, letters of comment, and studies. It conducted its own survey of attorneys, witnesses, jurors, and court personnel through the Office of the State Court Coordinator. A separate survey was taken of judges by the Florida Conference of Circuit Judges. The court also studied the experience of 6 States that had, by 1979, adopted rules relating to electronic coverage of trials, as well as that of the 10 other States that, like Florida, were experimenting with such coverage.

Following its review of this material, the Florida Supreme Court concluded

> that, on balance, there [was] more to be gained than lost by permitting electronic media coverage of judicial proceedings subject to standards for such coverage.

[ ] The Florida court was of the view that, because of the significant effect of the courts on the day-to-day lives of the citizenry, it was essential that the people have confidence in the process. It felt that broadcast coverage of trials would contribute to wider public acceptance and understanding of decisions. [ ] Consequently, after revising the 1977 guidelines to reflect its evaluation of the pilot program, the Florida Supreme Court promulgated a revised Canon 3A(7). [ ] The Canon provides:

> Subject at all times to the authority of the presiding judge to (i) control the conduct of proceedings before the court, (ii) ensure decorum and prevent distractions, and (iii) ensure the fair administration of justice in the pending cause, electronic media and still photography coverage of public judicial proceedings in the appellate and trial courts of this state shall be allowed in accordance with standards of conduct and technology promulgated by the Supreme Court of Florida.

[ ]

The implementing guidelines specify in detail the kind of electronic equipment to be used and the manner of its use. [ ] For example, no more than one television camera and only one camera technician are allowed. Existing recording systems used by court reporters are used by broadcasters for audio pickup. Where more than one broadcast news organization seeks to cover a trial, the media must pool coverage. No artificial lighting is allowed. The equipment is positioned in a fixed location, and it may not be moved during trial. Videotaping equipment must be remote from the courtroom. Film, videotape, and lenses may not be changed while the court is in session. No audio recording of conferences between lawyers, between parties and counsel, or at the bench is permitted. The judge has sole and plenary discretion to exclude coverage of certain witnesses, and the jury may not be filmed. The judge has discretionary power to forbid coverage whenever satisfied that coverage may have a deleterious effect on the paramount right of the defendant to a fair trial. The Florida Supreme Court has the right to revise these rules as experience dictates, or indeed to bar all broadcast coverage or photography in courtrooms.

In July, 1977, appellants were charged with conspiracy to commit burglary, grand larceny, and possession of burglary tools. The counts covered breaking and entering a well-known Miami Beach restaurant.

The details of the alleged criminal conduct are not relevant to the issue before us, but several aspects of the case distinguish it from a routine burglary. At the time of their arrest, appellants were Miami Beach policemen. The State's principal witness was John Sion, an amateur radio operator who, by sheer chance, had overheard and recorded conversations between the appellants over their police walkie-talkie radios during the burglary. Not surprisingly, these novel factors attracted the attention of the media.

By pretrial motion, counsel for the appellants sought to have experimental Canon 3A(7) declared unconstitutional on its face and as applied. The trial court denied relief, but certified the issue to the Florida Supreme Court. However, the Supreme Court declined to rule on the question, on the ground that it was not directly relevant to the criminal charges against the appellants. [ ]

After several additional fruitless attempts by the appellants to prevent electronic coverage of the trial, the jury was selected. At *voir dire,* the appellants' counsel asked each prospective juror whether he or she would be able to be "fair and impartial" despite the presence of a television camera during some, or all, of the trial. Each juror selected responded that such coverage would not affect his or her consideration in any way. A television camera recorded the *voir dire.*

A defense motion to sequester the jury because of the television coverage was denied by the trial judge. However, the court instructed the jury not to watch or read anything about the case in the media and suggested that jurors "avoid the local news and watch only the national news on television." [ ] Subsequently, defense counsel requested that the witnesses be instructed not to watch any television accounts of testimony presented at trial. The trial court declined to give such an instruction, for "no witness' testimony was [being] reported or televised [on the evening news] in any way." [ ]

A television camera was in place for one entire afternoon, during which the State presented the testimony of Sion, its chief witness. No camera was present for the presentation of any part of the case for the defense. The camera returned to cover closing arguments. Only 2 minutes and 55 seconds of the trial below were broadcast -- and those depicted only the prosecution's side of the case.

The jury returned a guilty verdict on all counts. Appellants moved for a new trial, claiming that, because of the television coverage, they had been denied a fair and impartial trial. No evidence of specific prejudice was tendered.

The Florida District Court of Appeal affirmed the convictions. It declined to discuss the facial validity of Canon 3A(7); it reasoned that the Florida Supreme Court, having decided to permit television coverage of criminal trials on an experimental basis, had implicitly determined that such coverage did not violate the Federal or State Constitutions. Nonetheless, the District Court of Appeal did agree to certify the question of the facial constitutionality of Canon 3A(7) to the Florida Supreme Court. The District Court of Appeal found no evidence in the trial record to indicate that the presence of a television camera had hampered appellants in presenting their case or had deprived them of an impartial jury.

The Florida Supreme Court denied review, holding that the appeal, which was limited to a challenge to Canon 3A(7), was moot by reason of its decision in *In re Petition of Post-Newsweek Stations, Florida, Inc.* [ ], rendered shortly after the decision of the District Court of Appeal.

II

At the outset, it is important to note that, in promulgating the revised Canon 3A(7), the Florida Supreme Court pointedly rejected any state or federal constitutional right of access on the part of photographers or the broadcast media to televise or electronically record and thereafter disseminate court proceedings. It carefully framed its holding as follows:

> While we have concluded that the due process clause does not prohibit electronic media coverage of judicial proceedings *per se,* by the same token, we reject the argument of the [Post-Newsweek stations] that the first and sixth amendments to the United States Constitution mandate entry of the electronic media into judicial proceedings.

[ ]

The Florida court relied on our holding in *Nixon v. Warner Communications, Inc.* [ ], where we said:

> In the first place, . . . there is no constitutional right to have [live witness] testimony recorded and broadcast. Second, while the guarantee of a public trial, in the words of Mr. Justice Black, is "a safeguard against any attempt to employ our courts as instruments- of persecution," it confers no special benefit on the press. Nor does the Sixth Amendment require that the trial - - or any part of it -- be broadcast live or on tape to the public. The requirement of a public trial is satisfied by the opportunity of members of the public and the press to attend the trial and to report what they have observed.

[ ]

The Florida Supreme Court predicated the revised Canon 3A(7) upon its supervisory authority over the Florida courts and not upon any constitutional imperative. Hence, we have before us only the limited question of the Florida Supreme Court's authority to promulgate the

266

Canon for the trial of cases in Florida courts.

This Court has no supervisory jurisdiction over state courts, and, in reviewing a state court judgment, we are confined to evaluating it in relation to the Federal Constitution.

III

Appellants rely chiefly on [ ], and Chief Justice Warren's separate concurring opinion in that case. They argue that the televising of criminal trials is inherently a denial of due process, and they read *Estes* as announcing a *per se* constitutional rule to that effect.

Chief Justice Warren's concurring opinion, in which he was joined by Justices Douglas and Goldberg, indeed provides some support for the appellants' position:

> While I join the Court's opinion and agree that the televising of criminal trials is inherently a denial of due process, I desire to express additional views on why this is so. In doing this, I wish to emphasize that our condemnation of televised criminal trials is not based on generalities or abstract fears. The record in this case presents a vivid illustration of the inherent prejudice of televised criminal trials, and supports our conclusion that this is the appropriate time to make a definitive appraisal of television in the courtroom.

[ ] If appellants' reading of *Estes* were correct, we would be obliged to apply that holding and reverse the judgment under review.

The six separate opinions in *Estes* must be examined carefully to evaluate the claim that it represents a *per se* constitutional rule forbidding all electronic coverage. Chief Justice Warren and Justices Douglas and Goldberg joined Justice Clark's opinion announcing the judgment, thereby creating only a plurality. Justice Harlan provided the fifth vote necessary in support of the judgment. In a separate opinion, he pointedly limited his concurrence:

> I concur in the opinion of the Court, subject, however, to the reservations and only to the extent indicated in this opinion.

[ ] A careful analysis of Justice Harlan's opinion is therefore fundamental to an understanding of the ultimate holding of *Estes*.

Justice Harlan began by observing that the question of the constitutional permissibility of televised trials was one fraught with unusual difficulty:

> Permitting television in the courtroom undeniably has mischievous potentialities for intruding upon the detached atmosphere which should always surround the judicial process. Forbidding this innovation, however, would doubtless impinge upon one of the valued attributes of our federalism by preventing the states from pursuing a novel course of procedural experimentation. My conclusion is that there is no

constitutional requirement that television be allowed in the courtroom, and, *at least as to a notorious criminal trial such as this one, the considerations against allowing television in the courtroom so far outweigh the countervailing factors advanced in its support as to require a holding that what was done in this case infringed the fundamental right to a fair trial* assured by the Due Process Clause of the Fourteenth Amendment.

[ ]

He then proceeded to catalog what he perceived as the inherent dangers of televised trials.

> In the context of a trial of intense public interest, there is certainly a strong possibility that the timid or reluctant witness, for whom a court appearance, even at its traditional best, is a harrowing affair, will become more timid or reluctant when he finds that he will also be appearing before a "hidden audience" of unknown, but large, dimensions. There is certainly a strong possibility that the "cocky" witness having a thirst for the limelight will become more "cocky" under the influence of television. And who can say that the juror who is gratified by having been chosen for a front-line case, an ambitious prosecutor, a publicity-minded defense attorney, and even a conscientious judge will not stray, albeit unconsciously, from doing what "comes naturally" into pluming themselves for a satisfactory television "performance"?

[ ] Justice Harlan faced squarely the reality that these possibilities carry "grave potentialities for distorting the integrity of the judicial process," and that, although such distortions may produce no telltale signs, "their effects may be far more pervasive and deleterious than the physical disruptions which all would concede would vitiate a conviction." [ ] The "countervailing factors" alluded to by Justice Harlan were, as here, the educational and informational value to the public.

JUSTICE STEWART, joined by JUSTICES Black, BRENNAN, and WHITE in dissent, concluded that no prejudice had been shown and that *Estes'* Fourteenth Amendment rights had not been violated. While expressing reservations not unlike those of Justice Harlan and those of Chief Justice Warren, the dissent expressed unwillingness to "escalate this personal view into a *per se* constitutional rule." [ ] The four dissenters disagreed both with the *per se* rule embodied in the plurality opinion of Justice Clark and with the judgment of the Court that "the *circumstances of [that]* trial led to a denial of [*Estes'*] Fourteenth Amendment rights." [ ]

Parsing the six opinions in *Estes,* one is left with a sense of doubt as to precisely how much of Justice Clark's opinion was joined in, and supported by, Justice Harlan. In an area charged with constitutional nuances, perhaps more should not be expected. Nonetheless, it is fair to say that Justice Harlan viewed the holding as limited to the proposition that "*what was done in this case* infringed the fundamental right to a fair trial assured by the Due Process Clause of the Fourteenth Amendment" [ ], he went on:

268

> *At the present juncture,* I can only conclude that televised trials, *at least in cases like this one,* possess such capabilities for interfering with the even course of the judicial process that they are constitutionally banned.

[ ] Justice Harlan's opinion, upon which analysis of the constitutional holding of *Estes* turns, must be read as defining the scope of that holding; we conclude that *Estes* is not to be read as announcing a constitutional rule barring still photographic, radio, and television coverage in all cases and under all circumstances. It does not stand as an absolute ban on state experimentation with an evolving technology, which, in terms of modes of mass communication, was in its relative infancy in 1964, and is, even now, in a stage of continuing change.

IV

Since we are satisfied that *Estes* did not announce a constitutional rule that all photographic or broadcast coverage of criminal trials is inherently a denial of due process, we turn to consideration, as a matter of first impression, of the appellants' suggestion that we now promulgate such a *per se* rule.

A

Any criminal case that generates a great deal of publicity presents some risks that the publicity may compromise the right of the defendant to a fair trial. Trial courts must be especially vigilant to guard against any impairment of the defendant's right to a verdict based solely upon the evidence and the relevant law. Over the years, courts have developed a range of curative devices to prevent publicity about a trial from infecting jury deliberations. [ ]

An absolute constitutional ban on broadcast coverage of trials cannot be justified simply because there is a danger that, in some cases, prejudicial broadcast accounts of pretrial and trial events may impair the ability of jurors to decide the issue of guilt or innocence uninfluenced by extraneous matter. The risk of juror prejudice in some cases does not justify an absolute ban on news coverage of trials by the printed media; so also the risk of such prejudice does not warrant an absolute constitutional ban on all broadcast coverage. A case attracts a high level of public attention because of its intrinsic interest to the public and the manner of reporting the event. The risk of juror prejudice is present in any publication of a trial, but the appropriate safeguard against such prejudice is the defendant's right to demonstrate that the media's coverage of his case -- be it printed or broadcast -- compromised the ability of the particular jury that heard the case to adjudicate fairly. [ ]

B

As we noted earlier, the concurring opinions in *Estes* expressed concern that the very presence of media cameras and recording devices at a trial inescapably gives rise to an adverse psychological impact on the participants in the trial. This kind of general psychological prejudice, allegedly present whenever there is broadcast coverage of a trial, is different from the more particularized problem of prejudicial impact discussed earlier. If it could be demonstrated that the mere presence of photographic and recording equipment and the knowledge that the event would be broadcast invariably and uniformly affected the conduct of participants so as to impair fundamental fairness, our task would be simple; prohibition of broadcast coverage of trials would be required.

In confronting the difficult and sensitive question of the potential psychological prejudice associated with broadcast coverage of trials, we have been aided by *amici* briefs submitted by various state officers involved in law enforcement, the Conference of Chief Justices, and the Attorneys General of 17 States in support of continuing experimentation such as that embarked upon by Florida, and by the American College of Trial Lawyers, and various members of the defense bar representing essentially the views expressed by the concurring Justices in *Estes*.

Not unimportant to the position asserted by Florida and other states is the change in television technology since 1962, when *Estes* was tried. It is urged, and some empirical data are presented, that many of the negative factors found in *Estes* -- cumbersome equipment, cables, distracting lighting, numerous camera technicians -- are less substantial factors today than they were at that time.

It is also significant that safeguards have been built into the experimental programs in state courts, and into the Florida program, to avoid some of the most egregious problems envisioned by the six opinions in the *Estes* case. Florida admonishes its courts to take special pains to protect certain witnesses -- for example, children, victims of sex crimes, some informants, and even the very timid witness or party -- from the glare of publicity and the tensions of being "on camera." [ ]

The Florida guidelines place on trial judges positive obligations to be on guard to protect the fundamental right of the accused to a fair trial. The Florida Canon, being one of the few permitting broadcast coverage of criminal trials over the objection of the accused, raises problems not present in the rules of other states. Inherent in electronic coverage of a trial is the risk that the very awareness by the accused of the coverage and the contemplated broadcast may adversely affect the conduct of the participants and the fairness of the trial, yet leave no evidence of how the conduct or the trial's fairness was affected. Given this danger, it is significant that Florida requires that objections of the accused to coverage be heard and considered on the record by the trial court. [ ] In addition to providing a record for appellate review, a pretrial hearing enables a defendant to advance the basis of his objection to broadcast coverage and allows the trial court to define the steps necessary to minimize or eliminate the risks of prejudice to the accused. Experiments such as the one presented here may well increase the number of appeals by adding a new basis for claims to reverse, but this is a risk Florida has chosen to take after preliminary experimentation. Here, the record does not indicate that appellants requested an evidentiary hearing to show adverse impact or injury. Nor does the record reveal anything more than generalized allegations of prejudice.

Nonetheless, it is clear that the general issue of the psychological impact of broadcast coverage upon the participants in a trial, and particularly upon the defendant, is still a subject of sharp debate -- as the *amici* briefs of the American College of Trial Lawyers and others of the trial bar in opposition to Florida's experiment demonstrate. These *amici* state the view that the concerns expressed by the concurring opinions in *Estes* [   ] have been borne out by actual experience. Comprehensive empirical data are still not available -- at least on some aspects of the problem. For example, the *amici* brief of the Attorneys General concedes:

> The defendant's interests in not being harassed and in being able to concentrate on the proceedings and confer effectively with his attorney are crucial aspects of a fair trial. There is not much data on defendant's reactions to televised trials available now, but what there is indicates that it is possible to regulate the media so that their presence does not weigh heavily on the defendant. *Particular attention should be paid to this area of concern as study of televised trials continues.*

[   ] The experimental status of electronic coverage of trials is also emphasized by the *amicus* brief of the Conference of Chief Justices:

> Examination and reexamination, by state courts, of the in-court presence of the electronic news media, *vel non,* is an exercise of authority reserved to the states under our federalism.

[ ]

Whatever may be the "mischievous potentialities [of broadcast coverage] for intruding upon the detached atmosphere which should always surround the judicial process," [   ], at present, no one has been able to present empirical data sufficient to establish that the mere presence of the broadcast media inherently has an adverse effect on that process. [   ] The appellants have offered nothing to demonstrate that their trial was subtly tainted by broadcast coverage -- let alone that all broadcast trials would be so tainted. [   ]

Where, as here, we cannot say that a denial of due process automatically results from activity authorized by a state, the admonition of Justice Brandeis, dissenting in *New State Ice Co. v. Liebmann* [   ], is relevant:

> To stay experimentation in things social and economic is a grave responsibility. Denial of the right to experiment may be fraught with serious consequences to the Nation. It is one of the happy incidents of the federal system that a single courageous State may, if its citizens choose, serve as a laboratory; and try novel social and economic experiments without risk to the rest of the country. This Court has the power to prevent an experiment. We may strike down the statute which embodies it on the

271

ground that, in our opinion, the measure is arbitrary, capricious, or unreasonable. . . . But in the exercise of this high power, we must be ever on our guard, lest we erect our prejudices into legal principles. If we would guide by the light of reason, we must let our minds be bold.

[ ] This concept of federalism, echoed by the states favoring Florida's experiment, must guide our decision.

C

Amici members of the defense bar, [ ], vigorously contend that displaying the accused on television is, in itself, a denial of due process. [ ] This was a source of concern to Chief Justice Warren and Justice Harlan in *Estes:* that coverage of select cases "singles out certain defendants and subjects them to trials under prejudicial conditions not experienced by others." [ ] Selection of which trials, or parts of trials, to broadcast will inevitably be made not by judges, but by the media, and will be governed by such factors as the nature of the crime and the status and position of the accused -- or of the victim; the effect may be to titillate, rather than to educate and inform. The unanswered question is whether electronic coverage will bring public humiliation upon the accused with such randomness that it will evoke due process concerns by being "unusual in the same way that being struck by lighting" is "unusual." [ ] Societies and political systems, that, from time to time, have put on "Yankee Stadium" "show trials" tell more about the power of the state than about its concern for the decent administration of justice -- with every citizen receiving the same kind of justice.

The concurring opinion of Chief Justice Warren, joined by Justices Douglas and Goldberg, in *Estes* can fairly be read as viewing the very broadcast of some trials as potentially a form of punishment in itself -- a punishment before guilt. This concern is far from trivial. But whether coverage of a few trials will, in practice, be the equivalent of a "Yankee Stadium" setting -- which Justice Harlan likened to the public pillory long abandoned as a barbaric perversion of decent justice -- must also await the continuing experimentation.

D

To say that the appellants have not demonstrated that broadcast coverage is inherently a denial of due process is not to say that the appellants were, in fact, accorded all of the protections of due process in their trial. As noted earlier, a defendant has the right on review to show that the media's coverage of his case -- printed or broadcast -- compromised the ability of the jury to judge him fairly. Alternatively, a defendant might show that broadcast coverage of his particular case had an adverse impact on the trial participants sufficient to constitute a denial of due process. Neither showing was made in this case.

To demonstrate prejudice in a specific case, a defendant must show something more than juror awareness that the trial is such as to attract the attention of broadcasters. [ ] No doubt the very presence of a camera in the courtroom made the jurors aware that the trial was thought to be of sufficient interest to the public to warrant coverage. Jurors, forbidden to watch all broadcasts, would have had no way of knowing that only fleeting seconds of the proceeding would be reproduced. But the appellants have not attempted to show with any specificity that the presence of cameras impaired the ability of the jurors to decide the case on only the evidence before them, or that their trial was affected adversely by the impact on any of the participants of the presence of cameras and the prospect of broadcast.

Although not essential to our holding, we note that, at *voir dire*, the jurors were asked if the presence of the camera would in any way compromise their ability to consider the case. Each answered that the camera would not prevent him or her from considering the case solely on the merits. [ ] The trial court instructed the jurors not to watch television accounts of the trial, [ ], and the appellants do not contend that any juror violated this instruction. The appellants have offered no evidence that any participant in this case was affected by the presence of cameras. In short, there is no showing that the trial was compromised by television coverage, as was the case in *Estes*.

V

It is not necessary either to ignore or to discount the potential danger to the fairness of a trial in a particular case in order to conclude that Florida may permit the electronic media to cover trials in its state courts. Dangers lurk in this, as in most experiments, but unless we were to conclude that television coverage under all conditions is prohibited by the Constitution, the states must be free to experiment. We are not empowered by the Constitution to oversee or harness state procedural experimentation; only when the state action infringes fundamental guarantees are we authorized to intervene. We must assume state courts will be alert to any factors that impair the fundamental rights of the accused.

The Florida program is inherently evolutional in nature; the initial project has provided guidance for the new canons which can be changed at will, and application of which is subject to control by the trial judge. The risk of prejudice to particular defendants is ever present, and must be examined carefully as cases arise. Nothing of the "Roman circus" or "Yankee Stadium" atmosphere, as in *Estes,* prevailed here, however, nor have appellants attempted to show that the unsequestered jury was exposed to "sensational" coverage, in the sense of *Estes* or of *Sheppard v. Maxwell* [ ]. Absent a showing of prejudice of constitutional dimensions to these defendants, there is no reason for this Court either to endorse or to invalidate Florida's experiment.

In this setting, because this Court has no supervisory authority over state courts, our review is confined to whether there is a constitutional violation. We hold that the Constitution does not prohibit a state from experimenting with the program authorized by revised Canon 3A(7).

273

Affirmed.

JUSTICE STEVENS took no part in the decision of this case.

In *Sheppard v. Maxwell* (MCLE, page 453) the Supreme Court held in an 8-1 decision that Dr. Sam Sheppard's 14th Amendment due process rights were violated by the massive, highly prejudicial publicity during his trial for murder. This case served as a lightning rod for many state courts to close criminal trials, although that was not the message communicated by the Supreme Court. The Court suggested several remedies to counter the effects of such publicity, including a continuance of the trial, a new trial and sequestration of the jury. Although the Supreme Court indicated that the trial judge in the case should have imposed greater restrictions on the presence of the news media in the courtroom, the Court did not favor restrictive orders on actual publication.

Sheppard v. Maxwell

Argued February 28, 1966
Decided June 6, 1966

384 U.S. 333, 86 S.Ct. 1507, 16 L.Ed.2d 600, 1 Med.L.Rptr. 1220

CERTIORARI TO THE UNITED STATES COURT OF APPEALS FOR THE SIXTH CIRCUIT

Syllabus

Petitioner's wife was bludgeoned to death July 4, 1954. From the outset officials focused suspicion on petitioner, who was arrested on a murder charge July 30 and indicted August 17. His trial began October 18 and terminated with his conviction December 21, 1954. During the entire pretrial period, virulent and incriminating publicity about petitioner and the murder made the case notorious, and the news media frequently aired charges and countercharges besides those for which petitioner was tried. Three months before trial, he was examined for more than five hours without counsel in a televised three-day inquest conducted before an audience of several hundred spectators in a gymnasium. Over three weeks before trial, the newspapers published the names and addresses of prospective jurors causing them to receive letters and telephone calls about the case. The trial began two weeks before a hotly contested election at which the chief prosecutor and the trial judge were candidates for judgeships. Newsmen were allowed to take over almost the entire small courtroom, hounding petitioner and most of the participants. Twenty reporters were assigned seats by the court within the bar and in close proximity to the jury and counsel, precluding privacy between petitioner and his counsel. The movement of the reporters in the courtroom caused frequent confusion and disrupted the trial, and, in the corridors and elsewhere in and around the courthouse, they were allowed free rein by the trial judge. A broadcasting station was assigned space next to the jury room. Before the jurors began deliberations they were not sequestered, and had access to all news media, though the court made "suggestions" and "requests" that the jurors not expose themselves to comment about the case. Though they were sequestered during the five days and four nights of their deliberations, the jurors were allowed to make inadequately supervised telephone calls during that period. Pervasive publicity was given to the case throughout the trial, much of it involving incriminating matter not introduced at the trial, and the jurors were thrust into the role of celebrities. At least some of the publicity deluge reached the jurors. At the very inception of the proceedings and later, the trial judge announced that neither he nor anyone else could restrict the prejudicial news accounts. Despite his awareness of the excessive pretrial publicity, the trial judge failed to take effective measures against the massive publicity, which continued throughout the trial, or to take adequate steps to control the conduct of the trial. The petitioner filed a habeas corpus petition contending that he did not receive a fair trial. The District Court granted the writ. The Court of Appeals reversed.

Held:

1. The massive, pervasive, and prejudicial publicity attending petitioner's prosecution prevented him from receiving a fair trial consistent with the Due Process Clause of the Fourteenth Amendment.

(a) Though freedom of discussion should be given the widest range compatible with the fair and orderly administration of justice, it must not be allowed to divert a trial from its purpose of adjudicating controversies according to legal procedures based on evidence received only in open court.

(b) Identifiable prejudice to the accused need not be shown if, as in *Estes v. Texas* [ ], and even more so in this case, the totality of the circumstances raises the probability of prejudice.

(c) The trial court failed to invoke procedures which would have guaranteed petitioner a fair trial, such as adopting stricter rules for use of the courtroom by newsmen as petitioner's counsel requested, limiting their number, and more closely supervising their courtroom conduct. The court should also have insulated the witnesses; controlled the release of leads, information, and gossip to the press by police officers, witnesses, and counsel; proscribed extrajudicial statements by any lawyer, witness, party, or court official divulging prejudicial matters, and requested the appropriate city and county officials to regulate release of information by their employees.

2. The case is remanded to the District Court with instructions to release petitioner from custody unless he is tried again within a reasonable time.

346 F.2d 707, reversed and remanded.

This federal habeas corpus application involves the question whether Sheppard was deprived of a fair trial in his state conviction for the second-degree murder of his wife because of the trial judge's failure to protect Sheppard sufficiently from the massive, pervasive and prejudicial publicity that attended his prosecution. The United States District Court held that he was not afforded a fair trial, and granted the writ subject to the State's right to put Sheppard to trial again [ ]. The Court of Appeals for the Sixth Circuit reversed by a divided vote [ ]. We granted certiorari [ ]. We have concluded that Sheppard did not receive a fair trial consistent with the Due Process Clause of the Fourteenth Amendment and, therefore, reverse the judgment.

I

Marilyn Sheppard, petitioner's pregnant wife, was bludgeoned to death in the upstairs bedroom of their lakeshore home in Bay Village, Ohio, a suburb of Cleveland. On the day of the tragedy, July 4, 1954, Sheppard pieced together for several local officials the following story: he and his wife had entertained neighborhood friends, the Aherns, on the previous evening at their home. After dinner, they watched television in the living room. Sheppard became drowsy and dozed off to sleep on a couch. Later, Marilyn partially awoke him saying that she was going to bed. The next thing he remembered, was hearing his wife cry out in the early morning hours. He hurried upstairs and, in the dim light from the hall, saw a "form" standing next to his wife's bed. A s he struggled with the "form," he was struck on the back of the neck and rendered unconscious. On regaining his senses, he found himself on the floor next to his wife's bed. He rose, looked at her, took her pulse and "felt that she was gone." He then went to his son's room and found him unmolested. Hearing a noise, he hurried downstairs. He saw a "form" running out the door and pursued it to the lake shore. He grappled with it on the beach, and again lost consciousness. Upon his recovery, he was lying face down with the lower portion of his body in the water. He returned to his home, checked the pulse on his wife's neck, and "determined or thought that she was gone." He then went downstairs and called a neighbor, Mayor Houk of Bay Village. The Mayor and his wife came over at once, found Sheppard slumped in an easy chair downstairs and asked, "What happened?" Sheppard replied: "I don't know, but somebody ought to try to do something for Marilyn." Mrs. Houk immediately went up to the bedroom. The Mayor told Sheppard, "Get hold of yourself. Can you tell me what happened?" Sheppard then related the above-outlined events. After Mrs. Houk discovered the body, the Mayor called the local police, Dr. Richard Sheppard, petitioner's brother, and the Aherns. The local police were the first to arrive. They, in turn, notified the Coroner and Cleveland police. Richard Sheppard then arrived, determined that Marilyn was dead, examined his brother's injuries, and removed him to the nearby clinic operated by the Sheppard family. When the Coroner, the Cleveland police and other officials arrived, the house and surrounding area were thoroughly searched, the rooms of the house were photographed, and many persons, including the Houks and the Aherns, were interrogated. The Sheppard home and premises were taken into "protective custody," and remained so until after the trial.

From the outset, officials focused suspicion on Sheppard. After a search of the house and premises on the morning of the tragedy, Dr. Gerber, the Coroner, is reported -- and it is undenied -- to have tod his men, "Well, it is evident the doctor did this, so let's go get the confession out of him." He proceeded to interrogate and examine Sheppard while the latter was under sedation in his hospital room. On the same occasion, the Coroner was given the clothes Sheppard wore at the time of the tragedy, together with the personal items in them. Later that, afternoon Chief Eaton and two Cleveland police officers interrogated Sheppard at some length, confronting him with evidence, and demanding explanations. Asked by Officer Shotke to take a lie detector test, Sheppard said he would if it were reliable. Shotke replied that it was "infallible," and "you might as well tell us all about it now." At the end of the interrogation, Shotke told Sheppard: "I think you killed your wife." Still later in the same afternoon, a physician sent by the Coroner was permitted to make a detailed examination of Sheppard. Until the Coroner's inquest on July 22, at which time he was subpoenaed, Sheppard made himself available for frequent and extended questioning without the presence of an attorney.

On July 7, the day of Marilyn Sheppard's funeral, a newspaper story appeared in which Assistant County Attorney Mahon -- later the chief prosecutor of Sheppard -- sharply criticized the refusal of the Sheppard family to permit his immediate questioning. From there on, headline stories repeatedly stressed Sheppard's lack of cooperation with the police and other officials. Under the headline "Testify Now In Death, Bay Doctor Is Ordered," one story described a visit by Coroner Gerber and four police officers to the hospital on July 8. When Sheppard insisted that his lawyer be present, the Coroner wrote out a subpoena and served it on him. Sheppard then agreed to submit to questioning without counsel, and the subpoena was torn up. The officers questioned him for several hours. On July 9, Sheppard, at the request of the Coroner, reenacted the tragedy at his home before the Coroner, police officers, and a group of newsmen, who apparently were invited by the Coroner. The home was locked, so that Sheppard was obliged to wait outside until the Coroner arrived. Sheppard's performance was reported in detail by the news media, along with photographs. The newspapers also played up Sheppard's refusal to take a lie detector test and "the protective ring" thrown up by his family. Front-page newspaper headlines announced on the same day that "Doctor Balks At Lie Test; Retells Story." A column opposite that story contained an "exclusive" interview with Sheppard headlined: "'Loved My Wife, She Loved Me,' Sheppard Tells News Reporter." The next day, another headline story disclosed that Sheppard had "again late yesterday refused to take a lie detector test," and quoted an Assistant County Attorney as saying that, "at the end of a nine-hour questioning of Dr. Sheppard, I felt he was now ruling [a test] out completely." But subsequent newspaper articles reported that the Coroner was still pushing Sheppard for a lie detector test. More stories appeared when Sheppard would not allow authorities to inject him with "truth serum."

On the 20th, the "editorial artillery" opened fire with a front-page charge that somebody is "getting away with murder." The editorial attributed the ineptness of the investigation to

> friendships, relationships, hired lawyers, a husband who ought to have been subjected instantly to the same third-degree to which any other person under similar circumstances is subjected. . . .

The following day, July 21, another page-one editorial was headed: "Why No Inquest? Do It Now, Dr. Gerber." The Coroner called an inquest the same day, and subpoenaed Sheppard. It was staged the next day in a school gymnasium; the Coroner presided with the County Prosecutor as his advisor and two detectives as bailiffs. In the front of the room was a long table occupied by reporters, television and radio personnel, and broadcasting equipment. The hearing was broadcast with live microphones placed at the Coroner's seat and the witness stand. A swarm of reporters and photographers attended. Sheppard was brought into the room by police who searched him in full view of several hundred spectators. Sheppard's counsel were present during the three-day inquest, but were not permitted to participate. When Sheppard's chief counsel attempted to place some documents in the record, he was forcibly ejected from the room by the Coroner, who received cheers, hugs, and kisses from ladies in the audience. Sheppard was questioned for five and one-half hours about his actions on the night of the murder, his married life, and a love affair with Susan Hayes. At the end of the hearing, the Coroner announced that he "could" order Sheppard held for the grand jury, but did not do so.

Throughout this period, the newspapers emphasized evidence that tended to incriminate Sheppard and pointed out discrepancies in his statements to authorities. At the same time, Sheppard made many public statements to the press, and wrote feature articles asserting his innocence. During the inquest on July 26, a headline in large type stated: "Kerr [Captain of the Cleveland Police] Urges Sheppard's Arrest." In the story, Detective McArthur

> disclosed that scientific tests at the Sheppard home have definitely established that the killer washed off a trail of blood from the murder bedroom to the downstairs section,

a circumstance casting doubt on Sheppard's accounts of the murder. No such evidence was produced at trial. The newspapers also delved into Sheppard's personal life. Articles stressed his extramarital love affairs as a motive for the crime. The newspapers portrayed Sheppard as a Lothario, fully explored his relationship with Susan Hayes, and named a number of other women who were allegedly involved with him. The testimony at trial never showed that Sheppard had any illicit relationships besides the one with Susan Hayes.

On July 28, an editorial entitled "Why Don't Police Quiz Top Suspect" demanded that Sheppard be taken to police headquarters. It described him in the following language:

> Now proved under oath to be a liar, still free to go about his business, shielded by his family, protected by a smart lawyer who has made monkeys of the police and authorities, carrying a gun part of the time, left free to do whatever he pleases. . . .

A front-page editorial on July 30 asked: "Why Isn't Sam Sheppard in Jail?" It was later titled "Quit Stalling -- Bring Him In." After calling Sheppard "the most unusual murder suspect ever seen around these parts," the article said that, "[e]xcept for some superficial questioning during Coroner Sam Gerber's inquest, he has been scot-free of any official grilling. . . ." It asserted that he was "surrounded by an iron curtain of protection [and] concealment."

That night, at 10 o'clock, Sheppard was arrested at his father's home on a charge of murder. He was taken to the Bay Village City Hall, where hundreds of people, newscasters, photographers and reporters were awaiting his arrival. He was immediately arraigned -- having been denied a temporary delay to secure the presence of counsel -- and bound over to the grand jury.

The publicity then grew in intensity until his indictment on August 17. Typical of the coverage during this period is a front-page interview entitled: "DR. SAM: `I Wish There Was Something I Could Get Off My Chest -- but There Isn't.'" Unfavorable publicity included items such as a cartoon of the body of a sphinx with Sheppard's head and the legend below: "`I Will Do Everything In My Power to Help Solve This Terrible Murder.' -- Dr. Sam Sheppard." Headlines announced, *inter alia,* that: "Doctor Evidence is Ready for Jury," "Corrigan Tactics Stall Quizzing," "Sheppard 'Gay Set' Is Revealed By Houk," "Blood Is Found In Garage," "New Murder Evidence Is Found, Police Claim," "Dr. Sam Faces Quiz At Jail On Marilyn's Fear Of Him." On August 18, an article appeared under the headline "Dr. Sam Writes His Own Story." And reproduced across the entire front page was a portion of the typed statement signed by Sheppard:

> I am not guilty of the murder of my wife, Marilyn. How could I, who have been trained to help people and devoted my life to saving life, commit such a terrible and revolting crime?

We do not detail the coverage further. There are five volumes filled with similar clippings from each of the three Cleveland newspapers covering the period from the murder until Sheppard's conviction in December, 1954. The record includes no excerpts from newscasts on radio and television, but, since space was reserved in the courtroom for these media, we assume that their coverage was equally large.

280

With this background, the case came on for trial two weeks before the November general election at which the chief prosecutor was a candidate for common pleas judge and the trial judge, Judge Blythin, was a candidate to succeed himself. Twenty-five days before the case was set, 75 veniremen were called as prospective jurors. All three Cleveland newspapers published the names and addresses of the veniremen. As a consequence, anonymous letters and telephone calls, as well as calls from friends, regarding the impending prosecution were received by all of the prospective jurors. The selection of the jury began on October 18, 1954.

The courtroom in which the trial was held measured 26 by 48 feet. A long temporary table was set up inside the bar, in back of the single counsel table. It ran the width of the courtroom, parallel to the bar railing, with one end less than three feet from the jury box. Approximately 20 representatives of newspapers and wire services were assigned seats at this table by the court. Behind the bar railing there were four rows of benches. These seats were likewise assigned by the court for the entire trial. The first row was occupied by representatives of television and radio stations, and the second and third rows by reporters from out-of-town newspapers and magazines. One side of the last row, which accommodated 14 people, was assigned to Sheppard's family, and the other to Marilyn's. The public was permitted to fill vacancies in this row on special passes only. Representatives of the news media also used all the rooms on the courtroom floor, including the room where cases were ordinarily called and assigned for trial. Private telephone lines and telegraphic equipment were installed in these rooms so that reports from the trial could be speeded to the papers. Station WSRS was permitted to set up broadcasting facilities on the third floor of the courthouse next door to the jury room, where the jury rested during recesses in the trial and deliberated. Newscasts were made from this room throughout the trial, and while the jury reached its verdict.

On the sidewalk and steps in front of the courthouse, television and newsreel cameras were occasionally used to take motion pictures of the participants in the trial, including the jury and the judge. Indeed, one television broadcast carried a staged interview of the judge as he entered the courthouse. In the corridors outside the courtroom, there was a host of photographers and television personnel with flash cameras, portable lights and motion picture cameras. This group photographed the prospective jurors during selection of the jury. After the trial opened, the witnesses, counsel, and jurors were photographed and televised whenever they entered or left the courtroom. Sheppard was brought to the courtroom about 10 minutes before each session began; he was surrounded by reporters and extensively photographed for the newspapers and television. A rule of court prohibited picture-taking in the courtroom during the actual sessions of the court, but no restraints were put on photographers during recesses, which were taken once each morning and afternoon, with a longer period for lunch.

All of these arrangements with the news media and their massive coverage of the trial continued during the entire nine weeks of the trial. The courtroom remained crowded to capacity with representatives of news media. Their movement in and out of the courtroom often caused so much confusion that, despite the loudspeaker system installed in the courtroom, it was difficult for the witnesses and counsel to be heard. Furthermore, the reporters clustered within the bar of the small courtroom made confidential talk among Sheppard and his counsel almost impossible during the proceedings. They frequently had to leave the courtroom to obtain privacy. And many times when counsel wished to raise a point with the judge out of the hearing of the jury, it was necessary to move to the judge's chambers. Even then, news media representatives so packed the judge's anteroom that counsel could hardly return from the chambers to the courtroom. The reporters vied with each other to find out what counsel and the judge had discussed, and often these matters later appeared in newspapers accessible to the jury.

The daily record of the proceedings was made available to the newspapers, and the testimony of each witness was printed verbatim in the local editions, along with objections of counsel, and rulings by the judge. Pictures of Sheppard, the judge, counsel, pertinent witnesses, and the jury often accompanied the daily newspaper and television accounts. At times, the newspapers published photographs of exhibits introduced at the trial, and the rooms of Sheppard's house were featured, along with relevant testimony.

The jurors themselves were constantly exposed to the news media. Every juror except one testified at *voir dire* to reading about the case in the Cleveland papers or to having heard broadcasts about it. Seven of the 12 jurors who rendered the verdict had one or more Cleveland papers delivered in their home; the remaining jurors were not interrogated on the point. Nor were there questions as to radios or television sets in the jurors' homes, but we must assume that most of them owned such conveniences. As the selection of the jury progressed, individual pictures of prospective members appeared daily. During the trial, pictures of the jury appeared over 40 times in the Cleveland papers alone. The court permitted photographers to take pictures of the jury in the box, and individual pictures of the members in the jury room. One newspaper ran pictures of the jurors at the Sheppard home when they went there to view the scene of the murder. Another paper featured the home life of an alternate juror. The day before the verdict was rendered -- while the jurors were at lunch and sequestered by two bailiffs -- the jury was separated into two groups to pose for photographs which appeared in the newspapers.

III

We now reach the conduct of the trial. While the intense publicity continued unabated, it is sufficient to relate only the more flagrant episodes:

282

1. On October 9, 1954, nine days before the case went to trial, an editorial in one of the newspapers criticized defense counsel's random poll of people on the streets as to their opinion of Sheppard's guilt or innocence in an effort to use the resulting statistics to show the necessity for change of venue. The article said the survey "smacks of mass jury tampering," called on defense counsel to drop it, and stated that the bar association should do something about it. It characterized the poll as "nonjudicial, nonlegal, and nonsense." The article was called to the attention of the court, but no action was taken.

2. On the second day of *voir dire* examination, a debate was staged and broadcast live over WHK radio. The participants, newspaper reporters, accused Sheppard's counsel of throwing roadblocks in the way of the prosecution and asserted that Sheppard conceded his guilt by hiring a prominent criminal lawyer. Sheppard's counsel objected to this broadcast and requested a continuance, but the judge denied the motion. When counsel asked the court to give some protection from such events, the judge replied that "WHK doesn't have much coverage," and that

> [a]fter all, we are not trying this case by radio or in newspapers or any other means. We confine ourselves seriously to it in this courtroom, and do the very best we can.

3. While the jury was being selected, a two-inch headline asked: "But Who Will Speak for Marilyn?" The front-page story spoke of the "perfect face" of the accused. "Study that face as long as you want. Never will you get from it a hint of what might be the answer. . . ." The two brothers of the accused were described as

> Prosperous, poised. His two sisters-in law. Smart, chic, well groomed. His elderly father. Courtly, reserved. A perfect type for the patriarch of a staunch clan.

The author then noted Marilyn Sheppard was "still off-stage," and that she was an only child whose mother died when she was very young and whose father had no interest in the case. But the author -- through quotes from Detective Chief James McArthur -- assured readers that the prosecution's exhibits would speak for Marilyn. "Her story," McArthur stated, "will come into this courtroom through our witnesses." The article ends:

> Then you realize how what and who is missing from the perfect setting will be supplied.

> How in the Big Case justice will be done.

> Justice to Sam Sheppard.

> And to Marilyn Sheppard.

4. As has been mentioned, the jury viewed the scene of the murder on the first day of the trial. Hundreds of reporters, cameramen and

onlookers were there, and one representative of the news media was permitted to accompany the jury while it inspected the Sheppard home. The time of the jury's visit was revealed so far in advance that one of the newspapers was able to rent a helicopter and fly over the house taking pictures of the jurors on their tour.

5. On November 19, a Cleveland police officer gave testimony that tended to contradict details in the written statement Sheppard made to the Cleveland police. Two days later, in a broadcast heard over Station WHK in Cleveland, Robert Considine likened Sheppard to a perjurer and compared the episode to Alger Hiss' confrontation with Whittaker Chambers. Though defense counsel asked the judge to question the jury to ascertain how many heard the broadcast, the court refused to do so. The judge also overruled the motion for continuance based on the same ground, saying:

> Well, I don't know, we can't stop people, in any event, listening to it. It is a matter of free speech, and the court can't control everybody. . . . We are not going to harass the jury every morning. . . . I t is getting to the point where if we do it every morning, we are suspecting the jury. I have confidence in this jury. . . .

6. On November 24, a story appeared under an eight-column headline: "Sam Called A `Jekyll-Hyde' By Marilyn, Cousin To Testify." It related that Marilyn had recently told friends that Sheppard was a "Dr. Jekyll and Mr. Hyde" character. No such testimony was ever produced at the trial. The story went on to announce:

> The prosecution has a "bombshell witness" on tap who will testify to Dr. Sam's display of fiery temper -- countering the defense claim that the defendant is a gentle physician with an even disposition.

Defense counsel made motions for change of venue, continuance and mistrial, but they were denied. No action was taken by the court.

7. When the trial was in its seventh week, Walter Winchell broadcast over WXEL television and WJW radio that Carole Beasley, who was under arrest in New York City for robbery, had stated that, as Sheppard's mistress, she had borne him a child. The defense asked that the jury be queried on the broadcast. Two jurors admitted in open court that they had heard it. The judge asked each: "Would that have any effect upon your judgment?" Both replied, "No." This was accepted by the judge as sufficient; he merely asked the jury to "pay no attention whatever to that type of scavenging. . . . Let's confine ourselves to this courtroom, if you please." In answer to the motion for mistrial, the judge said:

> Well, even, so, Mr. Corrigan, how are you ever going to prevent those things, in any event? I don't justify them at all. I think it is outrageous, but in a sense, it is outrageous even if there were no trial here. The trial has nothing to do with it in the Court's mind, as far as its outrage is concerned, but --

> Mr. CORRIGAN: I don't know what effect it had on the mind of any of

these jurors, and I can't find out unless inquiry is made.

The COURT: How would you ever, in any jury, avoid that kind of a thing?

8. On December 9, while Sheppard was on the witness stand, he testified that he had been mistreated by Cleveland detectives after his arrest. Although he was not at the trial, Captain Kerr of the Homicide Bureau issued a press statement denying Sheppard's allegations which appeared under the headline: "'Bare-faced Liar,' Kerr Says of Sam." Captain Kerr never appeared as a witness at the trial.

9. After the case was submitted to the jury, it was sequestered for its deliberations, which took five days and four nights. After the verdict, defense counsel ascertained that the jurors had been allowed to make telephone calls to their homes every day while they were sequestered at the hotel. Although the telephones had been removed from the jurors' rooms, the jurors were permitted to use the phones in the bailiffs' rooms. The calls were placed by the jurors themselves; no record was kept of the jurors who made calls, the telephone numbers or the parties called. The bailiffs sat in the room where they could hear only the jurors' end of the conversation. The court had not instructed the bailiffs to prevent such calls. By a subsequent motion, defense counsel urged that this ground alone warranted a new trial, but the motion was overruled, and no evidence was taken on the question.

IV

The principle that justice cannot survive behind walls of silence has long been reflected in the "Anglo-American distrust for secret trials." [ ] A responsible press has always been regarded as the handmaiden of effective judicial administration, especially in the criminal field. Its function in this regard is documented by an impressive record of service over several centuries. The press does not simply publish information about trials, but guards against the miscarriage of justice by subjecting the police, prosecutors, and judicial processes to extensive public scrutiny and criticism. This Court has, therefore, been unwilling to place any direct limitations on the freedom traditionally exercised by the news media for "[w]hat transpires in the courtroom is public property." [ ] The

> unqualified prohibitions laid down by the framers were intended to give to liberty of the press . . . the broadest scope that could be countenanced in an orderly society.

[ ] And where there was "no threat or menace to the integrity of the trial," *Craig v. Harney, supra* [ ], we have consistently required that the press have a free hand, even though we sometimes deplored its sensationalism.

But the Court has also pointed out that "[l]egal trials are not like elections, to be won through the use of the meeting-hall, the radio, and the newspaper." [ ] And the Court has insisted that no one be punished

for a crime without "a charge fairly made and fairly tried in a public tribunal free of prejudice, passion, excitement, and tyrannical power."
[ ]

> Freedom of discussion should be given the widest range compatible with the essential requirement of the fair and orderly administration of justice.

[ ] But it must not be allowed to divert the trial from the

> very purpose of a court system . . . to adjudicate controversies, both criminal and civil, in the calmness and solemnity of the courtroom according to legal procedures.

[ ] Among these "legal procedures" is the requirement that the jury's verdict be based on evidence received in open court, not from outside sources. Thus, in *Marshall v. United States* [ ], we set aside a federal conviction where the jurors were exposed, "through news accounts," to information that was not admitted at trial. We held that the prejudice from such material "may indeed be greater" than when it is part of the prosecution's evidence, "for it is then not tempered by protective procedures." [ ] At the same time, we did not consider dispositive the statement of each juror

> that he would not be influenced by the news articles, that he could decide the case only on the evidence of record, and that he felt no prejudice against petitioner as a result of the articles.

[ ] Likewise, in *Irvin v. Dowd* [ ], even though each juror indicated that he could render an impartial verdict despite exposure to prejudicial newspaper articles, we set aside the conviction, holding:

> With his life at stake, it is not requiring too much that petitioner be tried in an atmosphere undisturbed by so huge a wave of public passion. . . .

[ ]

The undeviating rule of this Court was expressed by Mr. Justice Holmes over half a century ago in *Patterson v. Colorado* [ ]:

> The theory of our system is that the conclusions to be reached in a case will be induced only by evidence and argument in open court, and not by any outside influence, whether of private talk or public print.

Moreover, "the burden of showing essential unfairness . . . as a demonstrable reality" [ ] need not be undertaken when television has exposed the community "repeatedly and in depth to the spectacle of [the accused] personally confessing in detail to the crimes with which he was later to be charged." [ ] In *Turner v. Louisiana* [ ], two key witnesses were deputy sheriffs who doubled as jury shepherds during the trial. The deputies swore that they had not talked to the jurors about the case, but the Court nonetheless held that,

> even if it could be assumed that the deputies never did discuss the case directly with any members of the jury, it would be blinking reality not to recognize the extreme prejudice inherent in this continual association. . . .

[ ]

Only last Term, in *Estes v. Texas* [ ], we set aside a conviction despite the absence of any showing of prejudice. We said there:

> It is true that, in most cases involving claims of due process deprivations, we require a showing of identifiable prejudice to the accused. Nevertheless, at times, a procedure employed by the State involves such a probability that prejudice will result that it is deemed inherently lacking in due process.

[ ] And we cited with approval the language of MR. JUSTICE BLACK for the Court in *In re Murchison* [ ], that "our system of law has always endeavored to prevent even the probability of unfairness."

V

It is clear that the totality of circumstances in this case also warrants such an approach. Unlike Estes, Sheppard was not granted a change of venue to a locale away from where the publicity originated; nor was his jury sequestered. The Estes jury saw none of the television broadcasts from the courtroom. On the contrary, the Sheppard jurors were subjected to newspaper, radio, and television coverage of the trial while not taking part in the proceedings. They were allowed to go their separate ways outside of the courtroom, without adequate directions not to read or listen to anything concerning the case. The judge's "admonitions" at the beginning of the trial are representative:

> I would suggest to you and caution you that you do not read any newspapers during the progress of this trial, that you do not listen to radio comments, nor watch or listen to television comments, insofar as this case is concerned. You will feel very much better as the trial proceeds. . . . I am sure that we shall all feel very much better if we do not indulge in any newspaper reading or listening to any comments whatever about the matter while the case is in progress. After it is all over, you can read it all to your heart's content. . . .

At intervals during the trial, the judge simply repeated his "suggestions" and "requests" that the jurors not expose themselves to comment upon the case. Moreover, the jurors were thrust into the role of celebrities by the judge's failure to insulate them from reporters and photographers. [ ] The numerous pictures of the jurors, with their addresses, which appeared in the newspapers before and during the trial itself exposed them to expressions of opinion from both cranks and friends. The fact that anonymous letters had been received by prospective jurors should have made the judge aware that this publicity seriously threatened the jurors' privacy.

The press coverage of the Estes trial was not nearly as massive and pervasive as the attention given by the Cleveland newspapers and broadcasting stations to Sheppard's prosecution. Sheppard stood indicted for the murder of his wife; the State was demanding the death penalty. For months, the virulent publicity about Sheppard and the murder had made the case notorious. Charges and countercharges were aired in the news media besides those for which Sheppard was called to trial. In addition, only three months before trial, Sheppard was examined for more than five hours without counsel during a three-day inquest which ended in a public brawl. The inquest was televised live from a high school gymnasium seating hundreds of people. Furthermore, the trial began two weeks before a hotly contested election at which both Chief Prosecutor Mahon and Judge Blythin were candidates for judgeships.

While we cannot say that Sheppard was denied due process by the judge's refusal to take precautions against the influence of pretrial publicity alone, the court's later rulings must be considered against the setting in which the trial was held. In light of this background, we believe that the arrangements made by the judge with the news media caused Sheppard to be deprived of that "judicial serenity and calm to which [he] was entitled." [ ] The fact is that bedlam reigned at the courthouse during the trial, and newsmen took over practically the entire courtroom, hounding most of the participants in the trial, especially Sheppard. At a temporary table within a few feet of the jury box and counsel table sat some 20 reporters, staring at Sheppard and taking notes. The erection of a press table for reporters inside the bar is unprecedented. The bar of the court is reserved for counsel, providing them a safe place in which to keep papers and exhibits and to confer privately with client and co-counsel. It is designed to protect the witness and the jury from any distractions, intrusions or influences, and to permit bench discussions of the judge's rulings away from the hearing of the public and the jury. Having assigned almost all of the available seats in the courtroom to the news media, the judge lost his ability to supervise that environment. The movement of the reporters in and out of the courtroom caused frequent confusion and disruption of the trial. And the record reveals constant commotion within the bar. Moreover, the judge gave the throng of newsmen gathered in the corridors of the courthouse absolute free rein. Participants in the trial, including the jury, were forced to run a gauntlet of reporters and photographers each time they entered or left the courtroom. The total lack of consideration for the privacy of the jury was demonstrated by the assignment to a broadcasting station of space next to the jury room on the floor above the courtroom, as well as the fact that jurors were allowed to make telephone calls during their five-day deliberation.

VI

There can be no question about the nature of the publicity which surrounded Sheppard's trial. We agree, as did the Court of Appeals, with the findings in Judge Bell's opinion for the Ohio Supreme Court:

> Murder and mystery, society, sex and suspense were combined in this case in such a manner as to intrigue and captivate the public fancy to a degree perhaps unparalleled in recent annals. Throughout the pre-indictment investigation, the subsequent legal skirmishes, and the nine-

288

week trial, circulation-conscious editors catered to the insatiable interest of the American public in the bizarre. . . . In this atmosphere of a "Roman holiday" for the news media, Sam Sheppard stood trial for his life.

[ ] Indeed, every court that has considered this case, save the court that tried it, has deplored the manner in which the news media inflamed and prejudiced the public.

Much of the material printed or broadcast during the trial was never heard from the witness stand, such as the charges that Sheppard had purposely impeded the murder investigation, and must be guilty, since he had hired a prominent criminal lawyer; that Sheppard was a perjurer; that he had sexual relations with numerous women; that his slain wife had characterized him as a "Jekyll-Hyde"; that he was "a bare-faced liar" because of his testimony as to police treatment; and, finally, that a woman convict claimed Sheppard to be the father of her illegitimate child. As the trial progressed, the newspapers summarized and interpreted the evidence, devoting particular attention to the material that incriminated Sheppard, and often drew unwarranted inferences from testimony. At one point, a front-page picture of Mrs. Sheppard's blood-stained pillow was published after being "doctored" to show more clearly an alleged imprint of a surgical instrument.

Nor is there doubt that this deluge of publicity reached at least some of the jury. On the only occasion that the jury was queried, two jurors admitted in open court to hearing the highly inflammatory charge that a prison inmate claimed Sheppard as the father of her illegitimate child. Despite the extent and nature of the publicity to which the jury was exposed during trial, the judge refused defense counsel's other requests that the jurors be asked whether they had read or heard specific prejudicial comment about the case, including the incidents we have previously summarized. In these circumstances, we can assume that some of this material reached members of the jury. [ ]

VII

The court's fundamental error is compounded by the holding that it lacked power to control the publicity about the trial. From the very inception of the proceedings, the judge announced that neither he nor anyone else could restrict prejudicial news accounts. And he reiterated this view on numerous occasions. Since he viewed the news media as his target, the judge never considered other means that are often utilized to reduce the appearance of prejudicial material and to protect the jury from outside influence. We conclude that these procedures would have been sufficient to guarantee Sheppard a fair trial, and so do not consider what sanctions might be available against a recalcitrant press, nor the charges of bias now made against the state trial judge.

The carnival atmosphere at trial could easily have been avoided, since the courtroom and courthouse premises are subject to the control of the court. As we stressed in *Estes*, the presence of the press at judicial proceedings must be limited when it is apparent that the accused might otherwise be prejudiced or disadvantaged. Bearing in mind the massive pretrial publicity, the judge should have adopted stricter rules governing the use of the courtroom by newsmen, as Sheppard's counsel requested. The number of reporters in the courtroom itself could have been limited at the first sign that their presence would disrupt the trial. They certainly should not have been placed inside the bar. Furthermore, the judge should have more closely regulated the conduct of newsmen in the courtroom. For instance, the judge belatedly asked them not to handle and photograph trial exhibits lying on the counsel table during recesses.

Secondly, the court should have insulated the witnesses. All of the newspapers and radio stations apparently interviewed prospective witnesses at will, and in many instances disclosed their testimony. A typical example was the publication of numerous statements by Susan Hayes, before her appearance in court, regarding her love affair with Sheppard. Although the witnesses were barred from the courtroom during the trial, the full verbatim testimony was available to them in the press. This completely nullified the judge's imposition of the rule. [ ]

Thirdly, the court should have made some effort to control the release of leads, information, and gossip to the press by police officers, witnesses, and the counsel for both sides. Much of the information thus disclosed was inaccurate, leading to groundless rumors and confusion. That the judge was aware of his responsibility in this respect may be seen from his warning to Steve Sheppard, the accused's brother, who had apparently made public statements in an attempt to discredit testimony for the prosecution. The judge made this statement in the presence of the jury:

> Now, the Court wants to say a word. That he was told -- he has not read anything about it at all -- but he was informed that Dr. Steve Sheppard, who has been granted the privilege of remaining in the courtroom during the trial, has been trying the case in the newspapers and making rather uncomplimentary comments about the testimony of the witnesses for the State.

> Let it be now understood that, if Dr. Steve Sheppard wishes to use the newspapers to try his case while we are trying it here, he will be barred from remaining in the courtroom during the progress of the trial if he is to be a witness in the case.

> The Court appreciates he cannot deny Steve Sheppard the right of free speech, but he can deny him the . . . privilege of being in the courtroom if he wants to avail himself of that method during the progress of the trial.

Defense counsel immediately brought to the court's attention the tremendous amount of publicity in the Cleveland press that "misrepresented entirely the testimony" in the case. Under such circumstances, the judge should have at least warned the newspapers to check the accuracy of their accounts. And it is obvious that the judge should have further sought to alleviate this problem by imposing control

290

over the statements made to the news media by counsel, witnesses, and especially the Coroner and police officers. The prosecution repeatedly made evidence available to the news media which was never offered in the trial. Much of the "evidence" disseminated in this fashion was clearly inadmissible. The exclusion of such evidence in court is rendered meaningless when news media make it available to the public. For example, the publicity about Sheppard's refusal to take a lie detector test came directly from police officers and the Coroner. The story that Sheppard had been called a "Jekyll-Hyde" personality by his wife was attributed to a prosecution witness. No such testimony was given. The further report that there was "a 'bombshell witness' on tap" who would testify as to Sheppard's "fiery temper" could only have emanated from the prosecution. Moreover, the newspapers described in detail clues that had been found by the police, but not put into the record.

The fact that many of the prejudicial news items can be traced to the prosecution as well as the defense aggravates the judge's failure to take any action. [ ] Effective control of these sources -- concededly within the court's power -- might well have prevented the divulgence of inaccurate information, rumors, and accusations that made up much of the inflammatory publicity, at least after Sheppard's indictment.

More specifically, the trial court might well have proscribed extrajudicial statements by any lawyer, party, witness, or court official which divulged prejudicial matters, such as the refusal of Sheppard to submit to interrogation or take any lie detector tests; any statement made by Sheppard to officials; the identity of prospective witnesses or their probable testimony; any belief in guilt or innocence; or like statements concerning the merits of the case [ ], in which the court interpreted Canon 20 of the American Bar Association's Canons of Professional Ethics to prohibit such statements. Being advised of the great public interest in the case, the mass coverage of the press, and the potential prejudicial impact of publicity, the court could also have requested the appropriate city and county officials to promulgate a regulation with respect to dissemination of information about the case by their employees. In addition, reporters who wrote or broadcast prejudicial stories could have been warned as to the impropriety of publishing material not introduced in the proceedings. The judge was put on notice of such events by defense counsel's complaint about the WHK broadcast on the second day of trial. [ ] In this manner, Sheppard's right to a trial free from outside interference would have been given added protection without corresponding curtailment of the news media. Had the judge, the other officers of the court, and the police placed the interest of justice first, the news media would have soon learned to be content with the task of reporting the case as it unfolded in the courtroom -- not pieced together from extrajudicial statements.

From the cases coming here, we note that unfair and prejudicial news comment on pending trials has become increasingly prevalent. Due process requires that the accused receive a trial by an impartial jury free from outside influences. Given the pervasiveness of modern

291

communications and the difficulty of effacing prejudicial publicity from the minds of the jurors, the trial courts must take strong measures to ensure that the balance is never weighed against the accused. And appellate tribunals have the duty to make an independent evaluation of the circumstances. Of course, there is nothing that proscribes the press from reporting events that transpire in the courtroom. But where there is a reasonable likelihood that prejudicial news prior to trial will prevent a fair trial, the judge should continue the case until the threat abates, or transfer it to another county not so permeated with publicity. In addition, sequestration of the jury was something the judge should have raised *sua sponte* with counsel. If publicity during the proceedings threatens the fairness of the trial, a new trial should be ordered. But we must remember that reversals are but palliatives; the cure lies in those remedial measures that will prevent the prejudice at its inception. The courts must take such steps by rule and regulation that will protect their processes from prejudicial outside interferences. Neither prosecutors, counsel for defense, the accused, witnesses, court staff nor enforcement officers coming under the jurisdiction of the court should be permitted to frustrate its function. Collaboration between counsel and the press as to information affecting the fairness of a criminal trial is not only subject to regulation, but is highly censurable, and worthy of disciplinary measures.

Since the state trial judge did not fulfill his duty to protect Sheppard from the inherently prejudicial publicity which saturated the community and to control disruptive influences in the courtroom, we must reverse the denial of the habeas petition. The case is remanded to the District Court with instructions to issue the writ and order that Sheppard be released from custody unless the State puts him to its charges again within a reasonable time.

It is so ordered.

MR. JUSTICE BLACK dissents.

In *Campbell v. Acuff-Rose Music, Inc.* (MCLE, page 532) the Supreme Court found that a "2 Live Crew" parody of the song, "Oh, Pretty Woman," was not presumptively unfair use under the Copyright Act of 1976 and therefore not an infringement. In reaching its decision, the Court applied the four factors of fair use set out in Section 107 of the Copyright Act. This case illustrates how courts are expected to assess a copyrighted work in determining whether a defendant to an infringement suit can claim fair use.

Campbell v. Acuff-Rose Music, Inc.

Argued November 9, 1993
Decided March 7, 1994

510 U.S. 569, 114 S.Ct. 1164, 127 L.Ed.2d 500, 22 Med.L.Rptr. 1353

CERTIORARI TO THE UNITED STATES COURT OF APPEALS FOR THE SIXTH CIRCUIT

Syllabus

Respondent Acuff-Rose Music, Inc., filed suit against petitioners, the members of the rap music group 2 Live Crew and their record company, claiming that 2 Live Crew's song, "Pretty Woman," infringed Acuff-Rose's copyright in Roy Orbison's rock ballad, "Oh Pretty Woman." The District Court granted summary judgment for 2 Live Crew, holding that its song was a parody that made fair use of the original song. *See* Copyright Act of 1976, 17 U.S.C. § 107. The Court of Appeals reversed and remanded, holding that the commercial nature of the parody rendered it presumptively unfair under the first of four factors relevant under § 107; that, by taking the "heart" of the original and making it the "heart" of a new work, 2 Live Crew had, qualitatively, taken too much under the third § 107 factor; and that market harm for purposes of the fourth § 107 factor had been established by a presumption attaching to commercial uses.

Held: 2 Live Crew's commercial parody may be a fair use within the meaning of § 107.

(a) Section 107, which provides that "the fair use of a copyrighted work . . . for purposes such as criticism [or] comment . . . is not an infringement . . . ," continues the common law tradition of fair use adjudication, and requires case-by-case analysis, rather than bright-line rules. The statutory examples of permissible uses provide only general guidance. The four statutory factors are to be explored and weighed together in light of copyright's purpose of promoting science and the arts.

(b) Parody, like other comment and criticism, may claim fair use. Under the first of the four § 107 factors, "the purpose and character of the use, including whether such use is of a commercial nature . . . ," the enquiry focuses on whether the new work merely supersedes the objects of the original creation, or whether and to what extent it is "transformative," altering the original with new expression, meaning, or message. The more transformative the new work, the less will be the significance of other factors, like commercialism, that may weigh against a finding of fair use. The heart of any parodist's claim to quote from existing material is the use of some elements of a prior author's composition to create a new one that, at least in part, comments on that author's work. But that tells courts little about where to draw the line. Thus, like other uses, parody has to work its way through the relevant factors.

(c) The Court of Appeals properly assumed that 2 Live Crew's song contains parody commenting on and criticizing the original work, but erred in giving virtually dispositive weight to the commercial nature of that parody by way of a presumption, ostensibly culled from *Sony Corp. of America v. Universal City Studios, Inc.* [ ], that "every commercial use of copyrighted material is presumptively . . . unfair. . . ." The statute makes clear that a work's commercial nature is only one element of the first factor enquiry into its purpose and character, and *Sony* itself called for no hard evidentiary presumption. The Court of Appeals' rule runs counter to *Sony* and to the long common law tradition of fair use adjudication.

(d) The second § 107 factor, "the nature of the copyrighted work," is not much help in resolving this and other parody cases, since parodies almost invariably copy publicly known, expressive works, like the Orbison song here.

(e) The Court of Appeals erred in holding that, as a matter of law, 2 Live Crew copied excessively from the Orbison original under the third § 107 factor, which asks whether "the amount and substantiality of the portion used in relation to the copyrighted work as a whole" are reasonable in relation to the copying's purpose. Even if 2 Live Crew's copying of the original's first line of lyrics and characteristic opening bass riff may be said to go to the original's "heart," that heart is what most readily conjures up the song for parody, and it is the heart at which parody takes aim. Moreover, 2 Live Crew thereafter departed markedly from the Orbison lyrics and produced otherwise distinctive music. As to the lyrics, the copying was not excessive in relation to the song's parodic purpose. As to the music, this Court expresses no opinion whether repetition of the bass riff is excessive copying, but remands to permit evaluation of the amount taken, in light of the song's parodic purpose and character, its transformative elements, and considerations of the potential for market substitution.

(f) The Court of Appeals erred in resolving the fourth § 107 factor, "the effect of the use upon the potential market for or value of the copyrighted work," by presuming, in reliance on *Sony* [ ], the likelihood of significant market harm based on 2 Live Crew's use for commercial gain. No "presumption" or inference of market harm that might find support in *Sony* is applicable to a case involving something beyond mere duplication for commercial purposes. The cognizable harm is market substitution, not any harm from criticism. As to parody pure and simple, it is unlikely that the work will act as a substitute for the original, since the two works usually serve different market functions. The fourth factor requires courts also to consider the potential market for derivative works. [ ] If the later work has cognizable substitution effects in protectable markets for derivative works, the law will look beyond the criticism to the work's other elements. 2 Live Crew's song comprises not only parody, but also rap music. The absence of evidence or affidavits addressing the effect of 2 Live Crew's song on the derivative market for a nonparody, rap version of "Oh, Pretty Woman" disentitled 2 Live Crew, as the proponent of the affirmative defense of fair use, to summary judgment.

972 F.2d 1429, reversed and remanded.

SOUTER, J., delivered the opinion for a unanimous Court. Kennedy, J., filed a concurring opinion.

SOUTER, J., lead opinion

We are called upon to decide whether 2 Live Crew's commercial parody of Roy Orbison's song, "Oh, Pretty Woman," may be a fair use within the meaning of the Copyright Act of 1976, 17 U.S.C. § 107 [ ]. Although the District Court granted summary judgment for 2 Live Crew, the Court of Appeals reversed, holding the defense of fair use barred by the song's commercial character and excessive borrowing. Because we hold that a parody's commercial character is only one element to be weighed in a fair use enquiry, and that insufficient consideration was given to the nature of parody in weighing the degree of copying, we reverse and remand.

I

In 1964, Roy Orbison and William Dees wrote a rock ballad called "Oh, Pretty Woman" and assigned their rights in it to respondent Acuff-Rose Music, Inc. [ ] Acuff-Rose registered the song for copyright protection.

Petitioners Luther R. Campbell, Christopher Wongwon, Mark Ross, and David Hobbs, are collectively known as 2 Live Crew, a popular rap music group. In 1989, Campbell wrote a song entitled "Pretty Woman," which he later described in an affidavit as intended, "through comical lyrics, to satirize the original work. . . ." [ ] On July 5, 1989, 2 Live Crew's manager informed Acuff-Rose that 2 Live Crew had written a parody of "Oh, Pretty Woman," that they would afford all credit for ownership and authorship of the original song to Acuff-Rose, Dees, and Orbison, and that they were willing to pay a fee for the use they wished to make of it. Enclosed with the letter were a copy of the lyrics and a recording of 2 Live Crew's song. [   ] Acuff-Rose's agent refused permission, stating that "I am aware of the success enjoyed by 'The 2 Live Crews', but I must inform you that we cannot permit the use of a parody of 'Oh, Pretty Woman.'" [ ] Nonetheless, in June or July, 1989, 2 Live Crew released records, cassette tapes, and compact discs of "Pretty Woman" in a collection of songs entitled "As Clean As They Wanna Be." The albums and compact discs identify the authors of "Pretty Woman" as Orbison and Dees and its publisher as Acuff-Rose.

Almost a year later, after nearly a quarter of a million copies of the recording had been sold, Acuff-Rose sued 2 Live Crew and its record company, Luke Skyywalker Records, for copyright infringement. The District Court granted summary judgment for 2 Live Crew, reasoning that the commercial purpose of 2 Live Crew's song was no bar to fair use; that 2 Live Crew's version was a parody, which "quickly degenerates into a play on words, substituting predictable lyrics with shocking ones" to show "how bland and banal the Orbison song" is; that 2 Live Crew had taken no more than was necessary to "conjure up" the original in order to parody it; and that it was "extremely unlikely that 2 Live Crew's song could adversely affect the market for the original." [ ] The District Court weighed these factors and held that 2 Live Crew's song made fair use of Orbison's original. [ ]

The Court of Appeals for the Sixth Circuit reversed and remanded. [ ]. Although it assumed for the purpose of its opinion that 2 Live Crew's song was a parody of the Orbison original, the Court of Appeals thought the District Court had put too little emphasis on the fact that "every commercial use . . . is presumptively . . . unfair," [ ], and it held that "the admittedly commercial nature" of the parody "requires the conclusion" that the first of four factors relevant under the statute weighs against a finding of fair use. [ ] Next, the Court of Appeals determined that, by "taking the heart of the original and making it the heart of a new work," 2 Live Crew had, qualitatively, taken too much. [ ] Finally, after noting that the effect on the potential market for the original (and the market for derivative works) is "undoubtedly the single most important element of fair use" [ ], the Court of Appeals faulted the District Court for "refus[ing] to indulge the presumption" that "harm for purposes of the fair use analysis has been established by the presumption attaching to commercial uses." [ ] In sum, the court concluded that its "blatantly commercial purpose . . . prevents this parody from being a fair use." [ ]

We granted certiorari [   ] to determine whether 2 Live Crew's commercial parody could be a fair use.

II

It is uncontested here that 2 Live Crew's song would be an infringement of Acuff-Rose's rights in "Oh, Pretty Woman," under the Copyright Act of 1976 [ ], but for a finding of fair use through parody. From the infancy of copyright protection, some opportunity for fair use of copyrighted materials has been thought necessary to fulfill copyright's very purpose, "[t]o promote the Progress of Science and useful Arts. . . ." U.S.Const., Art. I, § 8, cl. 8. For as Justice Story explained,

> [i]n truth, in literature, in science and in art, there are, and can be, few, if any, things, which in an abstract sense, are strictly new and original throughout. Every book in literature, science and art, borrows, and must necessarily borrow, and use much which was well known and used before.

[ ] Similarly, Lord Ellenborough expressed the inherent tension in the need simultaneously to protect copyrighted material and to allow others to build upon it when he wrote, "while I shall think myself bound to secure every man in the enjoyment of his copyright, one must not put manacles upon science." [ ] In copyright cases brought under the Statute of Anne of 1710, English courts held that in some instances "fair abridgements" would not infringe an author's rights [ ], and although the First Congress enacted our initial copyright statute, Act of May 31, 1790 [ ] without any explicit reference to "fair use," as it later came to be known, the doctrine was recognized by the American courts nonetheless.

In *Folsom v. Marsh*, Justice Story distilled the essence of law and methodology from the earlier cases:

> look to the nature and objects of the selections made, the quantity and value of the materials used, and the degree in which the use may prejudice the sale, or diminish the profits, or supersede the objects, of the original work.

[ ] Thus expressed, fair use remained exclusively judge-made doctrine until the passage of the 1976 Copyright Act, in which Story's summary is discernible:

> § 107. Limitations on exclusive rights: Fair use
>
> Notwithstanding the provisions of sections 106 and 106A, the fair use of a copyrighted work, including such use by reproduction in copies or phonorecords or by any other means specified by that section, for purposes such as criticism, comment, news reporting, teaching (including multiple copies for classroom use), scholarship, or research, is not an infringement of copyright. In determining whether the use made of a work in any particular case is a fair use the factors to be considered shall include --
>
> (1) the purpose and character of the use, including whether such use is of a commercial nature or is for nonprofit educational purposes;
>
> (2) the nature of the copyrighted work;
>
> (3) the amount and substantiality of the portion used in relation to the copyrighted work as a whole; and
>
> (4) the effect of the use upon the potential market for or value of the copyrighted work.
>
> The fact that a work is unpublished shall not itself bar a finding of fair

use if such finding is made upon consideration of all the above factors.

17 U.S.C. § 107 [ ] Congress meant § 107 "to restate the present judicial doctrine of fair use, not to change, narrow, or enlarge it in any way" and intended that courts continue the common law tradition of fair use adjudication. [ ] The fair use doctrine thus

> permits [and requires] courts to avoid rigid application of the copyright statute when, on occasion, it would stifle the very creativity which that law is designed to foster.

[ ]

The task is not to be simplified with bright-line rules, for the statute, like the doctrine it recognizes, calls for case-by-case analysis. [ ] The text employs the terms "including" and "such as" in the preamble paragraph to indicate the "illustrative and not limitative" function of the examples given, § 101; [ ] which thus provide only general guidance about the sorts of copying that courts and Congress most commonly had found to be fair uses. Nor may the four statutory factors be treated in isolation, one from another. All are to be explored, and the results weighed together, in light of the purposes of copyright. [ ]

A

The first factor in a fair use enquiry is "the purpose and character of the use, including whether such use is of a commercial nature or is for nonprofit educational purposes." § 107(1). This factor draws on Justice Story's formulation, "the nature and objects of the selections made." [ ] The enquiry here may be guided by the examples given in the preamble to § 107, looking to whether the use is for criticism, or comment, or news reporting, and the like, *see* § 107. The central purpose of this investigation is to see, in Justice Story's words, whether the new work merely "supersede[s] the objects" of the original creation [ ], or instead adds something new, with a further purpose or different character, altering the first with new expression, meaning, or message; it asks, in other words, whether and to what extent the new work is "transformative." [ ] Although such transformative use is not absolutely necessary for a finding of fair use [ ], the goal of copyright, to promote science and the arts, is generally furthered by the creation of transformative works. Such works thus lie at the heart of the fair use doctrine's guarantee of breathing space within the confines of copyright [ ], and the more transformative the new work, the less will be the significance of other factors, like commercialism, that may weigh against a finding of fair use.

This Court has only once before even considered whether parody may be fair use, and that time issued no opinion because of the Court's equal division. [ ] Suffice it to say now that parody has an obvious claim to transformative value, as Acuff-Rose itself does not deny. Like less ostensibly humorous forms of criticism, it can provide social benefit, by shedding light on an earlier work, and, in the process, creating a new one. We thus line up with the courts that have held that parody, like other comment or criticism, may claim fair use under § 107. [ ] The germ of parody lies in the definition of the Greek *parodeia,* quoted in Judge Nelson's Court of Appeals dissent, as "a song sung alongside another."   [ ] Modern dictionaries accordingly describe a parody as a "literary or artistic work that imitates the characteristic style of an author or a work for comic effect or ridicule," or as a "composition in prose or verse in which the characteristic turns of thought and phrase in an author or class of authors are imitated in such a way as to make them appear ridiculous." For the purposes of copyright law, the nub of the definitions, and the heart of any parodist's claim to quote from existing material, is the use of some elements of a prior author's composition to create a new one that, at least in part, comments on that author's works. [ ] If, on the contrary, the commentary has no critical bearing on the substance or style of the original composition, which the alleged infringer merely uses to get attention or to avoid the drudgery in working up something fresh, the claim to fairness in borrowing from another's work diminishes accordingly (if it does not vanish), and other factors, like the extent of its commerciality, loom larger. Parody needs to mimic an original to make its point, and so has some claim to use the creation of its victim's (or collective victims') imagination, whereas satire can stand on its own two feet and so requires justification for the very act of borrowing. [ ]

The fact that parody can claim legitimacy for some appropriation does not, of course, tell either parodist or judge much about where to draw the line. Like a book review quoting the copyrighted material criticized, parody may or may not be fair use, and petitioner's suggestion that any parodic use is presumptively fair has no more justification in law or fact than the equally hopeful claim that any use for news reporting should be presumed fair [   ] The Act has no hint of an evidentiary preference for parodists over their victims, and no workable presumption for parody could take account of the fact that parody often shades into satire when society is lampooned through its creative artifacts, or that a work may contain both parodic and nonparodic elements. Accordingly, parody, like any other use, has to work its way through the relevant factors, and be judged case by case, in light of the ends of the copyright law.

Here, the District Court held, and the Court of Appeals assumed, that 2 Live Crew's "Pretty Woman" contains parody, commenting on and criticizing the original work, whatever it may have to say about society at large. As the District Court remarked, the words of 2 Live Crew's song copy the original's first line, but then

> quickly degenerat[e] into a play on words, substituting predictable lyrics with shocking ones . . . [that] derisively demonstrat[e] how bland and banal the Orbison song seems to them.

[ ] Judge Nelson, dissenting below, came to the same conclusion, that the 2 Live Crew song "was clearly intended to ridicule the white-bread

original" and

> reminds us that sexual congress with nameless streetwalkers is not necessarily the stuff of romance, and is not necessarily without its consequences. The singers (there are several) have the same thing on their minds as did the lonely man with the nasal voice, but here there is no hint of wine and roses.

[ ] Although the majority below had difficulty discerning any criticism of the original in 2 Live Crew's song, it assumed for purposes of its opinion that there was some. [ ]

We have less difficulty in finding that critical element in 2 Live Crew's song than the Court of Appeals did, although, having found it, we will not take the further step of evaluating its quality. The threshold question when fair use is raised in defense of parody is whether a parodic character may reasonably be perceived. Whether, going beyond that, parody is in good taste or bad does not and should not matter to fair use. As Justice Holmes explained,

> [i]t would be a dangerous undertaking for persons trained only to the law to constitute themselves final judges of the worth of [a work], outside of the narrowest and most obvious limits. At the one extreme, some works of genius would be sure to miss appreciation. Their very novelty would make them repulsive until the public had learned the new language in which their author spoke.

[ ] ...

While we might not assign a high rank to the parodic element here, we think it fair to say that 2 Live Crew's song reasonably could be perceived as commenting on the original or criticizing it, to some degree. 2 Live Crew juxtaposes the romantic musings of a man whose fantasy comes true with degrading taunts, a bawdy demand for sex, and a sigh of relief from paternal responsibility. The later words can be taken as a comment on the naivete of the original of an earlier day, as a rejection of its sentiment that ignores the ugliness of street life and the debasement that it signifies. It is this joinder of reference and ridicule that marks off the author's choice of parody from the other types of comment and criticism that traditionally have had a claim to fair use protection as transformative works.

The Court of Appeals, however, immediately cut short the enquiry into 2 Live Crew's fair use claim by confining its treatment of the first factor essentially to one relevant fact, the commercial nature of the use. The court then inflated the significance of this fact by applying a presumption ostensibly culled from *Sony,* that "every commercial use of copyrighted material is presumptively . . . unfair. . . ." [ ] In giving virtually dispositive weight to the commercial nature of the parody, the Court of Appeals erred.

The language of the statute makes clear that the commercial or nonprofit educational purpose of a work is only one element of the first factor enquiry into its purpose and character. Section 107(1) uses the term "including" to begin the dependent clause referring to commercial use, and the main clause speaks of a broader investigation into "purpose and character." As we explained in *Harper & Row,* Congress resisted attempts to narrow the ambit of this traditional enquiry by adopting categories of presumptively fair use, and it urged courts to preserve the breadth of their traditionally ample view of the universe of relevant evidence. [ ] Accordingly, the mere fact that a use is educational and not for profit does not insulate it from a finding of infringement, any more than the commercial character of a use bars a finding of fairness. If, indeed, commerciality carried presumptive force against a finding of fairness, the presumption would swallow nearly all of the illustrative uses listed in the preamble paragraph of § 107, including news reporting, comment, criticism, teaching, scholarship, and research, since these activities "are generally conducted for profit in this country." [ ] Congress could not have intended such a rule, which certainly is not inferable from the common law cases, arising as they did from the world of letters in which Samuel Johnson could pronounce that "[n]o man but a blockhead ever wrote except for money." [ ]

Sony itself called for no hard evidentiary presumption. There, we emphasized the need for a "sensitive balancing of interests" [ ], noted that Congress had "eschewed a rigid, bright-line approach to fair use" [ ], and stated that the commercial or nonprofit educational character of a work is "not conclusive" [ ], but rather a fact to be "weighed along with other[s] in fair use decisions." [ ] The Court of Appeals' elevation of one sentence from *Sony* to a *per se* rule thus runs as much counter to *Sony* itself as to the long common law tradition of fair use adjudication. Rather, as we explained in *Harper & Row, Sony* stands for the proposition that the "fact that a publication was commercial as opposed to nonprofit is a separate factor that tends to weigh against a finding of fair use." [ ] But that is all, and the fact that even the force of that tendency will vary with the context is a further reason against elevating commerciality to hard presumptive significance. The use, for example, of a copyrighted work to advertise a product, even in a parody, will be entitled to less indulgence under the first factor of the fair use enquiry than the sale of a parody for its own sake, let alone one performed a single time by students in school. [ ]

B

The second statutory factor, "the nature of the copyrighted work," § 107(2), draws on Justice Story's expression, the "value of the materials used." [ ] This factor calls for recognition that some works are closer to the core of intended copyright protection than others, with the consequence that fair use is more difficult to establish when the former works are copied. [ ] … We agree with both the District Court and the Court of Appeals that the Orbison original's creative expression for public dissemination falls within the core of the copyright's protective purposes. [ ] This fact, however, is not much help in this case, or ever likely to help

301

much in separating the fair use sheep from the infringing goats in a parody case, since parodies almost invariably copy publicly known, expressive works.

C

The third factor asks whether "the amount and substantiality of the portion used in relation to the copyrighted work as a whole," § 107(3) (or, in Justice Story's words, "the quantity and value of the materials used," [ ]are reasonable in relation to the purpose of the copying. Here, attention turns to the persuasiveness of a parodist's justification for the particular copying done, and the enquiry will harken back to the first of the statutory factors, for, as in prior cases, we recognize that the extent of permissible copying varies with the purpose and character of the use. [ ] ... The facts bearing on this factor will also tend to address the fourth, by revealing the degree to which the parody may serve as a market substitute for the original or potentially licensed derivatives. [ ]

The District Court considered the song's parodic purpose in finding that 2 Live Crew had not helped themselves overmuch. [ ] The Court of Appeals disagreed, stating that

> [w]hile it may not be inappropriate to find that no more was taken than necessary, the copying was qualitatively substantial. . . . We conclude that taking the heart of the original and making it the heart of a new work was to purloin a substantial portion of the essence of the original.

[ ]

The Court of Appeals is, of course, correct that this factor calls for thought not only about the quantity of the materials used, but about their quality and importance, too. In *Harper & Row,* for example, the Nation had taken only some 300 words out of President Ford's memoirs, but we signalled the significance of the quotations in finding them to amount to "the heart of the book," the part most likely to be newsworthy and important in licensing serialization. [ ] We also agree with the Court of Appeals that whether "a substantial portion of the infringing work was copied verbatim" from the copyrighted work is a relevant question [ ], for it may reveal a dearth of transformative character or purpose under the first factor, or a greater likelihood of market harm under the fourth; a work composed primarily of an original, particularly its heart, with little added or changed, is more likely to be a merely superseding use, fulfilling demand for the original.

Where we part company with the court below is in applying these guides to parody, and in particular to parody in the song before us. Parody presents a difficult case. Parody's humor, or in any event its comment, necessarily springs from recognizable allusion to its object through distorted imitation. Its art lies in the tension between a known original and its parodic twin. When parody takes aim at a particular original work, the parody must be able to "conjure up" at least enough of that original to make the object of its critical wit recognizable. [ ] What

302

makes for this recognition is quotation of the original's most distinctive or memorable features, which the parodist can be sure the audience will know. Once enough has been taken to assure identification, how much more is reasonable will depend, say, on the extent to which the song's overriding purpose and character is to parody the original or, in contrast, the likelihood that the parody may serve as a market substitute for the original. But using some characteristic features cannot be avoided.

We think the Court of Appeals was insufficiently appreciative of parody's need for the recognizable sight or sound when it ruled 2 Live Crew's use unreasonable as a matter of law. It is true, of course, that 2 Live Crew copied the characteristic opening bass riff (or musical phrase) of the original, and true that the words of the first line copy the Orbison lyrics. But if quotation of the opening riff and the first line may be said to go to the "heart" of the original, the heart is also what most readily conjures up the song for parody, and it is the heart at which parody takes aim. Copying does not become excessive in relation to parodic purpose merely because the portion taken was the original's heart. If 2 Live Crew had copied a significantly less memorable part of the original, it is difficult to see how its parodic character would have come through. [ ]

This is not, of course, to say that anyone who calls himself a parodist can skim the cream and get away scot free. In parody, as in news reporting [ ], context is everything, and the question of fairness asks what else the parodist did besides go to the heart of the original. It is significant that 2 Live Crew not only copied the first line of the original, but thereafter departed markedly from the Orbison lyrics for its own ends. 2 Live Crew not only copied the bass riff and repeated it, but also produced otherwise distinctive sounds, interposing "scraper" noise, overlaying the music with solos in different keys, and altering the drum beat. [ ] This is not a case, then, where "a substantial portion" of the parody itself is composed of a "verbatim" copying of the original. It is not, that is, a case where the parody is so insubstantial, as compared to the copying, that the third factor must be resolved as a matter of law against the parodists.

Suffice it to say here that, as to the lyrics, we think the Court of Appeals correctly suggested that "no more was taken than necessary" [ ], but just for that reason, we fail to see how the copying can be excessive in relation to its parodic purpose, even if the portion taken is the original's "heart." As to the music, we express no opinion whether repetition of the bass riff is excessive copying, and we remand to permit evaluation of the amount taken, in light of the song's parodic purpose and character, its transformative elements, and considerations of the potential for market substitution sketched more fully below.

D

The fourth fair use factor is "the effect of the use upon the potential market for or value of the copyrighted work." § 107(4). It requires courts to consider not only the extent of market harm caused by the particular actions of the alleged infringer, but also

> whether unrestricted and widespread conduct of the sort engaged in by the defendant . . . would result in a substantially adverse impact on the potential market

for the original. [ ] The enquiry "must take account not only of harm to the original, but also of harm to the market for derivative works." [ ]

Since fair use is an affirmative defense, its proponent would have difficulty carrying the burden of demonstrating fair use without favorable evidence about relevant markets. In moving for summary judgment, 2 Live Crew left themselves at just such a disadvantage when they failed to address the effect on the market for rap derivatives, and confined themselves to uncontroverted submissions that there was no likely effect on the market for the original. They did not, however, thereby subject themselves to the evidentiary presumption applied by the Court of Appeals. In assessing the likelihood of significant market harm, the Court of Appeals quoted from language in *Sony* that

> "[i]f the intended use is for commercial gain, that likelihood may be presumed. But if it is for a noncommercial purpose, the likelihood must be demonstrated."

[ ] The court reasoned that, because "the use of the copyrighted work is wholly commercial, . . . we presume a likelihood of future harm to Acuff-Rose exists." [ ] In so doing, the court resolved the fourth factor against 2 Live Crew, just as it had the first, by applying a presumption about the effect of commercial use, a presumption which as applied here we hold to be error.

No "presumption" or inference of market harm that might find support in *Sony* is applicable to a case involving something beyond mere duplication for commercial purposes. *Sony's* discussion of a presumption contrasts a context of verbatim copying of the original in its entirety for commercial purposes, with the noncommercial context of *Sony* itself (home copying of television programming). In the former circumstances, what *Sony* said simply makes common sense: when a commercial use amounts to mere duplication of the entirety of an original, it clearly "supersede[s] the objects" [ ], of the original and serves as a market replacement for it, making it likely that cognizable market harm to the original will occur. [ ] But when, on the contrary, the second use is transformative, market substitution is at least less certain, and market harm may not be so readily inferred. Indeed, as to parody pure and simple, it is more likely that the new work will not affect the market for the original in a way cognizable under this factor, that is, by acting as a substitute for it ("supersed[ing] [its] objects"). [ ] This is so because the parody and the original usually serve different market functions. [ ]

We do not, of course, suggest that a parody may not harm the market at all, but when a lethal parody, like a scathing theater review, kills demand for the original, it does not produce a harm cognizable under the Copyright Act. Because "parody may quite legitimately aim at garroting the original, destroying it commercially as well as artistically" [ ], the role of the courts is to distinguish between "[b]iting criticism [that merely] suppresses demand [and] copyright infringement[, which] usurps it." [ ]

This distinction between potentially remediable displacement and unremediable disparagement is reflected in the rule that there is no protectable derivative market for criticism. The market for potential derivative uses includes only those that creators of original works would in general develop or license others to develop. Yet the unlikelihood that creators of imaginative works will license critical reviews or lampoons of their own productions removes such uses from the very notion of a potential licensing market. "People ask . . . for criticism, but they only want praise." [ ] Thus, to the extent that the opinion below may be read to have considered harm to the market for parodies of "Oh, Pretty Woman" [ ], the court erred. [ ]

In explaining why the law recognizes no derivative market for critical works, including parody, we have, of course, been speaking of the later work as if it had nothing but a critical aspect (*i.e.,* "parody pure and simple" [ ]. But the later work may have a more complex character, with effects not only in the arena of criticism but also in protectable markets for derivative works, too. In that sort of case, the law looks beyond the criticism to the other elements of the work, as it does here. 2 Live Crew's song comprises not only parody but also rap music, and the derivative market for rap music is a proper focus of enquiry [ ]. Evidence of substantial harm to it would weigh against a finding of fair use, because the licensing of derivatives is an important economic incentive to the creation of originals. [ ] Of course, the only harm to derivatives that need concern us, as discussed above, is the harm of market substitution. The fact that a parody may impair the market for derivative uses by the very effectiveness of its critical commentary is no more relevant under copyright than the like threat to the original market.

Although 2 Live Crew submitted uncontroverted affidavits on the question of market harm to the original, neither they nor Acuff-Rose introduced evidence or affidavits addressing the likely effect of 2 Live Crew's parodic rap song on the market for a non-parody, rap version of "Oh, Pretty Woman." And while Acuff-Rose would have us find evidence of a rap market in the very facts that 2 Live Crew recorded a rap parody of "Oh, Pretty Woman" and another rap group sought a license to record a rap derivative, there was no evidence that a potential rap market was harmed in any way by 2 Live Crew's parody, rap version. The fact that 2 Live Crew's parody sold as part of a collection of rap songs says very little about the parody's effect on a market for a rap version of the original, either of the music alone or of the music with its lyrics. The District Court essentially passed on this issue, observing that Acuff-Rose is free to record "whatever version of the original it desires" [ ]; the Court of

Appeals went the other way by erroneous presumption. Contrary to each treatment, it is impossible to deal with the fourth factor except by recognizing that a silent record on an important factor bearing on fair use disentitled the proponent of the defense, 2 Live Crew, to summary judgment. The evidentiary hole will doubtless be plugged on remand.

III

It was error for the Court of Appeals to conclude that the commercial nature of 2 Live Crew's parody of "Oh, Pretty Woman" rendered it presumptively unfair. No such evidentiary presumption is available to address either the first factor, the character and purpose of the use, or the fourth, market harm, in determining whether a transformative use, such as parody, is a fair one. The court also erred in holding that 2 Live Crew had necessarily copied excessively from the Orbison original, considering the parodic purpose of the use. We therefore reverse the judgment of the Court of Appeals and remand for further proceedings consistent with this opinion.

Appendix A
"Oh, Pretty Woman" by Roy Orbison and William Dees

Pretty Woman, walking down the street,
Pretty Woman, the kind I like to meet,
Pretty Woman, I don't believe you,
   you're not the truth,
No one could look as good as you
Mercy
Pretty Woman, won't you pardon me,
Pretty Woman, I couldn't help but see,
Pretty Woman, that you look lovely as can be
Are you lonely just like me?
Pretty Woman, stop a while,
Pretty Woman, talk a while,
Pretty Woman give your smile to me
Pretty woman, yeah, yeah, yeah
Pretty Woman, look my way,
Pretty Woman, say you'll stay with me
Cause I need you, I'll treat you right
Come to me baby, Be mine tonight
Pretty Woman, don't walk on by,
Pretty Woman, don't make me cry,
Pretty Woman, don't walk away,
Hey, O.K.
If that's the way it must be, O.K.
I guess I'll go on home, it's late
There'll be tomorrow night, but wait!
What do I see
Is she walking back to me?
Yeah, she's walking back to me!
Oh, Pretty Woman.

Appendix B
"Pretty Woman" as Recorded by 2 Live Crew

Pretty woman walkin' down the street
Pretty woman girl you look so sweet
Pretty woman you bring me down to that knee
Pretty woman you make me wanna beg please
Oh, pretty woman
Big hairy woman you need to shave that stuff
Big hairy woman you know I bet it's tough
Big hairy woman all that hair it ain't legit
Cause you look like "Cousin It"
Big hairy woman
Bald headed woman girl your hair won't grow
Bald headed woman you got a teeny weeny afro
Bald headed woman you know your hair could look nice
Bald headed woman first you got to roll it with rice
Bald headed woman here, let me get this hunk of biz for ya
Ya know what I'm saying you look better than rice a roni
Oh bald headed woman
Big hairy woman come on in
And don't forget your bald headed friend
Hey pretty woman let the boys
Jump in
Two timin' woman girl you know you ain't right
Two timin' woman you's out with my boy last night
Two timin' woman that takes a load off my mind
Two timin' woman now I know the baby ain't mine
Oh, two timin' woman
Oh pretty woman

In *Miller v. California* (MCLE, page 567), the Supreme Court reaffirmed in a split (5-4) decision that that obscenity did not enjoy 1st Amendment protection and established a 3-prong conjunctive test that is still recognized as the standard for determining whether a particular work is obscene. Individual states may define "patently offensive," but they may punish or impose prior restraint only on materials depict hardcore sexual conduct and pass all three prongs of the test. The Court also said that contemporary community standards apply, not national standards, as had been presumed in the past. The test grants considerable leeway to the government in banning sexually-oriented materials.

Miller v. California

Argued January 18-19, 1972
Reargued November 7, 1972
Decided June 21, 1973

413 U.S. 15, 93 S.Ct. 2607, 37 L.Ed.2d 822, 1 Med.L.Rptr. 1130

APPEAL FROM THE APPELLATE DEPARTMENT,
SUPERIOR COURT
OF CALIFORNIA, COUNTY OF ORANGE

Syllabus

Appellant was convicted of mailing unsolicited sexually explicit material in violation of a California statute that approximately incorporated the obscenity test formulated in *Memoirs v. Massachusetts* [ ] (plurality opinion). The trial court instructed the jury to evaluate the materials by the contemporary community standards of California. Appellant's conviction was affirmed on appeal. In lieu of the obscenity criteria enunciated by the *Memoirs* plurality, it is *held*:

1. Obscene material is not protected by the First Amendment. *Roth v. United States* [ ], reaffirmed. A work may be subject to state regulation where that work, taken as a whole, appeals to the prurient interest in sex; portrays, in a patently offensive way, sexual conduct specifically defined by the applicable state law; and, taken as a whole, does not have serious literary, artistic, political, or scientific value.

2. The basic guidelines for the trier of fact must be: (a) whether "the average person, applying contemporary community standards" would find that the work, taken as a whole, appeals to the prurient interest, *Roth, supra* [ ], (b) whether the work depicts or describes, in a patently offensive way, sexual conduct specifically defined by the applicable state

law, and (c) whether the work, taken as a whole, lacks serious literary, artistic, political, or scientific value. If a state obscenity law is thus limited, First Amendment values are adequately protected by ultimate independent appellate review of constitutional claims when necessary.

3. The test of "utterly without redeeming social value" articulated in *Memoirs, supra,* is rejected as a constitutional standard.

4. The jury may measure the essentially factual issues of prurient appeal and patent offensiveness by the standard that prevails in the forum community, and need not employ a "national standard."

Vacated and remanded.

BURGER, C.J., delivered the opinion of the Court, in which WHITE, BLACKMUN, POWELL, and REHNQUIST, JJ., joined. DOUGLAS, J., filed a dissenting opinion. BRENNAN, J., filed a dissenting opinion, in which STEWART and MARSHALL, JJ., joined.

BURGER, J., lead opinion

This is one of a group of "obscenity-pornography" cases being reviewed by the Court in a reexamination of standards enunciated in earlier cases involving what Mr. Justice Harlan called "the intractable obscenity problem." [ ]

Appellant conducted a mass mailing campaign to advertise the sale of illustrated books, euphemistically called "adult" material. After a jury trial, he was convicted of violating California Penal Code § 311.2(a), a misdemeanor, by knowingly distributing obscene matter, and the Appellate Department, Superior Court of California, County of Orange, summarily affirmed the judgment without opinion. Appellant's conviction was specifically based on his conduct in causing five unsolicited advertising brochures to be sent through the mail in an envelope addressed to a restaurant in Newport Beach, California. The envelope was opened by the manager of the restaurant and his mother. They had not requested the brochures; they complained to the police.

The brochures advertise four books entitled "Intercourse," "Man-Woman," "Sex Orgies Illustrated," and "An Illustrated History of Pornography," and a film entitled "Marital Intercourse." While the brochures contain some descriptive printed material, primarily they consist of pictures and drawings very explicitly depicting men and women in groups of two or more engaging in a variety of sexual activities, with genitals often prominently displayed.

I

This case involves the application of a State's criminal obscenity statute to a situation in which sexually explicit materials have been thrust by aggressive sales action upon unwilling recipients who had in no way indicated any desire to receive such materials. This Court has recognized that the States have a legitimate interest in prohibiting

309

dissemination or exhibition of obscene material when the mode of dissemination carries with it a significant danger of offending the sensibilities of unwilling recipients or of exposure to juveniles. [ ] It is in this context that we are called on to define the standards which must be used to identify obscene material that a State may regulate without infringing on the First Amendment as applicable to the States through the Fourteenth Amendment.

The dissent of MR. JUSTICE BRENNAN reviews the background of the obscenity problem, but since the Court now undertakes to formulate standards more concrete than those in the past, it is useful for us to focus on two of the landmark cases in the somewhat tortured history of the Court's obscenity decisions. In *Roth v. United States* [ ], the Court sustained a conviction under a federal statute punishing the mailing of "obscene, lewd, lascivious or filthy . . ." materials. The key to that holding was the Court's rejection of the claim that obscene materials were protected by the First Amendment. Five Justices joined in the opinion stating:

> All ideas having even the slightest redeeming social importance -- unorthodox ideas, controversial ideas, even ideas hateful to the prevailing climate of opinion -- have the full protection of the [First Amendment] guaranties, unless excludable because they encroach upon the limited area of more important interests. But implicit in the history of the First Amendment is the rejection of obscenity as utterly without redeeming social importance. . . . This is the same judgment expressed by this Court in GO>*Chaplinsky v. New Hampshire* [ ]:

> . . . There are certain well defined and narrowly limited classes of speech, the prevention and punishment of which have never been thought to raise any Constitutional problem. *These include the lewd and obscene. . . . It has been well observed that such utterances are no essential part of any exposition of ideas, and are of such slight social value as a step to truth that any benefit that may be derived from them is clearly outweighed by the social interest in order and morality. . . .*

[Emphasis by Court in *Roth* opinion.]

> We hold that obscenity is not within the area of constitutionally protected speech or press.

[ ]

Nine years later, in *Memoirs v. Massachusetts* [ ], the Court veered sharply away from the *Roth* concept and, with only three Justices in the plurality opinion, articulated a new test of obscenity. The plurality held that, under the *Roth* definition,

> as elaborated in subsequent cases, three elements must coalesce: it must be established that (a) the dominant theme of the material, taken as a whole, appeals to a prurient interest in sex; (b) the material is patently offensive because it affronts contemporary community standards relating to the description or representation of sexual matters; and (c) the material is

utterly without redeeming social value.

[ ] The sharpness of the break with *Roth,* represented by the third element of the *Memoirs* test and emphasized by MR. JUSTICE WHITE's dissent [ ], was further underscored when the *Memoirs* plurality went on to state:

> The Supreme Judicial Court erred in holding that a book need not be "unqualifiedly worthless before it can be deemed obscene." A book cannot be proscribed unless it is found to be *utterly* without redeeming social value.

[ ]

While *Roth* presumed "obscenity" to be "utterly without redeeming social importance," *Memoirs* required that to prove obscenity it must be affirmatively established that the material is "*utterly* without redeeming social value." Thus, even as they repeated the words of *Roth,* the *Memoirs* plurality produced a drastically altered test that called on the prosecution to prove a negative, *i.e.,* that the material was "*utterly* without redeeming social value" -- a burden virtually impossible to discharge under our criminal standards of proof. Such considerations caused Mr. Justice Harlan to wonder if the "*utterly* without redeeming social value" test had any meaning at all. [ ]

Apart from the initial formulation in the *Roth* case, no majority of the Court has at any given time been able to agree on a standard to determine what constitutes obscene, pornographic material subject to regulation under the States' police power. [ ] We have seen "a variety of views among the members of the Court unmatched in any other course of constitutional adjudication." [ ] This is not remarkable, for in the area of freedom of speech and press the courts must always remain sensitive to any infringement on genuinely serious literary, artistic, political, or scientific expression. This is an area in which there are few eternal verities.

The case we now review was tried on the theory that the California Penal Code § 311 approximately incorporates the three-stage *Memoirs* test, *supra.* But now the *Memoirs* test has been abandoned as unworkable by its author, and no Member of the Court today supports the *Memoirs* formulation.

II

This much has been categorically settled by the Court, that obscene material is unprotected by the First Amendment. [ ] "The First and Fourteenth Amendments have never been treated as absolutes ... " [ ] We acknowledge, however, the inherent dangers of undertaking to regulate any form of expression. State statutes designed to regulate obscene materials must be carefully limited. [ ] As a result, we now confine the permissible scope of such regulation to works which depict or describe sexual conduct. That conduct must be specifically defined by

311

the applicable state law, as written or authoritatively construed. A state offense must also be limited to works which, taken as a whole, appeal to the prurient interest in sex, which portray sexual conduct in a patently offensive way, and which, taken as a whole, do not have serious literary, artistic, political, or scientific value.

The basic guidelines for the trier of fact must be: (a) whether "the average person, applying contemporary community standards" would find that the work, taken as a whole, appeals to the prurient interest [ ]; (b) whether the work depicts or describes, in a patently offensive way, sexual conduct specifically defined by the applicable state law; and (c) whether the work, taken as a whole, lacks serious literary, artistic, political, or scientific value. We do not adopt as a constitutional standard the "utterly without redeeming social value" test of *Memoirs v. Massachusetts* [ ]; that concept has never commanded the adherence of more than three Justices at one time. [ ] If a state law that regulates obscene material is thus limited, as written or construed, the First Amendment values applicable to the States through the Fourteenth Amendment are adequately protected by the ultimate power of appellate courts to conduct an independent review of constitutional claims when necessary. [ ] We emphasize that it is not our function to propose regulatory schemes for the States. That must await their concrete legislative efforts. It is possible, however, to give a few plain examples of what a state statute could define for regulation under part (b) of the standard announced in this opinion, *supra:*

(a) Patently offensive representations or descriptions of ultimate sexual acts, normal or perverted, actual or simulated.

(b) Patently offensive representations or descriptions of masturbation, excretory functions, and lewd exhibition of the genitals.

Sex and nudity may not be exploited without limit by films or pictures exhibited or sold in places of public accommodation any more than live sex and nudity can be exhibited or sold without limit in such public places. At a minimum, prurient, patently offensive depiction or description of sexual conduct must have serious literary, artistic, political, or scientific value to merit First Amendment protection. [ ] For example, medical books for the education of physicians and related personnel necessarily use graphic illustrations and descriptions of human anatomy. In resolving the inevitably sensitive questions of fact and law, we must continue to rely on the jury system, accompanied by the safeguards that judges, rules of evidence, presumption of innocence, and other protective features provide, as we do with rape, murder, and a host of other offenses against society and its individual members.

MR. JUSTICE BRENNAN, author of the opinions of the Court, or the plurality opinions, in *Roth v. United States, supra; Jacobellis v. Ohio, supra; Ginzburg v. United States* [ ]; *Mishkin v. New York* [ ]; and *Memoirs v. Massachusetts, supra,* has abandoned his former position and now maintains that no formulation of this Court, the Congress, or the

States can adequately distinguish obscene material unprotected by the First Amendment from protected expression [ ] Paradoxically, MR. JUSTICE BRENNAN indicates that suppression of unprotected obscene material is permissible to avoid exposure to unconsenting adults, as in this case, and to juveniles, although he gives no indication of how the division between protected and nonprotected materials may be drawn with greater precision for these purposes than for regulation of commercial exposure to consenting adults only. Nor does he indicate where in the Constitution he finds the authority to distinguish between a willing "adult" one month past the state law age of majority and a willing "juvenile" one month younger.

Under the holdings announced today, no one will be subject to prosecution for the sale or exposure of obscene materials unless these materials depict or describe patently offensive "hard core" sexual conduct specifically defined by the regulating state law, as written or construed. We are satisfied that these specific prerequisites will provide fair notice to a dealer in such materials that his public and commercial activities may bring prosecution. [ ] If the inability to define regulated materials with ultimate, god-like precision altogether removes the power of the States or the Congress to regulate, then "hard core" pornography may be exposed without limit to the juvenile, the passerby, and the consenting adult alike, as, indeed, MR. JUSTICE DOUGLAS contends ... In this belief, however, MR. JUSTICE DOUGLAS now stands alone.

MR. JUSTICE BRENNAN also emphasizes "institutional stress" in justification of his change of view. Noting that "[t]he number of obscenity cases on our docket gives ample testimony to the burden that has been placed upon this Court," he quite rightly remarks that the examination of contested materials "is hardly a source of edification to the members of this Court." [ ] He also notes, and we agree, that "uncertainty of the standards creates a continuing source of tension between state and federal courts. . . ."

> The problem is . . . that one cannot say with certainty that material is obscene until at least five members of this Court, applying inevitably obscure standards, have pronounced it so.

[ ]

It is certainly true that the absence, since *Roth,* of a single majority view of this Court as to proper standards for testing obscenity has placed a strain on both state and federal courts. But today, for the first time since *Roth* was decided in 1957, a majority of this Court has agreed on concrete guidelines to isolate "hard core" pornography from expression protected by the First Amendment. Now we may abandon the casual practice of *Redrup v. New York* [ ], and attempt to provide positive guidance to federal and state courts alike.

This may not be an easy road, free from difficulty. But no amount of "fatigue" should lead us to adopt a convenient "institutional" rationale -- an absolutist, "anything goes" view of the First Amendment -- because it will lighten our burdens. "Such an abnegation of judicial supervision in this field would be inconsistent with our duty to uphold the constitutional guarantees." [ ] Nor should we remedy "tension between state and federal courts" by arbitrarily depriving the States of a power reserved to them under the Constitution, a power which they have enjoyed and exercised continuously from before the adoption of the First Amendment to this day. [ ]

> Our duty admits of no "substitute for facing up to the tough individual problems of constitutional judgment involved in every obscenity case." [ ]

[ ]

III

Under a National Constitution, fundamental First Amendment limitations on the powers of the States do not vary from community to community, but this does not mean that there are, or should or can be, fixed, uniform national standards of precisely what appeals to the "prurient interest" or is "patently offensive." These are essentially questions of fact, and our Nation is simply too big and too diverse for this Court to reasonably expect that such standards could be articulated for all 50 States in a single formulation, even assuming the prerequisite consensus exists. When triers of fact are asked to decide whether "the average person, applying contemporary community standards" would consider certain materials "prurient," it would be unrealistic to require that the answer be based on some abstract formulation. The adversary system, with lay jurors as the usual ultimate factfinders in criminal prosecutions, has historically permitted triers of fact to draw on the standards of their community, guided always by limiting instructions on the law. To require a State to structure obscenity proceedings around evidence of a *national* "community standard" would be an exercise in futility.

As noted before, this case was tried on the theory that the California obscenity statute sought to incorporate the tripartite test of *Memoirs*. This, a "national" standard of First Amendment protection enumerated by a plurality of this Court, was correctly regarded at the time of trial as limiting state prosecution under the controlling case law. The jury, however, was explicitly instructed that, in determining whether the "dominant theme of the material as a whole . . . appeals to the prurient interest," and, in determining whether the material "goes substantially beyond customary limits of candor and affronts contemporary community standards of decency," it was to apply "contemporary community standards of the State of California."

During the trial, both the prosecution and the defense assumed that the relevant "community standards" in making the factual determination of obscenity were those of the State of California, not some hypothetical standard of the entire United States of America. Defense counsel at trial never objected to the testimony of the State's expert on community standards or to the instructions of the trial judge on "state-wide" standards. On appeal to the Appellate Department, Superior Court of California, County of Orange, appellant for the first time contended that application of state, rather than national, standards violated the First and Fourteenth Amendments.

We conclude that neither the State's alleged failure to offer evidence of "national standards," nor the trial court's charge that the jury consider state community standards, were constitutional errors. Nothing in the First Amendment requires that a jury must consider hypothetical and unascertainable "national standards" when attempting to determine whether certain materials are obscene as a matter of fact. Mr. Chief Justice Warren pointedly commented in his dissent in *Jacobellis v. Ohio, supra* [ ]:

> It is my belief that, when the Court said in *Roth* that obscenity is to be defined by reference to "community standards," it meant community standards -- not a national standard, as is sometimes argued. I believe that there is no provable "national standard." . . . At all events, this Court has not been able to enunciate one, and it would be unreasonable to expect local courts to divine one.

It is neither realistic nor constitutionally sound to read the First Amendment as requiring that the people of Maine or Mississippi accept public depiction of conduct found tolerable in Las Vegas, or New York City. [ ] People in different States vary in their tastes and attitudes, and this diversity is not to be strangled by the absolutism of imposed uniformity. As the Court made clear in *Mishkin v. New York* [ ], the primary concern with requiring a jury to apply the standard of "the average person, applying contemporary community standards" is to be certain that, so far as material is not aimed at a deviant group, it will be judged by its impact on an average person, rather than a particularly susceptible or sensitive person -- or indeed a totally insensitive one. [ ] We hold that the requirement that the jury evaluate the materials with reference to "contemporary standards of the State of California" serves this protective purpose and is constitutionally adequate.

IV

The dissenting Justices sound the alarm of repression. But, in our view, to equate the free and robust exchange of ideas and political debate with commercial exploitation of obscene material demeans the grand conception of the First Amendment and its high purposes in the historic struggle for freedom. It is a "misuse of the great guarantees of free speech and free press. . . ." [ ] The First Amendment protects works which, taken as a whole, have serious literary, artistic, political, or scientific value, regardless of whether the government or a majority of the people approve of the ideas these works represent.

> The protection given speech and press was fashioned to assure unfettered interchange of *ideas* for the bringing about of political and social changes desired by the people,

315

[   ] But the public portrayal of hard-core sexual conduct for its own sake, and for the ensuing commercial gain, is a different matter.

There is no evidence, empirical or historical, that the stern 19th century American censorship of public distribution and display of material relating to sex [   ], in any way limited or affected expression of serious literary, artistic, political, or scientific ideas. On the contrary, it is beyond any question that the era following Thomas Jefferson to Theodore Roosevelt was an "extraordinarily vigorous period" not just in economics and politics, but in *belles lettres* and in "the outlying fields of social and political philosophies." We do not see the harsh hand of censorship of ideas -- good or bad, sound or unsound -- and "repression" of political liberty lurking in every state regulation of commercial exploitation of human interest in sex.

MR. JUSTICE BRENNAN finds "it is hard to see how state-ordered regimentation of our minds can ever be forestalled." [   ] These doleful anticipations assume that courts cannot distinguish commerce in ideas, protected by the First Amendment, from commercial exploitation of obscene material. Moreover, state regulation of hard-core pornography so as to make it unavailable to nonadults, a regulation which MR. JUSTICE BRENNAN finds constitutionally permissible, has all the elements of "censorship" for adults; indeed even more rigid enforcement techniques may be called for with such dichotomy of regulation. [   ] One can concede that the "sexual revolution" of recent years may have had useful byproducts in striking layers of prudery from a subject long irrationally kept from needed ventilation. But it does not follow that no regulation of patently offensive "hard core" materials is needed or permissible; civilized people do not allow unregulated access to heroin because it is a derivative of medicinal morphine.

In sum, we (a) reaffirm the *Roth* holding that obscene material is not protected by the First Amendment; (b) hold that such material can be regulated by the States, subject to the specific safeguards enunciated above, without a showing that the material is "utterly without redeeming social value"; and (c) hold that obscenity is to be determined by applying "contemporary community standards" [   ], not "national standards." The judgment of the Appellate Department of the Superior Court, Orange County, California, is vacated and the case remanded to that court for further proceedings not inconsistent with the First Amendment standards established by this opinion. [   ]

Vacated and remanded

In *Reno v. American Civil Liberties Union* (MCLE, page 584), the Supreme Court struck down in a 7-2 decision both the "indecent transmission" and the "patently offensive display" provisions of the Communications Decency Act of 1996 as a violation of the 1st Amendment. For 1st Amendment purposes, the Court distinguished regulation of the Internet from broadcast and cable regulation. In determining that the provisions were unconstitutional, the majority conducted a "strict scrutiny" analysis. The justices were particularly concerned with the breadth of the restrictions, especially the extent to which their vagueness swept in protected speech. The Court's ruling concerned only indecent speech, not obscenity, which can be banned in any medium, including the Internet.

Reno v. American Civil Liberties Union

Argued March 19, 1997
Decided June 26, 1997

521 U.S. 844, 117 S.Ct., 2329, 138 L.Ed.2d 874, 25 Med.L.Rptr. 1833

APPEAL FROM THE UNITED STATES DISTRICT COURT FOR THE EASTERN DISTRICT OF PENNSYLVANIA

Syllabus

Two provisions of the Communications Decency Act of 1996 (CDA or Act) seek to protect minors from harmful material on the Internet, an international network of interconnected computers that enables millions of people to communicate with one another in "cyberspace" and to access vast amounts of information from around the world. Title 47 U.S.C. § 223(a)(1)(B)(ii) (Supp. 1997) criminalizes the "knowing" transmission of "obscene or indecent" messages to any recipient under 18 years of age. Section 223(d) prohibits the "knowin[g]" sending or displaying to a person under 18 of any message

> that, in context, depicts or describes, in terms patently offensive as measured by contemporary community standards, sexual or excretory activities or organs.

Affirmative defenses are provided for those who take "good faith, . . . effective . . . actions" to restrict access by minors to the prohibited communications, § 223(e)(5)(A), and those who restrict such access by requiring certain designated forms of age proof, such as a verified credit card or an adult identification number, § 223(e)(5)(B). A number of plaintiffs filed suit challenging the constitutionality of §§ 223(a)(1) and 223(d). After making extensive findings of fact, a three-judge District Court convened pursuant to the Act entered a preliminary injunction against enforcement of both challenged provisions. The court's judgment enjoins the Government from enforcing § 223(a)(1)(B)'s prohibitions insofar as they relate to "indecent" communications, but expressly preserves the Government's right to investigate and prosecute the obscenity or child pornography activities prohibited therein. The injunction against enforcement of § 223(d) is unqualified because that section contains no separate reference to obscenity or child pornography. The Government appealed to this Court under the Act's special review provisions, arguing that the District Court erred in holding that the CDA violated both the First Amendment because it is overbroad and the Fifth Amendment because it is vague.

Held: The CDA's "indecent transmission" and "patently offensive display" provisions abridge "the freedom of speech" protected by the First Amendment.

(a) Although the CDA's vagueness is relevant to the First Amendment overbreadth inquiry, the judgment should be affirmed without reaching the Fifth Amendment issue.

(b) A close look at the precedents relied on by the Government -- *Ginsberg v. New York* [ ]; *FCC v. Pacifica Foundation* [ ]; and *Renton v. Playtime Theatres, Inc.* [ ] -- raises, rather than relieves, doubts about the CDA's constitutionality. The CDA differs from the various laws and orders upheld in those cases in many ways, including that it does not allow parents to consent to their children's use of restricted materials; is not limited to commercial transactions; fails to provide any definition of "indecent" and omits any requirement that "patently offensive" material lack socially redeeming value; neither limits its broad categorical prohibitions to particular times nor bases them on an evaluation by an agency familiar with the medium's unique characteristics; is punitive; applies to a medium that, unlike radio, receives full First Amendment protection; and cannot be properly analyzed as a form of time, place, and manner regulation because it is a content-based blanket restriction on speech. These precedents, then, do not require the Court to uphold the CDA, and are fully consistent with the application of the most stringent review of its provisions.

(c) The special factors recognized in some of the Court's cases as justifying regulation of the broadcast media -- the history of extensive government regulation of broadcasting [ ]; the scarcity of available frequencies at its inception [ ]; and its "invasive" nature [ ] -- are not present in cyberspace. Thus, these cases provide no basis for qualifying the level of First Amendment scrutiny that should be applied to the Internet.

(d) Regardless of whether the CDA is so vague that it violates the Fifth Amendment, the many ambiguities concerning the scope of its coverage render it problematic for First Amendment purposes. For instance, its use of the undefined terms "indecent" and "patently offensive" will provoke uncertainty among speakers about how the two standards relate to each other and just what they mean. The vagueness of such a content-based regulation [ ], coupled with its increased deterrent effect as a criminal statute [ ], raise special First Amendment concerns because of its obvious chilling effect on free speech. Contrary to the Government's argument, the CDA is not saved from vagueness by the fact that its "patently offensive" standard repeats the second part of the three-prong obscenity test set forth in *Miller v. California* [ ]. The second *Miller* prong reduces the inherent vagueness of its own "patently offensive" term by requiring that the proscribed material be "specifically defined by the applicable state law." In addition, the CDA applies only to "sexual conduct," whereas, the CDA prohibition extends also to "excretory activities" and "organs" of both a sexual and excretory nature. Each of *Miller's* other two prongs also critically limits the uncertain sweep of the obscenity definition. Just because a definition including three limitations is not vague, it does not follow that one of those limitations, standing alone, is not vague. The CDA's vagueness undermines the likelihood that it has been carefully tailored to the congressional goal of protecting minors from potentially harmful materials.

(e) The CDA lacks the precision that the First Amendment requires when a statute regulates the content of speech. Although the Government has an interest in protecting children from potentially harmful materials   [ ], the CDA pursues that interest by suppressing a large amount of speech that adults have a constitutional right to send and receive [ ]. Its breadth is wholly unprecedented. The CDA's burden on adult speech is unacceptable if less restrictive alternatives would be at least as effective in achieving the Act's legitimate purposes. [ ] The Government has not proved otherwise. On the other hand, the District Court found that currently available *user-based* software suggests that a reasonably effective method by which *parents* can prevent their children from accessing material which the *parents* believe is inappropriate will soon be widely available. Moreover, the arguments in this Court referred to possible alternatives such as requiring that indecent material be "tagged" to facilitate parental control, making exceptions for messages with artistic or educational value, providing some tolerance for parental choice, and regulating some portions of the Internet differently than others. Particularly in the light of the absence of any detailed congressional findings, or even hearings addressing the CDA's special problems, the Court is persuaded that the CDA is not narrowly tailored.

(f) The Government's three additional arguments for sustaining the CDA's affirmative prohibitions are rejected. First, the contention that the Act is constitutional because it leaves open ample "alternative channels" of communication is unpersuasive because the CDA regulates speech on the basis of its content, so that a "time, place, and manner" analysis is inapplicable. [ ] Second, the assertion that the CDA's "knowledge" and "specific person" requirements significantly restrict its permissible application to communications to persons the sender knows to be under 18 is untenable, given that most Internet forums are open to all comers and that even the strongest reading of the "specific person" requirement would confer broad powers of censorship, in the form of a "heckler's veto," upon any opponent of indecent speech. Finally, there is no textual support for the submission that material having scientific, educational, or other redeeming social value will necessarily fall outside the CDA's prohibitions.

(g) The § 223(e)(5) defenses do not constitute the sort of "narrow tailoring" that would save the CDA. The Government's argument that transmitters may take protective "good faith actio[n]" by "tagging" their indecent communications in a way that would indicate their contents, thus permitting recipients to block their reception with appropriate software, is illusory, given the requirement that such action be "effective": the proposed screening software does not currently exist, but, even if it did, there would be no way of knowing whether a potential recipient would actually block the encoded material. The Government also failed to prove that § 223(b)(5)'s verification defense would significantly reduce the CDA's heavy burden on adult speech. Although such verification is actually being used by some commercial providers of sexually explicit material, the District Court's findings indicate that it is not economically feasible for most noncommercial speakers.

(h) The Government's argument that this Court should preserve the CDA's constitutionality by honoring its severability clause, § 608, and by construing nonseverable terms narrowly, is acceptable in only one respect. Because obscene speech may be banned totally [ ], and § 223(a)'s restriction of "obscene" material enjoys a textual manifestation separate from that for "indecent" material, the Court can sever the term "or indecent" from the statute, leaving the rest of § 223(a) standing.

(i) The Government's argument that its "significant" interest in fostering the Internet's growth provides an independent basis for upholding the CDA's constitutionality is singularly unpersuasive. The dramatic expansion of this new forum contradicts the factual basis underlying this contention: that the unregulated availability of "indecent" and "patently offensive" material is driving people away from the Internet.

929 F.Supp. 824, affirmed.

STEVENS, J., delivered the opinion of the Court, in which SCALIA, KENNEDY, SOUTER, THOMAS, GINSBURG, and BREYER, JJ., joined. O'CONNOR, J., filed an opinion concurring in the judgment in part and dissenting in part, in which REHNQUIST, C.J., joined.

STEVENS, J., lead opinion

At issue is the constitutionality of two statutory provisions enacted to protect minors from "indecent" and "patently offensive" communications on the Internet. Notwithstanding the legitimacy and importance of the congressional goal of protecting children from harmful materials, we agree with the three-judge District Court that the statute abridges "the freedom of speech" protected by the First Amendment.

I

The District Court made extensive findings of fact, most of which were based on a detailed stipulation prepared by the parties. [ ] The findings describe the character and the dimensions of the Internet, the availability of sexually explicit material in that medium, and the problems confronting age verification for recipients of Internet communications. Because those findings provide the underpinnings for the legal issues, we begin with a summary of the undisputed facts.

The Internet

The Internet is an international network of interconnected computers. It is the outgrowth of what began in 1969 as a military program called "ARPANET," which was designed to enable computers operated by the military, defense contractors, and universities conducting defense-related research to communicate with one another by redundant channels even if some portions of the network were damaged in a war. While the ARPANET no longer exists, it provided an example for the development of a number of civilian networks that, eventually linking with each other, now enable tens of millions of people to communicate with one another and to access vast amounts of information from around the world. The Internet is "a unique and wholly new medium of worldwide human communication."

The Internet has experienced "extraordinary growth." The number of "host" computers -- those that store information and relay communications -- increased from about 300 in 1981 to approximately 9,400,000 by the time of the trial in 1996. Roughly 60% of these hosts are located in the United States. About 40 million people used the Internet at the time of trial, a number that is expected to mushroom to 200 million by 1999.

Individuals can obtain access to the Internet from many different sources, generally hosts themselves or entities with a host affiliation. Most colleges and universities provide access for their students and faculty; many corporations provide their employees with access through an office network; many communities and local libraries provide free access; and an increasing number of storefront "computer coffee shops" provide access for a small hourly fee. Several major national "online services" such as America Online, CompuServe, the Microsoft Network, and Prodigy offer access to their own extensive proprietary networks as well as a link to the much larger resources of the Internet. These commercial online services had almost 12 million individual subscribers at the time of trial.

Anyone with access to the Internet may take advantage of a wide variety of communication and information retrieval methods. These methods are constantly evolving and difficult to categorize precisely. But, as presently constituted, those most relevant to this case are

321

electronic mail ("e-mail"), automatic mailing list services ("mail exploders," sometimes referred to as "listservs"), "newsgroups," "chat rooms," and the "World Wide Web." All of these methods can be used to transmit text; most can transmit sound, pictures, and moving video images. Taken together, these tools constitute a unique medium -- known to its users as "cyberspace" -- located in no particular geographical location but available to anyone, anywhere in the world, with access to the Internet.

E-mail enables an individual to send an electronic message -- generally akin to a note or letter -- to another individual or to a group of addressees. The message is generally stored electronically, sometimes waiting for the recipient to check her "mailbox" and sometimes making its receipt known through some type of prompt. A mail exploder is a sort of e-mail group. Subscribers can send messages to a common e-mail address, which then forwards the message to the group's other subscribers. Newsgroups also serve groups of regular participants, but these postings may be read by others as well. There are thousands of such groups, each serving to foster an exchange of information or opinion on a particular topic running the gamut from, say, the music of Wagner to Balkan politics to AIDS prevention to the Chicago Bulls. About 100,000 new messages are posted every day. In most newsgroups, postings are automatically purged at regular intervals. In addition to posting a message that can be read later, two or more individuals wishing to communicate more immediately can enter a chat room to engage in real-time dialogue -- in other words, by typing messages to one another that appear almost immediately on the others' computer screens. The District Court found that, at any given time, "tens of thousands of users are engaging in conversations on a huge range of subjects." It is "no exaggeration to conclude that the content on the Internet is as diverse as human thought."

The best known category of communication over the Internet is the World Wide Web, which allows users to search for and retrieve information stored in remote computers, as well as, in some cases, to communicate back to designated sites. In concrete terms, the Web consists of a vast number of documents stored in different computers all over the world. Some of these documents are simply files containing information. However, more elaborate documents, commonly known as Web "pages," are also prevalent. Each has its own address -- "rather like a telephone number." Web pages frequently contain information, and sometimes allow the viewer to communicate with the page's (or "site's") author. They generally also contain "links" to other documents created by that site's author or to other (generally) related sites. Typically, the links are either blue or underlined text -- sometimes images.

Navigating the Web is relatively straightforward. A user may either type the address of a known page or enter one or more keywords into a commercial "search engine" in an effort to locate sites on a subject of interest. A particular Web page may contain the information sought by the "surfer," or, through its links, it may be an avenue to other documents located anywhere on the Internet. Users generally explore a given Web page, or move to another, by clicking a computer "mouse" on one of the page's icons or links. Access to most Web pages is freely available, but some allow access only to those who have purchased the right from a commercial provider. The Web is thus comparable, from the readers' viewpoint, to both a vast library including millions of readily available and indexed publications and a sprawling mall offering goods and services.

From the publishers' point of view, it constitutes a vast platform from which to address and hear from a worldwide audience of millions of readers, viewers, researchers, and buyers. Any person or organization with a computer connected to the Internet can "publish" information. Publishers include government agencies, educational institutions, commercial entities, advocacy groups, and individuals. Publishers may either make their material available to the entire pool of Internet users or confine access to a selected group, such as those willing to pay for the privilege.

> No single organization controls any membership in the Web, nor is there any centralized point from which individual Web sites or services can be blocked from the Web.

Sexually Explicit Material

Sexually explicit material on the Internet includes text, pictures, and chat, and "extends from the modestly titillating to the hardest-core." These files are created, named, and posted in the same manner as material that is not sexually explicit, and may be accessed either deliberately or unintentionally during the course of an imprecise search. "Once a provider posts its content on the Internet, it cannot prevent that content from entering any community." Thus, for example,

> when the UCRCalifornia Museum of Photography posts to its Web site nudes by Edward Weston and Robert Mapplethorpe to announce that its new exhibit will travel to Baltimore and New York City, those images are available not only in Los Angeles, Baltimore, and New York City, but also in Cincinnati, Mobile, or Beijing -- wherever Internet users live. Similarly, the safer sex instructions that Critical Path posts to its Web site, written in street language so that the teenage receiver can understand them, are available not just in Philadelphia, but also in Provo and Prague.

Some of the communications over the Internet that originate in foreign countries are also sexually explicit.

Though such material is widely available, users seldom encounter such content accidentally.

> document's title or a description of the document will usually appear before the document itself . . . and in many cases the user will receive detailed information about a site's content before he or she need take the step to access the document. Almost all sexually explicit images are preceded by warnings as to the content.

323

For that reason, the "odds are slim" that a user would enter a sexually explicit site by accident. Unlike communications received by radio or television,

> the receipt of information on the Internet requires a series of affirmative steps more deliberate and directed than merely turning a dial. A child requires some sophistication and some ability to read to retrieve material and thereby to use the Internet unattended.

Systems have been developed to help parents control the material that may be available on a home computer with Internet access. A system may either limit a computer's access to an approved list of sources that have been identified as containing no adult material, it may block designated inappropriate sites, or it may attempt to block messages containing identifiable objectionable features.

> Although parental control software currently can screen for certain suggestive words or for known sexually explicit sites, it cannot now screen for sexually explicit images.

Nevertheless, the evidence indicates that

> a reasonably effective method by which parents can prevent their children from accessing sexually explicit and other material which parents may believe is inappropriate for their children will soon be available.

Age Verification

The problem of age verification differs for different uses of the Internet. The District Court categorically determined that there

> is no effective way to determine the identity or the age of a user who is accessing material through e-mail, mail exploders, newsgroups or chat rooms.

The Government offered no evidence that there was a reliable way to screen recipients and participants in such fora for age. Moreover, even if it were technologically feasible to block minors' access to newsgroups and chat rooms containing discussions of art, politics or other subjects that potentially elicit "indecent" or "patently offensive" contributions, it would not be possible to block their access to that material and "still allow them access to the remaining content, even if the overwhelming majority of that content was not indecent."

Technology exists by which an operator of a Web site may condition access on the verification of requested information such as a credit card number or an adult password. Credit card verification is only feasible, however, either in connection with a commercial transaction in which the card is used, or by payment to a verification agency. Using credit card possession as a surrogate for proof of age would impose costs on noncommercial Web sites that would require many of them to shut down. For that reason, at the time of the trial, credit card verification was "effectively unavailable to a substantial number of Internet content

324

providers." [ ] Moreover, the imposition of such a requirement "would completely bar adults who do not have a credit card and lack the resources to obtain one from accessing any blocked material."

Commercial pornographic sites that charge their users for access have assigned them passwords as a method of age verification. The record does not contain any evidence concerning the reliability of these technologies. Even if passwords are effective for commercial purveyors of indecent material, the District Court found that an adult password requirement would impose significant burdens on noncommercial sites, both because they would discourage users from accessing their sites and because the cost of creating and maintaining such screening systems would be "beyond their reach."

In sum, the District Court found:

> Even if credit card verification or adult password verification were implemented, the Government presented no testimony as to how such systems could ensure that the user of the password or credit card is in fact over 18. The burdens imposed by credit card verification and adult password verification systems make them effectively unavailable to a substantial number of Internet content providers.

[ ]

II

The Telecommunications Act of 1996 [ ] was an unusually important legislative enactment. As stated on the first of its 103 pages, its primary purpose was to reduce regulation and encourage "the rapid deployment of new telecommunications technologies." The major components of the statute have nothing to do with the Internet; they were designed to promote competition in the local telephone service market, the multichannel video market, and the market for over-the-air broadcasting. The Act includes seven Titles, six of which are the product of extensive committee hearings and the subject of discussion in Reports prepared by Committees of the Senate and the House of Representatives. By contrast, Title V -- known as the "Communications Decency Act of 1996" (CDA) -- contains provisions that were either added in executive committee after the hearings were concluded or as amendments offered during floor debate on the legislation. An amendment offered in the Senate was the source of the two statutory provisions challenged in this case. They are informally described as the "indecent transmission" provision and the "patently offensive display" provision.

The first, 47 U.S.C. § 223(a) [ ], prohibits the knowing transmission of obscene or indecent messages to any recipient under 18 years of age. It provides in pertinent part:

(a) Whoever --

(1) in interstate or foreign communications-

325

* * * *

(B) by means of a telecommunications device knowingly --

(i) makes, creates, or solicits, and

(ii) initiates the transmission of,

any comment, request, suggestion, proposal, image, or other communication which is obscene or indecent, knowing that the recipient of the communication is under 18 years of age, regardless of whether the maker of such communication placed the call or initiated the communication;

* * * *

(2) knowingly permits any telecommunications facility under his control to be used for any activity prohibited by paragraph (1) with the intent that it be used for such activity,

shall be fined under Title 18, or imprisoned not more than two years, or both.

The second provision, § 223(d), prohibits the knowing sending or displaying of patently offensive messages in a manner that is available to a person under 18 years of age. It provides:

(d) Whoever --

(1) in interstate or foreign communications knowingly --

(A) uses an interactive computer service to send to a specific person or persons under 18 years of age, or

(B) uses any interactive computer service to display in a manner available to a person under 18 years of age,

any comment, request, suggestion, proposal, image, or other communication that, in context, depicts or describes, in terms patently offensive as measured by contemporary community standards, sexual or excretory activities or organs, regardless of whether the user of such service placed the call or initiated the communication; or

(2) knowingly permits any telecommunications facility under such person's control to be used for an activity prohibited by paragraph (1) with the intent that it be used for such activity,

shall be fined under Title 18, or imprisoned not more than two years, or both.

The breadth of these prohibitions is qualified by two affirmative defenses. *See* § 223(e)(5). One covers those who take "good faith, reasonable, effective, and appropriate actions" to restrict access by minors to the prohibited communications. § 223(e)(5)(A). The other covers those who restrict access to covered material by requiring certain designated forms of age proof, such as a verified credit card or an adult identification number or code. § 223(e)(5)(B).

III

On February 8, 1996, immediately after the President signed the statute, 20 plaintiffs filed suit against the Attorney General of the United States and the Department of Justice challenging the constitutionality of §§ 223(a)(1) and 223(d). A week later, based on his conclusion that the term "indecent" was too vague to provide the basis for a criminal prosecution, District Judge Buckwalter entered a temporary restraining order against enforcement of § 223(a)(1)(B)(ii) insofar as it applies to indecent communications. A second suit was then filed by 27 additional plaintiffs, the two cases were consolidated, and a three-judge District Court was convened pursuant to § 561 of the Act. After an evidentiary hearing, that Court entered a preliminary injunction against enforcement of both of the challenged provisions. Each of the three judges wrote a separate opinion, but their judgment was unanimous.

Chief Judge Sloviter doubted the strength of the Government's interest in regulating "the vast range of online material covered or potentially covered by the CDA," but acknowledged that the interest was "compelling" with respect to some of that material. [ ] She concluded, nonetheless, that the statute "sweeps more broadly than necessary and thereby chills the expression of adults" and that the terms "patently offensive" and "indecent" were "inherently vague." [ ] She also determined that the affirmative defenses were not "technologically or economically feasible for most providers," specifically considering and rejecting an argument that providers could avoid liability by "tagging" their material in a manner that would allow potential readers to screen out unwanted transmissions. [ ] Chief Judge Sloviter also rejected the Government's suggestion that the scope of the statute could be narrowed by construing it to apply only to commercial pornographers. [ ]

Judge Buckwalter concluded that the word "indecent" in § 223(a)(1)(B) and the terms "patently offensive" and "in context" in § 223(d)(1) were so vague that criminal enforcement of either section would violate the "fundamental constitutional principle" of "simple fairness" [ ], and the specific protections of the First and Fifth Amendments [ ]. He found no statutory basis for the Government's argument that the challenged provisions would be applied only to "pornographic" materials, noting that, unlike obscenity, "indecency has *not* been defined to exclude works of serious literary, artistic, political or scientific value." [ ] Moreover, the Government's claim that the work must be considered patently offensive "in context" was itself vague, because the relevant context might

> refer to, among other things, the nature of the communication as a whole, the time of day it was conveyed, the medium used, the identity of the speaker, or whether or not it is accompanied by appropriate warnings.

[ ] He believed that the unique nature of the Internet aggravated the

327

vagueness of the statute. [ ]

Judge Dalzell's review of "the special attributes of Internet communication" disclosed by the evidence convinced him that the First Amendment denies Congress the power to regulate the content of protected speech on the Internet. [ ] His opinion explained at length why he believed the Act would abridge significant protected speech, particularly by noncommercial speakers, while "[p]erversely, commercial pornographers would remain relatively unaffected." [ ] He construed our cases as requiring a "medium specific" approach to the analysis of the regulation of mass communication [ ] and concluded that the Internet -- as "the most participatory form of mass speech yet developed" [ ] -- is entitled to "the highest protection from governmental intrusion" [ ].

The judgment of the District Court enjoins the Government from enforcing the prohibitions in § 223(a)(1)(B) insofar as they relate to "indecent" communications, but expressly preserves the Government's right to investigate and prosecute the obscenity or child pornography activities prohibited therein. The injunction against enforcement of §§ 223(d)(1) and (2) is unqualified, because those provisions contain no separate reference to obscenity or child pornography.

The Government appealed under the Act's special review provisions, § 561 [ ], and we noted probable jurisdiction [ ]. In its appeal, the Government argues that the District Court erred in holding that the CDA violated both the First Amendment because it is overbroad and the Fifth Amendment because it is vague. While we discuss the vagueness of the CDA because of its relevance to the First Amendment overbreadth inquiry, we conclude that the judgment should be affirmed without reaching the Fifth Amendment issue. We begin our analysis by reviewing the principal authorities on which the Government relies. Then, after describing the overbreadth of the CDA, we consider the Government's specific contentions, including its submission that we save portions of the statute either by severance or by fashioning judicial limitations on the scope of its coverage.

IV

In arguing for reversal, the Government contends that the CDA is plainly constitutional under three of our prior decisions: (1) *Ginsberg v. New York* [ ]; (2) *FCC v. Pacifica Foundation* [ ]; and (3) *Renton v. Playtime Theatres, Inc.* [ ]. A close look at these cases, however, raises -- rather than relieves -- doubts concerning the constitutionality of the CDA.

In *Ginsberg,* we upheld the constitutionality of a New York statute that prohibited selling to minors under 17 years of age material that was considered obscene as to them even if not obscene as to adults. We rejected the defendant's broad submission that

> the scope of the constitutional freedom of expression secured to a citizen to
> read or see material concerned with sex cannot be made to depend on

whether the citizen is an adult or a minor.

[　] In rejecting that contention, we relied not only on the State's independent interest in the wellbeing of its youth, but also on our consistent recognition of the principle that

> the parents' claim to authority in their own household to direct the rearing of their children is basic in the structure of our society.{GO>31}

In four important respects, the statute upheld in *Ginsberg* was narrower than the CDA. First, we noted in *Ginsberg* that "the prohibition against sales to minors does not bar parents who so desire from purchasing the magazines for their children." [　] Under the CDA, by contrast, neither the parents' consent -- nor even their participation -- in the communication would avoid the application of the statute. Second, the New York statute applied only to commercial transactions [　], whereas the CDA contains no such limitation. Third, the New York statute cabined its definition of material that is harmful to minors with the requirement that it be "utterly without redeeming social importance for minors." [　] The CDA fails to provide us with any definition of the term "indecent" as used in § 223(a)(1) and, importantly, omits any requirement that the "patently offensive" material covered by § 223(d) lack serious literary, artistic, political, or scientific value. Fourth, the New York statute defined a minor as a person under the age of 17, whereas the CDA, in applying to all those under 18 years, includes an additional year of those nearest majority.

In *Pacifica,* we upheld a declaratory order of the Federal Communications Commission, holding that the broadcast of a recording of a 12-minute monologue entitled "Filthy Words" that had previously been delivered to a live audience "could have been the subject of administrative sanctions." [　] (internal quotations omitted). The Commission had found that the repetitive use of certain words referring to excretory or sexual activities or organs "in an afternoon broadcast when children are in the audience was patently offensive," and concluded that the monologue was indecent "as broadcast." [　] The respondent did not quarrel with the finding that the afternoon broadcast was patently offensive, but contended that it was not "indecent" within the meaning of the relevant statutes because it contained no prurient appeal. After rejecting respondent's statutory arguments, we confronted its two constitutional arguments: (1) that the Commission's construction of its authority to ban indecent speech was so broad that its order had to be set aside even if the broadcast at issue was unprotected; and (2) that, since the recording was not obscene, the First Amendment forbade any abridgement of the right to broadcast it on the radio.

In the portion of the lead opinion not joined by Justices Powell and Blackmun, the plurality stated that the First Amendment does not prohibit all governmental regulation that depends on the content of speech. [　] Accordingly, the availability of constitutional protection for a vulgar and offensive monologue that was not obscene depended on the context of the broadcast. [ ] Relying on the premise that "of all forms of communication" broadcasting had received the most limited First Amendment protection [ ], the Court concluded that the ease with which children may obtain access to broadcasts, "coupled with the concerns recognized in *Ginsberg,*" justified special treatment of indecent broadcasting. [ ]

As with the New York statute at issue in *Ginsberg,* there are significant differences between the order upheld in *Pacifica* and the CDA. First, the order in *Pacifica,* issued by an agency that had been regulating radio stations for decades, targeted a specific broadcast that represented a rather dramatic departure from traditional program content in order to designate when -- rather than whether -- it would be permissible to air such a program in that particular medium. The CDA's broad categorical prohibitions are not limited to particular times and are not dependent on any evaluation by an agency familiar with the unique characteristics of the Internet. Second, unlike the CDA, the Commission's declaratory order was not punitive; we expressly refused to decide whether the indecent broadcast "would justify a criminal prosecution." [ ] Finally, the Commission's order applied to a medium which as a matter of history had "received the most limited First Amendment protection" [ ], in large part because warnings could not adequately protect the listener from unexpected program content. The Internet, however, has no comparable history. Moreover, the District Court found that the risk of encountering indecent material by accident is remote because a series of affirmative steps is required to access specific material.

In *Renton,* we upheld a zoning ordinance that kept adult movie theatres out of residential neighborhoods. The ordinance was aimed, not at the content of the films shown in the theaters, but rather at the "secondary effects" -- such as crime and deteriorating property values -- that these theaters fostered: "`It is th[e] secondary effect which these zoning ordinances attempt to avoid, not the dissemination of "offensive" speech."' [ ] According to the Government, the CDA is constitutional because it constitutes a sort of "cyberzoning" on the Internet. But the CDA applies broadly to the entire universe of cyberspace. And the purpose of the CDA is to protect children from the primary effects of "indecent" and "patently offensive" speech, rather than any "secondary" effect of such speech. Thus, the CDA is a content-based blanket restriction on speech, and, as such, cannot be "properly analyzed as a form of time, place, and manner regulation." [ ] ... These precedents, then, surely do not require us to uphold the CDA and are fully consistent with the application of the most stringent review of its provisions.

V

In *Southeastern Promotions, Ltd. v. Conrad* [ ], we observed that "[e]ach medium of expression . . . may present its own problems." Thus, some of our cases have recognized special justifications for regulation of the broadcast media that are not applicable to other speakers [ ] In these cases, the Court relied on the history of extensive government regulation of the broadcast medium [ ].

Those factors are not present in cyberspace. Neither before nor after the enactment of the CDA have the vast democratic fora of the Internet been subject to the type of government supervision and regulation that has attended the broadcast industry. Moreover, the Internet is not as "invasive" as radio or television. The District Court specifically found that

> [c]ommunications over the Internet do not "invade" an individual's home or appear on one's computer screen unbidden. Users seldom encounter content "by accident."

[ ] It also found that "[a]lmost all sexually explicit images are preceded by warnings as to the content," and cited testimony that "'odds are slim' that a user would come across a sexually explicit sight by accident." [ ]

We distinguished *Pacifica* in *Sable* [ ] on just this basis. In *Sable*, a company engaged in the business of offering sexually oriented prerecorded telephone messages (popularly known as "dial-a-porn") challenged the constitutionality of an amendment to the Communications Act that imposed a blanket prohibition on indecent as well as obscene interstate commercial telephone messages. We held that the statute was constitutional insofar as it applied to obscene messages but invalid as applied to indecent messages. In attempting to justify the complete ban and criminalization of indecent commercial telephone messages, the Government relied on *Pacifica,* arguing that the ban was necessary to prevent children from gaining access to such messages. We agreed that "there is a compelling interest in protecting the physical and psychological wellbeing of minors" which extended to shielding them from indecent messages that are not obscene by adult standards [ ], but distinguished our "emphatically narrow holding" in *Pacifica* because it did not involve a complete ban and because it involved a different medium of communication [ ]. We explained that "the dial-it medium requires the listener to take affirmative steps to receive the communication." [ ] "Placing a telephone call," we continued, "is not the same as turning on a radio and being taken by surprise by an indecent message." [ ]

Finally, unlike the conditions that prevailed when Congress first authorized regulation of the broadcast spectrum, the Internet can hardly be considered a "scarce" expressive commodity. It provides relatively unlimited, low-cost capacity for communication of all kinds. The Government estimates that "[a]s many as 40 million people use the Internet today, and that figure is expected to grow to 200 million by 1999." This dynamic, multifaceted category of communication includes not only traditional print and news services, but also audio, video, and still images, as well as interactive, real-time dialogue. Through the use of chat rooms, any person with a phone line can become a town crier with a voice that resonates farther than it could from any soapbox. Through the use of Web pages, mail exploders, and newsgroups, the

331

same individual can become a pamphleteer. As the District Court found, "the content on the Internet is as diverse as human thought." [ ] We agree with its conclusion that our cases provide no basis for qualifying the level of First Amendment scrutiny that should be applied to this medium.

VI

Regardless of whether the CDA is so vague that it violates the Fifth Amendment, the many ambiguities concerning the scope of its coverage render it problematic for purposes of the First Amendment. For instance, each of the two parts of the CDA uses a different linguistic form. The first uses the word "indecent," 47 U.S.C. § 223(a) [ ], while the second speaks of material that,

> in context, depicts or describes, in terms patently offensive as measured by contemporary community standards, sexual or excretory activities or organs,

§ 223(d). Given the absence of a definition of either term, this difference in language will provoke uncertainty among speakers about how the two standards relate to each other and just what they mean. Could a speaker confidently assume that a serious discussion about birth control practices, homosexuality, the First Amendment issues raised by the Appendix to our *Pacifica* opinion, or the consequences of prison rape would not violate the CDA? This uncertainty undermines the likelihood that the CDA has been carefully tailored to the congressional goal of protecting minors from potentially harmful materials.

The vagueness of the CDA is a matter of special concern for two reasons. First, the CDA is a content-based regulation of speech. The vagueness of such a regulation raises special First Amendment concerns because of its obvious chilling effect on free speech. [ ] Second, the CDA is a criminal statute. In addition to the opprobrium and stigma of a criminal conviction, the CDA threatens violators with penalties including up to two years in prison for each act of violation. The severity of criminal sanctions may well cause speakers to remain silent rather than communicate even arguably unlawful words, ideas, and images. [ ] As a practical matter, this increased deterrent effect, coupled with the "risk of discriminatory enforcement" of vague regulations, poses greater First Amendment concerns than those implicated by the civil regulation reviewed in *Denver Area Ed. Telecommunications Consortium, Inc. v. FCC*

[ ]

The Government argues that the statute is no more vague than the obscenity standard this Court established in *Miller v. California* [ ]. But that is not so. In *Miller,* this Court reviewed a criminal conviction against a commercial vendor who mailed brochures containing pictures of sexually explicit activities to individuals who had not requested such materials. [ ] Having struggled for some time to establish a definition of obscenity, we set forth in *Miller* the test for obscenity that controls to this day:

> (a) whether the average person, applying contemporary community standards would find that the work, taken as a whole, appeals to the prurient interest; (b) whether the work depicts or describes, in a patently offensive way, sexual conduct specifically defined by the applicable state law; and (c) whether the work, taken as a whole, lacks serious literary, artistic, political, or scientific value.

[ ]

Because the CDA's "patently offensive" standard (and, we assume *arguendo,* its synonymous "indecent" standard) is one part of the three-prong *Miller* test, the Government reasons, it cannot be unconstitutionally vague.

The Government's assertion is incorrect as a matter of fact. The second prong of the *Miller* test -- the purportedly analogous standard -- contains a critical requirement that is omitted from the CDA: that the proscribed material be "specifically defined by the applicable state law." This requirement reduces the vagueness inherent in the open-ended term "patently offensive" as used in the CDA. Moreover, the *Miller* definition is limited to "sexual conduct," whereas the CDA extends also to include (1) "excretory activities" as well as (2) "organs" of both a sexual and excretory nature.

The Government's reasoning is also flawed. Just because a definition including three limitations is not vague, it does not follow that one of those limitations, standing by itself, is not vague. Each of *Miller's* additional two prongs -- (1) that, taken as a whole, the material appeal to the "prurient" interest, and (2) that it "lac[k] serious literary, artistic, political, or scientific value" -- critically limits the uncertain sweep of the obscenity definition. The second requirement is particularly important because, unlike the "patently offensive" and "prurient interest" criteria, it is not judged by contemporary community standards. [ ] This "societal value" requirement, absent in the CDA, allows appellate courts to impose some limitations and regularity on the definition by setting, as a matter of law, a national floor for socially redeeming value. The Government's contention that courts will be able to give such legal limitations to the CDA's standards is belied by *Miller's* own rationale for having juries determine whether material is "patently offensive" according to community standards: that such questions are essentially ones of *fact.*

In contrast to *Miller* and our other previous cases, the CDA thus presents a greater threat of censoring speech that, in fact, falls outside the statute's scope. Given the vague contours of the coverage of the statute, it unquestionably silences some speakers whose messages would be entitled to constitutional protection. That danger provides further reason for insisting that the statute not be overly broad. The CDA's burden on protected speech cannot be justified if it could be avoided by a more carefully drafted statute.

333

We are persuaded that the CDA lacks the precision that the First Amendment requires when a statute regulates the content of speech. In order to deny minors access to potentially harmful speech, the CDA effectively suppresses a large amount of speech that adults have a constitutional right to receive and to address to one another. That burden on adult speech is unacceptable if less restrictive alternatives would be at least as effective in achieving the legitimate purpose that the statute was enacted to serve.

In evaluating the free speech rights of adults, we have made it perfectly clear that "[s]exual expression which is indecent but not obscene is protected by the First Amendment." [ ] ... Indeed, *Pacifica* itself admonished that "the fact that society may find speech offensive is not a sufficient reason for suppressing it." [ ]

It is true that we have repeatedly recognized the governmental interest in protecting children from harmful materials. [ ] But that interest does not justify an unnecessarily broad suppression of speech addressed to adults. As we have explained, the Government may not "reduc[e] the adult population . . . to . . . only what is fit for children." [ ] [R]egardless of the strength of the government's interest" in protecting children, "[t]he level of discourse reaching a mailbox simply cannot be limited to that which would be suitable for a sandbox." [ ]

The District Court was correct to conclude that the CDA effectively resembles the ban on "dial-a-porn" invalidated in *Sable*. [ ] In *Sable* [ ] this Court rejected the argument that we should defer to the congressional judgment that nothing less than a total ban would be effective in preventing enterprising youngsters from gaining access to indecent communications. *Sable* thus made clear that the mere fact that a statutory regulation of speech was enacted for the important purpose of protecting children from exposure to sexually explicit material does not foreclose inquiry into its validity. As we pointed out last Term, that inquiry embodies an "overarching commitment" to make sure that Congress has designed its statute to accomplish its purpose "without imposing an unnecessarily great restriction on speech." [ ]

In arguing that the CDA does not so diminish adult communication, the Government relies on the incorrect factual premise that prohibiting a transmission whenever it is known that one of its recipients is a minor would not interfere with adult-to-adult communication. The findings of the District Court make clear that this premise is untenable. Given the size of the potential audience for most messages, in the absence of a viable age verification process, the sender must be charged with knowing that one or more minors will likely view it. Knowledge that, for instance, one or more members of a 100-person chat group will be minor -- and therefore that it would be a crime to send the group an indecent message -- would surely burden communication among adults.

The District Court found that at the time of trial existing technology did not include any effective method for a sender to prevent minors from obtaining access to its communications on the Internet without also denying access to adults. The Court found no effective way to determine the age of a user who is accessing material through e-mail, mail exploders, newsgroups, or chat rooms. [ ] As a practical matter, the Court also found that it would be prohibitively expensive for noncommercial -- as well as some commercial -- speakers who have Web sites to verify that their users are adults. [ ] These limitations must inevitably curtail a significant amount of adult communication on the Internet. By contrast, the District Court found that,

> [d]espite its limitations, currently available *user-based* software suggests that a reasonably effective method by which *parents* can prevent their children from accessing sexually explicit and other material which *parents* may believe is inappropriate for their children will soon be widely available. [ ]

The breadth of the CDA's coverage is wholly unprecedented. Unlike the regulations upheld in *Ginsberg* and *Pacifica,* the scope of the CDA is not limited to commercial speech or commercial entities. Its open-ended prohibitions embrace all nonprofit entities and individuals posting indecent messages or displaying them on their own computers in the presence of minors. The general, undefined terms "indecent" and "patently offensive" cover large amounts of nonpornographic material with serious educational or other value. Moreover, the "community standards" criterion as applied to the Internet means that any communication available to a nationwide audience will be judged by the standards of the community most likely to be offended by the message. The regulated subject matter includes any of the seven "dirty words" used in the *Pacifica* monologue, the use of which the Government's expert acknowledged could constitute a felony. [ ] It may also extend to discussions about prison rape or safe sexual practices, artistic images that include nude subjects, and arguably the card catalogue of the Carnegie Library.

For the purposes of our decision, we need neither accept nor reject the Government's submission that the First Amendment does not forbid a blanket prohibition on all "indecent" and "patently offensive" messages communicated to a 17-year old-no matter how much value the message may contain and regardless of parental approval. It is at least clear that the strength of the Government's interest in protecting minors is not equally strong throughout the coverage of this broad statute. Under the CDA, a parent allowing her 17-year-old to use the family computer to obtain information on the Internet that she, in her parental judgment, deems appropriate could face a lengthy prison term. *See* 47 U.S.C. § 223(a)(2) [ ] Similarly, a parent who sent his 17-year-old college freshman information on birth control via e-mail could be incarcerated even though neither he, his child, nor anyone in their home community, found the material "indecent" or "patently offensive," if the college town's community thought otherwise.

The breadth of this content-based restriction of speech imposes an especially heavy burden on the Government to explain why a less restrictive provision would not be as effective as the CDA. It has not done so. The arguments in this Court have referred to possible alternatives such as requiring that indecent material be "tagged" in a way that facilitates parental control of material coming into their homes, making exceptions for messages with artistic or educational value, providing some tolerance for parental choice, and regulating some portions of the Internet -- such as commercial web sites -- differently than others, such as chat rooms. Particularly in the light of the absence of any detailed findings by the Congress, or even hearings addressing the special problems of the CDA, we are persuaded that the CDA is not narrowly tailored if that requirement has any meaning at all.

VIII

In an attempt to curtail the CDA's facial overbreadth, the Government advances three additional arguments for sustaining the Act's affirmative prohibitions: (1) that the CDA is constitutional because it leaves open ample "alternative channels" of communication; (2) that the plain meaning of the Act's "knowledge" and "specific person" requirement significantly restricts its permissible applications; and (3) that the Act's prohibitions are "almost always" limited to material lacking redeeming social value.

The Government first contends that, even though the CDA effectively censors discourse on many of the Internet's modalities -- such as chat groups, newsgroups, and mail exploders -- it is nonetheless constitutional because it provides a "reasonable opportunity" for speakers to engage in the restricted speech on the World Wide Web. Brief for Appellants 39. This argument is unpersuasive, because the CDA regulates speech on the basis of its content. A "time, place, and manner" analysis is therefore inapplicable. [ ] It is thus immaterial whether such speech would be feasible on the Web (which, as the Government's own expert acknowledged, would cost up to $10,000 if the speaker's interests were not accommodated by an existing Web site, not including costs for database management and age verification). The Government's position is equivalent to arguing that a statute could ban leaflets on certain subjects as long as individuals are free to publish books. In invalidating a number of laws that banned leafletting on the streets *regardless of* their content -- we explained that

> one is not to have the exercise of his liberty of expression in appropriate places abridged on the plea that it may be exercised in some other place.

[ ]

The Government also asserts that the "knowledge" requirement of both §§ 223(a) and (d), especially when coupled with the "specific child" element found in § 223(d), saves the CDA from overbreadth. Because both sections prohibit the dissemination of indecent messages only to persons known to be under 18, the Government argues, it does not

336

require transmitters to

> refrain from communicating indecent material to adults; they need only
> refrain from disseminating such materials to persons they know to be under
> 18.

[ ] This argument ignores the fact that most Internet fora -- including
chat rooms, newsgroups, mail exploders, and the Web -- are open to all
comers. The Government's assertion that the knowledge requirement
somehow protects the communications of adults is therefore untenable.
Even the strongest reading of the "specific person" requirement of §
223(d) cannot save the statute. It would confer broad powers of
censorship, in the form of a "heckler's veto," upon any opponent of
indecent speech who might simply log on and inform the would-be
discoursers that his 17-year-old child -- a "specific person . . . under 18
years of age," 47 U.S.C. § 223(d)(1)(A) [ ] -- would be present.

Finally, we find no textual support for the Government's submission
that material having scientific, educational, or other redeeming social
value will necessarily fall outside the CDA's "patently offensive" and
"indecent" prohibitions. [ ]

IX

The Government's three remaining arguments focus on the defenses
provided in § 223(e)(5). First, relying on the "good faith, reasonable,
effective, and appropriate actions" provision, the Government suggests
that "tagging" provides a defense that saves the constitutionality of the
Act. The suggestion assumes that transmitters may encode their
indecent communications in a way that would indicate their contents,
thus permitting recipients to block their reception with appropriate
software. It is the requirement that the good faith action must be
"effective" that makes this defense illusory. The Government recognizes
that its proposed screening software does not currently exist. Even if it
did, there is no way to know whether a potential recipient will actually
block the encoded material. Without the impossible knowledge that
every guardian in America is screening for the "tag," the transmitter
could not reasonably rely on its action to be "effective."

For its second and third arguments concerning defenses -- which we
can consider together-the Government relies on the latter half of §
223(e)(5), which applies when the transmitter has restricted access by
requiring use of a verified credit card or adult identification. Such
verification is not only technologically available, but actually is used by
commercial providers of sexually explicit material. These providers,
therefore, would be protected by the defense. Under the findings of the
District Court, however, it is not economically feasible for most
noncommercial speakers to employ such verification. Accordingly, this
defense would not significantly narrow the statute's burden on
noncommercial speech. Even with respect to the commercial
pornographers that would be protected by the defense, the Government
failed to adduce any evidence that these verification techniques actually

337

preclude minors from posing as adults. Given that the risk of criminal sanctions "hovers over each content provider, like the proverbial sword of Damocles," the District Court correctly refused to rely on unproven future technology to save the statute. The Government thus failed to prove that the proffered defense would significantly reduce the heavy burden on adult speech produced by the prohibition on offensive displays.

We agree with the District Court's conclusion that the CDA places an unacceptably heavy burden on protected speech, and that the defenses do not constitute the sort of "narrow tailoring" that will save an otherwise patently invalid unconstitutional provision. In *Sable* [ ] we remarked that the speech restriction at issue there amounted to "'burn[ing] the house to roast the pig.'" The CDA, casting a far darker shadow over free speech, threatens to torch a large segment of the Internet community.

X

At oral argument, the Government relied heavily on its ultimate fall-back position: if this Court should conclude that the CDA is insufficiently tailored, it urged, we should save the statute's constitutionality by honoring the severability clause, *see* 47 U.S.C. § 608, and construing nonseverable terms narrowly. In only one respect is this argument acceptable.

A severability clause requires textual provisions that can be severed. We will follow § 608's guidance by leaving constitutional textual elements of the statute intact in the one place where they are, in fact, severable. The "indecency" provision, 47 U.S.C. § 223(a) [ ] applies to "any comment, request, suggestion, proposal, image, or other communication which is *obscene or indecent.*" (Emphasis added.) Appellees do not challenge the application of the statute to obscene speech, which, they acknowledge, can be banned totally because it enjoys no First Amendment protection. [ ] As set forth by the statute, the restriction of "obscene" material enjoys a textual manifestation separate from that for "indecent" material, which we have held unconstitutional. Therefore, we will sever the term "or indecent" from the statute, leaving the rest of § 223(a) standing. In no other respect, however, can § 223(a) or § 223(d) be saved by such a textual surgery.

The Government also draws on an additional, less traditional aspect of the CDA's severability clause, 47 U.S.C., § 608, which asks any reviewing court that holds the statute facially unconstitutional not to invalidate the CDA in application to "other persons or circumstances" that might be constitutionally permissible. It further invokes this Court's admonition that, absent "countervailing considerations," a statute should "be declared invalid to the extent it reaches too far, but otherwise left intact." [ ] There are two flaws in this argument.

First, the statute that grants our jurisdiction for this expedited review, 47 U.S.C. § 561 [ ], limits that jurisdictional grant to actions challenging the CDA "on its face." Consistent with § 561, the plaintiffs who brought this suit and the three-judge panel that decided it treated it as a facial challenge. We have no authority, in this particular posture, to convert this litigation into an "as-applied" challenge. Nor, given the vast array of plaintiffs, the range of their expressive activities, and the vagueness of the statute, would it be practicable to limit our holding to a judicially defined set of specific applications.

Second, one of the "countervailing considerations" mentioned in *Brockett* is present here. In considering a facial challenge, this Court may impose a limiting construction on a statute only if it is "readily susceptible" to such a construction. [ ] ... The open-ended character of the CDA provides no guidance whatever for limiting its coverage.

This case is therefore unlike those in which we have construed a statute narrowly because the text or other source of congressional intent identified a clear line that this Court could draw. [ ] ... Rather, our decision in *United States v. Treasury Employees* [ ] is applicable. In that case, we declined to

> dra[w] one or more lines between categories of speech covered by an overly broad statute, when Congress has sent inconsistent signals as to where the new line or lines should be drawn,

because doing so "involves a far more serious invasion of the legislative domain." This Court "will not rewrite a . . . law to conform it to constitutional requirements."[ ]

XI

In this Court, though not in the District Court, the Government asserts that -- in addition to its interest in protecting children -- its "[e]qually significant" interest in fostering the growth of the Internet provides an independent basis for upholding the constitutionality of the CDA. [ ] The Government apparently assumes that the unregulated availability of "indecent" and "patently offensive" material on the Internet is driving countless citizens away from the medium because of the risk of exposing themselves or their children to harmful material.

We find this argument singularly unpersuasive. The dramatic expansion of this new marketplace of ideas contradicts the factual basis of this contention. The record demonstrates that the growth of the Internet has been and continues to be phenomenal. As a matter of constitutional tradition, in the absence of evidence to the contrary, we presume that governmental regulation of the content of speech is more likely to interfere with the free exchange of ideas than to encourage it. The interest in encouraging freedom of expression in a democratic society outweighs any theoretical but unproven benefit of censorship.

For the foregoing reasons, the judgment of the district court is affirmed.

It is so ordered.